WINNER OF THE JULES AND FRANCES LANDRY AWARD FOR 2002

History • Travel

Still Fighting the Civil War

The American South and Southern History

DAVID GOLDFIELD

 Louisiana State University Press BATON ROUGE

Designer: Barbara Neely Bourgoyne
Typeface: Janson Text
Typesetter: Coghill Composition, Inc.
Printer and binder: Thomson-Shore, Inc.

"The Mill Mother's Song" by Ella May Wiggins is from *American Folksongs of Protest*, ed. John Greenway. Copyright © 1953 University of Pennsylvania Press. Reprinted by permission. "The Tall Men" by Donald Davidson is from his *Poems 1922–1961* (University of Minnesota Press, 1966). Reprinted by permission.

Library of Congress Cataloging-in-Publication Data

Goldfield, David R., 1944–
    Still fighting the Civil War : the American South and southern history / David Goldfield.
        p.   cm.
    Includes bibliographical references and index.
    ISBN 0-8071-2758-2 (cloth : alk. paper)
    1. Southern States—Civilization.   2. Southern States—Social conditions.   3. Southern States—History—Philosophy.   4. United States—History—Civil War, 1861–1865—Influence.   I. Title.

F209 .G65   2002
975'.041—dc21   2001050245

for Erik and Eleanor

Contents

Illustrations

Acknowledgments

This book has many parents. It rests on the work of scholars, journalists, and novelists. If I listed them all here, I would inevitably leave someone out, not to mention that I would reduce the pool of potential reviewers significantly. Embalmment of my sources in the endnotes is the best I can do.

Some of the professionals whose work is evident in this book are not acknowledged in the notes. Copy editor Sarah Richards Doerries made splendid suggestions that improved the flow of the manuscript. Archivists in the North Carolina Collection at the University of North Carolina at Chapel Hill, the Library of Congress, the Duke Divinity School Library, Clemson University, and the Virginia Historical Society shared their expertise. Don Veasey of the Birmingham Public Library, Jim Willard of North Carolina Historical Sites, Michael Rose and Betsy Ricks of the Atlanta History Center, Cathy Mundale and Karen Jefferson of the Robert W. Woodruff Library at the Atlanta University Center, and Heather A. Whitacre of the Museum of the Confederacy were particularly helpful. Staff at the Charlotte *Observer*, especially Don Hinshaw and talented artists Kevin Siers and Diedra Laird, and Mic Smith and Tom Spain at the Charleston (S.C.) *Post & Courier* offered generous support to my project. And speaking of support, there is no finer staff to work with than the folks at LSU Press.

The greatest gift to a historian is time; the time to engage in research, and the time to reflect, write, and rewrite. I have been fortunate to work in an environment at UNC-Charlotte that not only encourages my efforts but supports them, too. My history department colleagues, especially department chair John Smail, have indulged my work probably more than I deserve. And the university administration, particularly Dean Schley Lyons and Provost Denise Trauth, have supported this and other productions. Chancellor James H. Woodward has created an atmosphere that promotes both scholarship and collegiality. It is a pleasure to come to work.

Melinda H. Desmarais served as my graduate assistant for three years during the research and writing phases of the project. Her work with the *Journal of Urban History* proved invaluable to my efforts, enabling me to devote more of my time to this book. Her judgments were always correct and deadlines always met. At the same time, she carried on an extensive research agenda of her own, uncovering the role of black domestics in North Carolina textile towns before World War II.

I completed the manuscript while serving as the Fulbright Chair in American Studies at Uppsala University in Sweden. I am grateful to the Fulbright program and to Jeannette Lindström, Executive Director of the Swedish Fulbright Commission, for making this possible. I cannot say that Sweden provided any great insights into my work on the American South, but it did offer a relaxed environment and the time to shape the manuscript. Erik Åsard, Director of the Swedish Institute for North American Studies, was especially supportive of my project, and he offered several opportunities to inflict my ideas on colleagues. The American Seminar at Cambridge University, run by Tony Badger, also provided suggestions for my work in progress.

I have been especially blessed by a wonderful family. My father, Alex, with his stories of life in Memphis, generated my initial curiosity about the South. My sister, Joni Schwager, has been a source of good humor and fellowship, often presenting the northern "take" on my region. Without Marie-Louise Hedin, my wife, I doubt very much whether this page could have been written at this time. She has provided a stability and affection that has allowed me to sustain my work and my life. The South for her is really a foreign country. The contrast with her native Sweden has provided some interesting and occasionally humorous insights.

This is the first book I have written that my mother, Sarah, will not see. Through her struggles for life and against it she maintained a steadfast belief in me and a spiritual love of learning. Through her, I learned to appreciate good books, but especially good writing. May she rest peacefully.

Blaine Brownell is not related to me biologically as far as either of us can figure out, but he has been a brother to me for more than thirty years. Whenever I despaired about the South, I thought of Blaine, a Deep South native, and grew hopeful for the future.

This book, because of its grounding in history, is really about the future. I am proud to be a southerner, and though sorrow occasionally veils my optimism, I can see in my students and in my children, Erik and Eleanor, southerners born and bred, that a new, more inclusive South is forming. My pride in my region is my hope for my children and their generation. I dedicate this work with love and hope to Erik and Eleanor.

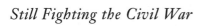
Still Fighting the Civil War

Introduction

If it can be said that there are many Souths, the fact remains that there is also one South.

—W. J. Cash, *The Mind of the South*

I live in a tolerable yet sometimes intolerable place. Its sensual climate lures the unsuspecting, and the grace, manners, and civility of its citizens impart a preternatural quietude that belies the storm beneath. Its culture is rich in music, food, conversation, and literature; yet it can be a barren place, a tundra of conformity, a murderer of imagination, inquiry, and innovation. Some who have loved it most deeply only to uncover the unpleasant reality have cast themselves, rather than the place, as the betrayer. For they have understood that the secret that lies beneath this place could, if broadcast, destroy it and them together. I am not immune to such feelings, though I grew up elsewhere. I have spent much more than half my life in the South, and I do not pretend to understand it yet. Perhaps I never will.

I do know that there is a war going on here. It is an ancient conflict, as war and time go in this country. The Civil War is like a ghost that has not yet made its peace and roams the land seeking solace, retribution, or vindication. It continues to exist, an event without temporal boundaries, an interminable struggle that has generated perhaps as many casualties since its alleged end in 1865 as during the four preceding years when armies clashed on the battlefield. For the society that became the South after 1865—and, truly, one could not speak of a distinct South before that time—the Civil War and the Reconstruction that followed shaped the form it takes today.

To justify the war, its great sacrifices, and its tragic conclusion, white southerners exalted the cause for which they fought. To that end, they rehabilitated the Old South and restored the principles upon which its civilization rested: white supremacy and patriarchy. Freedom was a dangerous thing; it ruined a slave and removed women from the protection of men. While all white southerners shared in fabricating a history out of necessity, white men, above all, elevated their own deeds during the war and their efforts to redeem the South afterward. Despite four years of fighting, after all, they had not only failed their cause of independence but had faltered in protecting their women and children and in keeping their slave families intact and working. Those who had slaves lost them, and many more lost their patrimony and self-respect. Southern white men could not live with failure and dishonor, so they manufactured a past that obviated both and returned their pride, dignity, and above all their control.

In this respect, white southerners responded as do many peoples of the world when confronted with tragedy and defeat. In the seventh century B.C. a young prince, Josiah, descended of King David, attained the throne of Judah. A small, poor nation with great plans to unify disparate territories under one ruler and one God required a history to justify its grand designs. That epic evolved into the Hebrew Bible, a text not so much historical record as ideological and theological tract designed "to appropriate the past for the present." But the one God could not protect Josiah and the people of Israel. The Egyptian pharaoh killed the ruler and enslaved his subjects. Not long after, Babylonians destroyed Judah and exiled its aristocracy. How to account for such a tragedy? Revise the epic to place the blame for the kingdom's downfall on an earlier ruler and promise that unconditional obedience to the covenant between God and the people will guarantee redemption and restoration: "If the people obey the commandments, they yet have a future." As theologian Phyllis Trible wrote, this new version of the story "spoke to the present; it served the needs of a defeated and dispossessed people." Though the promise of the return to glory and a rebuilt Temple never materialized, the Bible became the source of survival for a defeated people.[1]

The Bible underscores that history and memory are not distinct. They evolve from each other, and their interaction produces the flexibility that enables traditions to survive through centuries of change. Trible noted that "What 'actually happened' and what a people thought happened belong to a single historical process," and history and memory are indelibly "intertwined." Historians should seek to understand how the interrelationship has shaped people's lives and the society in which they live.[2]

The intersection of history and memory creates traditions, and traditions are central to a people's identity in that they give meaning to the present and offer hope for the future. Traditions banish time, connecting the past to the present until they are indiscernible. Leon Wieseltier, a Jew writing for *The New Republic*, states this idea simply: "In its liturgy and its ritual and its literature, my tradition makes the past into the present. . . . Tradition is an abolition of time and space."[3] The Jewish people have long since left Egypt, but their exodus still resonates in Jewish society, contributing to that society's sense of itself. Tradition is not predicated on secular concepts of time. If the past is always present, then why should the past become obsolete? If the past is essential for one's identity, then renouncing, forgetting, or ignoring that past shatters the self.

Tragedy is a central element to establishing and fostering tradition. It is why the past always seems immanent; it is a wound that must be salved, a loss that must be redeemed, and a reference point for all that comes after. What moves a people to the realm of tragedy is unmerited suffering, perhaps losing something precious like freedom or place. Memories of suffering and loss are burned into the consciousness and carried for generations; they give identity to the people. Occasionally, they are written down and become texts that serve as sacred guides to present behavior and action; more often they reveal themselves in laws and patterns of behavior and thought. The only thing greater than tragedy, of course, is overcoming it; this is the history, the legend, that people build nations upon. Conquering tragedy does not mean forgetting history; to the contrary, victory illuminates the tragedy, honors its victims, and blesses those who triumph. Sometimes the victory involves simple survival; sometimes it results from vanquishing a foe outright. Reversals of fortune supply the historical foundations for nations and peoples in texts as diverse as the Norse sagas and the New South renditions of the Civil War and Reconstruction. They gird citizens for future battles, render them vigilant against internal and external enemies, and generate vows never to lapse or regress, so help us God. These histories cloak the present with significance, a persistent pep talk from past generations to walk in the righteous path of ancestors: do not forget their sacrifice or courage, for to do otherwise would not only dishonor them but also destroy what we have gained.

Southern history is world history. And, as is the case with many places in the world, from fifteenth-century Spain to Germany of the 1930s, it is less the history itself than the uses to which citizens put that history, and the society created from those uses, that compound the tragedies of the past. Black and white southerners journeyed through the Civil War and Reconstruction together but fashioned different traditions from both events. Rather than sharing a common history, southern whites walled themselves away from their neighbors and, in the process, from each other. But white southerners are hardly the only people in history not to learn from their past. The question is, can we learn now? For in learning from the past, reconciliation will occur, and two people separated by a common history can move forward together to build their region, to build a nation. New traditions emerge from the remains of older verities that no longer serve their purpose.

The difficulty is that the past is more than merely a series of remembered events. It is the very core of a people's identity. The good news, though, is that neither the past nor the interpretation of it is unyielding. Changed circumstances, as occurred in the kingdom of Judah, can alter a people's course without destroying identity. As historian George B. Tindall has asserted, "to change is not necessarily to lose one's identity, to change sometimes is to find it."[4]

In the South we have not yet reached that point of mutual acquiescence in the separate yet common histories of black and white, man and woman. Yet the possibilities are greater than perhaps at any other time in our history, and there are already indications that a reconciled history can lead to a reconciled people.

The tradition, or historical perspective, that has defined the South for more than a century was created, like all traditions, to account for loss and prepare for redemption. As long as the tradition worked to achieve both objectives, it prevailed. And it still prevails, though in a more contested environment. What emerges from this contest will help determine the course of the South, and the nation, over the next century.

First it is important to recount and understand the traditional perspective of the Civil War and Reconstruction from which contemporary southern society derives much of its definition. It is a powerful narrative that succored a beaten people. The Civil War emerged in southern history as a heroic defense of Old South civilization and American constitutional principles, and the Reconstruction as a courageous battle against the despoilers of these values—blacks and Yankees alike—that concluded in triumph, or Redemption as the history calls it. Southern whites, but especially southern white men, used these perspectives to restore their control over African Americans and preserve their role as protectors of white women. Each responsibility reinforced the other. White women required protection, so blacks, especially black men, required controlling.

The interpretation of history is a reflection of the desire of people to control it and use it; like Josiah, to consolidate and legitimate their power. History, however, is neither immutable nor a closed system; it admits differing interpretations. The difficulty in establishing a "new" version of events is that this process requires wresting power from the people who have long controlled the past, or persuading them that alternative versions will not destroy but even perhaps enhance the prevailing view. A people who derive their identity from one particular version of history will likely defend that version as they would their homes and their families. They could no more deny this "past" than they could deny themselves.

In the South, as in ancient Israel, faith sealed this particular view of society and its people; not only the faith that this was the correct version of things but that it reflected the divine plan. Southern evangelical Protestantism became the accomplice to this historical version of racial and gender superiority. History was no longer a mere recitation of tradition; it took on the trappings of a biblical epic and became as holy, as unerring, and as immune to diverse interpretations as the Bible itself.

Some southerners, blacks foremost, rejected the new history and its implications. Periodically over the next century they would express their dissent, sometimes surreptitiously and sometimes forcefully, the latter at considerable personal peril. These new southern "rebels" railed not only against the position assigned them by white males' representation of southern history, but also against how that history had rendered them meaningful only as constructions of white male ideals. White men had become so dependent on and so accustomed to these constructions that they refought the battles of the Civil War and Reconstruction every time resistance appeared.

Another historical vision emerged that directly challenged the assumptions about the old view of the peoples of the South—especially of blacks and women—and about the Civil War and Reconstruction, from which that view derived. This vision stressed the commonality of all southerners, the shared culture and experiences that crossed racial and gender lines. It also demonstrated the possibility of preserving the memory of the Civil War without literally whitewashing the civilization that supported the southern cause, as well as the possibility that Reconstruction was an effort to make a southern society in which all citizens could pursue their dreams in a democratic and egalitarian society, not simply an era when former slaves sought dominion over government, economy, and white women. This concept of the Civil War and Reconstruction inferred a new version of the southerner, black and white. And that was both the purpose and the hope of the civil rights movement.

The more this historical perspective clashed against the traditional view, the more apparent it became that although southerners have shared a common place, they have not necessarily shared a common past. In the hard days after the Civil War, the white man saw in his black neighbor both the reason and the fact of his defeat. And in the years after 1865, many southern whites perceived their condition as a sentence in the purgatory of black and Yankee rule that ended only with a glorious Redemption. Black southerners viewed southern whites as the not-so-erstwhile enemy, and hailed Yankee soldiers, some of whom were black, as liberators rather than as oppressors, the Reconstruction as a time of golden possibility that turned to ashes through white subversion. These perspectives are difficult to reconcile, but they can be understood, acknowledged, and appreciated. And in that way, an accommodation can occur between the peoples of the South and their respective histories. Both are southern stories. And that is common ground enough.

It is this continuing historical consciousness, particularly how southerners have interpreted the Civil War and Reconstruction and then implemented that vision, that has set the South apart from the rest of the nation, though not apart from the world. As an urban, industrial nation grew to world power by the early twentieth century, the South looked backward, embracing a culture different from the diverse, democratic society that emerged up North. While southerners eagerly took on the latest inventions and crowed about their economic progress, their society rested on principles at odds with American ideals. Of course, Americans honored those ideals with a great deal of selectivity. But over the course of time, northern society became more inclusive, and the official version of American history reveled in the diversity and inclusiveness of that society. In the South, exclusivity, hierarchy, and homogeneity were actively promoted and legislated. If the cities of the North became the locus of the American Dream, however imperfect, then the South became America's nightmare, a place where a good portion of its population could never fulfill their aspirations.

This regional divergence of both history and its narrative has not escaped the notice of most Americans, even if historians habitually write epitaphs for

Dixie. Throughout our nation's history, the South has functioned, for good or ill, as a national mirror, an object of hate, love, and fantasy that rarely approached reality but nonetheless satisfied certain basic national needs. As a land of slavery, segregation, and disfranchisement, a place of predominantly rural poverty in a prosperous urban, industrial nation, the South has stood as a visible reminder that the benefits of American life do not extend to everyone. Though a hint of smug self-righteousness has often accompanied the comparison, the presence of this adverse South has propelled this nation to some of its finest moments.

At other times, northerners have looked upon the South as an idyllic land of grace and gentility, where personal character and charm counted more than bank accounts and business savvy; a region of unspoiled beauty, of small towns and large farms where the ills of urban civilization scarcely penetrated; of loyalty to family, God, and place as a counterpoise to a mobile, disjointed, secular society. As millions of immigrants poured into northern cities after 1900, the South's apparently peaceful race relations and homogeneous white population seemed ideal by contrast, a contrast that reflected northern fears and bigotry more than it did the reality of life in the early-twentieth-century South. White southerners cultivated these positive images even as they understood them to be exaggerations or outright fantasies; then again, they were living an artifice, and the promotion of the lie came naturally.

In the mid-1960s, when northerners discovered that they, too, had a racial problem, and as Vietnam and Watergate shattered national confidence, the South of dogs and fire hoses suddenly transformed into the South of peace and roses. National publications wrote features on the hospitality and gentility of the natives, the reconstructed race relations, and the Sunbelt prosperity; corresponding attributes seemed to disappear from the North. The revised images of the South told more about the narrator than the subject.

Vietnam is now a tourist destination, Newark is chic, and Watergate is a building where Monica Lewinsky was once a tenant. Americans feel much better about themselves and, consequently, worse about the South. Now, the nation is likely to see the South in more familiar terms, as the resident region of the nation's boobocracy; a receptacle of reprobate preachers, gun-toting toddlers, assorted Bravehearts rampaging against government, education, and the arts; and politicians who raise hogs and lower taxes. The region of all possibility in the 1970s has transformed into one of overhyped virtue and clandestine vice, which is to say that the South has not changed much even if the nation's perceptions have. It may be that the current national disfavor does the South a benefit as it forestalls yet again its ultimate merger into America. As historian Michael O'Brien opined, "regions die without a certain quota of misanthropy about the opinions held of them somewhere else."[5]

Northerners blowing into Atlanta for the 1996 Summer Olympic Games brought some widely perceived notions about the South along with their charge cards. They viewed southerners as "slow-moving," "racist," "ignorant," "genteel," "friendly," "still thinking the Civil War is in progress," and possessing "thick accents." One fellow from Michigan probably summarized the view of many of his colleagues when he confessed that he expected the South to be a place where "everyone had a southern drawl, had seen a UFO, ate grits, and made love to their sister." It is not clear what a follow-up might have revealed, but visitors may well have rationalized that Atlanta isn't the *real* South anyway. Georgians, after all, have been saying that for decades.

When Charlotte-based NationsBank merged with San Francisco's Bank of America in 1998 and moved its corporate headquarters to North Carolina, to Bay Area residents it was as if Dog Patch had conquered the Emerald City. The San Francisco *Chronicle* was beside itself: "Why should the headquarters of the new Bank of America move from San Francisco, home of the 49ers, haute cuisine and culture, to Charlotte, home to the Panthers expansion team, stock car racing and pork slathered in barbecue sauce?" The general idea was that San Francisco had culture and Charlotte had chitlins. As *Chronicle* columnist Ken Garcia confided, "The Bank of America merger is so frightening on so many levels that it's hard to grasp. . . . The new twin cities: San Francisco/Charlotte. What a concept: Pickled pigs' feet—the San Francisco treat." Charlotte Chamber of Commerce president Carroll Gray just shook his head and admitted that "We've struggled . . . for years [to] get people to come look at the city, because reputations die hard."[6]

Charlotte received San Francisco's cultural commentary with a mixture of unrestrained glee and indignant defiance. Dennis Rash, a NationsBank vice-president who has done probably more than any other individual to transform Charlotte from a series of suburban subdivisions to a gosh-honest city, retorted that a prime motivator of the merger was "to prove to the damn carpetbaggers that there was something intrinsically worthwhile about the South and we didn't need to tolerate their looking down their noses at Southerners." It was a motivation that an executive at Citigroup or Fleet of Boston would hardly harbor, let alone articulate. But, when you are still fighting the Civil War, you are still fighting.[7]

While some of the exchanges between the two cities assumed the tone of tongue-in-cheek saber rattling, there is a persistent image problem with respect to the South. When New York–based journalist Neil Strauss informed friends of his impending transfer to Nashville, they commiserated and urged him to think of it as spending a year abroad. Although African Americans feel as comfortable in the South as in any part of the country, some northern blacks maintain old stereotypes about the region. Journalist Kim McLarin, an African American, described the fear her black colleague expressed the first time she landed in Baton Rouge from New York. She admitted that most of her northern friends felt the same way, conjuring up images of "fat-bellied sheriffs, hooded sheets, fiery crosses burning in the night."[8]

As if the civil rights movement never occurred, the South continues to be the standard by which the rest of the country measures its own racial transgressions. When, in 1987, a group of white youths beat to death a young black man in the Howard Beach section of Queens, New York, then-mayor Ed Koch confessed to a national television audience that he would "expect this kind of thing to happen in the Deep South" and that the white attackers reminded him of "lynching parties that existed in the Deep South." When police officers in Riverside, California, pumped twenty-seven shots into a nineteen-year-old black woman even though she was apparently unconscious at the time in her car, a family friend noted in outrage that "this might as well be Mississippi."[9]

Southerners enjoy playing up to the less threatening of these stereotypes: a sort of contemporary version of "puttin' on ole massa." Although backers scuttled a "Gone With the Wind" theme park, visitors to the Atlanta Games could not help but notice the numerous Taras and other Deep South references in advertisements and names of shopping centers, movie theaters, and subdivisions. And the locals enjoy projecting an "aw shucks" attitude while they gobble up banks, land, and media empires from their erstwhile enemies. Much of southern literature these days continues to follow the "three F" school of writing—fishing, fighting, and fornicating (often expressed more colorfully)—long after such doings reflected the way most southerners lived. The novels of Larry Brown and Barry Hannah, for example, seem to caricature bad behavior, often in rural or small-town settings. Not that writers have a responsibility to write about the commonplace, but such bad-boy fiction is surprisingly dated, and dull in the bargain. The national press has hailed these writers as "realists," recalling a comment of Flannery O'Connor, herself a contributor to the image, that "anything that comes out of the South is going to be called grotesque by the northern reader, unless it *is* grotesque, in which case it is going to be called realistic."[10]

Though many of these stereotypes are overblown, there is a foundation of reality behind the perceptions. The current Yankee invasion, which has touched off another round of death watches for the South, is merely the latest in a long line of assaults the region and its people have absorbed, accommodated themselves to, or generally ignored since the end of Reconstruction. A poll conducted by the Institute for Research in Social Science at the University of North Carolina at Chapel Hill in 1999 indicated that, after more than two decades of significant northern in-migration, a majority of respondents in every southern state still viewed themselves as a distinctive category of American, as southerners. The perceptions ranged from 90 percent of the respondents in Mississippi to 51 percent in Florida. In states such as Georgia and North Carolina, recipients of great numbers of migrants, 81 percent and 80 percent of the respondents, respectively, identified themselves as southerners.[11]

As the poll implies, southerners are perhaps the most studied people in the United States. As Michael O'Brien has noted, various "regional organizations, study centers, periodicals, tourist pilgrimages, and bric-a-brac" analyze, research, or celebrate the South to an extent that is unique in America. And where else would a respected university press construct a Web site asking visitors to participate in an "Online Olympiad" to "Test Your Southern I.Q.!"? The questions range from the hallowed, such as "What is the name of the birthplace of Robert E. Lee?" (Stratford Hall in Westmoreland County, Virginia), to the obscure: "What state is the top exporter of collard greens?" (Georgia; the press noted with pride that half the collards go to New York City alone. At last, Gotham acquires cuisine.)[12]

Considerable empirical substantiation for southern difference reflects the region's history. The South, for example, remains the most violent section of the country, a legacy of the cult of honor in the Old South, where men derived status from their relationship to others and especially to the black slaves in their midst, and any question of that status turned an insult into a tragedy. It did not help that the cosmopolitan leaven of cities appeared late and inchoate. In a region dominated by farms and small towns, individuals could act beyond the law, or as the law itself. All eleven of the former Confederate states appear on the list of top twenty states in terms of homicide rate. Overall, the homicide rate in the South is almost double that of the Northeast, a ratio that has persisted since the nineteenth century.[13]

Race and religion also set the South apart from the rest of the country. In the spring of 1999, the Southern Focus Poll recorded that southerners still held more conservative racial views than the rest of the country concerning intermarriage, affirmative action, interracial dating, and general attitudes toward diversity. The Charlotte *Observer* reported poll results in May 1999 indicating significant differences in religious beliefs between southerners and other Americans. Nearly one-half of southern respondents read the Bible at home during the week, compared with less than one-third of non-southerners. Nearly one-third of southerners admitted that their ministers offered advice and guidance on political matters, compared with 18 percent of non-southerners. Almost two-thirds of the southern respondents agreed that some people are possessed by the Devil; 44 percent of non-southerners expressed that belief. Nearly one-half of southerners claimed that prayer had cured an illness in their lives, compared with 28 percent of non-southerners. And 48 percent of southern respondents agreed with the statement, "The U.S. is a Christian country and the government should make laws to keep it that way," while 32 percent of non-southerners agreed.[14]

Considering these differences, some of which are downright unpleasant, why would so many people move to the South? The amenities of southern life must outweigh the detractions. Besides, in the sprawling metropolitan areas that characterize the urban South, where the vast majority of new migrants arrive, it is easy to insulate oneself from southern culture and life; one may occasionally dip a toe in to test the cultural waters, knowing it is possible to draw back at any time. When "outsiders" engage their communities to demand better schools and improved and more-frequent services, do not flinch at huge bond issues or mild tax increases, express dissenting religious views, and wonder aloud why southerners still fight the Civil War, *then* the cultural distinctions become most apparent. Take a walk around New York City, Greenwich, Connecticut, or Bloomington, Minnesota, and you will find few people who refer to themselves as northerners. You are only a northerner when you move to the South. Then, suddenly, you have developed a new identity, no longer bound necessarily by ethnicity, religion, or even race. You are more than an outsider; you are a Yankee.

If southerners seem a bit prickly about these cultural encounters, it is a reflection of heightened awareness, of their "southernness," which comes into sharp relief in contact with non-southerners both in and outside the South. Which does not make us any less American. As with any ethnic group, it is possible to possess multiple allegiances and move easily back and forth through various cultural milieus. It is not a question of either/or, of being either an American or a southerner, though southern ethnicity is often so powerful, given the historical weight behind it, that it often trumps other identities.

The poll and statistical data, the numerous institutes and study centers, and the abundant perceptions and stereotypes about the South are surface manifestations of deeper distinctions between the South and the rest of the country. The surface, in fact, detracts from the underlying historical differences to such an extent that otherwise astute observers have dismissed the superficial expressions as the detritus of a moribund civilization. It is what journalist Edwin M. Yoder referred to as the "southernizing enterprise" of "obscurantism and self-caricature." Even the South's distinctive history seems more dim now, overshadowed by Sunbelt prosperity and the influence of a national diaspora southward. As new generations emerge, ever expanding the distance from the wellspring of southern identity—the Civil War and Reconstruction—it may be that the past no longer will seem present. But distance is much less important than the history itself; there is something different down in Dixie, the difference is real and deep, grounded in the region's distinctive past. As historian C. Vann Woodward declared, "The South's distinctive collective experience of the past . . . [is] the true source of Southern identity."[15]

So the South is different. Why is that important, other than for the sustenance of those research institutes? At the turn of the twenty-first century, the South is host to more than ten million people who have moved from outside the region. One out of every five southerners is not a native of the South. Since 1980 more people have moved into the South than into any other section of the country. These newcomers have arrived from the North and the West, and also from Latin America, Europe, and Asia. They have come, like most migrants, to find a better life. Some come because of jobs, others to reunite with family members, and still more to retire. Their success and satisfaction will depend, to some extent, on how they "fit in," always an important consideration for a southerner. And fitting in requires an understanding of the customs, frailties, strengths, and proclivities of the native population. If these newcomers go to bookstores, however, what they will see, as historian James C. Cobb noted in an eyeball survey of their shelves, is "a host of cutesy, one-sentence-per-page" works that merely feed caricatures—books on how to speak southern, eat southern, and understand southerners. They will learn very little. They will have gained some superficial knowledge and conclude that southerners, are, after all, superficial anyway.[16]

Yet the South's influence in the nation, and the world, extends beyond the population boom. The South is already leading the nation in generating new jobs and in population growth; its political influence is at its strongest since the 1850s, with leadership in the Congress, control of the White House, and a high profile in the federal judiciary (though with views more diverse than during the earlier period); and its cultural impact has been and will continue to be significant. The South has a major influence over key domestic issues, such as race relations, the role of religion in society and politics, the balance of federal power, and the federal budget and fiscal policy. What we will become as a nation in this century will depend very much on what happens in the South.

That is both encouraging and frightening: encouraging because the South and its people have demonstrated a great capacity to initiate and experience great change. A little more than half a century ago, a federal report tagged the South as the nation's "Number One economic problem."[17] Now it is the perceived showcase of economic prosperity. And, in less than half a century, a system of white supremacy that appeared invincible is vanishing. Those are good, even great, things. But, at the same time, there is a darkness in the southern soul; the time-ticking bomb called history that confounds and burdens the region still. The old regime may have relinquished its formal rule in 1965, but the remnants of its reign persist, as does a particular view of history and a religion that accompanies and gives strength to the old ideals, which are inimical to the national interest. That the South is still fighting the Civil War may be a quaint distinction that northerners and newcomers discover and that locals, despite themselves, frequently confirm, but it is more than a mere regional curiosity. It is a national concern demanding a serious look at this place I call home.

I begin with the past, which is still very much with us. To understand the grip of history, it is important to learn about southern religion. How history and faith have collaborated to shape southern society is the focus of chapters 2 and 3. How that collaboration determined and secured the position of blacks and women in the South, and how each, usually separately, attempted to extricate themselves and the South from the vise of the past, are the subjects of chapters 4 through 10. The book concludes with an accounting of the region's partial victories over the prevailing historical perspectives and an assessment of what may await in the future of the South.

Finally, a caveat: this is not a book about how southerners have remembered the Civil War and Reconstruction; it is not about whether or not the South is distinctive. Historians have written fine works on the memory of those events. The fact that history made the South different is hardly revelatory. I am more interested in relating *why* southerners have remembered the Civil War and Reconstruction as they have, and how these perspectives shaped an American region. My objective is not to provide a comprehensive history of the matter from 1865 to the present so much as to share a series of thoughts on the subject that will help both newcomers and long-time residents understand the South and, hopefully, each other. Professional historians may derive some enjoyment and, I hope, some insight into southern history from these pages, but I am writing primarily for my neighbors, not my colleagues. That is also a good marketing technique, as the former are considerably more numerous than the latter.

It is as much a cottage industry to declare the South's demise or its merger with the rest of America as it is to explain the region's distinctiveness.[18] The epitaph for Dixie is one of the longest-running pieces in American literature. When Charles Dudley Warner wrote in 1889 that "Southern society and Northern society are becoming every day more and more alike," he was hardly the first and certainly not the last to announce the imminent merger of the regions. As historian George B. Tindall has noted, "The belief that the South is forever disappearing has a long and honored tradition." This is a tired debate. Americans knew and still know that the South is a different place, even if they have not recognized that the region's distinctive history lay at the root of that difference. And, barring epidemic amnesia of the Civil War and Reconstruction, and of the century that followed these events, this difference is likely to persist. This may be good or bad for the rest of the United States. It all depends on history.[19]

The experience of the American South in accommodating, interpreting, and ultimately exalting its past since the Civil War is not a unique occurrence. Nations the world over have struggled with the results of dissolving distinctions between the sacred and the secular and of devising societies based on perspectives that admit no dissent and tolerate no deviation. The current global conflict is not between Islam on the one hand and Christianity and Judaism on the other. It is rather a battle between religious fundamentalism and modernity, between a closed, exclusive, and hierarchical society against an open, diverse, and fluid civilization. It is a battle in its outline, if not its scope, that we in the South understand very well.

1 *The Past Is*

If this war had smashed the southern world, it had left the essential southern mind and will—the mind and will arising from, corresponding to, and requiring this world—entirely unshaken. Rather, after the manner of defensive wars in general and particularly those fought against odds and with great stubbornness, it had operated enormously to fortify and confirm that mind and will.

—W. J. Cash, *The Mind of the South*

Although I was born more than half a century after the war was over, it was a living reality in my life. I grew up in one of the families whose people could not forget that we had been conquered, while most of our neighbors were black people whose grandparents had been liberated in the same conflict. Our two races, although inseparable in our daily lives, were kept apart by social custom, misinterpretation of Holy Scriptures, and the unchallenged law of the land. . . .

—Jimmy Carter, *An Hour Before Daylight*

One of the most frequent comments from newcomers and visitors alike is that the South is still fighting the Civil War. The immanence of the war is a given for a southerner, at least for white southerners. Southerners tend to live in multiple time zones. Past, present, and future are conflated, and the past is the most important of all. We are comfortable with this; it has become second nature. The title character of Mississippi writer Barry Hannah's novel *Ray* (1984) admits, "I live in so many centuries. Everybody is still alive."[1]

Some years ago I stood at the base of the massive equestrian statue of Robert E. Lee on Richmond's Monument Avenue. It was a bright Sunday summer morning, early but already suggesting the blazing heat to come. As I tried to position myself to take a photograph, I saw a well-dressed elderly gentleman shuffling toward me. He smiled, pointed up at the statue, and commented matter-of-factly before he ambled away, "Quite a man, isn't he." *Isn't* he? I should not have been surprised at the use of present tense in reference to a long-dead general, albeit a very special general. "There is no such thing really as was because the past is," William Faulkner wrote.[2] And so it is in the South. Southerners may live in the past, as some charge, but it is incontrovertible that the past lives in southerners. Ben Robertson, a South Carolina journalist in the 1930s and '40s, put it this way: "All about me, on every side, was age, and history was continuous. . . . I was Southern, I was old."[3]

In the South history is not learned; it is remembered, it is handed down like a family heirloom through generations. Much of this remembered past is no longer in history books, but it is valued all the more as a precious lifeline, ever more fragile, connecting southerners to the South and each other. The memories invariably begin with the Civil War. And how white southerners remembered the Civil War and its aftermath defined and distinguished the South for the next century.

It is tempting to read history backward and see North and South as distinctive regions since time began. From the first European settlements, it is true, North and South were never identical, any more than two children from the same family are exactly alike. Plantation slavery distinguished the South early in our nation's history, and that difference grew through the first half of the nineteenth century. But, as historian Stephen Nissenbaum wrote, the sectionalism derived from slavery was "not an outgrowth of fundamentally different social systems, but instead was integral to republican ideology and the conception of the federal system itself."[4] Put another way, the rhetoric of sectional antagonism often boiled down to which section espoused and practiced the Revolutionary ideals best. What galled southerners was not their difference from the North but that northerners refused to accept them as equal moral, political, and economic partners in the American enterprise.

When northerners and southerners defended their respective stands on sectional issues, they both appealed to the same time-honored nationalist and democratic sentiments. Southern secessionists believed they were the true keepers of the ideals that had inspired the American Revolution. They were merely re-creating a more perfect Union. It was not they, but the Republicans, who had sundered the old Union by subverting the Constitution's guarantee of liberty. Abraham Lincoln similarly appealed to nationalist themes, telling northerners that the United States was "the last best hope on earth."

Even when the Republicans won the election of 1860, secession was by no means inevitable. The debates over secession highlighted the divisions in southern society, between the states and within the states. Save for South Carolina, long in the forefront of radical sentiment in the region, dissent surfaced in all the southern states. Some states, such as Virginia, North Carolina, Tennessee, and Arkansas, seceded reluctantly only after the war began and President Lincoln asked them for troops. Kentuckians never could make up their minds one way or the other and remained tenuously in the Union for the duration of the war. Western Virginians could not abide their state's secession decision and pulled a secession of their own, declaring the separate state of West Virginia in 1863. In the meantime, residents of northern Alabama, eastern Tennessee, western North Carolina, and parts of Texas took up sporadic armed resistance to Confederate authority. The Heroes of America, a pro-Union group in North Carolina, may have had as many as ten thousand members by 1863. It was possible during that year of fierce fighting to visit southern mountain towns, Delta plantations, and Texas ranches and see the Stars and Stripes flying proudly.

Even loyal Confederates found it difficult to transfer that loyalty to a new central government. Most southerners had rarely ventured beyond their counties; family and friends were their primary frames of reference. They identified with their localities, perhaps their state, but rarely with an entity called "the South."[5] States' rights had been a great rallying cry for secession, and now southerners were called upon to sacrifice their local interests, wealth, and young men for a much broader cause. That was difficult; some governors balked at troop quotas, others withheld supplies, and many Confederates bickered with the government in Richmond. "Died of States' Rights" might arguably serve as the epitaph for the defeated Confederacy, at least according to one historian.[6] The South was not a united country as it fought for independence.

After the war, this changed. Robert Penn Warren's simple dictum, "The South was created at Appomattox," holds.[7] The war and defeat took a terrible toll on the South. From the outset, both sides depicted the conflict as a holy war. Julia Ward Howe's "Battle Hymn of the Republic" summarized the northern view that God would strike the South with "His terrible swift sword." Southerners, equally religious, claimed God's favor as well. Obviously, God could "choose" only one side in this conflict. From the white southerners' perspective, their defeat was more than a lost war; they had evidently fallen out of favor with God.

In addition to the terrible loneliness and abandonment such an event implied for a religious people, the physical destruction of the region testified to man's and God's wrath. The scorched-earth policies of General William T. Sherman and his comrades-in-arms not only eroded the southern will to fight but made recovery that much more difficult. There was no Marshall Plan to rescue the South. Union armies had destroyed two-thirds of the South's assessed wealth, two-fifths of the livestock, and one-quarter of the white men between the ages of twenty and forty. The invasion ruined half the South's farm machinery, destroyed many of its railroads, and shattered its industry. Northern wealth rose by 50 percent between 1860 and 1870; southern wealth declined by 60 percent. In 1860 the southern states possessed slightly less than one-third of the nation's wealth; by 1870 that share had declined to 12 percent.[8]

When the young Confederate soldiers—many were boys, really—hobbled home, some broken, a few relieved, many with a sense of ruined dreams and lives askew, they came to a familiar place, a homestead, a town; but the time was unfamiliar. A civilization had vanished; an order was undone, the future a blank of uncertainty. Though Union armies had foretold the war's outcome with victories at Gettysburg and Vicksburg in July 1863, the end nearly two years later still came as a blow, for hope is a hardy perennial, and faith is still stronger. Stories filled the Bible of the weak inheriting victory and more. One more miracle, Dear Lord, please.

The soldiers came home to women and children who also had suffered the shock of war and deprivation. The women had waved gaily at departing sons, brothers, husbands, and fathers; had knitted uniforms, tilled the soil, tended the wounded, and buried the dead; and had come to rail against the Confederate government for keeping their husbands, hoarding their food, and leaving them vulnerable to friend and foe alike. The chivalry that promised protection and shelter proved a thin reed in war; their men could guarantee neither. God had rendered His judgment, these women believed, and had pronounced the South guilty. "The demoralization is complete," a Georgia girl lamented.[9] But neither the meaning nor source of that guilt was altogether clear. Such riddles would await future decoding; in the meantime, food, livelihood, and life itself offered more than enough challenges.

It was easier to heal the body than to cure the mind. The holy war was lost, as was the civilization that drove it. White southerners confronted change, but change to what they knew not. Their worst fears and imaginations played wildly: Would the Negro work? Would the ex-slave seek vengeance? Would the Union soldiers maintain their subjects in permanent penury and fear? Would they persist in dependence as virtual slaves to their new black and federal masters?

For southern blacks, as for southern whites, time began in 1865. But to African Americans, the surrender at Appomattox marked the time of liberation, not capitulation. They greeted peace with celebration and began to craft a new lore from the wreckage of the old system. Georgia freedmen, for example, told a story, passed down into the twentieth century, of Abraham Lincoln walking through the dusty roads of Georgia in 1865, hailing the newly freed slaves and they him. Lincoln never visited Georgia, but the point of deliverance is more important than the accuracy of the occurrence, as is the fact that it revealed a significant divergence from the southern white "take" on the war's outcome.

As the freed slaves celebrated the Union victory, Confederates tried to live with defeat, but acceptance did not come easily. White southerners did not wait for answers; they fought back. *Reconstruction* is a misnomer; *Restoration* is a more accurate term to describe the events from the surrender at Appomattox in 1865 to the removal of the last federal troops from the South in 1877. Except for a brief three-year period, from 1867 to 1870, ex-Confederates reclaimed their region, their governments, and their dominion over their families and former slaves. It was a stunning reversal of fortune for the erstwhile Confederacy, so recently downtrodden, defeated, and demoralized. How could they have mustered the strength and will to restore so much of what the war had swept away?

Part of the answer is that the North allowed the ex-Confederates considerable leeway in governing themselves and in allowing them to govern others. But more significant, perhaps, was the mental alchemy white southerners performed on the war itself. They spun the straw of defeat into a golden mantle of victory. Not that they refused to accept the verdict of the war—the end of slavery and of southern independence—but they rejected the idea of defeat and the guilt such a result implied.

New Traditions

A rationale was born. White southerners elevated defeat into a heroic Lost Cause, their fallen comrades and faltering leaders into saintly figures, their crumbled society into the best place on earth, and their struggle to regain control over their lives and region into a victorious redemption. Memory offered salvation; they could not allow the past to slip into the past. They had to keep foremost the old proverb that the struggle of man against power is the struggle of memory against forgetting. And they remembered.[10]

Transforming defeat into a heroic cause, made more noble by loss than by victory, resolved some of the humiliation white southerners experienced in the years after the war. But such an artifice could not persist in a vacuum. It required context. That context was the Old South. For if the war was heroic, then so was the cause for which white southerners cast down their lives and fortunes. Recasting the war, they reformulated the Old South.

The invention of the Old South gave white southerners a tradition, a sense of continuity in a destabilized postwar world.[11] Returning from war, Confederate veterans entered a different world, a strange place with everything reversed, as if they were suddenly living in a mirror. From the simplicity of war to the complexity of life, soldiers groped for meaning and routine.[12] They found solace in the collective experience of war and the view of that war as it evolved into the Lost Cause. They needed a sterling vision of the Old South, a heroic war, and eventually a glorious Redemption to extract them from the mirror, to set things right—maybe not exactly like before, but tolerable, and maybe someday better. Now they could hope. By creating a history from the story of the Old South, the Civil War, and Reconstruction, they erected a legend to live by and for. Their history, like all good traditions, scrambled time, so that the war and Reconstruction became one event, an immediate and constant part of daily living, a reminder to do well and think right and remember that the legacy is watching.

White southerners often publicly professed good riddance to slavery in the postwar years, but they protested its shortcomings a bit too much. They cited the institution's burdens on masters and how it hampered the southern economy and limited opportunities for poorer whites. To hear them, one would think the Emancipation Proclamation liberated southern whites as much as black slaves. They rarely pronounced slavery a moral evil, however, for to do so would be to call the Cause into question. Instead, they created a memory of the Old South as a time of happy slaves, gracious masters, and beautiful, chaste women. The creation of an Edenic Old South heightened the tragedy of its destruction. Like the fall of ancient Greece, the demise of southern civilization dissolved the beauty, grace, learning, and civility that flourished under enlightened men. "In simple truth and beyond question," Virginia novelist George W. Bagby intoned in 1884, "there was in our Virginia country life a beauty, a simplicity, a purity and uprightness, a cordial and lavish hospitality, warmth and grace which shined in the lens of memory with a charm that passes all language at my command."[13]

In 1901 James Battle Avirett, a former Confederate chaplain who was once the master of a turpentine plantation, published a memoir, *The Old Plantation: How We Lived in Great House and Cabin Before the War*. The book purported to tell about Avirett's life on his estate in eastern North Carolina in the decade before the Civil War and how the war destroyed that existence. Avirett depicted an idyllic life for himself and his slaves, dedicating his book to "the memory of the old planter and his wife—the only real slaves on the old plantation of overgrown children." Unfortunately, Avirett's memory was much less a re-creation of plantation life than a fantasy, part of the full-blown rehabilitation of the Old South that had been underway since the end of Reconstruction. Avirett claimed in the book that his home and plantation perished during the war. In reality, the Civil War had nothing to do with Avirett's economic downfall: a fire consumed his house in 1851, and six years later, in desperate financial circumstances, Avirett sold his plantation.[14]

Avirett's document is not an example of selective remembrance; it is pure fabrication. By the time he wrote his memoir, the Civil War and Reconstruction had accumulated new legends to justify contemporary needs. New "traditions" appeared throughout the twentieth century. Among the most popular novels of the early 1900s were Thomas Dixon's *The Clansman* and *The Leopard's Spots*. Both idealized the Old South and chronicled a Reconstruction that occurred only in vivid imaginations; such fictions were shared by most white southerners (and by most white Americans) as fact. The refurbished history of the Old South, coupled with white perspectives on the Civil War and Reconstruction, forged a new national identity in the South, what D. W. Griffith would refer to in the title of his 1915 film adaptation of Dixon's work as *The Birth of a Nation*.

Neither Avirett's memoir nor Dixon's stories should be dismissed as the idle musings of reactionaries. The forward-looking publicity agents for a New South of great cities, industries, and commerce also paid homage to a sanitized Old South. This was not merely lip service to calm the doubts of those who feared the impact Yankee-style economic development on their traditional way of life. New South boosters avidly made the connection between their programs and their foundation in the Old South. The New South Creed of progress embraced an Old South Creed of tradition. Henry Grady, the cherubic Atlanta journalist who beat the drums of his city and region incessantly, offered no apologies for slavery and the civilization it supported. "The Northern man," he offered, "dealing with casual servants can hardly comprehend the friendliness that existed between the master and the slave." And, Grady continued, the warm relations between black and white had survived the war and distinguished the South's pursuit of progress. "It is the answer to abuse and slander," Grady professed. "It is the hope of our future."[15]

The Redeemers asserted that the best tribute to the Old South, and to the war and Redemption fought in its name, was to build a new South: to beat the Yankees at their own game, to build factories and cities and not corrupt the morals of the people or upset the racial, gender, and social balances derived from the vanished civilization. The New South Creed proved wonderfully compatible with the Old South Myth. The South would accept the industrial revolution, railroads, steam engines, and electricity, but southerners would adapt the modern world to its own purposes, ensuring the maintenance of white supremacy, patriarchy, and one-party rule. Like Bismarckian Germany, the late-nineteenth-century South marched forward to modernity, while looking backward to the past for its inspiration and guidance.

The New South promoters reveled in the Resurrection story. The South, paralleling Jesus, had risen from the dead of Reconstruction to the living Redemption. The southern economy could sustain that story and repeat it again and again. As Virginian Philip Alexander Bruce wrote in 1905, the story of the New South is "a vital narration of the progress of a mighty people, who, from adversity which as no other section of North America has ever experienced," had risen and "won the race with adverse fate and become the pride of the Union."[16]

By 1900 a multitude of new inventions connected the South to the rest of America and the world. In fashion, appliances, transportation conveyances, packaged foods, and domestic architecture, the urban South was virtually indistinguishable from cities of comparable size in the North. Some southern innovations became popular national phenomena. Jazz and blues wafted up from New Orleans and Memphis to Chicago and New York. James B. Duke, who built a tobacco empire, turned his resources and his curiosity to constructing an energy network, which provided the Carolina Piedmont with the cheapest electricity in the nation by 1920. And the looms powered by Duke's energy came to dominate the American textile industry in the 1920s, attracting yet another symbol of American ingenuity: Willis Carrier's air conditioning system, which debuted in a Belmont, North Carolina, textile plant in 1906.[17] And what is more American than Coca-Cola, the drink that Atlanta pharmacist James Pemberton hoped would cure a hangover and instead hooked a nation and eventually the world?

The South was hardly a backward place in 1900. Sure, there were backward places in the South, in the rural areas where agriculture failed, ignorance flourished, and poverty reigned. But in the cities, the go-getters, boosters, and flack men ripped, dug, built, promoted, and sold as quickly and as sharply as anyone in America. Yet they carefully cultivated and reinforced the prevailing views up North that the South remained a genteel land of moonlight and magnolias, a graceful counterpoint to the roiling North of immigrants, black migrants, and dirty, crowded cities. Or they let pass the image of the South as a pellagra-infested, incest-haunted, race-baiting, Bible-thumping, tobacco-chewing, eye-gouging region as different from the rest of America as the Congo was from Norway. Either way, the southern men on the make had the advantage. Not only did their view of the Old South and its society receive approbation up North, but northerners often underestimated their counterparts—to their economic and political peril.

As remarkable a chronicler and student of southern life as William Faulkner was, even he could not see through this duplicity. The Oxford master juxtaposed the faded, impotent, genteel aristocracy of the Old South, represented by the Sartoris family, with the crafty, beady-eyed degeneracy of the grasping Snopes clan—an Old South–New South diorama if there ever was one. The reality was that Snopes and Sartoris were one in the same. The new southerner affected a gentility of the old school while he lustily hankered after the main chance. The real Sartorises transformed with the times. They retained the trappings of the Old South, including the social and patriarchal system of that era, while adapting very well to the new economy.

These were not southern men in northern clothing. Though they craved profits and progress, they did so within the framework of white supremacy and patriarchy. They would not compromise that frame of reference, nor would they desist in deploying the Civil War and Reconstruction to justify the social system that grounded New South society. They operated happily within the infrastructure erected on the bones of Reconstruction: a weak state government and regulations, a deep belief in the sanctity of private property, and a fragile concept of the general welfare that dissolved on contact with the interests of political and economic leaders. They employed these elements to make a point: that the South was as good as any region, and that economic development would not only help them compete against the North but also release them from the dependence that had contributed to their defeat in the Civil War. For a white society that associated dependence with femininity and slavery, economic development was more than a way to get ahead and earn self-respect; it was a matter of honor, survival, and ultimate independence, a blueprint for getting even: avenge defeat and secure the Redemption. The New South Creed was, according to Charlotte journalist W. J. Cash, "a sort of new charge at Gettysburg which should finally and incontestably win for [the South] the right to be itself for which, in the last analysis, it had always fought."[18]

There was something familiar about this ardent thrust for economic power, with its fevered cotton-mill campaigns, census watches, enticements of new business, and inflation of progress—not so much in the activities themselves as in the process. It was Faulkner's Thomas Sutpen, hewing out a fortune from the tangled swamps of Mississippi, a man who stood as a metaphor for the ruthless exploitation of land and race in the Old South that led, like a Greek tragedy, to the destruction of that civilization. But white southerners, like the Bourbons, learned nothing and, in fact, wore destruction on their sleeves, the better to remind them to try harder next time.[19]

New South boosters promised that their version of modernity would, unlike that of their erstwhile enemies, rest on a foundation of grace, stability, and civility derived from the Old South heritage. These were traditions, unlike slavery, that white southerners could carry on after the war, that provided a direct behavioral link to a hallowed past and, because of that connection, were crucial to the maintenance of the New South. When Scarlett O'Hara attended a dance in Atlanta after the war, the music, the finery, and the manners threw her back to that blessed time. She realized, of course, that those years and that civilization were gone forever. But like the incandescence of a star long dead, the Old South could shine through in the "old forms." As Scarlett explained, "Everything in their old world had changed but the old forms. . . . The old usages went on, must go on, for the forms were all that were left to them."[20]

Old forms carried not only grace and civility forward to the New South but also the social relations implied in those forms. The forms required an elaborate etiquette that differed according to race, class, and gender. The etiquette reinforced traditional relationships of white male dominance and overall white supremacy. Patterns of speech, body language, hospitality, and the subjects of conversations composed the etiquette. Deviation from these patterns flouted tradition and threatened the entire social hierarchy of the New South. Glorification of the Old South not only elevated the Lost Cause but perpetuated antebellum social relations in the New South.

Manners also helped to gloss the gross inequalities and rough-hewn lives led by many southerners. Just as grace and gentility masked the violent, exploitive relationships of the Old South, so they covered inequities in the New. The very attributes New South boosters promoted to the world as endearingly southern proved as artificial as the raw social and racial relations they obscured. Etiquette was both a mental and visual barrier against unpleasantness. As South Carolina writer James McBride Dabbs noted, "all etiquette partly exists to enable people to live together closely without rubbing one another raw." Etiquette was also a means of control. Observable behavior reflected virtue or its absence. To be a "good Christian" was as much a behavioral norm as it was a religious statement. William Alexander Percy summarized it best when he wrote, "While good morals are all-important between the Lord and His creatures, what counts between one creature and another is good manners."[21]

White southerners would turn against the bearer of bad tidings, the critic, the malcontent. The best place on earth did not require reform; more than that, criticism was simply bad form. And form reflected upbringing and, above all, place. The Old South, recast into the New, served as a behavioral primer, a model for living life in a changed time so that time would not seem changed at all.

White southerners communicated these "traditions"—of the Old South, the Civil War, and Reconstruction—in various venues. Confederate president Jefferson Davis had given the charge to his and future generations to "keep the memories of our heroes green."[22] And they did. Veterans shared their stories at family gatherings and church picnics. Just after the war, women's memorial associations maintained the graves and the memories of the young men who perished fighting for their country. Public spectacles, commemorations, monuments, and the naming of streets, schools, and public buildings after martyrs and leaders offered visual representations of white southern history. Political contests, that most public of engagements in the South, offered opportunities to articulate the past and connect candidates' current endeavors to a storied and gloried history. Popular songs and hymns celebrated saints and martyrs to the Cause.

As subsequent generations of white southerners emerged, more removed from the actual events than their predecessors, the written word in textbooks, novels, memoirs, and monographs added to oral and visual traditions. The Southern Historical Society, founded in 1869, published scholarly papers defending the Confederacy. By the early 1900s the professional historical writings of William A. Dunning and U. B. Phillips told about an Old South of benevolent slavery, a Civil War fought for states' rights, and a Reconstruction that began in tragedy and ended in triumph with Redemption. Little differentiated the professional from the popular perspective. When Margaret Mitchell conducted research for *Gone With the Wind*, she diligently devoured half a century's worth of scholarly work in southern history, much of which found its way into her novel. Both her story and her sources were fiction. Only beginning in the 1930s and 1940s, with the pioneering work of historians C. Vann Woodward and John Hope Franklin, did southern historians challenge the traditional view of southern history, and not in earnest until the 1950s. But even then, the stories from the earlier era enveloped young white southerners, for whom the war and Redemption seemed more immediate than ever, preservation more important than before.

White southerners growing up in the early twentieth century noted how vivid the war and Redemption seemed to them in the stories created and recreated by their elders, in the books they read, the tableaux they viewed. The war and Redemption were as immanent as today and as impending as tomorrow. Novelist Mary Johnston, of the first postwar generation, recalled that her parents raised her "in a veritable battle cloud, an atmosphere of war stories, of continual reference to the men and to the deeds of gigantic struggle."[23]

Subsequent generations also heard and learned the heartfelt soliloquies; it was not enough to remember the past; it was necessary to *live* the past. The semblance of being there, of experiencing the pain and the glory, the martyrdom and the resurrection, made their preservation all the more precious. The sustenance of that Cause and that Redemption functioned both as a tribute to ancestors and a living memorial to the present, a gift that never stopped giving. Novelist Caroline Gordon grew up in Kentucky in the early 1900s, and as soon as she could carry a tune, she sang songs of praise for Confederate heroes interspersed by her grandmother's vivid commentary on battlefield exploits. As Gordon observed in the 1930s, "I do not think that my childhood experiences were very different from those of any southerner who is over thirty years old."[24]

Years later, when war and Reconstruction generations could no longer reach out to their children and grandchildren, the legacy of storytelling, the textbooks replete with the legends of the Cause and Redemption, and the physical and social world they inherited still surrounded their progeny. As if performing the Passion Play, white southerners repeated the exploits of the war over and over again: not the defeats, desertions, and dissent, but the heroism against great odds, the sacrifices when no more could be offered, and the lives lost for a cause greater than man. Southerners growing up in the first half of the twentieth century found dating the war difficult because their elders often discussed the conflict as if it had happened yesterday or was still in progress. Writer Willie Morris recalled frightening his maiden aunts in the 1940s with fabricated radio reports that the Yankees were coming. Margaret Mitchell confessed, "I heard so much about the fighting and hard times after the war that I firmly believed Mother and Father had been through it all instead of being born long afterward. In fact I was about ten years old before I learned the war hadn't ended shortly after I was born."[25]

Not only was the timing of the war uncertain to children coming of age enveloped in a "past" that was not quite past, but so was the outcome. James Eleazar, growing up in South Carolina in the early 1900s, did not learn that the South had lost the war until he was twelve years old: "And it was one of the saddest awakenings I ever had. For hours on end I had listened to Grandpa tell of whipping the lard out of the Yankees on a dozen battlefields." But the loss, Eleazar would learn, was only a temporary setback.[26] So pervasive was the tendency to idealize the war and repeat its events like a rosary that even Yankees who settled in the region adopted the stories as their own. Shirley Abbott wrote that her father recounted the heroic deeds of the war incessantly even though he hailed from Indiana and his ancestors had fought proudly in the Union Army.[27]

The histories made a lasting impression. George Wallace remembered his time as a fifteen-year-old page in the Alabama legislature, stealing out of the State House in Montgomery one sultry morning and standing on the star where Jefferson Davis was sworn in as president of the Confederacy, and how he would one day stand on that sacred spot, and how he would shield it from the bootheels of President John F. Kennedy's men when they came calling on him a century after Gettysburg.[28]

The Confederate monument erected in Yazoo City, Mississippi, in 1909 by the United Daughters of the Confederacy (UDC) bears the inscription, "As at Thermopylae, the greater glory was to the vanquished."[29] In the southern alchemy that turned failure to glory, here lay the soul of the New South. For southerners, like the ancient Spartans whom Xerxes' army had cut to ribbons, the outcome paled before the Cause. The civilization destroyed by the Union forces may have vanished, but its principles were immortal. The monuments that grew up, first of the leaders, then of the common soldiers, in every courthouse square in the South, reflected this noble lineage. They also indicated that the embodiment of these principles lay with the white South and, more particularly, with the white male South, embronzed in steadfast glory, gazing northward.

The recasting of the Civil War began before the ink dried on the surrender document. William Pittman Lumpkin enlisted in the Confederate army at the age of fifteen in 1864. Less than a year later, as he walked back to his Georgia home, he had reinvented himself as William *Wallace* Lumpkin, after the thirteenth-century Scottish patriot later immortalized in the film *Braveheart*. Like the first William Wallace, Lumpkin would not readily submit to rule by superior force, and that example girded his postwar life and the lives of countless other southern white men.[30]

Honor was to remember and follow the example of those who sacrificed; dishonor to forget and walk the path of the enemy. Orthodoxy mattered, both in civil and religious terms: the public symbols of sacrifice were etched into the southern landscape in the numerous statues, monuments, and consecrated grounds; on the lips of political leaders who reminded their neighbors of that sacrifice and how close they came to suffering the ultimate defeat of Yankee and black rule; in the books and articles they read, primers for remembrance, Aesops' fables for the masses, with the moral always evident and always the same.

The Orthodox Church

The Cause became holy. As Christ was sacrificed on the cross, so the South was crucified. But, like Jesus, the South would rise again. When the last federal troops left the region in 1877, southerners referred to the event as the Redemption, its leaders as Redeemers. Redeeming what? Redeeming the Old South of memory and, in the process, self-respect for whites and a rationale for the sacrifice of war and their bitter defeat. The words captured well the holy status southerners accorded the war, their crucifixion.[31]

The metaphors white southerners marshaled to re-create their past explicitly depicted their struggle as a religious movement. The war assumed a sacred quality, its heroes were martyrs, and even its outcome reflected God's grace. Pastors preached, "He loveth whom He chastiseth," and congregations branded this message into their souls. The generic portraits of Confederate soldiers, wan and doomed, that graced white southern homes in the decades after the war resembled Jesus in gray. As medieval townspeople erected statues to the saints, white southerners built monuments to their fallen heroes. By 1900 scarcely a southern town existed without a statue or memorial to the Confederate soldiers as a permanent reminder of the heroic conflict.

Leaders such as Robert E. Lee, Thomas "Stonewall" Jackson, and the much-maligned Jefferson Davis were elevated from heroes to saints. Their writings became holy writ; monuments became icons; cemeteries became shrines; white southerners made "pilgrimages" to Richmond's Monument Avenue and to Davis's home, Beauvoir, in Biloxi, Mississippi.

You would think that the exaltation of death and defeat would generate depression, but it proved exhilarating to southern society. Father Abram Ryan, Confederate chaplain, put the feeling in verse: "There's grandeur in grave / There's glory in gloom."[32] The war forced austerity onto southerners. They would make stoicism a virtue and mourning a moral obligation. The North could go about its secular business; the South would wear the thorny crown with pride.

Postwar life became a test of southern worthiness to receive God's favor. The Bible offered numerous examples of how unmerited suffering was redemptive. And it was the Bible and religion that inspired white southerners to endure as a testament to their heroic past. From the nation's least-churched region, the South became, after the war, the most church-going part of the Union. Evangelical Protestantism flourished as never before. The hard-boiled, fire-and-brimstone Calvinism that had dried up in New England generations earlier was resurrected and flourished in the postwar South. Religion and history merged; history—the Old South, the war, and the war's Redemption—ratified faith; and faith sanctified history.

Like their religion, white southerners proclaimed their history forcefully and publicly—in public art, in symbols, in pronouncements from the pulpit, the press, the stump, and the classroom. Convert the unconverted, pray for those who cannot bring themselves to the altar of the Lost Cause, but do not suffer these fools kindly, for they are damned. And we will cast them out from fellowship and keep them apart until they recant and rejoin the fold. For the creation of a heaven on earth can admit of no dissent, cannot allow the flight of thought known as opinion, much less of doubt. As Christ died for our sins, so did those young men in gray. And we cannot lapse in our love and devotion for either, else we are lost and doomed forever.

Just as the Bible allowed only one interpretation, history followed orthodoxy. Evangelical Protestantism blended into evangelical history. If history were holy, then those who lived in the present must strive to emulate the past. With one interpretation of history, there could be only one emulation. History became part of a white southerner's religion. As Virginian James Branch Cabell wrote at the turn of the twentieth century, "no history is a matter of record; it is a matter of faith."[33]

Orthodoxy created tyranny. W. J. Cash, a native of Shelby, North Carolina, grew up amid the paraphernalia and propaganda of the Lost Cause and Redemption. Yet, unlike most of his contemporaries, the contrast between the perfect society those traditions depicted and the society as he viewed it tormented him. Moving to Charlotte and working as a journalist in the heart of the booster-charged New South, the burdens of history and the authoritarian frame of mind nurtured by that history led Cash to write *The Mind of the South*. It was as if, Cash thought, the South were still at war, under a state of siege, where "criticism, analysis, detachment took on the aspect of high and aggravated treason." So solid was this orthodoxy that Cash felt confident to write about *the* mind of the South.[34] So troubled by his betrayal of his home, and so fearful of the consequences of that betrayal, Cash took his own life soon after his book was published.

The South where Cash grew up in the early twentieth century was not a nuanced place; unchallenged verities prevailed, and woe to those who demurred. Original thought, imagination, inquiry, and doubt were banished, at least from the public realm. Privately, one could muse at the contradictions between fact and fancy and between Christianity and white supremacy, but best to avoid public disclosure. In public (indistinct from private in the South), it was best not to divulge anything. Exude complacency and satisfaction.

So southerners lived buried, or what writer Ellen Glasgow called "sheltered," lives, which she defined as the "effort of one human being to stand between another and life." The surface civility, the gracious manners, and the oral traditions handed down from the Civil War and Reconstruction generation provided a comforting and confining refuge for southern whites, a throwback to the fondly remembered Old South, a shelter to blind them to the inequities of their remembered past and the racial, social, and gender divisions that such visionary history and its application generated. Glasgow's prototype of a southern gentleman, Civil War veteran General David Archibald, sacrificed love and the career he wanted—all for appearances. He lived the life other people expected of him, that of the southern gentleman. As Glasgow summarized Archibald's life, "For thirty years he had sacrificed his youth, his middle age, his dreams, his imagination, all the vital instincts that make a man, to the moral earnestness of tradition. . . . He had been a good citizen, a successful lawyer, a faithful husband, an indulgent father; he had been, indeed, everything but himself."[35]

The irony was that this tradition was a recent construct, scarcely out of the cradle when General Archibald came home from the war; it was no real tradition at all but rather a manufactured history woven from wishes, lies, and necessity and passed off as gospel.

Those who dared to break the spell, or merely to question it, suffered. Newspaper editors, preachers, teachers, or anyone who voiced dissent found that his business mysteriously dropped off, or her neighbors grew cold, or he suddenly became expendable at the bank or the school. Violence rarely enforced the status quo; it was unnecessary, at least against white people. To be cast from the tribe, to be shunned, ignored, rendered penurious—these were sufficient means to dissuade the thinker. Loneliness is a heavy burden.

The war may have become immortal, but rigor mortis settled in the southern mind. Faith did not admit inquiry; inquiry brought discord and disharmony; better to avoid it. For generations the South lagged in educational achievement and in the quality of its academic institutions. Part of this resulted from poverty, but part derived from design. Thinking threatened history, and history remained one of the few luxuries left to the South after the war. Thinking implied some cognizance of the future, but the South's future could only mirror the "past." And thinking sometimes produced change, and change was anathema: How could you change perfection?

To reify life before the war, to rescue meaning from defeat, and to depict its aftermath as a glorious struggle for redemption was preferable to the alternative: facing the awful lessons of loss and death. Heroism is preferable to humdrum. The South became a façade, a showcase under which lay an abyss of deceit and denial.

With heroes larger than life and their exploits greater than legends, the past became perfect, and white southerners, living in the imperfect present, visited their history as often as possible, until present and past became indistinguishable. Even today it does not take much to tease a Civil War story from southerners who go back a few generations, and even from those who don't go back at all. Worship of the past accounts, in part, for the importance of genealogy in the South. Alabama writer Florence King claimed her grandmother was such a genealogy buff that she had traced her ancestry back to Jesus and could thus lay claim to God as kin.[36]

Southerners' fascination with their forbears accounts also for the importance of cemeteries in the southern landscape—family plots, churchyard graves, and grander private and public cemeteries. Shirley Abbott related that "within our family there was no such thing as a person who did not matter. We all mattered, and the dead most of all." Go to any southern town and no matter how dingy or dilapidated the houses and businesses, the cemetery will likely be spruced up with lawns, pebbled walks, flowers, and shaded avenues of the dead. Southerners regularly visit cemeteries to converse with their relatives. Mississippian Will Percy explained his fondness for the cemetery near his home: "I come here not infrequently because it is restful and comforting. I am with my own people."[37]

Southerners notice the lack of ancestor worship when they move from the region, as Mississippi writer Eudora Welty observed: "I missed that when I lived in other parts of the country. People were friends but had no sense of their ancestors. No one was interested."[38] "Who are your people?" is likely to be one of the first questions a southerner will ask a newcomer. And, if the last name rings a bell—and southerners are very good with names; it's a fulltime occupation for some—there will likely be a discourse on the origin of the name, its bearers, and, most important, where those so-named have lived or moved. Natives are keenly interested in newcomers' ancestries, not to be intrusive or judgmental, but as part of the process of "placing." Names mean families and families mean ancestors and ancestors mean traditions and traditions mean you're OK.

So history is tied up not only with faith but with family as well. And just as you would not blaspheme God, you would not trash your family. The selective and positive version of history is thus carried down from generation to generation. Selective history reads out conflicting accounts that reduce heroes to mortals and events to, well, events. You can believe segregation is beneficial for both races, that slavery had some good points, and that whatever is southern is best. You can also read new material in, if it reinforces conventional historical wisdom. "Tradition" can include "anything anybody can remember being done for as long as a generation."[39]

This is not to say that northerners had no sense of the past or that they did not use history as a means to justify the ends of a rapidly urbanizing and industrializing society in the late nineteenth century. The myth of the Old South, after all, originated in the imagination of northerners before the Civil War. And the North generally subscribed to the white South's view of Reconstruction. But northerners' adoption of history was pragmatic, not pervasive. There were too few blacks, too many liberated women, and too many religions to build a rigid hierarchy on race, gender, and religious orthodoxy. And history had been considerably kinder to the North.

What distinguished white southerners from other Americans is that they set about to create a heritage, not to re-create a history. As historian John R. Gillis observed, heritage is a process by which "the past is domesticated, made familiar." Heritage forges "a sense of continuity where none exists," as between the Old South and the New.[40] Through the reinterpretation of the Old South and the fabrication of the story of the Civil War and Reconstruction, white southerners developed "traditions" that served as the building blocks of a distinctive "national" heritage. Appeals to truth or reality will rarely shake believers, because heritage is above all a faith, and white southerners engaged their religion to support their historical perspective. Heritage, for white southerners, was not merely a convenient rendering of the past to salve troubled minds and hearts; it was a divinely inspired vision that captured the white southern soul.

As comforting as heritage was, however, it proffered a false salvation. "A faith in heritage," Gillis warned, "can easily produce murderous fanaticism." White southerners did not go quite that far in acting out their historical fantasy, though murder and fanaticism were never far from the surface of southern life in the century after Reconstruction and occasionally punctured the veneer of civility. Instead, there existed what John Stuart Mill in another context termed "the tyranny of prevailing opinion and feeling."[41] Dissent implied much more than a disagreement over historical interpretation; it involved heresy and subverted the existing order.

Although democratic in form and superficially adhering to the general rules of the republic, the South after Reconstruction resembled an authoritarian regime. Visitors could not immediately discern authority's manifestations, though white supremacy and one-party politics provided strong hints in that direction. Southern whites successfully masked their society from outsiders, most of whom wanted to believe the positive about their fellow white Americans. White southerners were unfailingly hospitable and pridefully pointed out docile blacks, cooperative white labor, and no trouble whatsoever as evidence of the consensus and happiness in southern society (implying at the same time a disdain for the discordant, bordering-on-chaos, polyglot cities of the North). There were no jackbooted thugs in the street, though they did appear from time to time. No; it was more a dictatorship of the mind, a stifling self-censorship, a cutoff of inquiry, a dismissal of doubt; it was children growing up living other people's memories, not of the past but the legend of the past. It took much more courage to be a rebel than a Rebel. Conformity became not the easy way out but the only way in. Conformity brought a comforting order, but, as Ralph Waldo Emerson warned, conformity "loves not realities and creators, but names and customs."[42] Names and customs, genealogy and manners, became the glue that sealed the continuity and immutability of southern history and the society it created.

W. J. Cash called the intellectual support for this regime the "savage ideal . . . whereunder dissent and variety are completely suppressed and men become, in all their attitudes, professions, and actions, virtual replicas of one another." Cash attributed the ideal to the "conflict with the Yankee," with the Civil War at its center. But it was not the war itself, or its aftermath, that created the distinctive South; it was what white southerners made of those historical events and how they transformed history into heritage, how the Confederacy passed from defeat to divinity.[43]

The isolation chamber of the mind tightened after 1890. As the Civil War generation aged, younger men and women stepped forward to preserve memories in the amber of texts, monuments, folklore, and song. The United Daughters of the Confederacy and the Sons of Confederate Veterans memorialized the war, mourned Reconstruction, and cast flowers before battle heroes, those still-living links to glory. Commemorate, celebrate, orate, but do not think. As Hannah Arendt argued, "The ideal subject of totalitarian rule is not the convinced Nazi or the convinced Communist, but people for whom the distinction between fact and fiction and the distinction between true and false no longer exists."[44] The Old South became a *Gone With the Wind* set; the Civil War, a Lost Cause; and Reconstruction, a time of suffering and ultimate redemption always in danger of reversal at the slightest dissent.

Cash captured the prevailing mind-set well, a mind-set as valid in his Depression-era South as it was a generation earlier despite the South's growing cities, industries, and connections with the rest of the country and the world.

His insights resulted as much from the journalist's keen eye for observation as from his personal, tortured experience as an outsider, a dissenter, an outcast in his own hometown, which refused long after his death to honor him but whose leading citizens erected a statue to another hometown lad, the writer Thomas Dixon. Even now. So Cash wrote from both professional analysis and personal anguish. The typical white southerner, he believed, was addicted to "violence, intolerance, aversion and suspicion toward new ideas, an incapacity for analysis, an inclination to act from feeling rather than thought, an exaggerated individualism and a too narrow concept of social responsibility, attachment to fictions and false values, above all too great attachment to racial values and a tendency to justify cruelty and injustice in the name of these values, sentimentality and a lack of realism."[45]

Not a happy portrait. Yet few in the South thought about it, much less had the insight and courage to hold it up to fellow southerners. Southern newspapers comforted their readers, preachers blessed and forgave their congregations, and teachers reinforced that this was the greatest place on earth, let no one say or think otherwise. Contrary views, if they filtered into the region at all, were dismissed as Yankee infections that required large doses of denial. Espousal of adverse doctrines implied a kinship to the enemy, an attempt to undermine tradition and render the South helpless once again.

All these characteristics fit in with northerners' general perception of the South as America's "other place." The region's relative isolation and poverty between the 1890s and the 1930s limited outside contact and thus preserved the traditions of history from outside scrutiny and interference. But by the time of World War II, the more Americans learned about the South, the more they disliked. The millions of servicemen who filtered into the South to train for the war arrived with preconceived notions fired by the huge national success of the movie *Gone With the Wind*. The South they encountered, a land of cloying heat and humidity, and even more smothering prejudice and astounding ignorance, oozed through the gracious hospitality.

Seeing was believing, and the closer Americans came to the South the worse they thought of it. Indicative of this trend prior to midcentury was a best-selling portrait of postwar America, *Inside U.S.A.* (1947), by John Gunther. The journalist traversed the nation in the heady, optimistic days following World War II, but his depiction of the South exuded anything but optimism. "Once or twice," he reported, "traveling from town to town I felt that I wasn't in the United States at all, but in some utterly foreign land. . . . The South highlights almost every American problem. . . . The South contains a great number of pronouncedly schizoid people; the whole region is a land of paranoia, full of the mentally sick; most Southerners feel a deep necessity to hate something, if necessary even themselves." As for civil liberties, "the South is probably the darkest place in the nation." Perhaps the contrast between the just-won victory over fascism and the social structure of the American South touched a raw nerve in Gunther, but his view fit in with the growing mainstream impression of the South in the years between the end of the war and the beginning of the civil rights movement.[46]

This should not imply that the South from the decades after the Civil War to the end of World War II existed as a fortress impenetrable by outside ideas and things. The South was very much "with it" during these decades, much more so than many observers give the region credit for. Southerners accepted, even embraced, modern innovations, but as Mississippi writer Stark Young observed in 1930, "We . . . create our own attitude toward" the machine and invention.[47] Hydroelectric power in the early twentieth century fueled a burgeoning textile industry, but that industry reinforced traditional social, racial, and gender hierarchies crafted after the Civil War. Rapid urbanization after 1890 helped to institutionalize rather than weaken white supremacy. What need was there for racial segregation by law in the sparsely populated countryside? But in a city, with higher population densities, trolleys, elevators, public buildings, and sidewalks, whites implemented systematic separation of the races to ensure and reinforce their own dominance. The modern city provided the supreme laboratory to carry out the ideals of white superiority. The very landscape of the city—its neighborhoods, its infrastructure, its public spaces, such as parks and playgrounds—cried out, "Inequality!" "White supremacy!"

The South seemed to mimic George Orwell's characterization of English culture as "an everlasting animal stretching into the future and the past, and, like all living things, having the power to change out of recognition and yet remain the same." Mark Twain, who straddled the border between North and South, understood the region well but in the end could not make sense of its post–Civil War incarnation. To Twain, the South was an exotic mix of the modern and the traditional, though how the mix came out in a compound he was unable to say. As he noted somewhat exasperatingly in *Life on the Mississippi* (1883), the South was "practical common sense, progressive ideas, and progressive works, mixed up with the duel, the inflated speech, and the jejune romanticism of an absurd past that is dead."[48]

In the city the heavy hand of bigotry wore kid gloves, the better to hide the mean fist, at least to casual observers who did not look deeper than the emerging social clubs of Atlanta and Charlotte or beyond the gentility of gracious hospitality, soft voices, warm handshakes, and "y'all come back now, heah?" Or beyond the staged race relations, that etiquette of rules and boundaries for discourse. Manners convinced not only outsiders that grace and civility ruled in the South; more important, they convinced white southerners themselves. They surveyed the cities and saw not wildly disparate lives and fortunes but harmony, everyone in his place and a place for everyone.

Counterculture

Alternative histories existed all along. African Americans and some white women could not accept their places in southern society. Those other freedom fighters, the four million ex-slaves, had a prominent place in the new narrative, though they would have been willing to say no thank you if the Redeemers had allowed them a voice. To black southerners, the Civil War and Reconstruction represented a fundamental meaning to their lives as well, but one very different from that of their white neighbors. White women shared the despair and heartbreak of their men, but the experience of war had left them ambivalent, both about the past the war obviated and the future that may yet require them to assume new roles. If African Americans and white women could not somehow change the myths, or at least expose them as such, their roles would be fixed. That was hurtful not only to blacks and white women but to the South as a whole, for it is not possible to construct a society on a lie without poisoning its development. Political, educational, and economic institutions must work to perpetuate the lie. That is the way authoritarian regimes work.

Between 1865 and 1945 southern religious leaders, educators, women, and African Americans pointed to the discrepancies between prevailing wisdom and current reality, and a few offered alternatives. Their incremental approach—suggesting interracial dialogues, increased funding for black education, expansion of women's presence in education and the professions, or research into southern society to demonstrate that the region had problems—attained some minor victories but few significant alterations in prevailing traditions. More-direct challenges, especially from African Americans, such as boycotts, litigation, and individual protests directed at Jim Crow, occurred at great peril. But their very existence bespoke a determination to escape a smothering history.

From the perspective of contemporaries, the small challenges were heroic efforts, individuals and organizations stepping onto the battlefield, braving the fire of tradition, and risking reputations—even lives. Many became torchbearers at noon, proponents of the obvious, advocates of evolution, opponents of child labor and lynching. Yet even these modest stances were fraught with struggle, and their proponents comforted and cautioned themselves with the view that any beneficial change must come slowly and must be framed in traditional rhetoric. So change came slowly, and heritage endured.

Privately, some white southerners anguished over their region and the prevailing historical consensus that had burdened themselves and their neighbors. They knew exactly what was happening. They wanted the South to tell a new story. Southerners such as writer Katharine Du Pre Lumpkin, whose father had taken on the name, if not the legacy, of William Wallace, longed for the "plain . . . truths" of a revised southern history that provided a more visible place for women and a more honest account of blacks. A southern literary renaissance emerging in the 1920s and epitomized by William Faulkner exposed the bankruptcy of the Old South, the debilitating impact of obsessions with racial purity, and the hypocrisy of postwar life. But Faulkner's neighbors dismissed him, the Jackson (Mississippi) *Daily News* calling him "a propagandist of degradation and properly belong[ing] to the privy school of literature." And the writing was fiction, after all.[49]

The less subtle prose of novelist Thomas Wolfe and journalist W. J. Cash earned those writers much greater opprobrium from their neighbors. They may have been prophets in New York and Stockholm, but they were nothing more than "trashy" writers to white southerners. Eventually, both retreated into private despair. As a saddened Ellen Glasgow wrote in 1921, "There are few places in the world richer in color and inspiration than our own South— yet because of the stagnant air, the absence of critical values, the flaunting of borrowed flags, the facile cult of the cheap and showy, art has languished among us. . . . For the glory of men as of nations is measured not by the strength with which they cling to the past, but by the courage with which they adventure into the future. . . . [Genius] means a departure from tribal forms and images. It means a creation of new standards and new ideals of beauty and new rules of conduct."[50] But, for the foreseeable future, the South would march forward with its gaze firmly fixed on a past that never existed but served as the basis for existence.

Though the foreseeable future seemed indistinguishable from the lived past at the end of World War II, the rumblings of the previous decades grew louder. Some southerners became less willing to suffer in silence, hide their feelings in novels or diaries, mask their deep-seated misgivings behind social-science research or milquetoast reform efforts, or gently remind their neighbors that southern society ought to serve Christianity, not vice versa. Maybe it was the war against fascism that brought the contradictions of the South to bolder relief; or maybe it was all the young men, black and white, going off to other places, learning new things, and meeting new people; or maybe it was simply the optimism and yearning for change after years of Depression and war. Once you admit to other visions, the vision that you hold may become less clear.

The spirit surfaced in many places, but consider the exchanges that occurred in Georgia in 1946 between state legislators seeking to restrict black voting and witnesses urging them not to do so. The witnesses, needless to say, were all white, and they were well aware that what ailed the South was not white supremacy per se but the particular historical perspective that required it; change the history and you change the South. A young soldier, R. W. Hayes, testified to save "Georgia from its Reconstruction complex. If the Negro was good enough to carry a gun in the war, and pay taxes, he should vote." Perhaps the most striking witness was Helen Dortch Longstreet, the widow of Confederate General James Longstreet. If ever a tie existed between the Old South and the New, she was that connection. Mrs. Longstreet testified not as a relic but as a person answering, as she put it, "the call of duty within my soul." She urged the legislators to rise up "against this monstrous measure," which would "set up a dictatorship under the lying guise of white supremacy." Her husband and his comrades fought for many things, some despicable, but surely they did not fight to establish a republic of lies. Yet such wisdom was lost on the Georgia gentlemen as they pushed through their restrictions with virtual unanimity. Still, the widow's testimony was extraordinary, for here was a living link with a hallowed past become hollow, and she had exposed it as such. And, as a woman, she must have understood that such comments might very well remove the protection, community, and bonds of kinship shared by all white southerners of the mid-twentieth century. But she said it anyway.[51]

The Georgia legislators won the day, but the Confederate widow augured the future. The civil rights movement shattered prevailing verities. By the 1960s other versions of southern history challenged traditional perspectives that equated the Old South with grace, charm, and manners and cast the Civil War as a glorious, if tragic, battle for southern independence, ignoring or minimizing the role of slavery, and that Reconstruction involved the redemption of the South from freedmen and Yankees.

It proved difficult for southern whites to let go of this past in favor of other perspectives of the Old South and the Civil War, and to see the tragedy of Reconstruction as not the oppression of the white South but the blasted dreams of southern blacks. The past had become so much of part of them that it became their identity. As with any ethnic group, the collection of myths, facts, and symbols told more than a story of the past; it illuminated what people were and are. Besides, fantasy is preferable to a reality that was often cruel and unforgiving; some southern whites could not see how the liberation of Southern blacks implied anything other than a blow to pride and status. And the vaunted prosperity of the Sunbelt that followed the civil rights victories often proved elusive to working-class whites as an economy changing both nationally and globally left ghost towns, empty factories and warehouses, and tens of thousands of low-paying service jobs that boosted employment statistics but not paychecks. What was in it for them?

It was easy to point out that liberation eventually benefits everyone, and that a booming economy ultimately can translate into better education, which will provide better-paying jobs that will benefit all. But southerners were not accustomed to think in terms of the future. Their gaze, at least that of the whites among them, remained fixed in the past, and their political leaders kept it there. The political transformation to a two-party region did little to educate voters about the potential of cooperation and reconciliation. The Republicans merely picked up the old Democratic refrain, packaged it with acceptable phrases, and with a wink and a nod grew their constituency accordingly.

The new historical vision offered by the civil rights movement has not replaced the old construction manufactured from the experiences of the Civil War and Reconstruction. The American ideal, that we are a nation built on the proposition that all men are created equal and that we govern by the consent of the governed, is there for the taking, and most southerners would and have readily ascribed to it. But without adopting a new version of southern history, the merger with the national ideal is unconvincing, a layering without any change in perspective. Nor is it sufficient to suggest, as many have, that if only southerners could distill the positive from southern history—the grace and charm of the Old South, the heroism of the Civil War, and the aspirations of both simple blacks and whites after the war—then the South could give to the rest of the nation a leaven to its crass materialism, a humility check to self-absorbed invulnerability, and an idea that progress is not always a straight line up toward the future.

The South can offer nothing of the sort. The booster ethic and the mindless accumulation of property bereft of social conscience has, if anything, experienced greater acceptance in the South than in other parts of the country. The gospel of prosperity is preached in the pulpit, where pastors reaffirm the complacency of congregations convinced of their own righteousness and the lostness of others. State and local recruiters hawk their workers, their land, and their treasuries to employers who will care just as much as government about the welfare of their new labor force and the new communities in which they have located.

The cackling of southern warhawks in the Vietnam era, the quick tendency to resolve disputes by resort to violence, the swiftness in imposing the death penalty, and a nation-leading incidence of child and spousal abuse reflect nothing of the genteel past or the lesson of humility the Civil War allegedly imparted to a defeated region. In fact, white southerners have not only misread their history; they have ignored whatever positive lessons it might have disclosed to a more enlightened citizenry.

The view of the Civil War as a holy battle to preserve a gifted civilization, the failure of which elevated the martyrdom of its defenders and the nobility of its cause, influenced the perception of Reconstruction as a struggle to restore the South to the kind of power and society that preceded the war. One followed from the other and formed a whole in forging the historical myth that dominated the South for a century, a myth that is with us still, both in legacy and reality. The view suited southern white men especially well. Historical renovation became necessary after the Civil War because the southern white man was ultimately a failure; he had lost the war for independence, destroying slavery in the process, and had failed to protect his family from fear, poverty, and death. Considering the roles expected of white nineteenth-century American males, these failures were crushing. History became the elixir of the mind—not merely a rationale but a prescription for daily living. If the day is past to recover either independence or slavery, then let us, through whatever means we can muster, restore white dominion over black. And, at the same time, let us reassert and reestablish our role as masters of our households and protectors of our women, especially from black men.

Who were these white men? Southern white men, after all, were rarely lockstep in thought and action. The Civil War uncovered significant fissures in southern white society. Few Confederate states escaped internal violence and dissent. But to the white leaders who "redeemed" the South after 1877— the Black Belt planters and urban merchants and industrialists—racial solidarity was essential for both their persistence as leaders and for the triumph of their view of southern history which, in turn, legitimized their leadership and transformed their failure into victory. The racial and gender ideals derived from this perspective were directed as much toward maintaining white solidarity as ensuring the subservience of blacks and women. These ideals enabled white leaders to strike a heroic pose, and by dint of the common color, they could impart this posture of honor to all whites.

History thus became more than a rationalization for failure; it became a way to order society and the people in it. And history's connection with those in power in heaven and on earth rendered it sacrosanct, beyond challenge. It was not so much that southern society after the Civil War became defined by white supremacy as it drew its identity from a history that required the domination of white men. That domination, in turn, enabled their version of history to prevail. Southern history since the Civil War has revolved around those who sought to preserve a particular vision of the war and Reconstruction and those who dared to offer alternative histories. This is the history of that history.

2   God-Haunted

The South in a way made a religion of its history.
      —Richard M. Weaver, "The South and the American Union"

It would come to this: a liberating religion would turn confining and harsh, as hard as the lives of the people whose faith rode on the promise of ever after, not here and now. Their evangelical ancestors would scarcely recognize them. For in the forest clearings and towns of the late-eighteenth-century South, the young, unmarried preachers spoke the Gospel and demanded their listeners to question all earthly authority, all hierarchy of man, all family ties, and all institutions derived therefrom. They treated women and African Americans as equals and expected the like from their congregations: all were equal before Christ. The Baptist and Methodist itinerants unsettled the complacent, challenged the norm, urged people to question, and held open the possibility and beauty of grace if they did. Most of all, they gave America one of its greatest gifts: religious freedom.[1]

Things change; young, zealous preachers grow old and give way to a new generation. People move to town. Respectability replaces righteousness; prosperity softens opposition to that which makes men prosper. And a religious movement comes in from the outside to become part of a culture. More converts mean more power to God, and to churches and their ministers. No need to offend; soften the Gospel; encourage, don't despise; comfort, don't confront; sins may be easily expiated, just reenlist and everything will work out fine. Convert the slaves, don't free them. Teach your wives and daughters their proper roles; don't encourage their independence. It's God's plan.

Today's religious homogeneity in the South belies a past of great diversity. Before the American Revolution, the southern colonies hosted Protestants of various persuasions, Jews, Catholics, and a good number of Moslem slaves. This spiritual mélange was unplanned, and the Anglican Church, which served as the established church of the colonial South, did not encourage it. But the Anglicans were much less finicky about religious dissent than were their Puritan brethren in New England, who came to the New World for religious freedom, got it, and then promptly denied it to everyone else. Practicing Anglicans, almost an oxymoron in some parts of the colonial South, viewed the church more as an appendage to their social and economic status than as an integral part of their lives. They held Anglican ministers in low esteem, and a number of colonial divines lived down to that estimation. British North America was a distant and dangerous territory; ambitious, talented, and pious Anglican clerics avoided the place.

Word of religious toleration, or at least grudging acceptance, in parts of North America spread quickly, especially among Jews and Catholics, who were outcasts in many areas of the Atlantic world. By the time of the Revolution, Charleston boasted the largest Jewish population in the western hemisphere, and more Roman Catholics resided in the southern colonies than anywhere else in British North America.

As early as the 1730s, evangelical Protestant groups that had encountered hostility in New England and the Middle Colonies began to migrate south. Scotch-Irish Presbyterians and German Moravians set out on the Great Wagon Road, which stretched from eastern Pennsylvania, down the Shenandoah Valley, and into the Carolina Piedmont. Settling along this natural highway, they cultivated farms and founded towns. They became the backbone of the southern yeomanry.

While these groups created little notice or concern (except among the Indians), another Protestant band stirred up trouble. Few settlers among the nominally Anglican majority had arrived in the southern colonies for religious freedom; most came to make money. When they made their fortunes, they enjoyed themselves with lavish entertaining, fine English manufactured goods, and extravagant food and drink. They partied a lot. And they seldom allowed Sundays or holidays to interfere with a good time. But a religious enthusiasm known as the Great Awakening swept through the colonies in the 1740s, and by the 1760s Baptists, the most zealous exponents of a new spirituality and morality, grew their following large and strong enough to confront the Anglican majority in a very forceful manner.

The Baptists' appeal was simple, especially to people residing apart from the more-settled coastal areas. They offered fellowship and promised salvation no matter how humble a person's station. They preached equality for black and white, man and woman. They also preached against the excess they witnessed around them: the repeated violations of the sanctity of the Sabbath, rampant profanity, alcoholism, and physical abuse. Eighteenth-century colonists believed in a God-ordained hierarchy; rank carried privileges. Baptists did not think that way. They advocated equality before the eyes of God, pure and simple; their loud attacks on personal behavior generated great resentment among nonbelievers. A Virginian complained that a Baptist "cannot meet a man upon the road, but they must ram a text of Scripture down his throat."[2] These were not folks who appeared on many guest lists.

Baptists were not merely annoying; they were dangerous. Aside from challenging colonial financial support for the Anglican Church, their advocacy of equality had dire implications for a slave-based society. Baptists offered not only fellowship to lonely homesteaders but also a sense of dignity and worth in the eyes of God. They replaced the social hierarchy with a much simpler order: man (or woman) and God. That was it; all else was vanity.

The conversion experience was central to Baptist theology. Conversion occurred when an individual came forward to confess sin and ask forgiveness. Baptists illuminated sin; they fixated on it. They amassed a long list of spiritual transgressions; guilt played a major role in the conversion process. They challenged lifestyle, they challenged authority, and they gained converts.

The American Revolution was the ultimate attack on authority; not surprisingly, Baptists, though less than 10 percent of the southern population at the time, played an important role in supplying the spiritual undergirding of an essentially secular movement. As early as 1776 Virginia Baptists lobbied for the disestablishment of state churches and for complete religious freedom. Baptists promoted the novel (at the time) concept of church-state separation. Their argument was not that religion would confuse and poison politics, but that the state would infect churches and religion. Baptists viewed religion as an individual decision: a covenant between man and God. Government, by its nature, is collective and seeks to bring into a community everything and everyone under its control. These ideas were crucial in convincing Thomas Jefferson and James Madison to author Virginia's unprecedented statute on religious freedom, as well as the First Amendment to the Constitution of 1787. In great part, as a nation we owe our principles of religious freedom and the separation of church and state to southern Baptists.

After the Revolution, Baptists, soon joined by Methodists and Presbyterians, continued to preach austerity and equality. Some preachers went so far as to advocate freedom for slaves as the logical extension of evangelical theology. In the meantime, the tenets of the new religion and the new nation continued to coincide and win converts for the evangelicals. In 1800, at a crossroads clearing in Kentucky called Cane Ridge, the evangelical denominations came together to sponsor a massive revival that may have drawn as many as twenty thousand people in what was still a sparsely inhabited frontier. The enthusiasm generated by the revival, the fellowship it offered, and the equality it preached spread throughout the South, touching not only modest farmers and craftsmen but prominent planters and merchants as well. The disorder, violence, and uncertainty of the frontier South demanded an order that the British Empire and the Anglican Church no longer provided. The message of self-control and godliness preached by lay evangelical ministers touched the hearts and souls of their listeners as it imparted meaning to their lives.

As evangelical Protestantism surged through the South after Cane Ridge, it made a particularly strong impression on slaves. Masters were initially ambivalent about the evangelicals' ministry to the slaves. The message of equality before God troubled them, and the antislavery position of Baptists and Methodists in the North fueled a guilt-by-association mentality among some slave owners. But in the decades after Cane Ridge, the evangelical denominations and slave owners reached an accommodation: southern evangelical ministers blessed slavery in exchange for conversions. Masters not only opened their homes and field churches to evangelical ministers; they opened their slave quarters as well.

Logic held that slaves would reject evangelical Christianity as another white-ordered cultural trapping designed to foster obedience and subservience, or at least that slaves would only feign its adoption. But slaves embraced Christianity and turned it to their own uses. The Bible contained passages that suited their condition and aspirations; whatever spin ministers or planters put on it, Jesus was more like the slave than the master. The story of Exodus reflected the hope of all slaves, and it provided the theme for spirituals and the promise of deliverance. Slaves memorized the words from Malachi 2:10: "Have we not one Father? Hath not one God created Us?"

From what they did not like or could not use of evangelical Protestantism, slaves created their own variations. Evangelicals stressed the importance of individualism, but slaves interpreted Christianity as a community religion, strengthening the bonds of family through faith. They viewed their destinies collectively rather than as individuals. Slaves worshiped in a more emotional and intense style than did many white evangelicals, a fact that drove some white congregations to invite blacks to leave and form their own churches despite misgivings that slaves might wander from the Gospel According to White Ministers. Even if they spent Sunday morning praying with whites, later in the day blacks walked into the forest under an arbor, or gathered in the quarters, or crowded into church basements in the towns to praise the Lord in their own way. Whites often knew about these meetings but usually allowed them to continue, preferring to have their slaves in worship rather than idle or drunk on the Sabbath, and choosing to believe that good Christians would make good slaves.

The surreptitious services often had extrareligious purposes. Southern states prohibited blacks from learning to read or write. Under the guise of wanting to read the Bible, numerous slaves were lifted to literacy. These gatherings also fostered concepts of community, with individuals and families helping each other, tracking down lost relatives, or sharing news of important changes in plantation life. Increasingly during the early decades of the nineteenth century, blacks formed their own churches, either with the reluctant blessing of whites or in towns and cities where free blacks pooled limited resources to open houses of worship. By the time of the Civil War, blacks had embraced their evangelical churches as key institutions in their lives. The church remained one of the few places relatively free of white influence, where black preachers could expound on the Gospel and receive respect as leaders. The black church's great influence in the civil rights movement of the 1950s and 1960s owed a great deal to its origins in the era of slavery.

Black evangelicals had more choices than to worship under the surveillance of white masters or off by themselves. In the nonplantation areas of the South, primitive evangelical congregations of a few dozen members each dotted the landscape. For a congregation-based denomination such as the Baptists', establishing a church required no formal appeals or permissions: just gather the neighbors, put a few boards together, and get someone who's good at speaking and knows the Bible. The idea of a seminary-trained preacher was rarely entertained in and around small settlements, and if it were, many thought it unnecessary. These churches accepted all comers, and, whether slave or free, black or white, they addressed each other as "Brother" and "Sister." Occasionally, predominantly white churches heard black preachers.

Some historians have argued that both the style of worship and manner of preaching in black churches derived, in part, from African religions. While shards of African culture were imbedded in black Christianity, the most significant influence on the black church came from the rich cross-fertilization between white and black evangelicals. The oratorical style of chanting sermons, the freedom of congregants to call out to the preachers or to other worshipers as the Spirit moved them, and the highly emotional singing that many associate with black churches initially appeared in white congregations in the years after Cane Ridge. The association with Africa occurred because whites began to tone down their services while blacks retained the more intense style of worship. White Baptists came to look upon raucous singing, dancing, and up-tempo music as carry-overs from "primitive" African cultures. Blacks viewed these rituals as expressions of divine presence.

White evangelicals grew more conservative during the course of the nineteenth century. They began to stress biblical notions of order and hierarchy as opposed to ideals of human equality. Slaves owed masters obedience and, as the apostles Paul and Peter taught, wives and children owed husbands and fathers similar deference. The shift to a theology that complemented rather than challenged the prevailing culture helped to bring more members into evangelical congregations. During the 1830s the South's population grew by 30 percent, while church membership increased by 60 percent.

Though evangelicals increasingly tailored their doctrines to southern culture, they remained adamant about maintaining the separation of church and state. A Methodist minister in North Carolina remarked during the 1830s that "Sometimes it is true, a union of Church and State has been effected, but God has refused to approve the junction. In every instance the Church has suffered loss, and much mischief." An editorial in Richmond's Methodist *Christian Advocate* around the same time warned that allowing the church to become a platform for the espousal of a particular political viewpoint was "at once dangerous to the State and the liberty of the citizens."[3]

Religious trends in antebellum America ran against this view. Many antislavery advocates drew their views from evangelical Protestantism. Although at first they disdained political involvement, by the 1840s some discussed the benefits of supporting candidates for office. Two antislavery parties, the Liberty Party and the Free Soil Party, emerged in that decade, and in 1854 the Republican Party formed. All three parties attracted a significant evangelical contingent. They shared an intolerance for immigrants, especially Roman Catholics, and a strong antisouthern bias fueled by their hatred of slavery.

The injection of evangelical religion into northern politics dramatically changed the nature of those politics. The essence of the democratic process is compromise, the give and take of opposing views, rather than the imposition of a particular viewpoint. The diversity of American society, the differing religious and ethnic groups, requires such adjustments in order for the political process to work. The system is imperfect, and a compromise of principles is often necessary. Eventually, if enough people see the wisdom of a certain policy, then that other element of democratic politics—the will of the majority—kicks in.

The problem with northern evangelicals influencing political candidates and parties was not the lack of merit in their cause (the abolition of slavery). The difficulty lay in their inability to compromise. The Bible and God are not subject to relativism. One stood either with the evangelicals or against them; one was either good or evil. All southerners, therefore, were evil, because the South supported an evil institution. Compromise would be not only impolitic; it would be sinful. Political contests assumed the character of morality plays. As one New England evangelical warned on the eve of the 1856 presidential election, the people's choice lay between "the bloodstained ticket of the Democratic party . . . or the Republican ticket designated by the God of peace and purity as the one that shall smile upon you."[4] A simple choice. When Abraham Lincoln intoned that the nation could not exist half slave and half free, from an evangelical standpoint that was less political rhetoric than prophecy.

Southern evangelical churchmen rushed to the defense of their region, their neighbors, and themselves, similarly politicizing religious issues and vice versa. The major national evangelical denominations, the Baptists, Methodists, and Presbyterians, had split into northern and southern branches by the time of the Civil War. Only within the past decade have the Methodists and Presbyterians reconciled. The Baptists remain proudly sectional, but considering the atomistic nature of the Baptist faith, that is less a regional than a theological statement. In any case, the Old South tradition of the separation of church and state dissolved amid the sectional crisis. The evangelical denominations that had steadily come to identify more with southern culture than with God embraced southern traditions all the more heartily.

Southern whites, stung by northern evangelical criticism, moved closer to their own evangelical churches and teachings. Sermons against drink, sexual transgression, and other forms of illicit behavior, which preachers had delivered for decades, began to leave their mark. The more northerners depicted southerners as evil, the more the white southerner sought to live the virtuous life. Some slaveholders attempted to sanitize the institution of slavery by adhering to ministers' pleas to sanctify slave marriages, avoid the splitting of families, and resist corporal punishment.

When southerners went to war, they believed they were fighting for a just society, sanctified by God and blessed by the clergy. Had not First Jeremiah predicted the outcome? "Then the Lord said unto me, out of the North an evil shall break forth upon the inhabitants of the land, and they shall fight against thee, but they shall not prevail against thee; for I am with thee."

Northerners, of course, believed God was on *their* side. When President Lincoln added the abolition of slavery as a war objective, the conflict's distinction between good and evil became even sharper for northern evangelicals and southerners alike. But only one side would win. The loser would not only shoulder the burden of defeat but would need to explain how a God-chosen people could suffer so.

As Union victories mounted, preachers became as common as camp followers in Confederate bivouacs all across the South; the good chance of dying, combined with the threat of divine abandonment, spurred a host of conversions. Yet not all soldiers appreciated the priestly intervention. As one complained, "We sometimes feel more as if we were in a camp-meeting than in the army expecting to meet an enemy." But for most, the religious intermissions provided solace. The scenes of war proved horrible to an essentially civilian army. "I have not power to describe the scene. It beggars all description," a Confederate infantryman wrote home after his first battle.[5]

When the end came northerners were assured that God had blessed them. The South had sinned, and slavery was at the root of that sin. Some southerners shared that conviction. A North Carolinian cried at the end of the war, "Oh, our God! What sins we must have been guilty of that we should be so humiliated by Thee now!" A Virginia woman pointed to slavery as the sin of the South's downfall and rejoiced that "we white people are no longer permitted to go on in such wickedness, heaping up more and more wrath of God upon our devoted heads."[6]

Blessed Defeat

In a religious age, when prayer came as naturally as breathing, when the Lord walked alongside the young soldier and held the hands of his family and protected his children, the sense that God had abandoned the South and its people fell hard and terrible. There had to be another explanation. So much sacrifice, so much valor, so much pain, and so much death and destruction seemed in itself to demonstrate an uncommon fealty to the Lord, not its absence. So failure became the faith of the South: faith that its history as a region and a people had a purpose that God would ultimately reveal. These were times of trial, the time before redemption. But how would this redemption occur?

The Bible answered in Jeremiah 6:16: "Thus saith the Lord . . . ask for the old paths, where is the good way, and walk therein, and ye shall find rest for your souls." The "old paths," the Old South, became the blueprint for the new. Just as religion had infested politics in the North before the war, now religion penetrated history in the South after the war. The past was no longer merely the past, a time to remember fondly, especially in the harsh present glare of defeat. No, the past was holy; the men who fought to preserve that past were crusaders, and those who destroyed the South must not be allowed to triumph. The Civil War was a great war, a defining conflict, but for white southerners it marked a beginning, not an end, for the end was a grace that would come only with redemption.

In defeat, whites recognized the path to their salvation; in liberation, blacks understood the awesome power of God to forge freedom out of blood and ruin. Neither took salvation for granted. Sin always lurked near the surface, set to divert the righteous from the path to heaven. The history of the war provided stark evidence of the presence of good and evil, and how close one came to the other. But as black and white interpreted the meaning of the Civil War and Reconstruction in different ways, the evangelical Protestantism that thrived among them proved divisive as well. For whites, religion became a hard thing, as hard as the lives they led, as hard as the memories they fashioned into history. It became a rigid faith, a mechanism for control and restriction rather than liberation and innovation. For blacks, evangelical Protestantism came forth as a joyful noise, an animated, living spiritual experience that confirmed their newfound freedom even as its promise remained unfulfilled. Their history alone over the previous decades confirmed the presence of God and his beneficence.

The lives of most white southerners after the war confirmed their religious beliefs. The difficult present, with the world turned topsy-turvy, with survival by no means certain, paled in comparison to the past. It became easy for white southerners to glorify the past; memories, real or fictional, provided comfort. For the majority of the population who lived in the countryside, their lives and the landscape around them provided spare testimony to their tenuous existence. Solace derived from church and family. They heard the stories of toil and unmerited suffering from their ministers; they did not expect much from this life. But they took consolation in God, each other, and their traditions, especially those traditions of the past: the people who came before them, the war and the Redemption.

The Bible is replete with stories of how unfaithfulness to God has resulted in disaster for people and nations. Josiah used the Deuteronomistic history to command fealty to one God and one ruler. Southern leaders would do the same. Life followed Scripture; Scripture, life. People will fall, tragedies will occur, but we will prevail. From Job: "Though He slay me, yet will I trust him." Adversity is the ultimate test of a steadfast faith.

Southerners not only accepted adversity; they wore it as a hair shirt of faith. A Georgia minister sermonized in 1866 that "it is better to be chastened than to be let alone." Thus chastened, the southerner moved closer to God. "Each link of the chain that enslaves," Father Abram Ryan wrote, "shall bind us the closer to thee." Southerners should take pride, not pity, in their defeat. In 1890 a Presbyterian minister observed that the Bible included accounts of God's chosen people led into captivity by heathen conquerors, "but that fact did not prove the heathen to be right in the cause nor that the Israelites were upholding a bad cause."[7]

As white evangelicals restored southern pride and dignity, they convinced themselves that the war had been part of a grand design, as one minister noted in 1866: "God is working out larger ends than those which concern us as a people."[8] God controlled southern history now, and as long as southerners followed Him, they and their region would achieve salvation.

The South transformed from defeated country to righteous republic, its sanctity confirmed not only by history and God but in contrast to the victorious Yankees. Southern writers and journalists published stories on northern corruption and the crowding of immigrants into violent, vice-infested cities to confirm southern moral and racial superiority. Northerners might build palaces of gold, but the South nurtured something more precious. Baptist minister Victor I. Masters wrote that southerners had "developed a great gentleness of spirit which was worth more than all the billions."[9]

White southerners consciously compared their history to the crucifixion and ascension of Jesus Christ: the Civil War and Reconstruction mirrored the death and resurrection of the Savior. In 1880 essayist Thomas Nelson Page summarized southern history since the war: "The South was dead and buried, and yet she rose again. The voice of God called her forth; she came clad in her grave-clothes, but living, and with her face uplifted to the heavens from which had sounded the call of her resurrection."[10]

Redemption carried with it a sacred responsibility. God had chosen southerners because of their unequivocal devotion to Him. They must not only worship Him but follow His will and plan for the South as well. To swerve from this path of righteousness would threaten both the individual's salvation and the South's redemption. Evangelical ministers and Democratic Party leaders constantly reminded their constituents of the propinquity of sin and the various forms it took: rival political parties, ideas and policies that challenged prevailing views of race and gender, and conflicting interpretations of southern history. Salvation required obedience and orthodoxy. Anything less could result in individual and societal destruction. Dissent was not merely a disagreement; it was the difference between redemption and damnation. The punishments meted out to heretics, therefore, must be severe; isolation, harassment, physical violence, or banishment awaited those who questioned or criticized.

Secular obedience and orthodoxy overcame a religious tradition once noted for its individuality. While the individual soul was still important, it became subsumed under the needs of the larger society. Private behavior became public concern, and public issues took on religious meaning.

Most religions are authoritarian and exclusive in the sense that they demand varying degrees of orthodoxy from their followers, and they distinguish themselves from other religions by promoting their tenets and doctrines as the one true way to grace. Evangelical Protestants are no better or worse than other religions in this regard, except for one fundamental difference: they are pressed by their faith to take their views public, not simply to *share* them with others, but to *persuade* anyone within listening distance to join them. In the marketplace of ideas that is America, this distinction is not particularly important. But the American South was not such a marketplace; it featured a religious monopoly supported by the state, tacitly or actively. This monopoly became inextricably bound to the South's culture and history and, therefore, to the identity of its people. The boundaries between public and private were weak and permeable in the South; the merger of religion and culture removed any remaining distinction.

Rituals of Faith

Rituals became very important in sustaining history and faith. Evangelical churches had historically eschewed ritual. They associated heavily orchestrated services with Episcopalians or, worse, Roman Catholics. Ritual stifled free spiritual expression and formalized what evangelicals believed was a very personal relationship between each church member and God. But as the emphasis of evangelical theology passed from the righteous individual to the righteous republic, some public demonstration of devotion became necessary, much as evangelical history required lavish public displays of the artifacts and representations of the Lost Cause. The church service, which emphasized individual conversion, could not project to the larger tableau of the community. Rituals became the medium for bonding community members to the orthodoxy of the Lost Cause and the racial and gender hierarchy that such a historical perspective implied. Eventually, the public spectacles of religion and history became indistinguishable. History and religion merged easily and fatefully.

Survivors placed wreaths and flowers on the graves of Confederate soldiers, the martyrs of the struggle. Local women erected a remarkable monument, still standing today, in Richmond's Hollywood Cemetery. Stone by stone, they crafted a rough-hewn pyramid to honor the war dead, much as medieval burghers carried stone by stone to construct the great cathedrals of Europe. Richmond became the Confederate Vatican, a city of shrines, highlighted by a broad avenue of statues depicting the heroes of the Lost Cause, including the sainted Robert E. Lee and the martyred Stonewall Jackson.

In 1875 Richmond served as the site of the first reunion of Confederate war veterans. The occasion coincided with the unveiling of a statue honoring Stonewall Jackson. A commemorative arch was decorated with the words "Warrior, Christian, Patriot." The Reverend Moses Drury Hoge delivered the major oration to the assembled crowd of fifty thousand, reminding his audience that "Defeat is the discipline which trains the truly heroic soul to further and better endeavors." After the monument was unveiled, the Richmond Philharmonic played Martin Luther's hymn "A Castle of Strength Is Our Lord."[11]

At St. Paul's Church in Richmond, where many of the Confederate leaders had worshiped, the congregation purchased new stained-glass windows that connected the story of the Confederacy to the stories of the Old Testament. "How Firm a Foundation" became the official Confederate hymn, sung at funerals and at veterans' gatherings. A group of veterans transformed "That Old-Time Religion" into "We Are Old-Time Confederates." And the last words that Stonewall Jackson spoke, "let us pass over the river, and rest under the shade of the trees," became a Methodist hymn.[12]

Southern women, historically active in church affairs and in keeping the family genealogy, extended their religious work to memorializing the Confederacy. They not only decorated graves but also supplied pictures of heroes for classrooms and materials for the celebration of Confederate Memorial Day. One woman compared herself to the biblical Mary and Martha, who "last at the cross and first at the grave brought their offerings of love." Much of this work became formalized in 1894 with the founding of the United Daughters of the Confederacy (UDC). Included among their earliest publications was the "U.D.C. Catechism for Children." Local chapters often took religious quotes as their motto, and a Texas member urged her sisters to guard their archives "even as the children of Israel did the Ark of the Covenant." Civil War heroes materialized in formal prayers. Southern evangelist J. William Jones opened veterans' gatherings appealing to the "God of Israel, God of the centuries, God of our forefathers, God of Jefferson Davis and Sidney Johnston and Robert E. Lee, and Stonewall Jackson, God of the Southern Confederacy."[13]

The links between God and the Confederacy, God and the South became so powerful that young children occasionally confused the two. When Father Abram Ryan spotted his young niece standing before a portrait of the crucifixion, he asked her if she knew who crucified Jesus. "Oh yes, I know," she answered, "the Yankees."[14] The younger generation soon became aware of the burden God had placed on them. They were to lead the South out of bondage to the promised land. Of the South's chosen people, the youth were the most chosen. Their childhoods were filled with the importance of behaving righteously, of never following the easiest path simply because it was easy, of the redemptive quality of suffering and the bearing of that suffering. Those who grew up in households that held such beliefs, or knew of those who did, sometimes looked back in sadness on how a beautiful religion could become so dour as to transform its youngest and most tender believers into spiritual automatons, as to destroy the adventure of inquiry in favor of a rote faith grounded in rote history.

In 1947 University of North Carolina sociologist Howard W. Odum wrote about his Uncle John's youngest daughter, who grew up in Georgia during and after the Civil War. "This little girl in her first years especially seemed a symbol of all that was beautiful and pleasureful. She sought out the simple flowers and shrubs and rocks on hillside and bluff and by the edge of rippling waters. She sang almost incessantly and danced and played with rare imagination." But the war interrupted her idyll; hardship and suffering followed. "She grew up," Odum wrote. "Pleasure was translated into service, religion became a merciless tyrant demanding all pleasure for itself. Love of Jesus was substituted for love of youth, the beauty of the spirit transcended the beauty of the body." She married and bore children, some of whom died. "Then typhoid fever, interpreted as punishment from God because of her secret aspirations for beauty and companionship. . . . In the latter days of her short span of years . . . there came the bitter confession that no longer would she sin, 'Gladly will I toil and suffer, Only let me walk with Thee.' "[15]

When the first white postwar generation came of age in the 1890s, their task was to rededicate the South to the righteous path set down by their parents and other veterans of the heroic war and Reconstruction. Soaring church membership reflected the seriousness with which they approached their mission. As late as 1860 only one of four white southerners claimed church membership. By 1890 the figure was one of two. Preachers remonstrated with their congregations about the importance of living a moral life, especially attending to their personal behavior. The South would be judged on the abstinence of its people, on its freedom from personal sin, they intoned.

It may seem odd that a religious revival in the 1890s occurred at the same time that lynchings, disfranchisement, and segregation by law secured white supremacy. But these controlling mechanisms included their own ritualistic qualities, which adherents directed toward the expiation of sin. Lynchings often assumed the pattern of a church service, with crowds gathering to watch the victim submit to a series of ordeals that ultimately ended with death; artifacts of the victim, either body parts or clothing, were distributed to the crowd as souvenirs. Photographs of these events often depicted neatly dressed white men and boys, some smiling, others with a look of resolution and satisfaction, as if they had just come from church and were about to dig into dinner on the grounds.[16] The frequency with which black victims were burned at the stake reflected the belief that a devil or heretic was receiving punishment from the righteous. Mark Twain, a veteran observer of all kinds of bizarre occurrences, which he often softened with wry humor, could not divert himself from the horror of southern lynchings. In 1901 he captured the ritualized qualities of these events, tallying the lynchings that occurred over the previous two years. Participants seemed to believe that with each leap of the flame, the South came closer to grace:

> Place the 203 [black victims] in a row, allowing 600 feet of space for each human torch, so that there may be viewing room around it for 5,000 Christian American men, women, and children, youths and maidens; make it night, for grim effect; have the show in a gradually rising plain, and let the course of the stake be uphill; the eye can then take in the whole line of twenty-four miles of blood-and-flesh bonfires unbroken. . . . All being ready now, and the darkness opaque, the stillness impressive—for there should be no sound but the soft moaning of the night wind and the muffled sobbing of the sacrifices—let all the far stretch of kerosene pyres be touched off simultaneously and the glare and the shrieks and the agonies burst heavenward to the Throne.[17]

Although racial segregation involved less-drastic rituals, it nevertheless carried implications similar to those of lynching. Separate and inferior accommodations for blacks, or no accommodations at all, implied the setting-right of a divine order of things; of putting blacks in their natural, God-given place and securing the topmost place for whites, also ordained by God. Southern whites not only derived advantage from merely being white; their subjugation of African Americans carried religious approbation as well.

By 1900 white evangelical Protestantism had become so immersed in southern culture that few whites perceived the inherent contradiction between Christianity and white supremacy. With white supremacy a key tenet of the secular order, it became an article of evangelical faith as well. Segregation and disfranchisement thus sanctified, whites implemented them with religious zeal. Supporters of white supremacy stressed the moral dimensions of racial separation and voting reform. Disorder, corruption, and sexual deviance would disappear. Temptations to sin were removed, and the righteous republic and its sentinels reigned supreme. In a stunning sectional reversal, the post–Civil War South assumed the cloak of the Republic of Virtue, with all the combative, mind-numbing, and judgmental qualities pertaining thereto.

Making Good Christians

The crusade for white supremacy was not the only holy war engaged by southern white leaders. The merging of public and private, of church and state, opened up an array of personal behaviors that came under the evangelical purview. A "good Christian" was someone who both believed and behaved well.[18] If etiquette reflected the divinely ordained superiority of white men over women and blacks, then other forms of public behavior should reflect the divine order as well. Though not all white supremacists supported the prohibition of alcohol, proponents of abstinence argued that it solidified white supremacy by reducing the likelihood of intoxicated African American men assaulting white women. Not incidentally, the abolition of alcohol would also curb disorderly behavior by poor whites and eliminate the social settings of low taverns and bars where working-class blacks and whites could mingle and cause trouble amongst themselves, or worse, between them and the "better sort." White supremacy, class, sex, booze, and God thus merged into a happy brew.

This is not to say that the crusade pursued a frivolous vice. Alcoholism was a genuine problem after the Civil War. The South led the nation in per capita alcohol consumption. The frequent attempt of pharmacists to concoct a cure for hangovers evinced southerners' prolific drinking habits. If one could not explain away defeat, poverty, and social chaos through theology, then the bottle was the next best resolution.

White supremacist motivations did not preclude middle-class blacks from entering the fray on the side of the teetotalers. Black ministers became involved, as did a number of middle-class African Americans in southern cities. The adverse impact of alcohol on families concerned them, too, but they also worried that alcoholism among lower-class blacks damaged the reputation of the entire race and served as an excuse to further reduce blacks' civil rights. It was not surprising that whites usually allowed blacks to vote when prohibition appeared on the ballot.

Beginning in the 1880s southern localities and states began to outlaw alcohol, so that by the time of national prohibition in 1919, much of the South was dry, at least officially. The "better sort" could always find a way to locate a drink, and moonshine producers filled large orders that federal revenue agents did little to deter. The prohibition movement produced the same type of hypocrisy and casual lawbreaking in the South that it would in the rest of the country during the 1920s. A difference was that the prohibition movement began much earlier and lasted considerably longer in the South (and persists to this day in some areas) than in any other region. It became part of a larger effort to cleanse southern society of sin, to make it worthy of its history and destiny.

The public profession of dryness was apparently sufficient to satisfy evangelical divines, even if they and their congregations took a "medicinal" nip every now and then. There is no indication, at any rate, that alcoholism became much less of a problem after banning the sale of alcohol. Writer Willie Morris's father noted that the only difference between Mississippi (a dry state) and Tennessee (mostly wet) during the 1930s was that in Tennessee a man could not buy liquor on Sunday. By that time "grocery stores" had popped up all over Mississippi, ostensibly selling a very limited supply of canned goods and a large inventory of liquor. As the saying went, "As long as the people of Mississippi can stagger to the polls, they'll vote dry." Prohibition campaigns often produced unintended humor. Evangelical ministers would hand out bumper stickers that read FOR THE SAKE OF MY FAMILY, VOTE DRY. Willie Morris reported that "the son of the most prosperous bootlegger drove around town in a new Buick with three of these bumper stickers plastered on front and back."[19]

Evangelical southerners continued their assault on personal behavior through Sunday "closing laws" and limits or outright bans on sports contests on the Sabbath. These battles did not necessarily reflect an urban-rural division. In fact, evangelists enjoyed preaching in southern cities because the larger concentrations of population meant more sin, more conversions, and more revenue for the evangelist. Many urban residents had just recently removed from farms and small towns and sought fellowship in the city and salve for their souls. Evangelists exposed their personal past as metaphors of the South's past: sin, recovery, and redemption.

Sam Jones, a reformed alcoholic, became the South's first major evangelist during the 1890s. Although he traveled throughout the region, city revivals were his favorite venues. A slight, pale man with a high-pitched voice, rumpled suits, and a tousled shock of hair, Jones hardly seemed the prototype of the spellbinding southern evangelist. But that he was. In the days before microphones, Jones could project his voice to the back of most halls and throughout a fairgrounds arena. He laid bare his sin-filled early years, building credibility and empathy with the audience that God could save anyone. Like the South, the white southerner could rise from poverty and sin—if only he would accept Jesus Christ as Lord. Forgiveness, salvation, and eternal happiness. Southerners are very forgiving; they want to assist in the process of salvation, and forgiving sin is a major step in that direction. From black Alabamians openly praising a redeemed George Wallace to Carolina congregants reaching out to fallen evangelist Jim Bakker, redemption is a major theme in the lives of southerners, just as it has infused southern history.

Jones's crusades were important for reinforcing the racial "reforms" of the 1890s and early 1900s, for reinforcing white historical perspectives on the war and Reconstruction and the racial system that emanated from such views, as well as for curbing sinful personal behavior. In 1890 Jones preached that "law and order, protection of life and property, can only be maintained in the South by the supremacy of the white man and [his] domination over the inferior race." If God had wanted the colored man to be equal to the white man, "he wouldn't have colored him at the start." On more specific issues, Jones was very much attuned to this time and audience. He favored "summary justice" against blacks in rape cases and supported disfranchisement as a reasonable solution "to the Negro question." Much to the dismay of Atlanta businessmen, he also supported Sunday closing laws and prohibition.[20]

Local evangelical ministers had mixed feelings about Jones. On the one hand, he stirred the spiritual ardor of their flocks, but on the other, he drew money and time away from their churches. Also, Jones preached an ecumenicism that was very advanced for his time and not endorsed by evangelical leaders. Catholic- and Jew-baiting were common tactics among some evangelical ministers. Jones believed, however, that the righteous republic should not exclude other religious traditions. A moral Atlanta, he declared, would occur with "every Protestant living up to his vows, every Catholic as devout as grace could make him, [and] every Jew come back to the God of his fathers and the ten commandments."[21]

Jones particularly angered ministers with his insistence on the equality of women and men. Most preachers admonished wives and daughters to follow the Pauline doctrine of women's subservience. Jones disagreed, noting that "women were not only the last at the Cross, and first at the Resurrection, but they have been in the forefront of every hard fought battle for Christ." He went so far as to endorse women in the pulpit, shunting aside St. Paul's insistence that "it is a shame for a woman to speak in public."[22]

In the meantime, the evangelical mainstream, fresh from smashing demon rum, launched a holy crusade in the 1920s against the teaching of evolution in the public schools. The shaping of young minds was a crucial aspect of the southern evangelical crusade. Orthodoxy required dominance over education.

As the wall separating church and state disappeared, ministers plumped for governments that would espouse Christian principles and enact Christian laws. Few politicians could expect to win office without providing credentials of church affiliation, evidence of faithful church attendance, and obligatory religious allusions in campaign speeches and literature. That children would pray in public schools was a given; it was not even debated. But the content of their lessons was another matter. Just as the United Daughters of the Confederacy urged schools to adopt textbooks sympathetic to the Lost Cause and the southern view of Reconstruction, so evangelicals sought to expel heretical ideas from science courses, especially Charles Darwin's theory of evolution.

According to evangelical divines, Darwin's theory was not only theologically incorrect; its widespread acceptance was responsible for most of the sin in the world. In a 1922 sermon, the Reverend Amazi Clarence Dixon of Raleigh, North Carolina, attributed World War I to Darwin's theory: because it emphasized the "struggle for existence" and "survival of the fittest," it gave "the strong and fit the scientific right to destroy the weak and unfit." Evolution was also responsible for the rising divorce rate, for it implied that marriage "came up from the beast and not down from God." More dangerous, the theory denied that government is descended from God. Dixon reasoned that "if the basis of government came from the jungle where brute force prevails, the Bolshevist rule by bullet and bayonet is scientific and the scientific mind ought to accept it." He concluded, the "theory of evolution robs a man of his dignity, marriage of its sanctity, government of its authority, the church of her power and Christ of His glory."[23]

The anti-evolution forces enjoyed some success in the South during the 1920s, the Scopes "Monkey Trial" in Dayton, Tennessee, in 1925 being one manifestation of the controversy. Though the movement peaked by 1930, it never really disappeared and would resurface in the 1980s and later. But the Monkey Trial and assorted battles over the issue in other southern states fixed the South in the national consciousness as a hopelessly backward and narrow-minded region. Some evangelicals, though, fought what they perceived as an unwarranted assault on education by religion. William Poteat, president of the Baptist-affiliated Wake Forest University, led the pro-evolution forces in North Carolina. He painstakingly demonstrated how acceptance of Darwin's theory was compatible with the Bible. Poteat and his colleagues narrowly beat back efforts to pass a state law against the teaching of evolution in North Carolina public schools.[24]

At the same time evangelical Protestants were launching their moral and political offensives, new evangelical sects emerged to challenge the mainline denominations. Although they differed in doctrine, the new sects shared a belief that the older groups had strayed from the early evangelical principles

of moral rectitude and individual salvation. Secular concerns and moral re-
lapses had seeped into the traditional evangelical congregations, they asserted.

Earlier in the twentieth century, in the mountains of Tennessee and North
Carolina, small groups of families gathered to worship in a simple style that
harked back to the early evangelical meetings in the clearings of forests,
where eager listeners first heard the gospel of Jesus Christ preached and
strove to live their lives accordingly. These Pentecostal or Holiness churches
believed in the miraculous as a way of life. Seized by the spirit, they spoke in
tongues; a few congregations handled snakes to prove the presence of the
Holy Spirit. They believed in faith healing and scorned modern medicine.
Rather than disappearing as the South became more modern and urban, they
grew *because* the South became more modern and urban.[25]

In their purest form, Pentecostal churches emphasize a rigid rule of conduct, as demanding as the original Baptists on the colonial Virginia frontier.
In 1937 the Pentecostal Holiness Church of Franklin Springs, Georgia, issued a "Discipline," or list of tenets for members to abide. The tenets, or
"rules," are heavily laden with behavioral prohibitions, such as, "All our
members are forbidden to hold memberships in or have fellowship with oath-
bound secret societies, social clubs, and corrupt partisan politics; to attend
places of worldly amusement, such as moving picture shows, baseball games,
picnics, circuses, dancing halls, county and state fairs . . . The use of tobacco
in any form is forbidden, also its growth; its sale as a merchant, and its manufacture as a proprietor. . . . The Church is utterly opposed to the manufacture, sale, and use of all intoxicants. . . . Filthiness of speech, foolish talking,
jesting, and speaking evil of others are also forbidden. . . . All of our members
are forbidden to follow immodest and extravagant styles of dressing, or to
wear needless ornamentation."[26]

The major evangelical denominations had become too immersed in the
world; they were serfs of culture instead of servants of faith. Given the con-
vergence of evangelical religion with evangelical history, the Pentecostals offered a telling assessment of the state of mainline southern Protestant
practice; but, despite their growing numbers, they could not turn most evangelicals back to their ascetic origins.

During the first third of the twentieth century, Pentecostals were one of
the few white evangelical groups in the South that encouraged interracial
worship. An early founder of the movement was black. Although their doctrines prohibited public advocacy of racial equality, black members were ac-

corded the same privileges and positions within the church as whites. And rarely did the demeaning racial etiquette and the coded language that accompanied it intrude into member relationships. Today, interracial congregations are typical in Pentecostal churches.

Black Branches

Despite some integration in southern evangelical churches, the vast majority of southern blacks worshiped by themselves. The war and Reconstruction affected black evangelicals very differently than they did southern whites. For blacks, the story of Exodus had come true. Deliverance had arrived. African Americans quickly severed remaining ties with white churches after the surrender. A.M.E. (African Methodist Episcopal) and A.M.E. Zion recruiters came south to establish schools and churches and invite their brethren to join. Black Baptists, and the Colored Methodist Episcopal church formed by an amicable withdrawal from the Southern Methodist church in 1870, absorbed tens of thousands of former slaves. Some of these denominations founded black colleges, such as Fisk University in Nashville and Morehouse College in Atlanta. Fraternal orders and mutual-benefit societies grew out of black churches to aid the larger black community. Like their white counterparts, African American ministers stressed the importance of personal probity. Their outreach work made black churches social as well as religious institutions. During Reconstruction, when blacks clung tightly, if precariously, to political power, several ministers entered the political arena. Richard H. Cain, for example, was elected to the U.S. House of Representatives from North Carolina, and Hiram R. Revels to the U.S. Senate from Mississippi.

Once segregation and disfranchisement became the law of the southern land, black churches assumed even greater importance in a black community thrown back on its own resources. The black church functioned as a school, a social-service agency, a recreational facility, a meeting place, and a religious institution. The religious role of the black church became indistinguishable from its social mission, derived not only out of necessity but from blacks' historical perspective of themselves as a chosen people. That black and white southerners held similar perspectives on their respective roles within God's plan, yet evolved very different versions of evangelical Protestantism, reflects both the tragedy of their separation and their divergent views of the Civil War and Reconstruction era.

The southern black version of evangelical Protestantism also indicated that the evangelical persuasion admitted to various interpretations and uses, regardless of what southern white evangelicals stated about the issue. Northern evangelical Protestants, for example, also assumed an imperfect society, but they believed that people, though sinful by nature, could aspire to and even attain perfection. Their southern counterparts agreed that human depravity existed, but they believed that their society was perfect; it was already "a divine ordering of affairs." A perfect society, of course, required no mending or inquiry to improve it.[27]

Still there existed a relatively small band of southern evangelicals who demurred from the prevailing religiocultural view, who questioned both the historical perspective of the post-Reconstruction era and their churches' blindness to the misery in its midst. They read the Bible differently than did most of their white colleagues, a heresy in itself. For them, the life of Jesus provided inspiration for reform, and through that inspiration another tradition of evangelical Protestantism emerged by the early twentieth century.

Dissenters

Frank W. Barnett edited the *Alabama Baptist* and used that organ to promote an array of reforms to improve society and the status of the lowly within it, rather than to control thought and behavior. The growth of cities and industries throughout the South left numerous problems unaddressed by evangelical churches, despite their influence in the region. They remained curiously silent on a number of issues, particularly child labor and working conditions. In 1907 Barnett urged the state legislature to pass a child labor bill, arguing that "The South is harboring a system of slavery more horrible than that which existed before the Civil War, or which now exists in the Siberian mines—the slavery of child labor. Children from five to twelve years of age, working twelve and fourteen hours a day; babies . . . tramping wearily all day, before flying and buzzing machinery, pitiful little wrecks of humanity that wring the hearts of all who behold their thraldom, save their brutish masters, the mill owners."[28]

The bill failed, and Barnett's attack on employers earned him remonstrance from other evangelicals for engaging in issues beyond the purview of

Christianity. Barnett disagreed. For one thing, the church's support of disfranchisement, segregation, and numerous measures to curb personal behavior had already mixed Christianity and politics. Furthermore, to stand idly by
while suffering occurred was un-Christian. Barnett rejected those who perceived Christianity "as if it were simply a question of private life, with no
social obligations."[29]

None spoke more meaningfully for the possibilities of evangelical Protestantism to break the stranglehold of religious and historical orthodoxy on the
South than the Methodist-dominated Southern Sociological Congress.
Founded in 1912, the congress supported an array of Progressive reforms
common around the country at the time, such as urban beautification, public
health, and combating the evils of alcoholism, vice, and child labor. But the
congress also promoted activities peculiar to the southern circumstance, particularly attacking the convict lease system, which subjected mostly black
prisoners to harsh living and working conditions, and dedicating itself to "the
solving of the race question in a spirit of helpfulness to the negro and of equal
justice to both races." This is hardly a bold statement, but in the context of
the times, when racial segregation and disfranchisement threatened to petrify
race relations, such a mild objective seemed radical in contrast. Congress
members adopted as their motto "The fatherhood of God and the brotherhood of man." Again, not a revolutionary concept, but in the context of the
early twentieth-century South, they preached a sermon on the edge.[30]

Congress members fervently supported scientific inquiry and the importance of opening the mind, and eventually the South, to new ideas. They embraced the relatively new discipline of sociology as a method to study
southern society and to devise appropriate remedies for the problems uncovered by empirical research. As part of this process, they urged young ministers to train in the field, especially in urban missions. The ministers applied
both sociology and the Gospel vigorously. They looked not merely to save
the souls of their congregants, but their bodies and minds as well. As Methodist minister James E. McCulloch wrote, the mission of the church "is not
simply to 'save souls' but to save men, women, and children—body, intellect,
and soul."[31]

More important than their preaching were their actions, however timid
their attempts at racial and social harmony might appear to us today. The
congress established the Committee on Negro Problems to foster cooperation between black and white ministers and professionals, pressed for the ab-

olition of lynching, and supported liberal-arts (not merely vocational) training for African American youngsters.

How could they get away with it? The answer is that this was church work, and southerners allowed ministers a little more leeway than they would politicians or university professors—or any secular individual. The Methodist ministers and their colleagues of the cloth (the congress included rabbis, priests, and clergy from other Protestant denominations) grounded their advocacy in the Bible, and white southerners knew that book and the life of Jesus: his ministry to the poor, his absence of bigotry even toward his enemies. In their minds, they connected the life of Jesus with their own and followed his teachings as best they could, even though the society they created contradicted many of his precepts. So they were willing to allow ministers to cast a wide net in the name of Jesus, provided that the basic racial and social foundations of their society remained undisturbed.

In rural areas, ministers provided leadership and sometimes the only education around. When political or social movements swept through the region, ministers in the small churches often used their connections to organize congregations to support candidates or causes benefiting small farmers, tenants, and sharecroppers. True, some divines ignored the worldly plight of their congregations, or they preached the Gospel according to the mill owner or the landlord. But others interpreted their calling differently. They stood with the Populists and preached to the assembled men, women, and children, many of whom had driven their wagons a far distance to hear the cause. These political rallies assumed the character of religious revivals, with converts casting off their political sins and declaring for the Populist Party. In the 1930s evangelical preachers in the impoverished Arkansas delta exhorted their listeners to join the Southern Tenant Farmers Union (STFU), which would transform their lives on earth as sure as the Gospel could guarantee their place in heaven. Entire congregations joined the STFU. In a society where history and religion merged into politics, these progressive ministers did not so much separate these elements as they offered different perspectives on them. They demonstrated that evangelical religion could become a weapon of change and for social justice.[32]

The good works of the southern church proceeded also because white women undertook a considerable portion of it. Though white men financially supported many of the church's outreach activities, they rarely engaged in those endeavors. That was woman's work. And woman's work, important as it was, remained unscrutinized as long as it stayed out of the public realm. So

Atlanta's Lily Hammond, a delegate to the Southern Sociological Congress from the Methodist Women's Home Mission Society, helped to establish schools and settlement houses in urban neighborhoods, much as social workers such as Jane Addams and Emily Dinwiddie opened facilities for recent immigrants in northern cities. In the South, the recipients of such aid were blacks and working-class whites. A colleague, Estelle Haskin of Nashville, worked with faculty and administrators at Fisk University, a black school in the city, to open Bethlehem House, which would provide day care, sewing, classes, and kindergartens for black women and children. Bethlehem House also served as a laboratory school for social workers.[33]

None of these activities upset the prevailing racial traditions of the South. But consider the fact that at a time when localities provided as little as they could for their African American citizens, such institutions and ministries served not only as witness to a Christian conscience but as necessary features of an urban environment that daily reminded blacks that their white fellow residents did not care about them and did not see them unless they stepped out of character and into trouble.

The ministry of the Southern Sociological Congress also testified to the growing urbanization of the South during the last decade of the nineteenth century and the first two decades of the twentieth. The institutional church— the church of outreach, good works, and racial reconciliation—existed primarily as an urban phenomenon. With a high birth rate and falling commodities prices spreading resources thinner, farm life proved increasingly precarious. Urban life offered the possibility for work, especially in textile mills and tobacco factories, and a host of commercial activities opened up with improved transportation.

The coming together of rural blacks and whites in cities instigated racial segregation laws in the 1890s and after. Church work, especially work carried out by women and through the Southern Sociological Congress, provided a rare opportunity for interracial contact, at least at the middle-class level. Such work was invaluable in its assistance of blacks in an increasingly hostile and uncaring environment.

What moved one preacher and follower to interpret the Gospel as a divine directive for change while others used it to sanctify the status quo? That is the difficult question, but be thankful that the text—the Bible—could bear different interpretations and inspirations. A white southerner did not write it. It was possible for some to unlock the chains of the society that purportedly lived by the Bible's rules. Southern writer Katharine Du Pre Lumpkin—

born in Georgia, raised in South Carolina, of a once-privileged slaveholding family—found in the Bible weapons to challenge her own beliefs. As she experienced her revelation and redemption: "We may point to religion, and the way it was turned around on itself—for me, I mean—so that its high authority was fallen back on to justify the very acts under which religion's felt demand I could first profane the sacred tabernacle of our racial beliefs and go on profaning it in subsequent years. . . ."[34] What exactly drove Lumpkin to use the Bible to support her sacrilege remains elusive. Most women (and men) of her social position and education never questioned the received fabric of southern society.

Such a lack of introspection was part of what made the South such a maddening place in the first half of the twentieth century, but it also provided some hope that liberation was possible and that, in the end, the religion that bound the South to a false past and a dim future would be the same faith that would break those bonds. Later generations of white southerners would wonder at their predecessors. Had they not read, "[God] hath made of one blood all nations of men to dwell on all the face of the earth" (Acts 17:26), or "There is neither Jew nor Greek, there is neither bond nor free, there is neither male nor female: for ye are all one in Christ Jesus" (Galatians 3:28)? Yet the South of slavery, segregation, and disfranchisement persisted, and though white evangelical Christians considered themselves people of the Book, these biblical remonstrances could not mean what they said. Had their religion become a nonthinking habit, whose unquestioning of it meant a questioning of nothing?

So indistinguishable had southern history and religion become by the mid–twentieth century that its perversion of the Bible went mostly unnoticed. For a people who pledged to live the word of God, they had stretched the text mightily. Country comedian Jerry Clower recalled from his Baptist boyhood in Amite County, Mississippi, that Sunday School taught "there'd be a black heaven and a white heaven." In 1946 the Mississippi Southern Baptist Convention reiterated its support for segregation, resolving:

> We sympathize with and aid all the forces that have in mind helping the minority group to help themselves where they are best fitted to serve, live and enjoy life, which we believe is with, for, and among themselves. We recognize the sovereign will of God in bringing to pass the various races of the world and that His purpose will best be served in keeping separate what He has separated, and joined what He has joined. We condemn any teaching, doctrine, or example

that is biased toward social equality wherever found as being contrary to the best interests of both races and a hindrance to the proper solution of the problem. . . . We call upon our religious leaders and statesmen to strive to keep the races pure that they may serve out the purpose for which God created them.[35]

This is not to say that Mississippi Baptists abandoned the blacks in their midst. Much as some plantation owners felt a sense of *noblesse oblige* toward their slaves, Baptists believed that "acting right" and "doing good" toward the state's African American population reflected the proper Christian response to race. Just as their ancestors brought the slaves to Christ, so they would now conquer their own prejudices for the benefit of Christian harmony.

Harmony came at a price. Once the civil rights movement emerged in the 1950s, scarcely a Baptist preacher in Mississippi dared to speak out against segregation. Most avoided racial topics altogether; some spoke weakly of the importance of law and order; and those who spoke out or who invited blacks to worship in their churches found themselves without congregations.[36]

Civil Religion and Civil Rights

The southern black evangelical church was another matter, though the constraints of the Jim Crow South had increasingly proscribed its role to social service more than activist community leadership. The alleged independence of black churches from whites was overrated: any black institution during the early decades of the twentieth century invited white scrutiny, and white-owned banks frequently held the mortgages of black churches. Black ministers often felt they served three masters: God, the black community, and white leaders, and they walked a thin line satisfying all three constituencies.

During the 1930s, black educator Benjamin Mays of Atlanta University surveyed more than one hundred ministers' sermons from a like number of urban black churches in the South. He discovered that only twenty-six sermons touched upon practical problems; the rest dealt with "other-worldly" topics. Most of the sermons, Mays found, were characterized more by pyrotechnics than by logic and intellect. He concluded that black clergy "encourage Negroes to feel that God will see to it that things work out all right; if not in this world, certainly in the world to come. They make God influential chiefly in the beyond, in preparing a home . . . where His suffering servants will be free of the trials and tribulations which beset them on earth."[37]

Several years later, when Swedish economist Gunnar Myrdal visited Savannah as part of his research on American race relations, he found that the city's black ministers were actively discouraging an African American voter-registration drive. As one pastor explained, "all we preachers is supposed to do is to preach the Lord and Savior Jesus Christ and Him Crucified, and that's all."[38]

Given this attitude, it is surprising that the black church and black ministers were in the forefront of the civil rights movement less than a decade later. The renewal of the black evangelical church resulted from two related factors. First, a new generation of ministers emerged, steeled by depression and war, confident that as a result of that war a new day was dawning in the South. These new pastors were often educated in the North, or at least better educated than their predecessors, and reflected more accurately the youth of their congregations. Second, church members pushed their leaders to take a more active role in social affairs. Black veterans returned from World War II dissatisfied with the racial status quo, and they looked to one of the few places where blacks had influence, the black church, for leadership.

As the black church moved to the front of the African American community, it set the tone for the civil rights movement as a moral and religious crusade. Under the church's aegis, the movement would not be violent, would not be exclusive, and would not be demeaning. When younger blacks began to turn away from church leadership after the mid-1960s, the movement for black civil rights took on a different and more diffuse tone. Whites, once welcomed, were shunned or expelled; violence, once abhorred, was now condoned under certain circumstances; and the chant of Black Power replaced the gospel of Jesus Christ. The moral high ground that blacks had attained during the movement's key years seemed less secure, and these new trends yielded fewer and less-imposing victories.

White churches during the civil rights movement played the role of James Joyce's God in *Portrait of the Artist as a Young Man*: "Within or behind or beyond his handiwork, invisible, refined out of existence, indifferent, paring his fingernails." As the civil rights movement reached its climax with the passage of the 1964 Civil Rights Act, effectively ending public segregation, Ralph McGill, editor of the Atlanta *Constitution*, wrote the epitaph for the white evangelicals' part in this revolution: "the Christian church has been merely a bit player in the greatest social revolution of our time."[39]

Ministers who spoke out often lost their pulpits. The Reverend Robert Blakely McNeill of Columbus, Georgia, for example, authored a mild article on race relations in *Look* magazine in May 1957, urging "creative contact" between the races to promote racial harmony and discharge Christian duty. The Southeast Georgia Presbytery stripped McNeill of his pastorate, and a leader in his congregation informed members, "now we must find a preacher with the right kind of religion." Three days later, the distressed forty-four-year-old McNeill suffered a near-fatal heart attack, prompting a member of the congregation to remark that the Lord finally had "taken care of him."[40]

In Macon, Georgia, a Baptist church fired its minister when he suggested that it might be Christian to allow blacks to join the worship service. When a black man showed up, the deacons formed a barrier in front of the door to prevent his entrance. A young man who witnessed the incident remembered seeing a small dog running in and out of the church while the deacons made their stand and noted the irony of the fact that a dog could enter their church, but a man could not.[41]

If ministers privately questioned the wisdom of segregation, they went public with those reservations at their peril. Congregants were rarely in advance of the pastor's thinking on the subject. Journalist Pat Watters recalled an Atlanta woman who supported Lester Maddox's gubernatorial campaign. The woman defended her choice of the arch-segregationist with a remark that people in other parts of the country would have considered a non sequitur: "Lester knows how to handle those niggers," she explained to Watters. "He's a very religious man."[42]

As a powerful institution within southern white society, the evangelical church had a considerable stake in maintaining the status quo. Intertwined as it was with the historical perspective that justified the racial and gender inequalities in southern society, it could not readily remove its blessing from that society without diminishing itself. By the mid-1950s the white Protestant church in the South was complacent and smug—a state church for the ruling race, growing more prosperous and more respectable. Its gaze was broad, maintaining a vigilant eye over personal behavior, thought, and expression; yet its vision was remarkably narrow, closed off from the most momentous moral issue of the time. As a young North Carolina evangelist, Billy Graham counseled in the mid-1950s, "the church should not answer questions the people aren't asking."[43]

The timidity of white clergymen both saddened and angered the black ministers who led the civil rights movement. When Martin Luther King Jr. wrote his famous letter from a Birmingham jail cell in April 1963, he was responding to a petition from the city's white ministers criticizing him for instigating demonstrations in that city. They charged that King was an outsider who had no business in the city and that his protests were untimely and demanded too much too soon. Such extremism, they argued, would hurt, not help, race relations in Birmingham.

Writing with a stubby pencil along the margins of the New York *Times* page on which the ministers' letter appeared, King composed a simple but eloquent reply. The sheer beauty of King's letter, as well as its deep grounding in southern black evangelical Protestantism, warrant quoting it at length. It contains the lessons of a lecture, the cadence of a sermon, and the devotion of a doxology. To the charge of being an "outside agitator," he wrote, "I am in Birmingham because injustice is here. Just as the prophets of the eighth century B.C. left their villages and carried their 'thus saith the Lord' far beyond the boundaries of their home towns . . . so am I compelled to carry the gospel of freedom beyond my own home town." To the clergymen's counsel of patience, King replied:

> We have waited for more than 340 years for our constitutional and God-given rights. . . . Perhaps it is easy for those who have never felt the stinging darts of segregation to say, "Wait." But when you have seen vicious mobs lynch your mothers and fathers at will and drown your sisters and brothers at whim; when you have seen hate-filled policemen curse, kick, and even kill your black brothers and sisters; when you see the vast majority of your twenty million Negro brothers smothering in an airtight cage of poverty in the midst of an affluent society; when you suddenly find your tongue twisted and your speech stammering as you seek to explain to your six-year-old daughter why she can't go to the public amusement park . . . and see tears welling up in her eyes . . . when you take a cross-country drive and find it necessary to sleep night after night in the uncomfortable corners of your automobile because no motel will accept you . . . when your first name becomes "nigger," your middle name becomes "boy" . . . and your last name becomes "John," and your wife and mother are never given the respected title "Mrs." . . . when you are forever fighting a degenerating sense of "nobodiness"—then you will understand why we find it difficult to wait.

In addressing the charge that he engaged in illegal actions, King made the distinction between just laws and unjust laws, labeling segregation an unjust law because it was sinful. He quoted theologian Paul Tillich that "sin was separation." King asked, "Is not segregation an existential expression of man's tragic separation, his awful estrangement, his terrible sinfulness?" As for the related question that his illegal demonstrations provoked violence,

King again phrased his response with a question: "Isn't this like condemning Jesus because his unique God-consciousness and never-ceasing devotion to God precipitated the evil act of crucifixion?" By framing his replies within a Christian context, King hoped not only to convince the clergymen of the righteousness of his cause, but also to demonstrate that their view was outside that context. This latter objective was evident in King's response to the charge of extremism. The question for King was not "whether we will be extremists, but what kind of extremists we will be. Will we be extremists for hate or for love?" He added that "Jesus Christ . . . was an extremist for love, truth, and goodness, and thereby rose above his environment. Perhaps the South, the nation, and the world are in dire need of creative extremists."[44]

King also expressed deep disappointment in the role of the white church in the South during the nine years since the *Brown v. Board of Education of Topeka* decision, a disappointment shared by the relatively few white ministers who dared speak out against segregation. Carlyle Marney of Myers Park Baptist Church in Charlotte was one such white cleric who regretted that "there's a social revolution under way, and Baptists in God's white hand have had precious little to do with it except when run over from the rear." The problem was not, as novelist Walker Percy noted, of "putting into practice the Judeo-Christian ethic [because] Christendom of a sort has already won." The problem was to expose the church and its congregants to a more expansive view of an ethic that did not "canonize the existing social and political structure."[45]

When modest desegregation was effected in several southern cities prior to 1964, either through local law or agreement, white evangelicals urged compliance. They did so not out of a sense of morality but because it was the law. White ministers evinced scant awareness from their pulpits that such changes corroborated rather than countered God's plan. As King continued in his letter, "I have heard numerous southern religious leaders admonish their worshipers to comply with a desegregation decision because it is the law. But I have longed to hear white ministers declare: 'Follow this decree because integration is morally right and because the Negro is your brother.' In the midst of blatant injustices inflicted upon the Negro, I have watched white churchmen stand on the sideline and mouth pious irrelevancies and sanctimonious trivialities. In the midst of a mighty struggle to rid our nation of racial and economic injustice, I have heard many ministers say: 'those are social issues with which the gospel has no real concern.'" King warned that "if today's church does not recapture the sacrificial spirit of the early church, it will lose its authenticity, forfeit the loyalty of millions, and be dismissed as an irrelevant social club with no meaning for the twentieth century."[46]

King did not want to conclude his letter with a catalogue of grievances against the South in general and white clergymen in particular. Instead, he closed with a vision: "One day, the South will know that when these disinherited children of God sat down at lunch counters, they were in reality standing up for what is best in the American dream and for the most sacred values in our Judeo-Christian heritage, thereby bringing our nation back to those great wells of democracy which were dug deep by the founding fathers in their formulation of the Constitution and the Declaration of Independence."[47]

The blending of the sacred and the secular had become a southern evangelical tradition. Whether or not the white clergy heeded King's words, they understood him. And so did numerous other white southerners for whom white supremacy was becoming a heavy burden of conscience. As journalist Ralph McGill noted in 1961, "all Southerners, save the most obtuse and insensitive, have long carried a private weight of guilt about the inequities of segregation." In a society laced with the daily presence of sin, black revelations of white supremacy's immorality weighed oppressively on some white southern evangelicals. South Carolina senator Ernest F. Hollings recalled that moment in his life when the verities of his history suddenly disappeared to reveal a different past. It came to him when he read King's letter from the Birmingham jail. Hollings admitted that "as governor, for four years I enforced those Jim Crow laws. I did not understand, I did not appreciate what King had in mind . . . until he wrote that letter. He opened my eyes and he set me free."[48]

True enough; such awareness and repentance may not have been general among white southerners, but numbers were not that important. What was important, especially for the continuation of racial reconciliation, was that at least a few whites attained enlightenment. Referring to God's pledge in Genesis not to destroy Sodom if only ten righteous people could be found there, German theologian Dietrich Bonhoeffer observed that God "is able to see the whole people in a few, just as he saw and reconciled in One the whole of humanity."[49] The civil rights movement in the South demonstrated that evangelical Protestantism, so long a prop for white southern culture, could serve a nobler, more inclusive cause.

The mission of the South to build a kingdom of God was no different in 1965 than it was in 1865. As God's chosen people, they would find a way. But if the objective was the same, the road now was much broader and the company traveling more diverse and more authentically southern, in that it included African Americans and whites who had lived and prayed apart for three centuries, but who, in the end, shared a common religion, history, and culture. That was southern blacks' greatest gift to their region and to its religion. But could these two evangelical traditions—black and white—merge in the coming years? Would the Civil War and Reconstruction continue to be both the historical and theological dividing line between black and white southerners?

3   Culture Protestants

> . . . being a culture religion has its darker side as well. The law of inertia operates so powerfully that one is never quite sure whether it is custom or conviction that controls or rules. Moreover, in a single-religion section of the country, separation of church and state at the local level is far more shibboleth than sure agenda.
> —Edwin Scott Gaustad, "North and South in American Religious History: Baptists and Beyond"

As the greatest religious movement in our nation's history wound down in the mid-1960s, the lessons of grace and redemption imparted by southern blacks did not go unchallenged into the hearts of white southerners. The evangelical Protestantism preached and practiced by the movement did not readily dissolve the myths of southern history and the religious justifications that supported them. White southerners were vigilant about false prophecy paraded as Gospel, and to some, the ideals of racial equality qualified as such.

In the decades that followed, evangelical Protestantism went upscale and suburban, its palaces of worship rivaling the great cathedrals of Europe in dimension, if not in style. Humbler houses have persisted, and within their walls remains the message of the ages, though somewhat less adorned than in the megachurches; but the message remains open to manipulation and interpretation, as always. The good news is that how the Gospel is interpreted (and by whom) matters to a great many people; that is also the bad news.

The great difficulty in shifting the South's historical perspective, and the religious dogma that supports it, is that such change requires southern whites to rethink both their history and their religion. When both are a matter of faith, and when faith is an indelible part of identity, that is a difficult thing to do, even if their black neighbors demonstrated that southern theology could be compatible with a more inclusive version of southern history. But the very changes wrought by southern blacks and their federal allies, along with the Sunbelt prosperity that accompanied the initial resolution of civil rights issues in the South, generated not only a revival of the traditional perspective of southern history, but a renewal of its religious partner as well.

History and religion have reinforced each other for so long in the South that white southerners have attained a comfort zone with respect to their version of evangelical Christianity. Like the history that raised white supremacy to a commandment, white evangelical Protestantism provided its adherents with a justification and a rationale for their beliefs and how they led their lives. Religion offered a bedrock, security, the glue that held society together, a safe harbor, and any other metaphors that could be dreamt up. But these were not mere metaphors; to southern white evangelicals, they were the thing itself.[1]

Because religion provided the civilizing force for their society, white southerners defended their faith with ferocious devotion. They swatted away conflicting ideas, denigrated inquiry, suppressed doubt, and girded their institutions to fight the battle for orthodoxy. Bob Jones Sr., a preacher from rural Alabama, founded his eponymous university (originally founded in Florida and now located in Greenville, South Carolina) in 1927 with the idea that parents who sent their children to his school could "go to sleep at night with no haunting fear that some skeptical teacher [would] steal the faith" of their offspring.[2]

Fright is a poor grounding for faith; it can lead to defensiveness and excessive reaction. "I think we are afraid of ourselves," South Carolina journalist Ben Robertson wrote in the 1940s. "I do not know whether we are intemperate because of our religion, or whether our religion is intemperate because of us. I know, though, that the basis of our character is derived from our spiritual outlook."[3] The fear of difference is driven by the fear of doubt: after living such a strictured life, following the tortured orthodoxies of custom and religion, could those struggles somehow have been in vain? Could a different path lead to the same salvation? If faith topples, all else goes with it.

Events from the 1960s onward built insecurity into an already defensive faith. The civil rights movement, Sunbelt migration, challenges to prevailing cultural norms from Supreme Court decisions on school prayer and abortion, and from the youthful counterculture, shook the complacency of southern white evangelicals. No longer isolated from the American religious main-stream—which is to say, the diversity of American religion—southern white evangelicals felt under siege. Changes in their own circumstances com-pounded the feeling. More of them had moved to the South's rapidly advanc-ing metropolitan areas, away from their families and the homogeneity of small towns and farms. They confronted the culture of their new surround-ings head on, and it frightened them, even as, and *because*, its material abun-dance proved alluring. The old conflict between sin and salvation, both in their personal lives and in the larger society where they now lived and worked, seemed ever more relevant. When the evangelical renewal came in earnest in the late 1970s, it was precisely in the urban and suburban South that it first flourished.

White southerners looked to the state for both validation and protection; the state in the South had historically nurtured southern religion as an ally in enforcing the prevailing views on the Civil War and Reconstruction, as well as the society derived from those views. The small religious minorities typi-cally went along. Jewish students sang as heartily as their Gentile classmates that "We Have a Friend in Jesus" and participated in school Easter pageants and Christmas plays. Strong in their faith, they endured these events as part of the cultural dues for living in the South and being left alone to pursue their own religion on their own time. As one chosen people to another, there was a tacit understanding that as long as one professed some religion, one could participate in community life on a roughly equal basis. Each year the Anti-Defamation League of the B'nai B'rith would report that the South experi-enced the fewest anti-Semitic attacks of all American regions. Southern fault lines ran along issues of race, not religion, and as long as one upheld the other, there was tolerance, if not respect. The South was so overwhelmingly peopled with evangelical Christians that the few dissenters in their midst seemed more curiosities than threats. But by the 1970s the loosening of racial strictures and the migration of northern Catholics and Jews emboldened the region's religious minorities to challenge the merger of church and state in the South and the promotion of religion as a daily spectacle that ignored or violated their own faiths. These legal attacks, coupled with cultural and de-mographic changes, led southern evangelicals to organize and mount a counterreformation.

In the late 1970s Jerry Falwell, a Southern Baptist minister from Lynchburg, Virginia, founded the Moral Majority. Falwell, a supporter of segregation during the 1950s, pastored a large congregation in Lynchburg and established Liberty College (now University) to promote a conservative Christian education and lifestyle. He envisioned the Moral Majority as more than a group of like-minded religious conservatives; he hoped to use the organization as a political force to promote an evangelical agenda including a constitutional amendment to ban abortions, legislation to allow prayer in public schools, and measures designed to enhance "traditional" families as opposed to single-parent households and gay couples. While the Moral Majority espoused a race-neutral program, its immediate popularity owed, in part, to whites' resentment of the growing power and militancy of African Americans. Its spokesmen denounced "welfare dependency" and single parenthood. Though the Moral Majority was national in scope, the South provided its greatest sustenance and support. And the growing economic vitality and political importance of the South gave southern evangelicals a national platform.[4]

The national "coming out" of southern evangelical Protestantism went well at first but began to falter by the late 1980s. Increasing scandals among televangelists (though not Falwell); the glaring contradiction of the evangelical platform, which denounced government control and intervention yet beseeched that same government to make laws institutionalizing behavior that evangelicals espoused; and the religious exclusivity of the evangelicals all caused the Moral Majority to shrink in consequence.

Not to be kept down, the southern evangelical spirit soon materialized in another political guise. In 1989 Pat Robertson, a Virginia Beach–based evangelist who had modest success in several Republican presidential primaries in 1988, formed the Christian Coalition. The new organization quickly became a crucial political arm of the Republican Party. The zeal and organizational abilities of its members, especially in the South, consumed party regulars and transformed the nature of southern Republicanism in several states. Its full-fledged emergence during the 1992 presidential election also elicited comments such as one by Randall Terry, founder of a militant anti-abortion organization called Operation Rescue: "to vote for Bill Clinton is to sin against God."[5] But, as with the Moral Majority, once the Christian Coalition's agenda and tactics became widely known, its national popularity slipped. By the late 1990s its financial base withered due to membership depletion and the loss of its tax exemption. Yet the group is still a critical component of southern Republicanism today.

The power of conservative evangelicals remains strong in the South, limiting the prospect of progressive change or challenge to the traditional historical perspective that grew alongside religious dogma. Disparate historical views cannot exist side by side in the minds of some white southerners, any more than they can admit other religions to their notion of theology. Many evangelicals view the world as a place starkly divided between good and evil, and any compromise with the latter amounts to the death of the former. Such an outlook served as a valid and effective discipline during the years after the Civil War, but its practice is problematical in a diverse society. Leighton Ford, a Presbyterian minister in Charlotte, stated that "It makes, I think, a great difference whether Christians use the name of Christ out of a need for control and power, rather than with a spirit of humility and a sense of our own need. The Jesus of Bethlehem, after all, came as a vulnerable baby, born to a downtrodden people, not in the palace of Caesar." Quoting Alan Jones, dean of Grace Cathedral in San Francisco, Ford concluded, "For a believer to urge the exclusive claims of Christ in a bullying, offensive, and triumphalist manner is to deny the very Spirit of the Christ one is proclaiming. Christ bullies no one. The Cross coerces no one."[6]

The rise and faltering of these theocratic movements over the past two decades exposed the underside of southern evangelical Protestantism to a national audience. The aversion of the movements to skeptical inquiry reflected a substitution of bias for belief. For many other religions, self-examination and inquiry are partners of faith, not its adversaries. Pope John Paul II's 1998 encyclical, "Faith and Reason," argues that the Creator gave us reason and we should be confident to use it; there are absolute truths, but reason will confirm rather than destroy them.[7] Openness to reason is a sign of maturity, of belief in one's ability to plumb the depths of doubt without fear of losing either face or faith. Theologian Erich Fromm has argued that dogmatism is basically an immature form of religion, an immaturity that confounds those outside the faith in particular. David Cohn, a Jewish writer from Greenville, Mississippi, spoke of his evangelical neighbors in puzzlement: "Faith, I felt, is the indissoluble love-marriage of intuition and reason, the mind confirming what the heart postulates. Certainly denial of the right to doubt in one field may lead to tyranny—denial of the right to doubt in all fields."[8]

It is this last point, the immersion of religious dogmatism into southern society in general, that has especially characterized the region to this day.

Religious fundamentalism encourages an "intellectual fundamentalism that has failed to train southerners to read, feel, or think with any sophistication." But sophisticated thought is not necessarily the issue here; rather, it is thought at all, inquiry, the ability to consider various perspectives.[9]

The issue of homosexuality tortures some congregations, for example, but many evangelicals feel secure in the notion that it is a sin, pure and simple, and the only remedy is conversion. As one letter writer to the Charlotte *Observer* declared, "What Christ says is morally wrong is morally wrong. Murdering is still a sin, stealing is still a sin, cheating is still a sin and homosexuality is *still a sin*." A minister agreed: "Homosexuality and other sins caused God to destroy Sodom, and they will cause the same thing to happen to this nation."[10] If southern history is not past, then the Bible is a living document as well.

This perspective also suggests a lack of respect for other faiths, because evangelicals believe there is only one Truth, only one way to attain heaven: through their faith. As Southern Baptist leader Bailey Smith noted in 1980 and again in 1987, "God doesn't hear the prayer of the Jew." This comment implies a certitude over a range of issues, from free trade to feminism. In response to a 1992 survey of churchgoers in Charlotte, North Carolina, a member of Northside Baptist Church admitted that "people who don't have a Christian background might think we're fanatical." She added not an apology but a confirmation: "Well, I guess we are. We have all the answers." As exasperating as such statements are to many people, especially to newcomers to the South, they are understandable in light of the fact that evangelical southerners believe they are uniquely chosen by God. Historian Charles Reagan Wilson explained, "the self-image of a chosen people leaves little room for self-criticism." Since the end of the Civil War, and because of the result of that war, white southern evangelicals have believed this with all their hearts and souls.[11]

Beginning in 1996 the Southern Baptist Convention (SBC) implemented specific organizational initiatives directed at converting Jews, Hindus, and other non-Christians. Regrettably, the response of these religions has been as combative and as unyielding as the evangelical directive. If people are secure in their faith, there should be little concern about conversion. The issue is not really theological; it is a political matter. The Baptists' proselytizing efforts imply a disrespect or a trivializing of other religions. Such attitudes contribute to and encourage religious violence and verbal attacks. That is the real danger of such outreach efforts: not that they will result in mass conversions but that they encourage some to express hatred and commit violence against religious communities different from their own.

Take, for example, the Herring family in Pike County, Alabama, whose circumstance offers a preview of what school prayer under evangelical direction might be like. Their three children are the only Jewish pupils in the county's public school system. Teachers forced the Herring children to bow their heads during Christian-influenced prayers and vowed to convert them. The Herrings endured swastikas painted on their lockers and physical harassment from fellow students who rationalized they were doing the Lord's work. On one occasion, eleven-year-old Sarah Herring reported that a minister visited her class (not an unusual occurrence in rural southern schools) "and said I was going to hell because I was not a Christian."

In fact, Pike County's schools are only nominally secular, nonsectarian institutions. Assemblies routinely open with Christian prayers and Scripture readings, the Gideons hand out Bibles to fifth-graders in their classrooms, and preachers regularly lecture students on morality. The Herrings have alleged (and the school superintendent admits) that an assistant principal in the high school forced fourteen-year-old Paul Herring to write an essay on "Why Jesus loves me." A teacher also ordered Paul to remove his Star of David because she thought it was a gang symbol. Students have admitted to the harassment, confirming incidents such as drawing swastikas on the Herrings' book bags. It took a federal lawsuit to force the school system to abandon the most overt expressions of religion in Pike County's public schools.[12]

Religious orthodoxy is the new racism in the South. It was always present, but now that evangelicism is under siege, its practitioners feel justified in striking out in the name of the Lord, as they once defended the ramparts of white supremacy. In June 2000 the U.S. Supreme Court struck down the practice of students' electing fellow students to offer prayers at the beginning of Friday night football games in Santa Fe, Texas. The families of two students who brought the suit, one Mormon, one Roman Catholic, had the good sense to request anonymity during the court proceedings. Thus challenged, the evangelicals lashed out in the name of the Lord, as the lone Jewish student in the high school discovered when his classmates, not knowing the plaintiffs in the case, chanted "Hitler missed one! No more Jews! Hitler missed one! He should have gotten you!" The taunts elevated into death threats, which the school superintendent dismissed as a teenage prank.[13]

A similar militancy attaches to the issue of teaching evolution in the public schools—a national controversy, to be sure, but with particular roots and expanse in the South. Access to public schools has been as important to the southern church as it had been to groups such as the United Daughters of the Confederacy. These were key venues in which to secure the message and lessons of history and faith; schools were extensions of homes. A high-school principal in Louisville blurted over the public address system that "evolution had been overthrown and no longer needed to be taught." The message apparently did not filter down to his teachers. Most teachers have found a way around the faith-based politics of creationists. High-school biology teachers in Alabama use a textbook with the following disclaimer placed there by the state board of education: "Evolution is a controversial theory some scientists present as scientific explanation for the origin of living things. . . . No one was present when life first appeared on earth. Therefore, any statement about life's origins should be considered as theory, not fact." Biology teachers, especially those in the state's more cosmopolitan and diverse metropolitan areas, generally ignore the caveat and teach evolution anyway. As one high-school teacher stated, "I tell them [the students] on the first day, 'We are going to learn about evolution, I do not care if you believe what I am saying, but you will learn.' " She added, "Most teachers just teach their stuff and ignore it [the disclaimer]." A rebellious spirit still prevails in the Old Confederacy.[14]

The promoters of religious orthodoxy in the public arena are not the only voices of faith in the South today, of course. Just as some evangelicals spearheaded reform movements earlier in this century, defying the prevailing religious culture, so there are those divines today who work to extricate southern Christianity from its culture-centered past. Tom Ehrich, an Episcopal priest (admittedly, not an evangelical) from Winston-Salem, North Carolina, urged his fellow southerners not to torture the Gospel to fit contemporary political ends. "Jesus," he wrote, "said nothing about abortion or homosexuality. He made but one reference to divorce. His comment concerning adultery was how we shouldn't judge each other." Then what *did* Jesus talk about? He talked about money, a topic most New South congregants could warm to, though perhaps not quite in the way Jesus had in mind. According to Ehrich, Jesus taught "the great burden that wealth places on the believer, the need to let go of wealth, the need to break our addiction to control, and the need to share." We have, in effect, baptized our ideas and opinions and made them God's. "We have created a God who wants what we want, who hates those whom we hate, who looks like us, talks like us, maybe even votes like us. . . . We aren't the first to build a golden calf." Ehrich concluded, "The Gospel is about dying to self and loving both God and neighbor, not about raising the victory flag of right opinion."[15]

Yet southerners are quite fond of flag-waving, from flags snapping from car antennae on football Saturdays, proclaiming, "My college is going to cream yours," to a mindless patriotism that, like most southern religion, asks no questions and generates no doubts. These folks know they are good people and know they follow Christ's admonition to love. They openly express their love for the sinner, their prayers for the wayward. As one letter writer advised, "As Christians we should love all people no matter their beliefs, but let's not pretend they are in good standing with God."[16] These are the same folks who clamor for prayer in the public schools, emphasizing the harmless yet cleansing nature of simple prayer—a valid sentiment to be sure, but can we trust religious observance to those who believe there is no faith other than their own? To admit others into their circle of faith on the basis of equality would be to destroy their own faith. Like in the Saturday football game (which many writers have described as religious), in religion there can be only one winner.

Evangelicals insist that their advocacy of school prayer and other religious intrusions into the public sphere is based on American ideals of religious freedom. But, in practice, the faith is often hostile to other religious traditions. What has happened in the South in recent years is an assault not on religion but the application of American Constitutional principles and the migration of Roman Catholics, Jews, Muslims, and others who expect protection, not disparagement, of their faith. The *Santa Fe* case revealed that southern evangelicals do not want parity; rather, they want a restoration of their uncontested dominance, in much the same way as the Redeemers of the 1870s sought to wrest control of their region from Yankee and African American usurpers. It also reflects the terrible uncertainty and doubt that has crept into this once-unchallenged faith. As one legal scholar noted after the *Santa Fe* ruling, "A faith that requires the support of a government is an infirm faith. If they demand an invocation of Jesus at a football game, and the right [of other religions] be damned, it must be because the invocations of Jesus at home, and in church, and in voluntary associations . . . are proving inadequate; and so they must pretend that what stands in the way of their Christian life are the rights of non-Christians." Religions "will flourish, or they will not flourish, according to the spiritual quality of their exertions. Politics is too puny to get in the way of the most exalted meanings."[17]

Recent statements of faith by the Southern Baptist Convention reflect this insecurity well. Thwarted by court decisions and threatened by the South's growing religious diversity, the SBC has worked to shore up the crumbling bastions of southern orthodoxy. In 1963 the SBC approved a resolution allowing women to be ordained as Baptist ministers. The declaration did not address whether a woman could lead a congregation, but ordination implied a step in that direction. The matter rested there until the June 2000 meeting of the SBC, where delegates ended the ambiguity and unequivocally resolved that "the office of pastor is limited to men as qualified by Scripture." The chairman of the drafting committee explained that "Southern Baptists, by practice as well as conviction, believe leadership is male." The resolution came two years after the SBC had called for women to subordinate themselves to their husbands: "A wife is to submit graciously to the servant leadership of her husband, even as the church willingly submits to the headship of Christ." The timing of these two resolutions—more than a generation after the SBC last addressed women's issues specifically—reflects the uncertainty of these men, not only about their women, but about their faith as well.

The assault on the autonomy of Southern Baptist women, more than the militancy over school prayer and evolution, has rousted some Baptists to break their ties to the SBC. The General Baptist Convention of Texas initiated a formal split in 2000. The Reverend Charles Wade, executive director of the Texas group, explained, "There's a partnership in Christian marriage. We're trying to say in our day any attempt to put women 'in their place' or somehow limit the contribution that women might have in church goes against the whole spirit of Christ." An SBC leader called the Texas action "an intentional rejection of a clear teaching of the Bible."[18]

As rancorous and distressing as these religious disputes may be to believers, eventually they will result in a better understanding and practice of the role of religion in contemporary southern society, a society markedly different from the one that formed after Reconstruction. This is not to say that religion will be less important, or less "southern," but it may attain the promise that reformers over the past century have held out for it: to help shape a more just, more inclusive society.

Regardless of the shape of this new southern religion, evangelical Protestants will continue to have a major voice in its development for some time to come. For all the in-migration, the South remains the least religiously diverse region of the country. More than 90 percent of southerners are evangelical Protestants. Religion is daily on the southern mind. A recent survey indicated that 94 percent of southerners pray regularly, a ratio well above the national average. Such frequency may reflect the fact that evangelicals believe they have a direct line to God, but it indicates more the immanence of God in their lives and how personal that relationship is.

When nonevangelicals move into a southern neighborhood, one of the first questions a neighbor will ask is "What church do you go to?" For most newcomers, the question seems intrusive. People from other parts of the country or the world are not less religious than their new neighbors, but religion for many people is a private matter worn in one's heart, not on one's sleeve. In contrast, the very nature of evangelical Protestantism is to spread the Bible's good news, the Gospel; evangelicals are demonstrative about their faith and very public, like their history. Some newcomers relish this homogeneity and the comfort of uniform patterns of thought and behavior such near unanimity implies. A woman who moved from Phoenix to Charlotte in 1997 confessed that the North Carolina city's "Christian climate" was one of the major attractions. As she explained her experience with diversity in Phoenix: "I just felt like my Christian faith was somewhat pressured in Phoenix. There is such a large number of people of other faiths there, it was felt you shouldn't emphasize any belief."[19]

It is still difficult to dissent in the South, and being outside evangelical Protestantism is a de facto dissent. In the larger cities of the region, religious dissenters generally go about unmolested, save for the occasional confession that Baptists are praying for Jews or seeking their conversion, or the identification of Catholics, Mormons, or Seventh-Day Adventists as cultists rather than fellow Christians. In smaller communities, however, difference can be dangerous; the same folks who view homosexuality as a sin agree that those who are not born-again Christians are sinners as well. In either case, tolerance is no virtue, for how can one tolerate sin?

There is an abiding faith among southern evangelicals that public behavior and public display can have a salutary effect on individual souls. The ubiquity of public prayer and the persistent efforts to post the Ten Commandments in visible public places are manifestations of this faith. But it is a faith untempered by reason, or at least by common sense, for it is doubtful most of the faithful could actually abide by these commandments. Number ten, about coveting, would have a serious impact on New South economic development. Or number four, keeping the Sabbath holy—what would happen to all those Sunday football games? If you follow Jesus' teachings closely, then number seven, about adultery, includes a lusting heart as a violation, and Jesus' equation of anger with murder would knock out number six as well.

While we're at it, there are many aspects of the Bible that evangelicals, despite their protests of literalism, do not take literally. What are we to make of the sixth chapter of Matthew's Gospel, where Jesus says, "And when thou prayest, thou shalt not be as the hypocrites are: for they love to pray standing in the synagogues and in the corners of the streets, that they may be seen of men. Verily I say unto you, they have their reward. But thou, when thou prayest, enter into thy closet, and when thou hast shut thy door, pray to thy Father which is in secret; and thy Father which seeth in secret shall reward thee openly"?

The evangelical tendency to make the private public ultimately has the effect of trivializing faith. When President George W. Bush Jr., a professed born-again Christian, occupied the State House in Austin, he designated June 11, 2000, as the Spirit of Americans with Disabilities Act Torch Relay Day across Texas. Governors do this sort of thing all the time and, except for the people or organizations targeted by these special "days," most citizens have no idea. More noticed, however, was the governor's declaration of June 10, 2000, as Jesus Day in Texas. The well-meaning governor, surprised at the outcry, including from some evangelical Protestants, protested that "people of all religions recognize Jesus Christ as an example of love, compassion, sacrifice, and service." Although the governor's claim of universality may be arguable, theologically it is off base. It is not Jesus' example of love that commands the worship of Christians. Christians worship Jesus because they believe he is the Son of God. For believers, "every day is Jesus Day." Anything less trivializes both Jesus and the Christian religion. But this is precisely what occurs when government meddles in religion: religion invariably suffers, and the support evangelical Protestantism has given to state and local governments in the South since the Reconstruction era is a mostly sad record of compliance and subordination. The old Baptists and Methodists challenged conformity, challenged the very society they sought to convert; their successors became too entrenched to distinguish themselves from the power of government and align themselves with the power of God. Worse, they believed they were doing God's bidding, not Caesar's.[20]

A key to restructuring southern religion and returning it to its historic roots is for evangelicals to conquer their fear, to become more assured of their own faith and their ability to resist rather than attack the forces they perceive as different and dangerous. As Bill Moyers, a Southern Baptist, has noted, "To see what others see, you don't have to give up your own faith. You just have to dig deeper into it. Because down there below doctrine and dogma, beneath the particularity of your individual experience, is the ultimate source of life, the common water table of humanity."[21]

There are enough examples in twentieth-century southern history of southern evangelical Protestantism as a positive force for change, tolerance, and improving the human condition to think that the current reaction is not the last theological word on the spiritual condition of southern society. It is important to keep in mind how evangelical Protestantism lifted up a defeated and despairing people and provided hope to those only recently released from bondage. Evangelical Protestantism's spiritual sustenance overcame the meager rations of daily life for both blacks and whites. True, many whites took this religion and shaped it toward their own particular ends. But there is a simple beauty in it, which, once tapped, can unleash a great deal of good in the region. The civil rights movement demonstrated that, as did the countless numbers of whites who worked throughout the twentieth century, especially with organizations such as the Southern Sociological Congress, the Commission on Interracial Cooperation, the Southern Regional Council, the Association of Southern Women for the Prevention of Lynching, the Young Women's Christian Association, and other groups. They promoted a living, working religion to improve southern society and risked physical, economic, and verbal abuse to do so. David Mathews, a former president of the University of Alabama, noted that "all our traditions are two-sided coins . . . the very tendencies that have made Southerners reactionary could, indeed, have at times made them progressive."[22]

Southerners who are still fighting the Civil War are still fighting themselves. In order for the past to become truly the past and not weigh heavily on the region and its people, the very sense of history and the strength of religious conviction that bound the South to that past are required to effect the change to a more promising future. For without a progressive religion, there will be no progressive history. The old prejudices conjured up by the Lost Cause and Reconstruction ideologies will continue to exist, even flourish, without a strong religious theology and action to the contrary.

4 Pretty Women

The Southern lady is not so much a real person as a utilitarian device for covering up ugly reality. What makes her powerful is not her own perfection but her ability to mask the imperfections of the world.
—Shirley Abbott, *Womenfolks: Growing Up Down South*

Southern women conformed to an ideal after the Civil War and Reconstruction. In the society ordered and arranged by white men, southern women, white and black, occupied a clearly defined place designed to serve and service white men, promote their ambitions, and ensure the tranquility and smooth operation of the domestic realm. The needs of history and the tenets of religion prescribed these roles, and thus bound by tradition and theology, southern women played out a constrained if important role in the New South. Yet that role allowed for some creativity, even in a society that detested innovation and rewarded orthodoxy. And, occasionally, brave and determined women stepped outside their appointed positions and struck at both their roles and the historical and religious rules that governed their society. Eventually, they would play a significant part in changing both.

The studied rehabilitation of the Old South, which helped to recast southern history and religion after the war, established the principles for the status of women and blacks in the New South. In the Old South era, slavery dictated the roles of black and white women. The presence of mulatto children throughout the South stood as a visible reminder of the sexual exploitation of black women by white men. The reminder weighed heavily on white women who saw unmistakable traces of their husbands, fathers, and sons in the slaves around them. Mulattoes also reminded black women, if such reminders were necessary, that they were powerless to combat the sexual advances of white men; they reminded black men that whites held the ultimate power over their wives and daughters. White women's position on the pedestal had placed them beyond sexual desire and their men above reproach. The Old South was a hothouse of sexual tensions and silent recriminations.

Marriage and slavery were institutions with similar features. Mary Chesnut, witnessing a slave auction in March 1861, spilled her thoughts on the matter into her diary: "this is not worse than the willing sale most women make of themselves in marriage nor can the consequences be worse—the Bible authorizes marriage and slavery—poor women!—poor slaves!"[1]

Men held a different perspective. To them, biblical approval of both slavery and marriage granted master/husbands the authority and responsibility for the welfare of women and slaves and sanctified their dependence. To the Reverend James Henry Thornwell of South Carolina, the Bible demonstrated unequivocally that "the relation of master and slave stands on the same foot with the other relations of life. We find masters exhorted in the same connection with husbands, parents, magistrates; and slaves exhorted in the same connection with wives, children, and subjects." From the male viewpoint, women, like slaves, required protection; they were dependents and were to be treated as such. As a South Carolina slaveholder noted, a "freeman is master of his own time and action. . . . To submit to a blow would be degrading to a freeman because he is the protector of himself." But it was "not degrading to a slave—neither is it . . . to a woman." The equation between slavery and marriage implied that threats against slavery menaced the institution of marriage as well. Virginia writer George Fitzhugh summarized the interrelationship bluntly in 1854: "marriage is too much like slavery not to be involved in its fate."[2]

The legal rights of women in the Old South reinforced their dependence. Once married, a woman lost all her property rights to her husband, except for one-third of the income from the property she brought into the marriage. Women could dispose of their property as they chose, and often they provided for the maintenance of their female children who would not be favored in their husbands' wills. If women did not marry, they retained full rights to their property. But southern society expected women to marry, and the pressure to do so was great. Women without property had little choice but to marry, given their very limited economic opportunities. As one struggling single teacher in Georgia complained, "It is indeed a hard lot for a penniless girl to go forth alone in this wide world to seek maintenance. . . . What can a poor timid woman do?"[3]

Aside from their limited property rights, married women had little legal standing in the Old South. As elsewhere in the United States, they could not vote or hold office. Few families valued education for their daughters beyond their learning to read the Bible. A Georgia legislator informed his colleagues that "all a young lady needs to know is how to weave clothes for her family and how to paint a daisy in water colors."[4] Many men doubted that women were capable of more, and, besides, anything more was irrelevant, unladylike, and apt to make for an unhappy home.

Women could scarcely savor their childhoods. They married young as a rule, typically as teenagers. They left the security of their homes for a new household and all the chores and responsibilities that came with it. If they were fortunate, they developed a circle of friends and relatives with whom they visited periodically. But the early nineteenth century was a time of great migration in the South. The soils of the Southeast had played out, and new lands opened in the Old Southwest. The fertile black belts of Georgia, Alabama, Mississippi, and Louisiana beckoned as the dark alluvial soil nurtured tall cotton and huge fortunes. Ambitious young men in Virginia and the Carolinas streamed westward with their slaves, household possessions, and wives.

For young white women, who rarely participated in the decision making that led to migration, the uprooting proved wrenching. They left kin, friends, and the churches that had provided emotional and spiritual sustenance for an untamed frontier and an isolated existence. Even when they ventured beyond farms and plantations, convention dictated that they always embark in the company of a man. Husbands were often gone for long periods of time on business, and the burdens of child rearing and managing servants and households fell on the wives. Correspondence substituted for conversation, but not for companionship. The difficulty and danger of traveling long distances in an era when a five-hundred-mile journey might consume the better part of a month made visits back home rare. Sarah Jane Lide Fountain cried that "my heart bleeds within me" when she thought of the "many tender cords that are now severed forever" as she left South Carolina for Alabama. A young North Carolina bride recently removed to Mississippi wrote wistfully to her mother, "It seems so unnatural for me to be living so far from you that I can never visit you or have the pleasure of your company at my house." Once in their new homes, these women became more dependent than ever on their men.[5]

At least these elite women had the benefit of slaves to assist them in setting up a new household. The majority of white women had no such assistance but worked side by side with their husbands in the fields while they maintained the household and child-rearing responsibilities as well. One woman recalled her farm work as a young mother and wife: "I was hollered outa bed at four o'clock and after I'd got the house cleaned up if I didn't go to the branch to wash, I went to the field to hoe. When I see the sun get to noon I went back to the house and cooked dinner. Then when I'd hung my dishrag on the plum bush outside the kitchen door I grabbed my splitbonnet and took back to the cornfield."[6] Almost everything on the farm was handmade. Women were responsible for making soap and clothes, canning fruits and vegetables, doing the wash over a large black pot heated underneath by a wood fire, drawing and carrying water from the well, and tending to infants and toddlers. All of this with only the sporadic help of friends and relatives, if that.

Women fortunate enough to live in towns were relieved of most of these tasks. They purchased food and some household products at markets and shops. Their lives also expanded with the opportunities offered by urban living: associations with other women and a variety of church work. Women found the evangelical church's emphasis on Christ-like qualities such as meekness and gentleness a consolation for their domestic role. But the church also offered an outlet to the community in good works and education. Men readily relinquished these activities to women, and to many of their spouses church was a respite not only from household chores but from men as well. Women accounted for a majority of the membership in antebellum southern urban churches, upwards of 80 percent in some congregations.[7]

Out of these churches came benevolent societies to aid poor families, especially women and children, who formed the vast majority of the southern poor. They established Sunday schools and mission societies to reach the unchurched. From these organizations came others, most notably temperance societies to combat alcoholism and spousal abuse. Women gave public addresses on these topics, always careful to couch their rhetoric in domestic and family metaphors.

Black women had few pretensions of a public role. White masters circumscribed the lives of the vast majority, who were slaves. The similarities between marriage and slavery, as well as the similar roles of female slaves and white women, did not create a bond of sisterhood. White women were not closet abolitionists, although a few sympathized with the plight of black women, particularly with their sexual exploitation and the ever present threat of being sold. Mistresses treated their slaves as poorly or as well as did masters. The alleged easy sexuality of black women both infuriated and attracted white women, for whom the expression of sexual pleasure was taboo. During the Civil War, when black women deserted plantations en masse, white mistresses complained about the loss of unfaithful servants much more often than they praised the ending of an institution to which their own dependence was so closely tied.

Perhaps the best insight we have into life as a slave woman comes from the memoirs of Harriet Jacobs, who escaped bondage in North Carolina in the 1840s, settled in New York, and became a leading abolitionist. She described her mistress, a Mrs. Flint, who "could sit in her easy chair and see a woman whipped till the blood trickled from every stroke of the lash." Mrs. Flint would also spit in the cooking pots once dinner was served to prevent the cook from sharing leftovers with her children.[8]

But it was Mr. Flint whom Jacobs feared most. When Jacobs became a teenager, Mr. Flint began to pressure her to have sex with him. She recounted her feelings of helplessness: "But where could I turn for protection? No matter whether the slave girl be as black as ebony or as fair as her mistress. In either case, there is no shadow of law to protect her from insult, from violence, or even from death; all these are inflicted by fiends who bear the shape of men."[9] Jacobs was fortunate to have escaped Flint's advances, but other slave girls were not.

The Woman's War

The Civil War afforded white women opportunities to contribute to southern society in a multitude of ways. At the outset, they threw themselves into the war effort. It was nothing less than what society expected them to do. Magazine articles urged women to maintain their role as exemplars of goodness for their men. If the violence of war debased men, then women must set the example of purity. The southern woman's moral example "makes the confederate soldier a gentleman of honor, courage, virtue and truth, instead of a cut-throat and vagabond," according to one magazine. And if the fortunes of war wavered, women would maintain the new nation's morale. Upon their narrow shoulders rested "the destinies of the Southern Confederacy," the Natchez (Mississippi) *Weekly Courier* declared.[10]

White southern women lined up behind their men and encouraged them to enlist and fight. A young Alabamian received a package from his fiancée containing a skirt, a petticoat, and a note demanding: "Wear these or volunteer!"[11] Few young men required such extreme prodding at the beginning of the war. But to see wives, daughters, and mothers give a glorious and upbeat send-off to the troops, smiling through their tears and dissembling as they had been taught to do from girlhood, gave heart to the departing young men.

Women with loved ones at the front flooded newspapers and periodicals with patriotic verse and songs. Stoicism emerged as a major theme for budding poets. As one woman wrote in the Richmond *Record* in September 1863, "The maid who binds her warrior's sash / And smiling, all her pain dissembles, / The mother who conceals her grief [had] shed as sacred blood as e'er / was poured upon the plain of battle." A Virginia woman confided to her diary in a similar vein: "we must learn the lesson which so many have to endure—to struggle against our feelings."[12] Southern white women were already experts in emotional concealment. Their anguish over their husbands' nocturnal visits to the slave quarters, their frustration at not being accepted as intellectual equals with men, their bitterness at the contradiction between the myth of leisure and the reality of hard work, and their awareness of society's expectations of women to offer uncomplaining support of their men had accustomed them to sacrificial silence.

As Confederate manpower and materiel needs became acute, southern white women took on new roles. Initially much of their work was merely an extension of domestic responsibilities. Women formed clubs to sew flags and uniforms, held benefits and auctions to raise money, and collected jewelry and other metallic valuables for the war effort. For the majority of southern white women, without slaves and without men, the war meant more labor. After putting children to bed, they went out to the fields, sometimes working by the light of the moon to complete the day's chores.

Some women amazed themselves with the tasks they now performed. Kate Cumming of Mobile, who would go on to become one of the most selfless and prominent Confederate nurses, enthused at the beginning of the war: "Women, who thought such things impossible, are making shoes and knitting socks. In every farm-house the spinning-wheel and loom is heard." In South Carolina, a farm woman noted as much in wonder as accomplishment, "I am a planter for the first time."[13]

Soon, however, the needs of the Confederacy drew women outside the home to fill positions vacated by men. They entered textile mills to make uniforms or munitions factories to manufacture cartridges, took government employment as clerks and secretaries, and taught school. And, like their northern counterparts, they entered the nursing profession. Nursing was a male profession prior to the war; women tending to men violated gender and sexual taboos in both North and South. The requirements of war eased prohibitions, more in the North than in the South at first, but soon southern women were volunteering in hospitals across the Confederacy. Phoebe Yates Pember, a prominent Jewish widow from Savannah, traveled to Richmond's Chimborazo Hospital and rose to a top administrative post there. To critics who wondered if women "must lose a certain amount of delicacy" nursing men, she retorted that "a woman must soar beyond the conventional modesty considered correct under different circumstances."[14]

For some white women, desperation eventually replaced devotion. The demands of farm work, the dangers of marauding Union troops and Confederate deserters, and the burdens of child rearing placed women in precarious positions. They wrote letters to husbands, brothers, and fathers at the front pleading with them to come home and save what little they had. They watched their children grow thin and wan and cry out in hunger, and yet they could do little. "My dear Edward," wrote one disconsolate farm wife, "I have always been proud of you, and since your connection with the Confederate army, I have been prouder of you than ever before. I would not have you do anything wrong for the world, but before God, Edward, unless you come home we must die."[15]

By 1864 women's changing attitudes about the war inspired daring actions that undermined Confederate military efforts. Women appropriated food supplies that they claimed merchants were hoarding. Some women helped deserting husbands or relatives elude Confederate authorities. In Randolph County, North Carolina, two women torched a barn belonging to a state official in charge of rounding up deserters. Such incidents convinced authorities that women were mainly responsible for the high desertion rate during 1864. A North Carolina official explained that "desertion takes place because desertion is encouraged. . . . And though the ladies may not be willing to concede the fact, they are nevertheless responsible . . . for the desertion in the army and the dissipation in the country."[16]

The effort that began as a sacred cause had disintegrated into fear and deprivation for some white women. They turned to work, to protest, and to religion. Some devoutly religious women looked upon their crumbling nation and concluded that God, not the Yankees, had rendered judgment on them. They believed that "God . . . would punish the Confederacy because it had not lived up to its own ideals—particularly its obligations to the women and children." As the women ministered to "the peculiar chant of pain," and as many public buildings became hospitals, the wails of the dying presaged the death of the Confederacy.[17]

Southern men had failed the great test of patriarchy: they had not protected their women and children from want and depredation. As Confederate defeats mounted and more white women and children found themselves refugees in their own land, some women turned a withering eye on the performance of their men. Responding to a series of southern losses in the West, one woman scolded, "If our soldiers continue to behave so disgracefully, we *women* had better take the field and send them home to raise chickens." A downcast column of Confederate soldiers retreating from Vicksburg heard women taunting as they passed: "We are disappointed in you!" When her husband, following military orders, left her during the siege of Atlanta, Julia Davidson wrote in fury, "The men of Atlanta have brought everlasting stain upon their name. Instead of remaining to defend their homes they have run & left Atlanta." In February 1865, Grace Elmore summarized both the puzzlement and the new reality: "How queer the times, the women can't count on the men at all to help them."[18]

The Confederacy's demise created a dilemma for white southern women. Their men had lost a holy war. A devastated region stood as mute testimony to men's failure in their roles as protectors and providers. Women had not fared well in the war either. In addition to losing sons, husbands, and fathers, they had assumed the burdens of managing farms and shops in a crumbling economy and in the midst of danger. Some women, especially those who resided on large plantations, found their circumstances changed dramatically for the worse. Others shouldered heavier burdens: without men to work the land, they feared losing small family farms; they feared marauding blacks or Yankees; and they feared the future. The optimism that characterized northern women after the war and led to women's rights organizations and suffrage movements was absent in the defeated South. Southern white women approached the postwar era with trepidation.

Support and Sacrifice

Southern white men had lost the war for independence, and with it their prewar lives and the institution of slavery. Surrounded by failure and hard circumstances, their families provided the support and reaffirmation they required. While some white women felt spite, disappointment, and even rage at their men's inability to protect them, love and caring typically overcame these feelings. Women bolstered men broken physically and mentally by the war: men who retreated into alcohol or lassitude, seized with a paralysis of failure, who came home to a world turned upside down, where blacks were free and a foreign army occupied their land. These women quietly assumed the role of protector and provider, taking jobs, managing family finances, and educating children. There were crops to put into the field, fences to mend, labor to hire, and livestock to be replaced. For many women, there were no men to support; one out of four Confederate recruits did not come home but died on the battlefield or in hospitals, camps, or prisons. They mourned and tried to sustain their families, relying on kin, selling (or losing) the family farm, taking in boarders, and eking out small incomes teaching, sewing, or writing for the local newspaper.

Traditionally responsible for maintaining contact with the family network, keeping track of genealogy, and memorializing ancestors, some women threw themselves into the work of preserving the memory of the Civil War. Aside from providing a much-needed outlet for frustration, fear, and grief, memorializing the Confederacy honored their men, present and past, who had fought for the cause. They tended graves, raised money for monuments, and volunteered to assist disabled veterans. Without a social-service network to support veterans, and without a generous pension system like the one Union soldiers enjoyed, the postwar South relied on its women as safety nets.

Preserving the Lost Cause and Reconstruction in stone and memory offered white women the opportunity to live up to expectations of their virtue, support their men, and find outlets for their talents. White women of the Old South had always served as record keepers, inscribing the family lineage in the heirloom Bible, collecting traditional folklore and music and teaching them to their children. It came as a natural, an honorable, calling to chronicle the heroic deeds of a dead civilization so that it and they might live again. It was a job only a woman could do. The women prayed, like Annie Laurie, the popular southern fictional heroine of the late nineteenth century, "for a man's power of forgetting," but with Annie they would feel "half a woman" if their prayers were answered. Like their men, these southern women had lost the war, but they would help shape its legacy.[19]

Ironically, their expanded calling in the field of historic preservation and creation sealed their subordinate position in the patriarchal hierarchy. Whether they forgave their men or not for failing their patriarchal duties during the war, many white southern women felt they had little choice but to trust in their men again. Patriarchy placed white women in an exalted position in a society struggling for legitimacy and sustenance. It assuaged some of the male failures of the war and, while it constrained white women's ambitions, it did not preclude a public career—provided a woman's work reinforced the patriarchy and white supremacy to which it was so closely connected. White men again secured the dependency of their women by constantly warning of freedmen, suddenly loosed from the discipline of slavery, becoming sex-crazed fiends. Much as the white man saw in the black man his own failure, so the white woman saw her own loss in the visual embodiment of why the life of the Old South could never exist again.[20]

This is not to say that white southern women did not express their disappointment in their men after the Civil War; they did so, but not directly. Scarlett O'Hara may have vowed never to be hungry again, but what she really meant was that she would never be so dependent on men again; her postwar career in the Atlanta lumber and real-estate businesses proved both her talent and her determination to remain independent. Other women wrote and taught and otherwise attempted to add to the household income, mostly out of necessity but also as a hedge against that awful dependence they had experienced during the war. Their activities in women's clubs and in organizations such as the United Daughters of the Confederacy helped preserve memory and promote the Lost Cause and Redemption. Though their efforts were supportive of patriarchy and white supremacy, they also justified the sacrifices they endured. For if southern white men performed heroically and courageously against long odds, then the sufferings of their families assumed the same tragic and heroic aspect, and it justified to some extent the conduct of southern men in leaving their women and children to the chances of war.

An inkling of this undercurrent of disappointment is apparent in the works of some popular postwar southern women novelists. They often depicted southern men negatively, especially in comparison to northern men. And they portrayed their southern heroines as intelligent, decisive, and creative. Mississippi writer Katharine Sherwood Bonner McDowell, who wrote under the nom de plume Sherwood Bonner, produced a popular novel set in a small Alabama town. *Like Unto Like* (1878) concerns the disintegrating engagement between northerner Roger Ellis and southerner Blythe Herndon. Though Herndon eventually decides not to marry, the main pressure on the relationship derives from their differences over race relations (Ellis is an abolitionist) and the strong opposition to the union by her unreconstructed grandmother. Bonner presents the townspeople as provincial, especially in their rejection of Ellis's racial views, and the grandmother's defense of the Confederacy as ludicrous. Blythe, on the other hand, is bright, self-determined, and bent on looking toward the future rather than trying to recount and relive the past.

Novelist Julia Magruder's criticisms of southern patriarchy and her admiration of the North were more direct than Bonner's. In her first novel, *Across the Chasm* (1885), she chronicled the romantic adventures of Margaret Trevennon, a nineteen-year-old Virginian on her first visit to Washington, D.C. Margaret is pursued by four suitors, including one northerner; the Yankee is the most virtuous of the quartet. The least appropriate suitor is the Confederate veteran, Major King, who looks awkward in his civilian suit and is arrogant and irritating to Margaret. The author clearly favors the work ethic of the northern architect, Louis Gaston, who, despite his wealth, continues to toil long hours at his architecture practice. He builds things, useful things, unlike the Confederate, who builds only memories. The other southern men, while decent, spend considerable time lounging around. Magruder's depiction of slavery also diverges from the contemporary white perspective: a black character relates how his first wife and daughter were sold away from him.[21]

Perhaps women could say in fiction what they dared not divulge in public. But the constraints on women's public behavior and the longings penned in their diaries and novels reflect a tension in the life of women in the New South. If southern women were masters of dissembling, they performed their public role well. They were not alone in living submerged lives. African Americans and some white men handled these dual roles in order to maintain their equilibrium, safety, and sanity. A dissenting underground existed in the New South, carefully hidden like a fast-flowing subterranean stream, silent and deep, seeking out an opening. Above all, the women could not let the men know; they must always strive for indirection. As novelist Bobbie Ann Mason noted, the behavior of southern women was "devious, depending on indirection, a fuzzy flirtation that relied on strategic hinting. Southern girls aren't taught to be real."[22] In turn, men demoted them to mental lightweights, flirts, dependent on men for most of the serious, important things in life. At least some white women let them think that way. But at what cost?

It would be a mistake to assume that all white women stifled their discontent, buried their talents and ambitions, and contented themselves with memorializing their men and immortalizing their history. These supporting and supportive roles emboldened some white women to embark on endeavors beyond the home out of necessity, desire, or both.

In 1851 seventeen-year-old Gertrude Clanton married fellow Georgian Jeff Thomas, son of a prominent planter. The Thomases lived prosperously before the war. But Jeff sank much of the family fortune into Confederate bonds, which became worthless in 1865. When he returned from the front, his wife reported that he was "cast down, utterly spirit-broken." She pulled her eldest son out of school to help on the family farm. As debts mounted, she used part of her dowry to cover them, knowing that this jeopardized her children's future. Her husband began to drink heavily. When she tried to discuss the family's financial situation with him, he cursed her. As she confided to her diary, "I might render my journal more spicy were I to relate conversations verbatim, but I omit the garniture with which Mr. Thomas clothes most of his remarks to render them emphatic, alas, a habit into which he has fallen since the war."[23]

Thomas blamed his financial woes on bad luck, but Gertrude thought otherwise: "I think a great deal of what we call bad luck is bad management. . . . there is no use talking about bad luck when one places themselves in the very way to produce that ill luck." Still, she sympathized with her husband's condition: "My poor dear husband has tried too hard."[24]

In 1878 Gertrude opened a school in her house to help the family finances. All the while, she regretted deeply that her children did not have the advantages or lifestyle she had enjoyed as a child. To earn more money, she sold refurbished dresses and hats and began to write a column for an Augusta newspaper. Her essays reflected interest in a wide variety of subjects, including education, temperance, and the Civil War. She joined the Women's Christian Temperance Union (WCTU) and the UDC and convinced her husband to move to Atlanta, where she could participate in many more activities. In 1899, at the age of sixty-five, Gertrude Thomas was elected president of the Georgia Woman Suffrage Association. In her presidential address, she spoke from her experiences: "Woman was not taken from the head of man—she is not his superior; she was not taken from his foot—she is not his inferior; but she was taken from his side, and there she should stand, his equal in the work of the world."[25]

The story of Gertrude Thomas is not offered as a typical example of white women's lives in the post–Civil War South. But it does reflect both the problems and possibilities women faced during the late nineteenth century in a broken region with broken men. They would not, nor could they, forsake their duty as wives and mothers to support their men; nor could they allow themselves to slip back into the comfortable yet confining role of antebellum housewife. But venturing out of that role required strength and stealth: strength to take on new challenges and stealth to make it appear as an extension of their domestic responsibilities. Gender relations, like race relations, were very tentative after the Civil War. Defeat shook men's sense of honor, and the aftermath of surrender—emancipation, occupation, and financial struggle—undermined men's dominance over blacks and women. They needed reassurance, not competition; subservience, not equality.

As the guardians of domestic tranquility and restoration, southern white women assumed a great responsibility. Reminders of women's domestic responsibilities and of the dangers of moving beyond them permeated regional culture after the war. The Reverend James H. McNeilly saluted Winnie Davis, Jefferson and Varina Davis's daughter, as a representation of the "old order of things," not a woman who desired to be "a competitor of man in the struggle of life, in the affairs of business." Even authors of innocuous cookbooks popular in the postwar South could not resist the opportunity to indoctrinate women. In the preface to her *Modern Domestic Cookery* (1871), Theresa Brown of South Carolina expounded on a common theme: "A woman may play like a professor, sing like a siren, possess the beauty of Arimida, yet a melancholy fate awaits her—her life will be one of gilded misery, if there does not exist the elements of a well-kept home." Brown criticized "external accomplishments" in particular. The *Dixie Cook Book* (1882) went so far as to warn women that inattention to domestic duties could result in marital infidelity, alcoholism, and delinquency: "A dirty kitchen and bad cooking have driven many a husband and son, and a daughter, too, from a home that should have been a refuge from temptation."[26]

The frequent retelling of Civil War and Reconstruction stories also served white men in their relations with white women. The white version of southern history created a new enemy, the black male, who enabled white men to fulfill their role as protector of white women, a role they had forfeited during the war and now could redeem. Elevating women also elevated white men to the noble cause of guardian and protector while simultaneously establishing the necessity for control over blacks. Thus was the Old South patriarchy restored. Sex connected gender and race: white men rode to the rescue of innocent white women threatened by black male sexual predators. The construction of this connection required the elevation of white women to incomparable levels of purity, which in turn demanded the emasculation of black males. During the Reconstruction era, sex entered politics whenever former slaves strove to advance their position in southern society; after Reconstruction, when white women looked to transfer their enhanced domestic roles into more public forums, supporting issues such as suffrage, child labor reform, and prohibition, white men joined sex and politics to banish women and their causes from the public arena.[27]

In the late 1860s when blacks in North Carolina pressed for integrated public schools, two Wilmington newspaper editors implored their male readers: "Think of it. You may die soon. Your wife and babes may be left without much of this world's goods. After you are gone, your children may be *forced* to go to school . . . with negroes. Your daughter, seventeen years old, may be compelled to recite with negro boys of twenty. They may make love to her, and call her pet names, and none can defend her."[28]

Perhaps the most telling creation in this campaign for the restoration of white male superiority was the emergence of the rape myth. The presence of mulattoes in the Old South testified to sexual liaisons between whites and blacks, typically involuntary unions between white masters and black female slaves. Occasionally reports surfaced of sexual encounters between black males and white females, some consensual, some not. Antebellum southern courts treated rape as they treated any crime committed by a black on a white: as a serious offense, sometimes deserving the death penalty, though most often resulting in the sale and transportation of the slave to another state. In the thousands of papers and diaries left by Old South planters, in newspaper accounts, and in court proceedings, there is no indication that blacks' raping white women was a fear of white society. During periodic frights of slave rebellion, whites sometimes conjured the specter of black men ravishing white women, but usually as part of a general rampage against the person and property of whites, not as a discrete offense.

After the Civil War, rape became an obsession with southern white males. Emancipation had overturned the existing racial order. In the slavery era, whites not only *felt* superior; the laws and institutions of southern society confirmed their superiority. After 1865 new laws and institutions would have to be drawn to reinvent the master-slave relationship under a new guise. As part of the reinvention of race and gender relations, the rape myth served several purposes. According to the tenets of the myth, freedom had dissolved the discipline of the black male; no longer constrained by the surveillance of white civilization, black men would revert to their base African instincts, among the most prevalent of which was an insatiable sexual appetite, especially for white women. The rape myth justified the controls, sometimes as horrific as lynchings, whites placed on blacks during the late nineteenth century.

The rape myth also helped to restore white males to their superior position over women. The new and improved version of southern womanhood, even more delicate and pristine than its antebellum ancestor, required greater protection. The defilement of a paragon of virtue and innocence represented an especially heinous crime, and from such a fate white men rose to protect white women, even if few women explicitly asked for the honor. Not incidentally, if a woman in such an exalted yet precarious position should fall, she would fall far and hard, which impressed upon her the importance of maintaining balance on her perch.[29]

White women faced a daunting task after 1865: They had to preserve the memory of the Lost Cause, shore up their men and their families, and often set out on new paths to accomplish both. When they succeeded, they had to moderate or abandon their ambitions and hide their new-found talents, or at least channel them into accepted behavior and activities. Women's success, one recent observer stated, "hinged on their ability to mask or blend their nonconformity with behavior that exhibited a profound respect for certain customs and traditions."[30] The act was on, the play begun.

Masks

By the 1890s, when a new generation of southern blacks and women advanced their respective causes of civil rights and suffrage, white men redoubled their efforts to maintain their status as protectors. Political campaigns paraded girls on floats dressed in immaculate white while banners fluttering above them cried out, PROTECT US.[31]

Protection came at a price. Women derived their identities from men. As helpless creatures, they required the presence of men; they could not show ambition, knowledge, or adverse emotions, as that would reflect poorly on their men and, ultimately, themselves. Their condition did not suit them for politics or any public profession or interest. Getting and securing a man, therefore, became the primary objective of young southern white women, a purpose that emphasized the skills of flirtation and beauty, superficial wiles that boosted the protective instincts of men. Hence the southern belle, an ideal that, not coincidentally, attained common currency during the late 1890s, when women became more active in public affairs. Southern writer

Ellen Glasgow, referring to this courtship dance, confessed, "I hate—I had always hated—the inherent falseness in [this] Southern tradition."[32]

Failure to engage these expectations resulted in a woman's being cast out, isolated from family, friends, and especially from men. So women retreated behind a mask. As Florence King noted, the ideal became a commandment: "*Thou shalt play dumb.* Men who have lost a war must feel superior to someone." The southern woman became like the southern black: a construction, "a utilitarian device for covering up ugly reality." But she also derived power, not from her own perfection, but from her "ability to mask the imperfections of the world." The southern woman became "a marble statue, beautiful and silent, eternally inspiring and eternally still."[33]

It was a difficult act to pull off, and those headstrong women who refused to play along suffered accordingly, turning away men, living in isolation and opprobrium, or going mad. If a woman strayed too far from convention, she suffered the ultimate injury: the loss of white men's protection. Fallen from the pedestal, she lost her femininity, her gender, her identity. Such was the penalty Scarlett O'Hara risked and ultimately paid for her determination not to allow men to mess up her life again; her interest in husband Frank Kennedy's business after the Civil War reflected as much her instincts for survival as her desire to achieve independence from want. Yet the interest disturbed Kennedy greatly. "It had begun to dawn on him," Margaret Mitchell wrote, "that this same sweet pretty little head was a 'good head for figures.' In fact, a much better one than his own and the knowledge was disquieting. . . . He felt there was something unbecoming about a woman understanding fractions and business matters and he believed that, should a woman be so unfortunate as to have such unladylike comprehension, she should pretend not to. . . . Added to it was the usual masculine disillusionment in discovering that a woman has a brain."[34]

Julia Peterkin, born in 1880 in Laurens County, South Carolina, grew up to become a well-respected writer, at least outside the South. She recalled from her upbringing being "taught early to conceal emotions, to make the same gestures in joy or sorrow lest we be criticized." But she could never bring herself to follow that dictum. She threw herself into her studies, defied her father to enter the teaching profession, and then emerged as a writer. Following the birth of her first child, her father, a physician, sterilized her with the consent of her husband, an incident that embittered Peterkin for the rest of her life. As she quoted from the Bible to express her tortured feelings: "I will wail and how, I will go stripped and naked; I will make a wailing like the dragons, and mourning as the owls. For her wound is incurable." Just a few months before her death in 1944, a guest asked Peterkin what her friends and neighbors thought of her many accomplishments. She replied, "They hated me."[35]

Nell Battle Lewis wrote for the Raleigh *News & Observer* in the 1920s. By that time, newspapers throughout the country employed female reporters but usually confined them to the society pages. Lewis was different. The daughter of a prominent Raleigh family, well-educated and outspoken, she had convinced her editors to give her a weekly column in which she would expound on the major issues of the day. The newspaper indulged Lewis because of her family connections and the hope that she would tire of bringing attention to herself outside the journalistic sphere for women. But the young reporter only grew bolder, authoring hard-hitting pieces on the role of women, religious fundamentalism, lynching, and race relations, subjects that few male writers would address in the daily press.

For her boldness, she lost the protection accorded white southern women. Lewis had, in the words of Alabama civil rights activist Virginia Durr, stepped outside "the Magic Circle." Once outside the boundaries of acceptable behavior, the veil of chivalry fell away to reveal the raw antagonism of the betrayed southern male. She parried the criticism and fought back, honoring in a poem those few who supported her crusades:

> It is a comfort to me, recollection
>> That ballyhoo quite patently absurd
> About the glories of your native section
>> Moved you to thumb your noses at the herd;
> I'm proud you wouldn't let them do your thinking,
>> The noisy boys who set the styles in thought,
> That, faced by facts which all the rest were blinking
>> You held opinions which you hadn't ought.
> I sing the small, perverse minority
>> That died unsung, unpopular, and free.

The lonely crusade proved too much for Lewis. Of her flouting southern convention she confided to a colleague, "I almost feel as if I had stuck a knife in a friend." She loved the South and criticized it to make it better, but it was not possible to love and disapprove at the same time. Southern love was unconditional: you accepted the South as it was and worked to keep it that way, or you remained silent. Lewis suffered a nervous breakdown and spent most of the late 1920s and early 1930s in and out of mental institutions. When she finally returned to the *News & Observer*, she came as an archconservative, preaching the gospel of segregation and promoting a bizarre religious mysticism.[36]

Lewis's unfortunate life and career affirms Virginia Durr's insight: there were only "three ways for a well-brought-up young southern white woman to go" during the first half of the twentieth century. She could conform, what Durr called "going with the wind." She could go crazy. Or she could rebel.[37] Lewis's attempt to rebel pushed her to each of the other alternatives.

Talent and independent thought in women were best concealed. Ellen Glasgow recalled that when a bound copy of her first book arrived, "I hid it under my pillow while a cousin . . . prattled beside my bed of the young men who had quarreled over the privilege of taking her to the . . . Cotillion." Glasgow's experience in the early twentieth century still obtained for writer Elizabeth Spencer, who grew up in Mississippi during the 1930s and '40s. Awakening to her talent as a writer while attending college in Jackson, she realized that she "was never cut out for the life I was supposed to live." When she received a contract for her first novel and called home with the news, the response was silence. "The news did not excite them. They had thought I might be engaged."[38]

For those with talent, the realization that they could not use it hit hard. One Little Rock woman remembered as a child her father saying to her and her sister, "It's a shame you were born girls." Another Little Rock woman, recalling the conventions of the 1920s and '30s, related that she "was never encouraged to pursue anything other than [to] be a wife, mother, have lovely manners . . . training in all the social amenities but nothing on training your mind for skills in other areas. . . . A Southern lady is . . . submissive, always gentle spoken, well groomed, versed in social amenities . . . [and] Southern ladies should be conformists."[39]

Such a confining existence drew the unstinting praise and devotion of men. A toast common in the 1880s and repeated for decades thereafter went something like this: "To Woman, lovely woman of the Southland, as pure and chaste as this sparkling water, as cold as this gleaming ice, we lift this cup, and we pledge our hearts and our lives to the protection of her virtue and chastity." But, as with much that is or was in the South, this simple, well-intentioned statement of love and fealty requires translation. And here we have it, courtesy of Florence King: "To woman, without whose purity and chastity we could never have justified slavery and segregation, without whose coldness we wouldn't have had the excuse we needed for messing around down in the slave cabins and getting plenty of poontang. We pledge our hearts and our lives to the protection of her virtue and chastity because they are the best political leverage we ever did see."[40]

Few writers have captured the essence of southern womanhood better than Stephen Vincent Benét. In this excerpt from his epic poem about the Civil War era, "John Brown's Body," Benét reveals the hard work, the studied circumspection, and the stifling banality of life as a woman of the South:

> She was at work by candlelight,
> She was at work in the dead of the night,
> Smoothing out troubles and healing schisms
> And doctoring phthisics and rheumatism,
> Guiding the cooking and watching the baking,
> The sewing, the soap- and candle-making,
> The brewing, the darning, the lady-daughters. . . .
> Her manner was gracious but hardly fervent
> And she seldom raised her voice to a servant.
> She was often mistaken, not often blind,
> And she knew the whole duty of womankind,
> To take the burden and have the power
> And seem like the well-protected flower,
> To manage a dozen industries
> With a casual gesture in scraps of ease,
> To hate the sin and to love the sinner
> And see that the gentlemen got their dinner . . .
> And always, always, to have the charm
> That makes the gentlemen take your arm
> But never the bright, unseemly spell
> That makes strange gentlemen love too well,
> Once you were married and settled down
> With a suitable gentleman of your own.
> . . .
> The requisite children, living and dead,
> To pity the fool and comfort the weak
> And always let the gentlemen speak . . .
> This was the creed that her mother taught her
> And the creed that she taught to every daughter.
> She knew her Bible—and how to flirt
> With a swansdown fan and brocade skirt.[41]

The institutions of southern society reinforced the prevailing perceptions of white women, most of whom lived in small, close-knit communities where kinship operated as a purveyor and enforcer of customs. The church also reinforced women's position. White women's place in southern society reflected not only social tradition but, like southern history, the working out of God's plan. Women heard Proverbs 31:27 often: "She looketh well to the ways of her household, and eateth not the bread of idleness." Julia Peterkin related that she was raised "to believe I had duties to God, men, myself, that to neglect or evade them would send my soul to hell." An identity existed between the expectations for a perfect woman and the expectations for a perfect Christian, with Christian perfection defined as obedience to the will of God. Ministers and others reminded women of the importance of inhabiting the "sphere to which God had appointed them."[42]

For the typical white woman living on a farm, the elevation to sainthood did not come with a surcease from toil, but profitable work had to appear as an extension of domestic responsibilities. So farm women raised chickens, harvested eggs, made butter, jams, and jellies, all of which offered opportunities to add cash to the family's usually meager income. In 1900 the federal government's Commission on Country Life concluded about southern farms that "whatever general hardships, such as poverty, isolation, lack of labor-saving devices, may exist on any given farm, the burden of these hardships falls more heavily on the farmer's wife than on the farmer himself. . . . Her life is more monotonous and the more isolated, no matter what the wealth or the poverty of the family may be."[43] This conclusion underscores the point that the construction of southern womanhood was fantasy, an ideal derived more from the needs of white men and their struggle to understand the Civil War and Reconstruction than from the reality of the New South.

Beneath the Pedestal

Black women were bound by similar artificial constructions, but the origins of their confinement and the status assigned to them differed from that of white women, reflecting both their race and gender. White men viewed black women as sensual, immoral, and possessing an unbounded sexual appetite. The vision evoked nocturnal visits to slave cabins, but the implication was rooted in the New South perspective on white women. The white woman's purity was all the more impressive and unassailable given the black woman's promiscuity, a condition that relieved the white man of both sexual restraint with respect to black women and contrition with respect to white women. Black women required not protection but control.

White men nevertheless thought little of placing black women in the most intimate contact with their children and families. They often idealized these black women as wise beyond their illiteracy, as good beyond goodness, and as devoted beyond what anyone had a right to expect. These caricatures appeared not only as figments of white imagination but on cereal and pancake boxes from the 1890s onward: a jolly, welcoming Aunt Jemima smiling out to her white charges. Mammy became more ubiquitous in whites' memory of the New South than she ever was in the reality of the Old South. Whereas white women lacked wisdom, appeared frail, and seemed overburdened by child rearing, mammy was robust, possessing of common sense, and energized rather than weakened by household responsibilities. She worked outside the home and apart from her own family, providing a counterpoint to the expectations for white women. In the process, she was unsexed and unfeminine, for only delicacy, superficiality, and beauty could be feminine, and those traits resided exclusively with white women.[44]

Black women labored under the dual handicaps of race and gender, under the conflicting perceptions of the white community and the perceptions of black men. White men's efforts to place black men into economically and socially dependent positions attacked black manhood, and their control over the labor of black women and, on occasion, their bodies, removed other perquisites of southern male dominance from blacks. Black men still attempted to assert themselves in their relationships with black women, sometimes violently, as black writers such as Zora Neale Hurston and Alice Walker have demonstrated. In *Their Eyes Were Watching God* (1937), Hurston's main character, Janie Mae Crawford, marries Joe Starks, who soon becomes the mayor of the small black north Florida community in which they reside. When some of the residents seek out Janie Mae for advice, Joe interjects, "Thank yuh fuy yo' compliments, but mah wife don't know nothin' 'bout no speech-makin'. Ah never married her for nothin' lak dat. She's uh woman and her place is in de home." On another occasion, Joe asks her, "Well, honey, how you lak bein' Mrs. Mayor? . . . Ah told you in de very first beginnin' dat Ah aimed tuh be uh big voice. You oughta be glad, 'cause dat makes uh big woman outa you."[45]

Janie's grandmother clues her in to the racial and gender hierarchy of the early twentieth-century South. "Honey," she confides, "de white man is de ruler of everything as fur as Ah been able tuh find out. Maybe it's some place way off in de ocean where de black man is in power, but we don't know nothin' but what we see. So de white man throw down de load and tell de nigger man tuh pick it up. He pick it up because he have to, but he don't tote it. He hand it to his womenfolks. De nigger woman is de mule uh de world so fur as Ah can see."[46]

Black women faced the same limitations on talent and ambition as their white sisters, though their options were even more circumscribed. The reasons for the restrictions reflected the realities of race relations in the early twentieth-century South more than the expectations of gender. Still, the result was the same for black women: an unrequited longing for something better, the knowledge that they possessed the ability to make something of themselves but lacked the prospects and support for doing so. Black North Carolina writer Mary Mebane, who grew up in Durham in the 1930s and '40s, felt the sting of her race and gender throughout her life. She was haunted by her status despite her literary accomplishments. Mebane eventually wound up penniless in a county welfare facility, where she died in 1991. As a teenager she resolved that her life would not consist of scrubbing "a hundred billion miles of tiled corridors" or washing "an equal number of dishes." But, as Mebane recalled, her mother told her to "get those foolish notions out of your head."[47]

In *Mary, Wayfarer: An Autobiography* (1983), Mebane, as a high-school teacher in Robinsonville, North Carolina, has an imaginary dialogue with an anonymous communal voice instructing her to accept her work and place: *"Why not you? . . . Others have come and have stayed, built homes and made stable lives for themselves. What makes you think that you're so much different from anybody else? Why are you so ambitious?"* Her church warns that her ambition springs from "vanity," while her family remonstrates, "you're getting beyond your raising." Her brother even suggests that her persistence will have her "end up in Goldsboro" (the location of the state mental institution). Still, Mary maintains her dreams: "Who is it that has ordained my place in life? Who has any right to tell me who I am, what I must do, what I must think, how I must view the world?" Unfortunately, Mebane never fully achieved her quest, nor attained peace with herself. Suffering from a loss of religious faith, clinical depression, and the aftermath of a rape by a family friend, she wandered from job to job until the end of her life.[48]

Despite these strictures, black and white southern women proved resourceful in stretching the boundaries of their roles and working to change

the society that bound them. The white and black middle class, though growing, was small, and the domestic responsibilities, the dangers of missteps, and
the concern over husbands' and fathers' reactions all weighed against agitation. But some women did take the chance, as much for their own edification
as for the cause of all women. The very act of engaging in public activities
changed women's perceptions of themselves, though those of the rest of
southern society remained more difficult to alter. At the same time, the myriad causes espoused by southern women, black and white, provided a firm
background of leadership, strategies, and experience leading up to the greatest and most difficult cause of all: civil rights.

Keepers of the Past with an Eye to the Future

The enhanced role of southern white women after the Civil War began, and
in some cases ended, with the past. The collective experience of war provided
the common history for all southern whites, regardless of their political positions before or during the conflict. Moving from family chroniclers to community memorialists, white women became the keepers of history, archangels
of the dead, ministers to the maimed, until living and dead merged into one
solemn, glorious, and holy story.

Perhaps most prominent among the associations given over to preserving
the memories of the war and Reconstruction was the United Daughters of
the Confederacy, the successor to the numerous Ladies' Memorial Associations that grew up in the South after the Civil War. Keeping alive the memories of the valorous war dead and their deeds remained a major focus of the
UDC, but members also emphasized the importance of Confederate women
and their sacrifices for the Cause: "Truly, those were days not only to try
men's souls, but to put to the test all that was greatest in the souls of the
women." As stated in the UDC's founding objectives, a central charge of the
organization was "to record the part taken by Southern women in patient
endurance of hardship and patriotic devotion during the struggle, and in un-
tiring efforts after the War during the reconstruction of the South."[49]

UDC women engaged in a variety of public causes to promote the Cause
and their role in it. They lobbied lawmakers for state archives and museums
to house and display the artifacts of the struggle; they interviewed former
soldiers to preserve their memories before they passed on; they sponsored
history texts to set the record straight and ensure that the grandsons and

granddaughters of the martyrs would learn the southern past, a past they were convinced the rest of the nation cared little about or was actively hostile toward. As their fathers and grandfathers strode to glory on the battlefield, they would wield the pen as a sword of redemption. The women erected monuments, thousands of them, moving them out from the cemeteries to the center of towns to bask among the living rather than the dead.

With increasing boldness, women spoke publicly, especially at rallies for Confederate veterans, whom they embraced with imagery reflecting their exalted position as chaste and sexless, yet at the same time, intentionally or not, alluring. Elizabeth Lumpkin, a UDC leader in South Carolina, proclaimed to the elderly soldiers who gathered like ragged remnants from a long-ago crusade, "I love you, you grand old men, who guarded with your lives the virgin whiteness of our South." The daughters could only envy the "honor our lovely mothers gloried in. . . . *they* could love and marry Confederate soldiers! . . . We can [only work for them] with tireless fingers . . . run with tireless feet."[50]

The young women who promoted the cause of a past remembered also promoted each other. Their efforts in education went beyond placing textbooks and influencing curriculum. Whatever the prevailing notions of women's limitations, women themselves remained convinced that "those who have brains are meant to use them," male and female alike. To that end, they established scholarships to enable young women to pursue higher education, a rare phenomenon in the South at the time. These passes were not merely to mediocre normal schools in the South, but to great institutions of higher education throughout the country, including Vassar College, Columbia University, and the University of Chicago.[51]

UDC women often linked their preservation and promotional efforts to white supremacy. From earliest memory they learned the lessons of the Lost Cause and Reconstruction, the dangers of "negro rule" and "negro domination." They enjoyed a privileged status precisely because of white supremacy, due both to their purity and their vulnerability to black sexual fiends. The birth of the UDC in the 1890s coincided with the acceleration of white-supremacy political campaigns. The two phenomena were hardly coincidental, as organizations such as the UDC reflected the coming of age of southern white women, daughters of the conflict, and of a new generation of southern white men determined to do their duty and preserve the redemption.

Many UDC members also belonged to women's clubs. Southern white women's clubs initially emerged in the 1880s as literary and self-learning groups but confederated into state organizations during the 1890s and came to espouse a wide range of reforms. The clubs and their regional and national networks opened southern white women to a wider world. In contact with sisters from across their respective states and with national organizations, hosts to discussions and lectures on a wide variety of public issues, and avid readers of current and historical works, they honed their expertise and moved into the public arena. The clubs served as adult education institutions for the white middle-class women of the South and as classrooms for political action. Although men occasionally wondered what went on at club meetings and periodically raised concerns about alien ideas filtering in from national temperance organizations or, worse, suffrage groups, the clubs generally supported prevailing views of history and southern society. Club women, in fact, played critical roles in formulating the evolving interpretation of the Civil War and Reconstruction and in supporting the ideals of white supremacy and patriarchy that flowed from those perspectives. Rather than viewing patriarchy as a restraint, many of these women used the pedestal as a liberating and empowering device that protected them, promoted their virtue, and, in some instances, provided a cover for bolder activities.

History played a key role in club activities. Club women listened to papers on the Old South describing "those leisurely days around which a certain halo lingers." They were avid consumers of black history, though with a particular slant. In 1908 the Old Homestead Club in South Carolina heard papers on "The Joys of Being a Negro." But this was no mere exercise in ratifying prevailing views of white supremacy and patriarchy. The women manufactured a history that gave themselves a prominent role. As one club member noted, "To the patient teachings and personal training of the Southern woman are due the civilization and Christianizing of the negro in America."[52]

Reading materials reflect both the clubs' interest in history and in promoting that history to the community. Thomas Dixon's books were popular works, discussed and read widely among club members. At the New Century Club in Columbia, South Carolina, Dixon's novels touched off a discussion recounting "the workings and object of the Ku Klux Klan, and the great part it played in the reclaiming of power by the white people." Together with the UDC, South Carolina club women pressed for the inclusion of southern poets and literature in children's reading lists—not only for white children, but for black children as well. African American youngsters learned Confederate songs and poems; they sang "Dixie," "Swanee River," and "My Old Kentucky Home."[53]

Club work and participation in organizations such as the WCTU and the UDC helped southern white women form their own political culture and perfect strategies to promote their projects with lawmakers, institutions, and at home. Their support of greater funding for education, health, and child-welfare legislation required a reversal of low-tax, low-service policies common throughout the South during the late nineteenth and early twentieth centuries. The women took care to frame their demands in maternalistic rhetoric, stressing that education and urban health and planning were extensions of women's dominion over the home, as the main beneficiaries would be children. Rarely did these women cross the color line; to do so would have cast doubt on their objectives and damaged the prospects for implementation, especially during the 1890s, when racial violence and the campaigns to disfranchise and segregate black southerners by law reached their pinnacle. If anything, white women and their organizations contributed to the charged racial climate, furthering their causes at the same time.[54]

The 1898 election campaign in North Carolina, which touched off a brutal riot against black citizens in the port city of Wilmington, elicited considerable involvement from middle-class white women. The immediate cause of the conflict resulted from an editorial in the city's black newspaper refuting whites' charges that the sexual predations of black men against white women both accounted for and justified lynching. Editor Alexander Manly argued that some relations between black men and white women were consensual and that white men should direct their efforts to protecting *all* women from the sexual advances of *all* men. But Manly's editorial was merely the spark that set off a conflagration that had been smoldering since 1896, when a combination of black and white Republicans and Populists won elections throughout North Carolina, including Wilmington, ousting Democrats. The white mob that rampaged through the black community took out their revenge on the city's African American population and overthrew the legally constituted administration, installing the Democrats in their stead.[55]

The Wilmington riot indicated the close connection between white supremacy and patriarchy, but events leading up to the revolt revealed that white women were hardly passive observers of the unfolding fray, standing back waiting for white men to rescue them. A letter to the Charlotte *Daily Observer* titled "A Southern Woman's Prayer" urged white men to end "negro domination." The writer continued, "How would you like for that fair young daughter of yours to have to get permission from three negroes to teach in the white free school?" Rebecca Cameron of Hillsboro, writing to her cousin Alfred Moore Waddell, a political leader, complained, "We have been amazed, confounded and bitterly ashamed of the acquiescence of the men of North Carolina at the existing conditions; and more than once have we asked: 'Where are the white men and the shotguns?' . . . I never thought to be ashamed of the manhood of North Carolina, but I am ashamed now."[56]

On another occasion, Cameron drew the connection between the white supremacy campaigns of the 1890s and earlier revolutionary movements in the South, as if the history of the oppression of white people formed one common strand from the British to the Yankees to the former slaves. She urged her cousin to "go forward to your work bloody though it may be, with the heartfelt approval of every good woman in the state. We say *Amen* to it as did our great grandmothers in '76 and our mothers in '61." At the end of the letter she confided, almost with joy, "I wish you could see Anna. She is fairly rampant and blood thirsty."[57] These are hardly the sentiments of delicate, pristine southern womanhood held above the fray of politics. Yet white supremacy, by moving white women to the center of public policy and interest, drew women into the battle, and some eagerly took up the charge.

Not all southern white women responded to the invocation in the same manner; the heated political campaign and its violent culmination drew opponents as well. Jane Cronly, daughter of a prominent Wilmington family, was moved to write an "Account of the Race Riot," which she never published. She wrote, "The negroes here [in Wilmington] are an excellent race, and under all the abuse which has been vented upon them for months they have gone quietly on and have been almost obsequiously polite as if to ward off the persecution." Cronly went so far as to draft letters to several northern newspapers, begging the editors to conceal her name if they published any or all. In one, she confided, "My conscience has reproached me ever since for not writing the truth for publication, but at first like others, I feared I might be asked to leave town if I were found out or that I might bring trouble upon my brothers who did much to prevent further lynching here that fatal night."[58]

White women generally supported white supremacy, either tacitly or actively. The racial and gender constructions derived from the Civil War and Reconstruction provided the basis for numerous white women's public careers in the postwar decades. Some white women, like Jane Cronly, perceived the connection between the limitations southern society imposed on their talents and ambitions and the subjugation of southern blacks. But the connections were not that obvious and, in fact, the opposite seemed to be the case: that white supremacy elevated white women. Besides, thought women, let the men have their racial obsessions; we have more important objectives to fulfill: not only to support our men, protect our children and those of others, improve our towns and cities, but also to better ourselves.

Suffering Suffrage

Even a national movement such as woman's suffrage took on a distinctive cast in the South, as white women sorted out the arguments for and against, and often took positions reflecting as much their view of race relations as their perspective on the proper rights of women, sometimes for strategic reasons. The suffrage movement represented a regional "coming out" for southern women, although the numbers actually engaged in the fight were small initially. Southern men rarely listened to reasoned arguments for woman's suffrage in the 1890s. At a time when they clamped down on black voting rights, they were not about to open the issue of the ballot for women. The call for federal legislation or a constitutional amendment to effect woman's suffrage alarmed southern white men. Not only were they in the process of solidifying states' rights, but any federal intervention on voting-rights issues threatened the region's move toward black disfranchisement and segregation by law. As Texas congressman Robert L. Henry explained, "If you submit this amendment the next request will be for a law to prohibit the States from passing 'Jim Crow' laws, separate-coach laws, separate schools, [and] separate churches. . . . The next demand will be to place a Federal ban on the States where the intermarriage of white and black races is prohibited."[59]

The volatile mixture of race and sex led white southern suffragists to steer clear of associating with black women who supported the right to vote. Texas suffragist Belle Critchett explained, "We want to help the colored people but just now it is a rather hard question."[60] White southern men had long associated women's rights with rights for African Americans. Before the Civil War, the emergence of female abolitionists in the North damaged the legitimacy of southern women's position in public discussion and reform activity. After the war, when northern churchwomen came south to establish schools for freed slaves, southern men wondered about their ulterior motives. A common story circulated that "Mrs. Harriet Beecher Stowe is going to establish a school in [the South] for the benefit of mulatto children that have been born in the South since its invasion by Yankee school-marms."[61] Southern white women who ventured across racial lines to work with and assist black suffragists risked such sexual innuendos. They also realized that once they achieved the vote, a crucial link between women's rights and white supremacy would be broken, and the one could then advance without being associated with or weighed down by the other.

Some southern women, though, viewed suffrage as a threat to their privileged place in society, especially their dominion over things domestic. Ida M. Darden, born in Texas in 1886, typified the antisuffragist viewpoint and, particularly, its relationship to white supremacy. Her opposition enabled her to exercise an unprecedented public role even to the point of running for Congress, an ironic candidacy considering her position on women in the political process. As she noted, "It would be sufficient political achievement for women that future rulers nurse at her breast, laugh in her arms and kneel at her feet. . . . If another vote were never cast and another law never passed, we could survive the ordeal, but without home, civilization would wither and die."[62]

Darden's conservative stands, and especially her views on suffrage, ironically positioned her to receive favorable consideration for a number of political appointments that women rarely received, such as lobbyist for the Texas Businessmen's Association, a post she utilized as a springboard to her failed congressional bid in 1932. During her later career, she served as a journalist and editor of a conservative newspaper and as a founder, in the 1950s, of the Houston Minute Women.[63]

Although states' rights and white supremacy threatened the suffrage movement in the South, perhaps the greatest obstacle was that women's political activism shattered the image of the pure and private woman that southern men had composed in the years since the war. Politics was a very public activity; political engagement would tarnish the image of southern women, they argued. Southern white men had fought a war, in part, to protect the innocence and chastity of southern women, both of which an active political role might threaten.

To combat this view, suffragists stressed that the right to vote was merely an extension of the domestic and private concerns women had always pursued. They asserted that women's votes would speed implementation of pro-family legislation, such as the elimination of child labor, the prohibition of alcohol, and the improvement of public education. Civic issues such as water and sewer construction, milk and meat inspection, and street lighting also came under the broad purview of family concerns. Patti Jacobs, president of the Alabama Equal Suffrage Association, summarized the connection between this broad conception of family concerns and the right to vote in a letter to the Birmingham *Age-Herald* in 1912:

> Nobody of women is more staunchly upholding the home than the woman suffragists, but we do not understand the home to mean the four walls in which we live. One after another the duties that formerly belonged exclusively to the individual household have become the common duties of the community. . . . The modern city is now a big, cooperative housekeeping business and what was the family's duty has been transferred to the municipality. . . . The ballot is the quickest, most effective, most dignified weapon which women may use to defend the home. So that when the assertion is made that "woman's place is in the home," we suffragists say, "Amen."[64]

Woman suffragists throughout the South picked up the refrain that the home transcended traditional boundaries and that the ballot offered the surest path to domestic tranquility. Sally Trueheart Williams of the Galveston Equal Suffrage Association wrote to her local newspaper in 1912 a virtual carbon copy of Jacobs' letter: "Housekeeping used to begin at home and end there. But time has changed all this. It begins now . . . in the public laundry, the grocery, the dairy, the meat market, or the candy stores; it only ends in the home. . . . The woman who keeps house must in a measure also keep the laundry, the grocery, the market, the dairy . . . and in asking for the right to vote they are following their housekeeping in the place where it is not being done, the polls."[65]

The suffragists' arguments reflected the accelerated pace of urbanization in the South during the late nineteenth and early twentieth centuries. Just as their circle of friends, associations, and interests expanded, so too did their domestic role outside the home. Their assertions were not mere contrivances to convince the doubtful but reflected their experiences. Still, their comments were calculated to convince other women that engagement in suffrage activities involved no violation of traditional roles, and to reassure men that women still knew their place, even if the geography of their place had expanded. Privately, suffragists looked upon the vote as a first major step toward equality, something they dared not divulge in public. As Galveston suffragist Cordia Sweeny wrote, her support of the ballot for women was driven by the fact that "I feel humiliated over the position of woman and the way she has been looked on in the past, as a slave or a plaything. I want to be neither, and want woman equal with man before my daughter grows up."[66]

Those who opposed woman's suffrage—and they counted for the vast majority of white southerners, male and female—understood the subtext of the domestic-sphere argument: that the right to vote was a giant step off the pedestal and into territory claimed exclusively by and for men. In opposing woman's suffrage, southern political leaders adopted a chivalrous tone, though their rhetoric belied deeper concerns. As Mississippi women pressed for the right to vote in the 1890s, a state political leader chided them, "Who would want to see pure, noble, lovely woman" lured from her "beautiful, modest, feminine sphere" and lowered to "the common level of a ward politician? Are the white men of Mississippi no longer men, that they must ask women to come to their rescue . . . ?"[67] At a time when the new generation of southern white men attempted to claim their mantle of greatness, the idea of women usurping or even sharing their political power and casting aside their protectors was indeed threatening, especially since it was to the political arena that white men looked to solidify their own supremacy.

An additional concern was that the vote for white women could upset the dominance of the Democratic Party, the party of Redemption. During the 1890s the popularity of the Farmer's Alliance and the Populist Party, which emerged from the Alliance movement, spread among the South's numerous small farmers and town artisans. The push for black disfranchisement derived in part from this political threat. The Populists openly courted women, who participated at all levels of party work, except as candidates for office. Women composed roughly a quarter of the party's membership in the South. Like their more affluent sisters in towns and cities, they did not view political activism as contradictory to their traditional domestic role. They perceived it instead as of a piece with their family and religious convictions. An Alabama woman asserted, "I am going to work for prohibition, the Alliance and for Jesus as long as I live." A Texas woman explained, "The Alliance has come to redeem woman from her enslaved condition. She is admitted into the organization as the equal of her brother, and the ostracism which has impeded her intellectual progress in the past is not met with."[68]

But the Alliance movement and the Populist Party fizzled, brought down by white supremacy and internal problems. Woman's suffrage experienced a similar fate, and were it not for the Nineteenth Amendment in 1920, southern states would have barred women from the voting booth for a considerable while longer. Only Tennessee ratified the amendment.

The woman's suffrage movement in the South was a halfway house between the pedestal and personhood. Not until the civil rights movement of the 1950s and 1960s would the move toward a more complete identity for southern women achieve significant progress. Yet woman's suffrage, measured against the progress that occurred in the decades following 1865, was a remarkable achievement. To get to the point of demanding equality in political life, southern white women served a lengthy but important apprenticeship that taught the basics of process, the importance of networking, and the types of strategies that worked in a white-male-dominated society.

Dedication of Robert E. Lee Equestrian Statue, Richmond, 1890. Richmond became the Confederate Vatican, a mixture of bronze, stone, and faith dedicated to the Lost Cause, a site for white pilgrims. *Courtesy Virginia Historical Society*

The 1915 film *Birth of a Nation*, adapted from Thomas Dixon's novel *The Clansman*, demonstrated how the southern interpretation of the Civil War and Reconstruction had become the national view by the early twentieth century. *Courtesy Library of Congress*

Old Catawba Hydroelectric Station, North Carolina, 1904. This station was part of James B. Duke's power-generating system that became the Southern Power Company in 1905, placing the South at the forefront of the new applications of electricity to manufacturing. These advances reinforced rather than challenged the racial or political status quo. *Courtesy Duke Energy Archives*

Mill air conditioning. The first application of the new technology of air conditioning was in southern textile mills. The objective of air conditioning had little to do with providing comfort to the region's residents. The purpose was to facilitate the production of textiles. Thread broke in hot weather, thus halting production. *Courtesy Levine Museum of the New South*

Pyramid at Hollywood Cemetery, Richmond, Virginia, lovingly and reverently erected by white women just after the Civil War to commemorate Confederate war dead. It continues to attract worshipers who leave mementos at its base. *Photo by Melinda H. Desmarais*

Confederate Memorial Day, Weddington, North Carolina, 1920. In small towns and large cities, white southerners commemorated the Confederacy apart from national holidays. Celebrations connected the present to the war era, often using religious imagery and rhetoric. This particular celebration occurred at a church. *Courtesy North Carolina Collection, University of North Carolina Library at Chapel Hill*

U. D. C.

CATECHISM FOR CHILDREN

What causes led to the war between the States, from 1861 to 1865?

The disregard, on the part of the States of the North, for the rights of the Southern or slave-holding States.

How was this shown?

By the passage of laws in the Northern States annulling the rights of the people of the South— rights that were given to them by the Constitution of the United States.

What were these rights?

The right to regulate their own affairs and to hold slaves as property.

Were the Southern States alone responsible for the existence of slavery?

No; slavery was introduced into the country in colonial times by the political authorities of Great Britain, Spain, France and the Dutch merchants, and in 1776—at the time of the Declaration of Independence—slavery existed in all of the thirteen colonies.

How many of the colonies held slaves when the federal constitution was adopted, in 1787?

All except one.

Did slavery exist among other civilized nations?

Yes, in most all; and our mother country, England, did not emancipate her slaves until 1843, when Parliament paid $200,000,000 to the owners.

—3—

United Daughters of the Confederacy (UDC), Galveston, Texas, 1904, "Catechism for Children." Mixing religious and historical symbolism, the UDC sought to relate the correct interpretations of the Old South, the Civil War, and Reconstruction to southern schoolchildren. Here is the UDC doctrine on slavery and the Old South. *Courtesy Museum of the Confederacy, Richmond, Virginia*

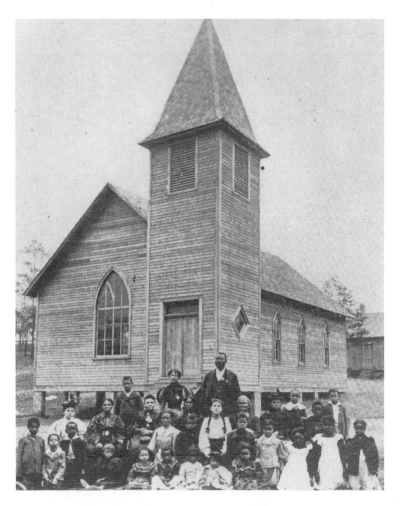

Colored Methodist Episcopal Church (CME), Hot Springs, Arkansas, 1925. The church functioned as the center for southern black communities during the Jim Crow era. It often served multiple purposes, and in smaller places, such as Hot Springs, it was the community's most imposing structure, a source of pride and symbol of visibility. *Courtesy Divinity School Library, Duke University. Photo found in C. H. Phillips's "The History of the Colored Methodist Episcopal Church in America: Comprising Its Organization, Subsequent Development, and Present Status" (Jackson, Tenn.: Publishing House CME Church, 1925)*

Icard, North Carolina, 2000. For some, Friday night football and school prayer are linked traditions regardless of federal court decisions. Evangelical Protestantism functions as a state religion in many parts of the South, but migration has challenged traditional perspectives on the relationship between church and state. *Photo by Jeff Willhelm; Courtesy Charlotte* Observer

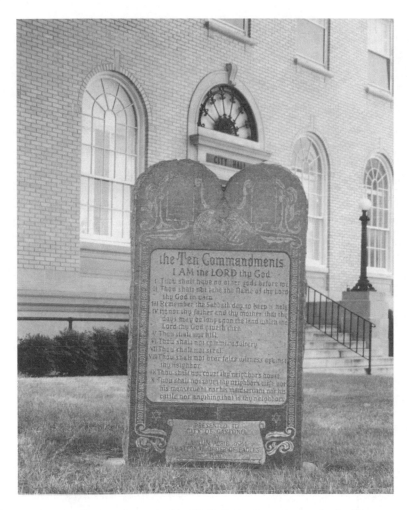

The Ten Commandments, Gastonia City Hall, 2001. Gastonia was ahead of the curve when it accepted this tablet in 1957, though it is unclear whether its presence has rendered local government more virtuous in Gastonia than elsewhere. *Photo by Melinda H. Desmarais*

Atlanta parade for woman's suffrage, 1913. Gradually moving into the public arena in the decades after the Civil War, some southern women campaigned for the right to vote as a necessity for achieving their reform agenda. Note also that the automobile provided a measure of independence for women of the New South. *Courtesy Atlanta History Center*

Young Women's Christian Association (YWCA) Women's Education Parade, Greensboro, North Carolina, 1908. The "Y" provided middle-class southern women with the opportunity to promote a variety of reforms, including higher education for women. *North Carolina Collection, University of North Carolina Library at Chapel Hill*

Textile worker, Union Point Mill, Greene County, Georgia, 1941. Contrary to the "ideal" of southern womanhood, many white women worked in the factories of the New South, a fact that compromised their social status and even their virtue in the eyes of white men in particular. *Courtesy Library of Congress*

Mrs. M. LaBlanc washing dishes in the kitchen of her home, Morganza, Louisiana, 1938. Staying home offered little respite from work, especially for women on farms and in small communities. Electricity and running water were rare in many parts of the rural South until after World War II. Their lives of hard toil belied the delicate image of southern women. *Courtesy Library of Congress*

"Lifting As We Climb": These 1918 graduates of the all-black Atlanta School of Social Work would go on to serve working-class blacks at institutions such as the Atlanta Neighborhood Union. *Neighborhood Union Collection, Box 14, Folder 29, Atlanta University Center, Robert W. Woodruff Library*

Charlotte Hawkins Brown instructing pupils at the Palmer Memorial Institute, Sedalia, North Carolina, 1947. Despite the realities of biracial living in the South, middle-class African Americans continued to strive and achieve in the hope that the future might be better. Note the gender separation and the presence of many light-skinned students. *Photo by Griffith J. Davis; Courtesy North Carolina Department of Archives and History*

Septima Clark and Rosa Parks at the Highlander Folk School, late 1950s. Civil rights leaders, especially women, learned strategies and experienced an integrated environment at Miles Horton's famous retreat in the mountains of East Tennessee. *Courtesy Highlander Center Archives*

White woman protesting hiring policies at a Birmingham department store, 1963. By the 1960s, an increasing number of whites, especially white women, began to join their black neighbors in actively demolishing Jim Crow. *Courtesy Birmingham Public Library (#639.1.2.1.28)*

5   Lady Insurrectionists

If maidens knew what good wives know / They never would care to wed.
—*Progressive Farmer*, 1887

It is one of the many ironies of a region steeped in irony that the same faith that blessed white supremacy also inspired the changes that undermined it. Not that those who took comfort from evangelical Christianity and shaped their faith to reshape the South felt they were engaged in heretical or radical activity. The teachings of the Bible that so permeated southern society showed them a way, and they took it.

The indirect route toward a distinctive voice and identity for southern women began at church, if for no other reason than that men delegated church work to their wives and daughters. Church also provided women an opportunity for sisterhood and a chance to develop strategies to outflank the men and the society that constricted them. A character in Nanci Kincaid's novel *Crossing Blood* (1992) explained, "*Church is the place where God and women get together to try and do something about the men in this world. It's where women get talked into loving men for spiritual reasons, since after a while they run out of any other reasons to do it.*"[1] Women in the evangelical denominations raised money for foreign missions beginning in the 1870s, supported schools, especially for poor children, and founded kindergartens throughout the South. Methodist women in particular organized an array of social programs. By 1890 they operated ten boarding schools, thirty-one day schools, and a hospital. Lucinda Helm led the Methodists' Woman's Department of Church Extension, which proffered aid to the children of Cuban immigrants in Florida as well as to poor white children of eastern Kentucky and Tennessee. Following the precedent of settlement houses in northern cities, Methodist women established "Wesley Houses" to provide poor urban children with basic educational skills, hygiene instruction, and recreational space.[2]

The women who led these efforts were often single or widowed. Although marriage and children were still the acceptable conditions of adult southern womanhood, the disruption of war and the death and maiming of tens of thousands of young men removed some of the stigma from a life without a man. No longer needing to obtain identity solely through a husband, these women constructed identities for themselves that stressed the importance of charity and good works for the numerous less fortunate individuals in the late-nineteenth-century South.

Most of these churchwomen resided in towns and cities, where their range of acquaintances were broad, and the labor-saving devices of urban life that by 1900 had brought electricity, indoor plumbing, appliances, and prepared foods to the urban South allowed them more time outside the home. If they could not obtain what they wanted from local shops, the Sears catalog enabled them to purchase the latest fashions and home furnishings from Chicago. These innovations accorded urban women much more independence and many more options than existed in the rural South. It is not surprising that Gertrude Thomas entreated her husband to move to Atlanta.

The Opening

Church activities drew southern white women into contact with the largest women's movement of the late nineteenth century, the Women's Christian Temperance Union. Southern women had promoted the benefits of temperance as a family issue since before the war, but in the late nineteenth century, a national organization emerged to advance the cause of alcohol abstention. Alcoholism was an especially acute problem in the postwar South, and southern women responded sympathetically to the evangelical strains and family programs of the WCTU. Many, such as Gertrude Thomas, had firsthand knowledge of the destructive capacity of drink.

Many women liked the emphasis the WCTU placed on political activism. Barred from either formal or informal entry into the political arena, southern women seized on the WCTU as a "respectable" back-door entry into the political world. Within a year of the founding of the Atlanta chapter of the WCTU, the Georgia legislature received six thousand petitions pleading for a local-option law. In the process of lobbying, women came to understand the workings and the importance of politics. From these activities, and from their contacts with women across the country, it was but a short step to advocating suffrage for southern women.[3]

Responding to the enthusiasm of southern women, the WCTU held its national convention in Atlanta in 1890. The spectacle of hundreds of women engaged in public speaking and public debate shocked many men, however sympathetic they were to the objectives of the organization. They attacked WCTU president Frances Willard for bringing women into the ministry in violation of biblical injunctions, and they feared that flirting with sacrilege would eventually push the women to advocate universal suffrage. They called upon the southern delegates to sever their ties with northern members, who obviously had deluded the naïve southern women into such unnatural activities. Southern women did not back down. The Georgia president of the WCTU responded to these charges: "As to 'dissolving' connection with our Northern sisters who have so long been our comrades in arms, it is not to be thought for a moment. The organization that was born of suffering and baptized with tears, that has stood together in unbroken ranks through years of trial, difficulties, opposition, persecution, discouragement, and numerous defeats will neither be intimidated or coerced into dissolution." As for the suffrage argument, she pointed out that no delegate had mentioned voting rights publicly, but now that "the question is thrust upon us for discussion and decision, let us pray God to direct bearing ourselves in a way worthy of our high calling in Christ Jesus."[4]

Southern women were on a mission. The temperance crusade provided license to use evangelical religion and women's role as preservers of domestic life to engage in activities southern white men had considered inappropriate at best and dangerous at worst. A woman in Opelousas, Louisiana, wrote to her local paper in 1894, "How if I see the liquor traffic . . . coiled and ready to spring at, crush and lure on to ruin and death, these, *my babies*, just as soon as they can creep far enough away from my arms—what shall I do? By using whatever weapon Providence places in my reach, and any weapon which helps us to protect our children is right and womanly;—if it is the tongue, wag it; if it is the pen, wield it; if it is joining in WCTU work, join it; if it is the ballot, cast it!" And, as if to throw down the gauntlet, she concluded, "So, my friend, the sphere you tell me to keep to takes me into everything."[5]

Such defiance came at a bad time for southern white men, who felt particularly importuned to protect the Great Restoration: to write white supremacy in stone and to strengthen their own dominance in southern society in general. But blacks pressed for their rights as well, equally eager to make the mark of a new generation. And the new southern woman strove for the same objective. Nurtured in a defeated region, raised on the edge of poverty, the new southern woman chafed under the constraints of the image men had created. Eleanor Foster Comegys of the Shreveport Woman's Club stated the demands of her generation forthrightly: "I want men to stop calling me a queen and treating me like an imbecile. I have a head as well as a heart, common sense as well as intuition."[6] Some women had expressed these sentiments before the Civil War, but privately. By the 1890s a few southern women were not afraid to utter them publicly.

Clubbing

Though most southern white women did not mount the battlements of temperance or suffrage in order to challenge the hierarchies created by white men, many white women contributed modestly to redefining their roles, hence enhancing the prospects for redefining their society. The women's club movement, like suffrage and the work with the WCTU, grew out of church activity. Beginning with individual congregations, the club movement eventually spread throughout denominations, states, and ultimately to the entire South, connecting with similar groups in the North. Though some members ventured into suffrage activities, most took a more conservative course, emphasizing self-improvement. But furthering their education and broadening their familiarity with current events, even if these activities reinforced prevailing views of the Lost Cause and the Redemption, expanded their notion of what they could accomplish. The personal became political.

Women who formed and joined clubs after the war did not foresee a career in crusading. They initially met more out of the need for companionship than to change society. Most clubs focused on self-improvement, such as the Atlanta History Class, whose members followed a curriculum designed by a Johns Hopkins University professor. In literary clubs, participants read and discussed books, and in diverse self-improvement clubs, women learned the finer points of elocution and debate to prepare them for public speaking. Though many of these activities focused on the Lost Cause and the Redemption as topics for discussion, reading, and debate, the women were soon attracted to other topics. An Arkansas club in 1900 debated the issue: "Resolved, That Women Are Incapacitated by Mental and Physical Conditions for a Business Career." As club minutes reveal, "the question was put to a vote and decided in the negative." Another literary club in Knoxville, Tennessee, discussed women writers such as Harriet Martineau and Hannah Moore. These seemingly harmless agendas did not allay men's fears that women's clubs were covers for more sinister activities. One gentleman complained that "he never saw any books in that club and he believed it concealed some secret political chicanery. . . . The whole thing was headed towards *votes for women.*"[7]

The gentleman's intuition was not far off. Although most club members did not suddenly dive into electoral politics, a few did; more became involved in social issues that went considerably beyond discussions of literature and history. They became interested in schools, child labor, health and sanitation matters, and prisons. Their reading and discussion opened up a new world, and they saw with a fresh vision how the realities of their society did not correspond to the images presented by its leaders. They formed networks with clubs throughout their states, and by the late 1890s almost all southern states included a woman's club federation. Although the Social Gospel, an outreach effort for the poor and disadvantaged undertaken by Protestant churches in northern cities, did not inspire similar work among the southern evangelical denominations, southern women took up the cause of civic betterment initially in their churches and then through larger secular organizations.

A glimpse into the early-twentieth-century activities of the Arkansas Federation of Women's Clubs, not the largest or most influential of the southern federations, provides some indication of the diverse activities undertaken by middle-class urban white women. The federation raised funds and successfully lobbied the state legislature to fund agricultural extension work to instruct rural housewives on the basics of canning, the benefits of sanitation, and the prudence of household and financial management. For town dwellers, federation women offered instruction on smart shopping, including a small pamphlet, "The Morals of Shopping," which included a sharp denunciation of unscrupulous merchants and urged customers to avoid clothing produced by exploited labor. Although many of these outreach programs had more than a tinge of class condescension about them, they provided important services for a neglected portion of the southern population.[8]

The programs also encouraged club women to familiarize themselves with issues that went beyond domestic advice, including pure-food and -drug standards, and health and sanitation questions. In Galveston, Texas, after a destructive hurricane decimated local government and services in 1900, women formed the Women's Health Protective Association (WHPA) in 1901, a group that succeeded in pushing the city to inspect food shops, housing, and dairies; enforce pure-food and -drug ordinances; initiate regular medical exams and hot lunches for schoolchildren; and establish medical clinics for the poor. Though they succeeded in most of their enterprises, the women clashed repeatedly with political leaders, who often retreated from confrontations with property and business owners affected by WHPA-sponsored regulations.[9]

Perhaps the most ambitious club crusade concerned child labor. In this contest, women battled powerful industrialists, politicians, and the families of workers whom they sought to help. In the North, child labor legislation advanced relatively quickly, as both organized labor and middle-class reformers worked together. In the South, however, a few church leaders and many women's clubs toiled alone. The Alabama Federation of Women's Clubs, formed in 1895, undertook the fight in that state. The federation had already coaxed the state legislature to pass a compulsory school attendance law; members had also lobbied successfully to place women on school boards; and they had introduced an array of reforms in the state's public school system, including kindergartens and vocational training programs. Their work on these issues honed their lobbying skills and cemented contacts with influential political leaders. Despite opposition from the state's important textile manufacturers, the federation helped to secure the passage of one of the first child labor laws in the nation.[10]

As their public skills improved, club women pushed for measures related specifically to women's rights. In 1894 a prominent club woman, Josephine Henry, published an article called "The New Woman of the New South" in the national magazine *Arena*, summarizing the work of southern women's clubs. "Southern women have in the past five years resorted in many states to their constitutional right of petition upon the question of property rights, 'age of consent,' and the licensed liquor laws. They have pleaded for admission into state universities, and asked for a division of state funds to establish industrial or reform schools for girls. . . . They have asked that women be placed on boards of all public institutions for the benefit of both sexes, and in many cases sought and obtained the county superintendency of public schools."[11]

As Henry's essay noted, southern women reformers not only worked to improve society by helping its less fortunate citizens, but struck boldly for themselves in the areas of property rights and higher education. The latter success was especially notable because very little in the way of higher education for women existed in the South in the late nineteenth century. Even the schools for women called colleges were scarcely better than two-year finishing schools for affluent girls. As late as 1903, only Randolph-Macon College in Virginia offered four years of college work for women. In that year a group of women in Knoxville, Tennessee, established the Southern Association of College Women to promote and raise the standards of women's higher education in the South. They argued that because public schools hired increasing numbers of young women as teachers, they should receive an appropriate education. By 1905 at least five southern states had established teacher-training colleges for women. Although homemaking and academic courses competed with each other, these colleges succeeded in preparing young women, many of whom came from families with modest incomes, for the profession of teaching. Despite this encouraging beginning, only six women's schools attained accreditation by 1917: Agnes Scott in Georgia, Converse College in South Carolina, Florida State, Randolph-Macon, H. Sophie Newcomb (associated with Tulane University), and Westhampton College (part of the University of Richmond).[12]

Education proved especially fertile ground for middle-class white women's ministrations. Their role in raising children enabled them to address pedagogical issues in the public sphere. By 1900 teaching had become a respectable profession for middle-class women as normal schools sprang up all over the South. In 1902 a group of middle-class white women in North Carolina's urban centers formed the Women's Association for the Betterment of Public School Houses after a failed effort to convince voters to raise taxes to pay for educational improvements. The association succeeded in bringing about physical improvements to school buildings and introduced innovative agricultural demonstration projects, as well as information on public health, hygiene, and proper sanitation. In the odd southern way of linking race, gender, and reform, the disfranchisement of blacks in 1900 in North Carolina helped the women's cause; they argued that the new literacy standards for voting required improved education and facilities for poor whites.[13]

White women tended to support, tacitly at least, the "settlement" of the race issue in the 1890s through segregation by law and disfranchisement. The accommodation cleared the legislative docket for their own agenda. The protective arguments white men often employed to push aside women's concerns held less resonance after 1900. The liberation of white women and the subjugation of African Americans were complementary. Reform in the early-twentieth-century South proved quite compatible with white supremacy.

Outside the club, churchwomen moved to a wider sphere of activity, especially in Methodist organizations. They began to challenge prevailing historical and racial traditions. Methodist women such as Lily Hammond contributed the shock troops for progressive work, especially in the urban South during the first two decades of the twentieth century. Belle Bennett, a colleague of Hammond's and a native of Richmond, Kentucky, established the Negro Chautauqua Assemblies and invited black leaders such as George Washington Carver and W. E. B. Du Bois to speak to integrated audiences. In the South after 1900 interracial dialogue diminished to a whisper, and black men and white women were scarcely mentioned in the same breath, let alone seated together in the same room. In that climate such activities were extraordinary, reflecting the commitment of a few urban women to break down the barriers between races and genders erected by the white men of the New South.[14]

These women applied their faith as readily as they observed it; they questioned their surroundings, believed in the new science, and took steps to change the immutable features of their society. They lived in the New South, in its cities amid the moil of commerce and industry. Some of what they witnessed frightened or repulsed them, so different it was from the places of their youth, even if they had grown up in town. Yet it mostly exhilarated them, provided wonderful laboratories for their work, and expanded their capabilities beyond the limited horizon their society had set for them. It was not that they no longer accepted their history or believed in the society that the past had created; rather, the past was much less important for them than the future. Their broader, deeper gaze did not contradict the Lost Cause and the Redemption as much as render it less relevant. They would eventually discover, however, that history cannot be set aside, despite its inconvenience; they would have to deal with it. When confrontation occurred in the 1950s and beyond, their apprenticeship would provide the experience necessary to engage it.

Women's Work

Though the growth of cities and industry provided the necessity and opportunities for reform, it also proved liberating both to the women who worked for change and those fresh from the countryside seeking their fortunes, or at least something better than their existence on the farm or in the small town. The growth of tobacco and textile manufacturing, the emergence of office work, and the importance of education in an increasingly urbanized society offered women of various backgrounds the opportunity for gainful employment outside the home and an array of causes to moderate the impact of urbanization and economic development on women and children from rural areas.

Though southern cities such as Atlanta, Charlotte, Nashville, Birmingham, and Dallas hardly challenged the supremacy of the urban Northeast and Midwest, they offered a variety of opportunities and attractions to women of any station during the early decades of the twentieth century. Rural life in the early-twentieth-century South lacked most modern amenities, from electricity to running water to cultural diversions. In the city, young women could take in a movie, whirl around a dance floor, attend schools of various levels and curricula, or visit an amusement park at the end of the trolley line. They could find a job in Rich's department store on Peachtree in Atlanta, or at Belk's on Tryon in Charlotte, and spend their days patrolling the aisles of these consumer palaces surrounded by the products of American industry and ingenuity, feeling themselves an integral part of modern life instead of on a stage set designed by and for someone else.

Office work provided an attractive occupational alternative for young women from the countryside, especially as schools began to offer vocational courses in typing and stenography. True, clerical jobs created a pink-collar ghetto in the city, but many recruits found work amid the clacking typewriters a welcome respite from the uncertainty and isolation of rural life. "All of us have a good time together" and "Such a nice boss, lovely office, and easy work" were typical comments of young women experiencing city life and work for the first time.[15]

The work, the amenities, and the attractions of urban life created new women: these were no longer farm girls or residents of confining small towns. Out in the larger world, they assumed an air of independence, relished their accomplishments, and strove against restrictions on their bodies and minds. These women also changed the cities. Traditional behaviors became less relevant in the more fluid world of the urban South. Writer Peter Taylor captured this change in a story he called "The Old Forest," set in Memphis in the 1930s and focused on a triangular relationship between two well-to-do long-time residents, Nat Ramsey and his fiancée Caroline Braxley, and a recent arrival from Arkansas, Lee Ann Deehart. Throughout the story, traditional conventions of men's and women's roles bound the actions of Ramsey and Braxley. But Lee Ann, emblematic of the new female working and middle classes, is different; her work encourages her independence both financially and intellectually. Caroline figures this out before Nat does and informs him with a combination of envy and wonder, "with girls like Lee Ann and Lucy and Betsy it's all different. They have made their break with the past. Each of them had the strength and intelligence to make the break for herself. . . . They occupy the real city of Memphis as none of the rest do. They treat men just as they please. And not the way men are treated in *our* circles. And men like them better for it. . . . Naturally we fear them."[16]

Fear did not transfix women like Caroline Braxley. They plunged into the work of easing the transition of these young women to urban life. Sometimes their tone and actions were condescending, but always they sought genuinely to improve the lot of working girls and, more generally, the city to which they came. In the process, they changed themselves.

The Young Women's Christian Association (YWCA) emerged as one of the earliest women's groups to offer young women from the countryside the protection and direction they needed, helping them to learn the ropes of urban life. The Y also quietly initiated the work of racial reconciliation.

Lucy Randolph Mason, a Virginia matron of impeccable lineage, granddaughter to a signer of the Declaration of Independence, could have lived out her years in the faded comfort of her Richmond home. In 1911, just shy of thirty years of age, looking not so much for a career as an outlet to give something of herself to a city she saw as wallowing in the past and a stranger to the present, she volunteered for the Richmond YWCA. Her special interest became the growing number of working black and white women coming to the city from the surrounding countryside with few skills and much naïveté, and ripe for exploitation. In 1914 the Y appointed her to the new position of industrial secretary, the first such appointment in the South. Active in the Southern Sociological Congress and later in the Virginia Commission for Interracial Cooperation, she became the general secretary for the Y in 1923 and dedicated her remaining years to the promotion of racial justice in the erstwhile capital of the Confederacy. By 1929 she had become notorious in some circles and considered an angel of mercy in others. Her genealogy shielded her somewhat from the opprobrium of her male peers, but not entirely. As black journalist Gordon Blaine Hancock wrote in 1929, Mason was "a young white woman who . . . braves criticism to champion the cause of the Negro race in general and the Richmond Negro in particular."[17]

When she was not working for racial justice, Mason stumped for workers' rights. During World War I, Mason served on the American Federation of Labor's Committee on Women in Industry and lobbied to improve Virginia's labor laws, especially promoting better working conditions and shorter hours for women, with modest success despite the vigorous opposition of industrialists and their political allies. But her most significant work in the 1920s was on the Negro Welfare Survey Committee, which issued a report on black life in Richmond, arguing in novel (for the time) and bold fashion that the city's African American population could attain economic equality if social relations between the races improved, a prospect most whites would scarcely entertain.

As a stream of white women moved from farms to towns and cities to take positions in the growing industries of the South, especially in textile towns up and down the Piedmont in a great industrial arc stretching from Richmond to Atlanta, reformers like Mason confronted new and significant problems. Before long, southern states such as North Carolina and Georgia had as high a rate of women working outside the home as did any other state in the nation. Factory work challenged traditional notions of southern womanhood in many ways. The work itself, cash employment, independence, time away from kin and friends, and most especially a life beyond the protection of white males scrambled traditional perceptions of southern white women.[18]

White rural men lost direct control of their women when they moved to the budding textile villages. Bosses and foremen controlled the work of young women and, on occasion, swapped promotions for sex. Life on the farm was typically a family affair; in the factory, directives came from outside the circle of kin. Since white men defined their independence in part by the degree of control they exercised over their families and the protection they afforded them, factory work and urban life in general created new relationships and threatened that independence. Young men also submitted to the routines of factory life and to the orders to themselves and their families from other men.[19]

Factory women, especially white women who worked in textiles, developed ambiguous reputations. The early sexual activity of girls in the mills was understood, if not widely discussed; at the same time, the image of pure white womanhood persisted. When the reality clashed with the ideal, trouble sometimes followed.[20]

Leo Frank, Texas-born, though raised in Brooklyn, managed a pencil factory in Atlanta. Thirteen-year-old Mary Phagan worked there. Her family had lost their farm and worked as tenants; she had moved to Atlanta to help support them. On Confederate Memorial Day 1913, someone robbed and murdered Mary as she left the factory to attend the parade downtown. Frank, a northern Jew who employed poor, white, Gentile southern girls, became the focus of the investigation. That a prosperous manager would rob and then kill a young employee made little sense, but rumors surfaced that Mary had been raped, a charge unsubstantiated by the medical examiner's report, though that same report implied that Mary may have been sexually active.

A jury convicted Frank and sentenced him to death, though much of the evidence pointed to a black janitor as the killer. Governor John Slaton, citing doubts about Frank's guilt, commuted the death sentence. But a group of twenty-five men, calling themselves the "Knights of Mary Phagan," pulled Frank from his cell in August 1915, drove to Marietta, Mary's home town, and lynched their prisoner. The lynching was less about an explosion of latent anti-Semitism than it was about control, control over young women and an assertion of independence among working-class men over white elites. It was about what every lynching was about: an exclamation of superiority.[21]

It is true that harsh working conditions existed in the pencil factory and in other operations that employed young white women. Simple things, such as lunch and bathroom breaks, promotions, working responsibilities, and overall treatment, were all negotiable and almost always in the hands of men. Sanitary conditions and adequate light and air were often wanting. Lila Mead Valentine, a prominent white reformer in Richmond during the 1920s, reported that "the heart of the woman today is stirred with pity for the laboring millions in sweatshops and factory work in terribly unsanitary conditions for starvation wages, for the young girls . . . who are sold into a condition worse than slavery."[22]

Factory women who protested often lost the patina of protection. Rumors circulated about sexual promiscuity or lesbian behavior, and bosses hired detectives to embellish the private lives of some of the more vocal operatives. Despite these dangers, white working women strove as hard for reform as their middle-class counterparts, but rarely from the parlor and lecture hall.

Their venues, their workplaces and neighborhoods, were often under the tight surveillance of management, and the very act of protest contradicted the alleged paternalism of the mills and the innocence and submission of white women.

Women and teenage girls organized unions and precipitated strikes, one of the most famous occurring at the Loray Mill in Gastonia, North Carolina, in 1929. A key issue in the strike was the plight of wage-earning mothers and their children. Participants created protest ballads, just as later civil rights workers composed songs for their movement. Few women leaders spoke more eloquently with music than did Ella May Wiggins, a spinner at American Mill No. 2 in Bessemer City, North Carolina. A single mother raising five children on nine dollars per week, she played a leading role in organizing strikers throughout Gaston County. Perhaps her most notable story song was "The Mill Mother's Song," which presents a portrait far different from the pedestaled white woman of the New South and stands as eloquent irony to the protection allegedly enjoyed by white women and children:

> We leave our home in the morning,
> We kiss our children goodbye,
> While we slave for the bosses
> Our children scream and cry.
>
> And when we draw our money
> Our grocery bills to pay,
> not a cent to spend for clothing,
> Not a cent to lay away.
>
> And on that very evening,
> Our little son will say:
> "I need some shoes, dear mother,
> And so does sister May."
>
> How it grieves the heart of a mother,
> You every one must know,
> But we can't buy for our children,
> Our wages are too low.
>
> It is for our little children
> That seem to us so dear,
> But for us nor them, dear workers,
> The bosses do not care.

> But understand, all workers,
> Our union they do fear,
> Let's stand together, workers,
> And have a union here.

Ella May presented not only a contradiction but a threat to the prevailing gender status quo. Company thugs gunned her down one evening as she returned from a union gathering. Ella May, in her own way, just like the well-positioned Nell Battle Lewis, suffered the fate of stepping outside the "magic circle" prescribed by her society. Despite the consequences, white women continued to push at the outer edges of the circle in the 1920s and '30s, with respect not only to white working women but to African Americans as well.[23]

False Chivalry

At church socials and, most often, at teas sponsored by the YWCA, black and white middle-class women met to discuss common issues. These affairs were staged carefully to avoid the appearance that the participants were challenging the color line. The women did not sit down and eat together; they mingled standing up. Apparently, vertical integration was acceptable.

White women engaged in more substantive contact after 1919, when the Southern Sociological Congress birthed the Commission on Interracial Cooperation. Women's club and church leaders, especially Methodists, immediately formed the Woman's Committee of the Interracial Commission and elected Jessie Daniel Ames of Texas as its leader. Ames viewed the committee as an opportunity to combat the rape myth that imprisoned both blacks and women. With the Nineteenth Amendment resolving the suffrage issue, and with progress on a variety of club projects, such as child labor legislation, increased funding for education, prison and sanitary reform, and civic regulations, Ames focused the committee's work on the eradication of the "false chivalry" of lynching. Ames worked tirelessly during the 1920s, and by 1930 she had built a network sufficiently extensive to establish the Association of Southern Women for the Prevention of Lynching (ASWPL).[24]

Lynching was a provocative subject in the South, connected as it was to racial and gender traditions derived from the white rendition of the Civil War and Reconstruction. The white women who joined Ames's group challenged racial and gender traditions and explicitly disavowed the need for white male protection. Lillian Smith captured the boldness of these "lady insurrection-ists," as she called them: "They said calmly that they were not afraid of being raped; as for their sacredness, they could take care of it themselves; they did not need the chivalry of a lynching to protect them and did not want it. Not only that . . . but they would personally do everything in their power to keep any Negro from being lynched."[25]

At the same time, the ASWPL was careful to frame its pronouncements in domestic metaphors to emphasize that southern femininity and opposition to lynching were compatible. Members promoted their cause in the conserva-tive rhetoric of domesticity and stressed their support for established institu-tions. The Georgia chapter of the ASWPL declared in 1931 that "the real victim of lynching is not so much the person done to death, but constituted and regularly established government. The crime is a greater menace to our homes, our children, and our country than any other."[26]

Ames achieved support for her cause by distributing pledge cards through-out the South asking men and women to sign an oath to eradicate lynching. By the late 1930s the ASWPL had accumulated forty thousand signatures, including those of the governors of every southern state and numerous law enforcement officers, who committed themselves to physically intervene if and when a lynch mob appeared in their communities.

Although the upswell of support for Ames's group reflected a widespread revulsion against extralegal violence, it is probable that most members of the ASWPL viewed their activism as a blow for white women as much as a way to ameliorate race relations. In leading the association, Ames consistently lec-tured against the double standard that "considers an assault by a white man as a moral lapse upon his part, better ignored and forgotten, while an assault by a Negro against a white woman is a hideous crime punishable with death by law or lynching."[27]

Not all southern women reformers crossed the color line. Attacking lynch-ing gave the appearance of defending black males, a posture that not only doomed antilynching legislation in the South, but also cast aspersions on the women who advocated such laws. But it was a measure of how far southern white women had come by 1930 that Ames could travel throughout the South speaking out on the subject of sexual exploitation and generate a large and active following. Although Ames could not convince a single southern state to adopt antilynching laws, the incidence of lynching declined significantly during the 1930s. In 1930, for example, mobs lynched twenty-one blacks in the South; in 1940 there were five black victims. And these five generated considerably more negative comment in the press than the larger number had ten years earlier. Whether this raised consciousness and declining mob rule resulted from Ames's efforts or from a combination of factors is unclear. But Ames was relentless in her crusade, and she reached the minds, if not the hearts, of many white southerners.[28]

By the 1930s southern middle-class white women stood between frustration and fulfillment. More than their husbands, middle-class women had become the main arbiters of high culture, fashion, and progressive thinking in the South. They enjoyed a latitude unknown by their mothers and grandmothers, entering professions, especially teaching; roaming the halls of legislatures and councils to promote numerous causes, often succeeding in these efforts; and writing, speaking out, and organizing for themselves and others.

Southern white women fought not only for themselves and against an ideal that relegated them to a secondary position, but also against the manufactured memory of the Civil War and Reconstruction. Considering the odds, their accomplishments in the half century after the end of Reconstruction are impressive. But they still lagged considerably behind their sisters in the North. Few southern colleges, other than those specifically designated as female schools, allowed women to enroll. Southern women were much less visible in business, the medical and legal professions, and in civil administration than their counterparts in the North. They were not less talented, nor less energetic, than their northern sisters, but they had considerably greater burdens to overcome. And even if they wanted to, southern white women rarely openly joined forces with black women. For the most part, each group operated alone, separated in the segregation that southern society imposed on both race and gender.

Lifting As We Climb

That separation was a shame. Black women, like their white counterparts, had built an impressive array of reform organizations. Their associations, however, worked parallel to, typically not in concert with, white women's groups. They worked in their own separate universes, producing minor victories but changing little in southern society. But they did change themselves, and they fought stereotypes, and they would eventually change a great deal together.

Like their white counterparts, one of the first tasks of black women after the Civil War was to reconstruct their families. Death or maiming did not sunder their ties of kin, but sale and separation did. So black women set out on roads across the South, or sent letters to where they thought family members might be. Often what they encountered was almost as painful as the separation. Laura Spicer located her husband, who was sold away from her before the war, only to have her spouse write, "I am married and my wife have two children, and if you and I meats it would make a very dissatisfied family." But clearly her memory tugged on his heart. In another letter he asked for "some of the children's hair in a separate paper with their names on the papers," and while he thought they should not see each other, he admitted, "The woman is not born that feels as near to me as you do. I thinks of you and my children every day of my life. My love to you never have failed." Many black women like Laura Spicer experienced not only the heartache of life without their dearest children, a husband, or a father, but the pain of knowing that family members, for reasons of new circumstances or old separations, remained inaccessible for all time.[29]

Black women also encountered some of the adjustment problems experienced by white women when their men returned from the war. It was less a homecoming from the battlefront than a release from slavery that inaugurated a new era of relations between black men and women. Black men were only titular heads of their families during the slavery era. They shared child-rearing responsibilities and discipline, and occasionally even their wives, with the master. Black children learned early that their fathers had little control over their own lives, let alone those of their offspring.

With emancipation, black men moved to assert control over their families, and, as they negotiated the extent of their new freedoms, that control became a key issue. They determined if and when their wives worked in the fields, and some blacks purposely withdrew their women from farm work to make that point both to themselves and white employers. Black men also strove to protect their women from white sexual exploitation. They sought the same protective role for themselves as white men exercised on behalf of white women. In 1866 black minister Henry McNeal Turner stated simply, *"All we ask of the white man is to let our ladies alone. . . .* The difficulty has heretofore been, *our ladies were not always at our own disposal."* Black women, however, preferred to be at no one's "disposal," and, as had white women, they attempted to negotiate the delicate balance between understanding the need of black males to serve as protectors and their own aspirations for independence.[30]

African American men moved to restrict black women's activities to the home or church and to keep the political arena a male-only domain. Laura Towne, a white school teacher on St. Helena Island, South Carolina, recorded in her diary with a mixture of disdain and bemusement how the island's black men worked to keep their women in the "proper place." Commenting about a meeting where men decided to bar women from attending a political gathering the following week, she noted, "It is too funny to see how much more jealous the men are of one kind of liberty they have achieved than of the other! Political freedom they are rather shy of, and ignorant of, but domestic freedom—the right, just found, to have their own way in their families and rule their wives—that is an inestimable privilege! Several speakers have been here who have advised the people to get the women into their proper place—never to tell them anything of their concerns, etc. etc.; and the notion of being bigger than woman generally, is just now influencing the conceit of the males to an amazing degree."[31]

For black males, fighting a losing battle for their political rights and against a prevailing stereotype that portrayed them as sexually aggressive and violent, controlling black women became a key issue for maintaining identity and self-respect. As white men increasingly defined their freedom and independence in the postwar South by the degree of their power over women and blacks, black men, who dared not assert their "maleness" against whites, focused their efforts at home, a cause not always shared by their spouses. For obvious reasons, black women did not feel the same compulsion as their white sisters to reconstruct the family along the lines of the model that prevailed before the Civil War. Viewing white men in particular as their oppressors, they saw no reason to relinquish their new and hard-won freedom to another group of men.

Yet middle-class black women at least shared with white women a dream of engagement, of uplift, of participation in a world increasingly closed to their men and shut tight for them as well in so many ways. Their reform efforts reflected the general trends of the time and the unwillingness to restrict themselves to roles assigned to them by men. Black middle-class women also fought against the public perception of themselves as promiscuous and lazy. "Usefulness" became the watchword of their efforts, especially as applied to their less fortunate sisters. As part of the effort to be useful, black women stressed the value of education, both for themselves and for working-class black women. Their families scraped together enough money, combined with northern philanthropy, to send their daughters to the black seminaries and colleges that sprang up in the post-Reconstruction South. Returning to their communities, they often married black professionals—doctors, attorneys, ministers, and teachers—and set out to work for the race. Their children, especially their daughters, adhered to a strict moral code and impeccable public behavior, as much to delineate their standing within the black community as to respond to the prevailing slanders against their gender by the white world. In the process, they created a black urban middle class that, in many respects, mimicked its white counterpart, with tastefully furnished homes, carriages, and the latest fashions. Such display underscored the ability of black women (and their men) to achieve, contradicting the white-supremacy dogma as well as the more particular canards about the slovenly character of black women.[32]

The work of middle-class black women commanded their duty and directed their lives. That work initially emanated from the church into the WCTU, following the same journey taken by white women. The WCTU afforded a range of opportunities for middle-class black women. First, the cause—the prohibition of alcohol—was relatively conservative and would thus not raise the suspicions of the white community. Second, temperance work enabled black middle-class women to distance themselves from the black working class, the typical targets of WCTU ministrations. Finally, work in the prohibition movement enabled black women to dream of an interracial sisterhood—an elusive goal but one that seemed attainable.[33]

Black middle-class women joined together in clubs and performed an array of social services for their communities. Some of these services were coordinated from the Washington, D.C., headquarters of the National Association of Colored Women (NACW), a federation of black women's clubs founded in 1896 with Mary Church Terrell as its president. The NACW, like its white counterpart, the General Federation of Women's Clubs, established in 1887, was a middle-class organization that focused on helping poor women and children. The NACW supported Mother's Clubs, mainly in the rural South, that established kindergartens and taught hygiene and the basics of modern housekeeping. Also like their white counterparts, black reformers occasionally bared their class condescension. A report from the Tuskegee, Alabama, Mother's Club, for example, boasted that it "had brought the light of knowledge and the gospel of cleanliness to hundreds of poor benighted sisters on the plantation."[34]

The NACW slogan, "Lifting as We Climb," encapsuled the dual purposes of middle-class black reform in this era. When the first biography of the

NACW's long-time leader Mary Church Terrell appeared, its title summarized her lifelong objective: *Mary Church Terrell, Respectable Person* (1959). As one prominent member noted, the work of the NACW "was an effort of the few competent on behalf of the many incompetent."[35] Such views were common among blacks who followed the teachings of W. E. B. Du Bois and his notion of a "Talented Tenth," an elite group of black men and women who would lead the race to full integration into American life. These assumptions rested on another assumption: that white southerners, especially the white men who held the economic and political power in the region, would appreciate their efforts and results and react positively. They did not; in fact, any example of black advancement or refinement, especially among black men, was likely to generate more hostility than admiration.

As with white women's clubs, initial activities of black women's clubs focused on self-improvement and then moved in ever wider circles to the broader community. Given the close connection between history and identity, black women also used the past to educate and edify. Black women's clubs, in their readings, discussions, and debates, emphasized American, not southern, identity. White southerners had denied the idea and meaning of "southern" for blacks, though they had shared the same land for more than two centuries. "Southern" meant white supremacy, slavery, and segregation. Black women's clubs firmly connected the story of southern blacks with American history, providing the foundation for the eventual reclamation of a black southern history. They celebrated and studied such notables as Frederick Douglass, Booker T. Washington, and W. E. B. Du Bois, as well as black women, such as poet Phyllis Wheatley and singer Marian Anderson. They read, wrote, and talked about black abolitionists and black Union soldiers. The Civil War was a war of liberation, not a Lost Cause, and the time that preceded it was not a golden era but a dark time in Egypt.

The gulf separating the historical visions of black and white southern women could not have been greater. As historian Joan Marie Johnson has noted, "one group celebrated the birthday of Lee, the other the life of Douglass. One group read Thomas Nelson Page [a writer who glorified the Old South] with tears in their eyes, while the other group read Du Bois with determination. One group vilified Harriet Beecher Stowe, and the other celebrated her birthday."[36]

As the black urban population increased in the South during the 1890s, club women directed more of their activities toward poor blacks, single women, and school children in the cities, again mirroring the efforts of white middle-class women. When black women with little education came to town, their options were limited to work as laundresses or domestics. Employers offered poor wages or sometimes none at all; white women occasionally reached into closets or cupboards and paid with clothes and food. Black women kept their dignity and what few workplace rights they had through informal, individual protests, deserting their employer's kitchen on the day of a dinner party, or losing, burning, or shredding an important garment. But such acts could not occur too often, as word of mouth and the need for references discouraged sustained or repeated acts of sabotage.

Nevertheless, black working-class women succeeded in establishing their own spaces and culture through leisure activities, though middle-class black women disapproved of some such pursuits, especially hanging out in juke joints. As historian Tera Hunter has interpreted these fervid nocturnal activities, they provided an outlet for working-class black women to "reclaim their bodies from appropriation as instruments of physical toil and redirect their energies toward other diversions."[37] But this lifestyle merely confirmed white stereotypes and deeply troubled middle-class black women who fought to erase such caricatures from the perception of the white South. The economic strictures of Jim Crow, and of white supremacy in general, tended to uphold prevailing notions in the white community about the character of black women, which, in turn, justified their subservient position and treatment.

If black middle-class women achieved mixed success with the working class, they hoped for better results with black youngsters. Nearly 40 percent of black club women were educators, as teaching remained one of the few professions open to black women in the South. Given their interest in education, it is not surprising that much of their local efforts were directed toward initiating or improving educational facilities and instruction for black children. Black women established the Gate City Kindergartens in Atlanta in 1905. In the absence of public-supported kindergartens for black youngsters, the Gate City organization filled an important need. To sustain the kindergartens, members held bake sales, track meets, dinners, and bazaars.[38]

Though whites controlled the curriculum and handed down the traditional history texts, black club women worked to place African American teachers in the classroom. Black women's clubs in South Carolina after World War I initiated a successful campaign to replace white teachers in black public schools with black instructors. The Confederate curriculum receded in favor of a broader, more positive instruction. One black teacher, Mamie Garvin Fields, recalled teaching her students in this period "America the Beautiful" and the Pledge of Allegiance. "My school was in the United States, after all, and not the Confederacy."[39]

The career of Charlotte Hawkins Brown revealed what at least one black teacher could accomplish in the age of Jim Crow. Though educated in New England, she returned to her native state of North Carolina to open a school for black youth in 1901. Plying her wealthy white female contacts in Massachusetts for money, and naming the school after a former Wellesley College president and mentor, Brown sustained the Alice Freeman Palmer Memorial Institute (PMI), where she stressed "the proper grooming, the gentle and cultivated speaking voice, the kindly courteous air." She hired top faculty from the leading black institutions of higher education of the era. By the 1930s PMI had evolved into a school for the "better classes" of blacks, preparing its students to succeed at major white universities in the North. PMI students took sojourns to France and England, enjoyed first-run movies at the campus movie house, and pursued Brown's objective to become "culturally secure." If well-brought-up and well-placed black children could not receive a decent education in the segregated South, Brown saw to it that PMI attained a level of education that exceeded many white public schools in the region. At the same time, the strict moral deportment and emphasis on manners at the school deflected white concerns and, it was Brown's hope, created different attitudes about the fitness of blacks to join fully in southern society.[40]

Though Brown attended a prominent northern school, the new cadre of black teachers often attended black colleges in the South. They provided the core for future club membership and work. Clubs formed at Spelman College in Atlanta, Fisk University in Nashville, and Hampton Institute in Hampton, Virginia. From this last institution, Jane Porter Barrett worked with faculty wives and alumni to open the first black settlement house in Virginia, the Locust Street Settlement. Barrett, a native of Athens, Georgia, who served as the bookkeeper for Hampton, hoped that her facility, and others like it throughout the urban South, would refine and redirect the energies and behavior of poor blacks toward middle-class values. If that happened, the image of blacks generally would improve and the entire race would benefit, particularly middle-class African American women.

Barrett's work took on the familiar dual dimension of uplift for the black poor and respectability for the middle-class. As Barrett explained, she hoped to teach people to "make a good clean home, whose inmates are honorable and upright." In her classes for mothers, she instructed her charges to keep their children off the streets and ensure that they "obey and give satisfaction at school." Esthetics were very important at the settlement house, as neatness and cleanliness reflected well on the entire race. Barrett talked about "the gospel of clean back yards." The house also taught families to grow vegetables to supplement meager diets.[41]

Lugenia Burns Hope of Atlanta established the Atlanta Neighborhood Union in 1908, and it quickly became one of the most ambitious black settlement houses in the South. Hope, the daughter of a prominent black educator and wife of Morehouse College president John Hope, declared that the Union promoted the "moral, social, intellectual and religious uplift of the community and the neighborhood in which the organization or its branches would be established." She divided the city into districts and set up Union branches in each, often managed by wives of Morehouse faculty. Projects included cleanup campaigns, the promotion of health care, improvement of schools and parks in black neighborhoods, and securing better police protection. Although the Union raised funds for many of these activities, its leaders believed that city government had a responsibility to the black community as well. Union members successfully lobbied both the Atlanta city government and the state legislature to appropriate money for the improvement of the wretched services in the city's black neighborhoods.

The Union also conducted research, reflecting its connection to Morehouse. Public health and cleanliness provided the focus for several key research initiatives. A Union survey of students' health in the Atlanta public schools in 1916, for example, led the women to establish a clinic that provided both health education and free medical treatment. As Hope explained, "There may after all be some relation between physical uncleanliness and moral uncleanliness."[42]

While white club women temporarily stepped down from their pedestals to redefine their usefulness to themselves and society, black women had always existed far beneath the pedestal. "Lifting as We Climb" involved both individual and racial objectives. Programs for protecting black women, such as establishing residences for single working women, reflected the need for sexual respectability for all black women. Their work for suffrage stressed the relationship between voting and personal respectability much more than their white sisters'. Black educator Nannie H. Burroughs argued for the ballot as "a weapon of moral defense." The African American woman needed the ballot, she implored, "to reckon with men who place no value upon her virtue."[43]

Black club women directed their programs as much at the public perception of black females, derived from the historical interpretations of the Civil War and Reconstruction, as to the needy of their race. In 1900 Mary Church Terrell summarized the role of black club women throughout the South: "Creating a healthful, wholesome public opinion in every community in which we are represented is one of the greatest services we can render. The duty of setting a high moral standard and living up to it devolves upon us as colored women."[44]

What made this task more onerous was that black women worked in an isolated world. White women drew on intimate (in both senses) relationships with white male economic and political leaders and created strategic alliances with white men to effect their goals. Black women, because they were black, had no quick entrée to white power. Nor could they afford to openly conspire with black men, for whom activism of any sort could mean doom both for themselves and their cause.

As lonely crusaders, black women considered themselves leaders of their race. They chastised bad habits among working-class black men, scolding them for trading votes for liquor or money, thereby providing whites with an opportunity to promote disfranchisement as an electoral reform. They complained about a poor work ethic, which provided employers with another excuse to close occupations to African American men. Recognizing that they were women in a male-dominated society, southern black club women did not stake claim to leadership because of moral superiority. They carefully placed their leadership role within the context of their domestic role. Mary Church Terrell declared that "the work which we hope to accomplish can be done better, we believe, by the mothers, wives, daughters, and sisters of our race than by the fathers, husbands, brothers, and sons." The reason, Terrell explained, was that women controlled the domestic sphere and "only through the home can people become really good and truly great." Of course, Terrell and her colleagues (and her white counterparts) defined "home" in the broadest of ways.[45]

Black club women also shared with their white sisters the belief that the first postwar generation would cast the mold for the race and the South for decades to come. They possessed a sense of mission and obligation that enabled them to pool the limited resources of the black community and provide an array of social and educational services that no one else would have provided. They were truly indispensable. We can marvel at the exuberance and confidence with which black educator Anna J. Cooper approached the challenges of an era that broke the dreams of many African Americans in the

South. She wrote in 1892 that her generation of black southerners had "a heritage unique in the ages," that despite the lengthening shadows of violence, segregation, and disfranchisement, she saw a shining light: "There is a quickening of the pulse, and a glowing of its self-consciousness. Aha, I can rival that! I can aspire to that! I can honor my name and vindicate my race!"[46] Cooper could not know, of course, the disappointment and heartbreak that lay ahead of her optimistic vision. Yet she and her sisters would not stop trying.

The importance of black middle-class women to the black community in general increased significantly with the disfranchisement of black men. Black women could not vote; with the added absence of their men from the political arena, coupled with the vigilance of whites against any political activity by black men, the women took over and became their communities' major political spokespersons. Black teachers lobbied for more school funding, civic clubs demanded improved sanitation and social services to the black community, and the women effected tentative alliances with white women, especially in YWCA activities, where women of both races shared common objectives such as public health and suffrage.

Black middle-class women held their communities together as best they could during the first half of the twentieth century. Their efforts to achieve personal respectability left white men unfazed as historical stereotypes persisted. Yet black women built a respectable and responsible middle class that served themselves and their communities well. Their organizational abilities, their leadership experiences, the networks they created among African Americans, and the tentative ties between themselves and white women provided an important base for bolder activities after World War II, when a new generation of black and white women challenged the iron grip of history.

6   A Woman's Movement

Woman had smelled the death in the word *segregation*—because she herself
had been segregated. Because of his unending secret enmity against woman,
[man had placed] her on a pedestal—segregating her . . . putting her always
and forever in her "place."
—Lillian Smith, "Man Born of Woman"

Most white southern women lived comfortably with prevailing views
of southern history. Their clubs espoused the Lost Cause and the Redemption, and their sisters subscribed to white supremacy and patriarchy. Their
reform efforts often employed white supremacy as a rhetorical strategy. Patriarchy may have been a velvet chain that enslaved their ambitions and talents, but it was soft and comfortable enough to allow for movement. Many
had made the best of it, building lives and even careers within the confines of
the South's peculiar historical vision. At some point, though, they would
begin to see the black in themselves, the limits, the duplicity, and even the
tragedy of a tortured past that still troubled the present and cast its deathlike
shadow over the future. Their work over the previous half century had prepared them for that moment.

The legacy of the first generation of post–Civil War women, black and
white, became evident in the years following World War II. The civil rights
movement owed a great deal to the work of black and white club women.
Although few club members of either race directly challenged segregation

prior to the 1940s, their work had sensitized them to the system's injustice. The campaigns against child labor, illiteracy, disease, and poverty accustomed women to social action, organization, lobbying techniques, and, above all, to the virtues and costs of courage.

World War II provided the impetus for bolder approaches to racial and gender issues in the South, and the Association of Southern Women for the Prevention of Lynching's organizational techniques and experiences frequently informed the women who took up the task of reform. The establishment of the Southern Regional Council in 1944, successor to the Commission on Interracial Cooperation, provided an important institutional step toward greater cooperation across racial lines. While the promise of a different racial future grew in the years immediately after World War II, so did southern white resistance, and women who attempted to challenge prevailing customs discovered that times had not changed much at all.

Off the Pedestal

Dorothy Tilly, like some white women of her social class in Atlanta during the 1940s, involved herself in church work, outreach to the poor, and promoting interracial dialogue. Since the early 1930s Tilly had participated in the reform activities of the ASWPL. And, like her mentor, Jessie Daniel Ames, she joined the new Southern Regional Council.

Tilly's work caught the eye of President Harry S. Truman, who appointed her as one of two southerners on the President's Committee on Civil Rights in 1945. The committee originated from a growing concern in Washington about racial violence in the South directed at returning black servicemen eager to put into practice what their superiors had preached during the war. The committee issued its report, *To Secure These Rights*, in 1947. It included a sweeping agenda for transforming race relations not only in the South but in the nation: an antilynching law, the abolition of the poll tax, laws to prevent voter-registration discrimination, desegregation of the armed forces, an end to segregation in Washington, D.C., and in interstate public transportation, the establishment of a permanent civil rights section within the Justice Department, and the withdrawal of federal funds to institutions practicing segregation. The recommendations went far beyond what white leaders in the South were prepared to discuss, let alone implement. Tilly endorsed all the proposals save the last, fearing damage to the South's struggling educational institutions.

Southern leaders roundly condemned the committee and the report. Tilly pushed on. In 1949, amid growing resistance in the South to President Truman's civil rights initiatives and the efforts of southern political leaders to link racial reconciliation with Communism, Tilly formed the Fellowship of the Concerned, an organization of women from churches and synagogues in the Southeast. The more she pressed for racial equality, the further she moved from the protection accorded her gender. Eventually she lost the guard altogether. Obscene callers harassed her day and night; she eventually moved a record player near her phone, and whenever a caller launched into a diatribe, she would play the Lord's Prayer. Atlanta mayor William B. Hartsfield, a friend of Tilly's, ordered a plainclothesman to follow Tilly and a police car to cruise her street during the night; he went so far as to have a streetlight installed in front of her house. Columnists held her up to ridicule, one denouncing her as "a parasite who while living upon funds furnished by the Methodist Church had rendered much of her service to the cause of Socialism and Communism." Such were the consequences of dissent. Tilly and the fellowship persisted, though, until her death in 1970.[1]

Other white women who took the bold step and challenged white supremacy found themselves not only bereft of male protection but the subject of sexual innuendo as well. The pedestaled woman offered white men the opportunity to protect them, confirming their manhood. If a woman rejected this construction, she no longer wanted white male protection and no longer feared black male sexuality. Ergo, she lusted after black men, condemning herself and absolving the white male of his protective role.

Virginia Durr, a white Alabamian who joined the Women's Society for Christian Service, a Methodist-supported social welfare organization, visited Mississippi senator James O. Eastland with a few of her colleagues in the 1940s to lobby against the poll tax. The tax, common throughout the South, excluded black voters, most of whom could not afford the fee. Miraculously, poor white voters often found their tax paid when they went to cast their ballots. Eastland chaired the Senate Judiciary Committee, which had the power to originate any legislation overturning the poll tax.

The meeting between the demure Methodist women and the courtly senator proceeded pleasantly until the women broached the subject of the poll tax. As Durr recalled, Eastland "jumped up. His face turned red. . . . And he screamed out, 'I know what you women want—black men laying on you!' "

The assertion came as a shock to the women, who hurriedly left the office without an apology from the senator. Virtue conveyed status to southern white women. To lose virtue meant to lose respectability and become an out-cast.[2]

These women activists represented a minority of white women's views in the South during the tense days of the 1950s, when the first major assaults against Jim Crow surfaced in the region's schools. For many working-class women imbued with the notion of their place as guardians of the family and the home—the school was an extension of the home—the threat of integration represented a threat to their children's status, and to their own as well. In a society where rank mattered, even if white leaders talked of racial solidarity, the threat of integration stood to obscure both racial and class distinctions in the same way that freedom after the Civil War threatened to overturn established social and racial relations. In both cases, nearly a century apart, the white reaction was swift and hard, and the screaming mothers straining at police barricades in New Orleans and Little Rock were there to protect their children above all else. They would battle fiercely for that future, even if the future was a lie based on a bigger lie.

Daughter of the Confederacy

Adolphine Terry reacted differently to the school crisis of the 1950s. Then again, she was different from most women, even of her social class. Terry was among those rare women in the post–World War II South who could engage in almost any outlandish behavior and retain her dignity, station, and the protective gauze of her gender. She was nearly seventy by the time Dorothy Tilly initiated the Fellowship of the Concerned, and southerners typically accorded older women a deep respect and a wider tolerance for eccentricity, almost to say, Sure, we'll allow odd behavior, but only if you are too old to make a difference. Terry did not seem the type to make much difference. The daughter of a slaveholder and Confederate veteran, she presided over the most prominent family in Little Rock, Arkansas. While she could have remained within the comfortable confines of family and friends, engaging in occasional charitable work and volunteering for various beneficial causes, she sought a broader world from the outset.

Terry attended Vassar College and resided for a number of years in Washington, D.C. Her time at Vassar proved a turning point in her education about herself and the place she came from. One evening she engaged in a heated dormitory discussion on lynching, concluding with the standard southern white justification that "if a black man rapes a white woman, he deserves to be lynched." But her roommate from Brooklyn didn't buy it. "You don't really believe that revenge on one poor black wretch is more important than maintaining a system of law and order for the whole community," she implored. The comment gave Terry pause: "I knew she was right. . . . It gave me an entirely different look . . . at the situation which we faced here in the South. . . . I think that was the beginning of my spiritual education and the beginning of wisdom, and learning not to accept a thing because everybody in the community was saying it."[3] Few southern women had the opportunity for such feedback. What they heard on a daily basis merely reinforced what they always had heard and would continue to hear in the future.

Once back in Little Rock, Terry threw herself into civic activism, founding the symphony orchestra, opening public libraries, reforming the juvenile court system, and working for woman's suffrage. She also served as an advisor to the local black chapter of the YWCA.

Her interaction with black Y members provided another educational opportunity for Terry. As she admitted, "We got more out of the experience than we gave." The black women "were the wives of professional men, and they provided us with an education. We, the daughters of Confederate veterans who had heard a great deal about the white side of the war, now learned of the suffering of the black population before, during and after the war, and of all the lacks from which they still suffered."[4] For the first time, Terry learned a different version of the Civil War and Reconstruction.

During the 1930s Terry became active in the ASWPL and lined up the support of women's groups throughout the state, such as the Methodist Woman's Missionary Society, the Arkansas Federation of Women's Clubs, and the Arkansas Democratic Women's Clubs. In 1939 Terry led the effort to form the Little Rock Housing Association to use federal funds to combat (mostly black) slum housing in the city. Little Rock became one of the first cities in the nation to apply for urban-renewal funds when that program appeared in 1949. The efforts of Terry and her colleagues helped to develop a progressive reputation for Little Rock with respect to race relations. Harry Bass, the black director of the Urban League, visited the city in 1952 and stated, "I've been in all the major cities of the South. And the race situation is better in Little Rock than anywhere else."[5]

During the 1950s, however, the fragile racial truce, constructed mostly on white terms, collapsed in Little Rock. In 1958 Arkansas governor Orval Faubus plunged the city into a crisis by closing its public schools to avoid racial desegregation. Civic leaders wrung their hands but dared not cross the popular governor. Privately, many believed Faubus was right. Adolphine Terry thought otherwise. Inviting other like-minded white women to her home and sitting beneath the portrait of her father decked out in his Confederate uniform, the seventy-six-year-old Terry established the Women's Emergency Committee to Open Our Schools (WEC). As she wrote to sympathetic newspaper editor Harry Ashmore, "The men have failed. It's time to call out the women."[6] Using the ASPWL as her inspiration, she formed the interracial group to lobby for the opening of public schools. By May 1959 the WEC included 1,400 women.

For many of the younger women in the group, it was their first taste of activism, as well as their first taste of the reaction that invariably accompanied stepping outside the protective circle. Kathryn Lambright, one of the younger members, recalled that before her work with the WEC she "was never encouraged to pursue anything other than [to] be a wife, mother, have lovely manners. . . . A Southern lady is . . . submissive, always gentle spoken, well groomed, versed in social amenities . . . [and] Southern ladies should be conformists."[7]

Men took turns making threatening phone calls to members, denouncing them as "nigger lovers," "race mixers," and "Communists." One bewildered man wrote to a member, "I'm absolutely dumbfounded at what you and Mrs. Terry are doing. I know her and I know she isn't a Jew or a Negro but . . . surely you are not white gentile." (She was.) Some of the women lost friends and noted a marked decline in social invitations. A few husbands lost business because of their wives' activities. Many women, fearful of their husbands' reactions, joined the WEC anonymously, and a few women experienced the ultimate casting out as their husbands filed for divorce. Yet many of the women felt as if they had no alternative, that if they did not speak up for education, no one else would, or worse, those women screaming hatred at the barricades would have the stage to themselves. As one member put it: "The men were afraid. . . . There were no leaders. They all chickened out. . . . They were afraid of losing money."[8]

Yet there were limits to Terry's activism. The WEC maintained racially separate chapters. And rarely did Terry or her members state the obvious: that racial segregation was morally wrong and the school system ought to desegregate as a moral imperative. Rather, they cast their arguments in prac-

tical terms, claiming the need to provide education for their children. Strategically, this was the safest route (though still fraught with peril), but the
absence of a publicly stated moral framework restricted the movement's
reach and its ultimate impact.

Still, Terry and the women of the WEC recognized that without the support of at least some white men, their efforts and good intentions would not,
by themselves, open the city's schools. They turned their gender roles into
weapons for change. The women invited male civic leaders to dinner, reason-
ing that "southern gentlemen have been taught to be courteous to their host-
ess, so when you give men food to eat they cannot be impolite to you and
they must do a favor in return." More boldly, the women organized a "SEX"
committee, "composed of beautiful young women who knew how to act
dumb and at the same time get the answers that they want," to persuade businessmen that closed schools damaged the city's economy.[9] In the same spirit,
Terry and her board recruited eight young women for a steering committee
to publicize their efforts, the point being that the media and the men were
more likely to pay attention to attractive and youthful women than to the
middle-aged matrons who initially organized the WEC. They lobbied in the
state legislature wearing high heels, white gloves, and demur dresses to ac-
centuate their femininity. Some lawmakers remained unimpressed and bri-
dled at the idea of any woman engaging in political activity, especially on
behalf of a cause that could lead to integration. State Representative Paul Van
Dalsem complained that these women had too much time on their hands and
pointed with pride at women in his rural district: "We keep them barefooted
and pregnant. And if that doesn't work, then we give them an extra cow to
milk."[10]

Irene Samuel, one of the group's leaders, went so far as to suggest that
wives withhold sex until their husbands agreed to publicly denounce the
school closings. "I don't know how widely used [Samuel's suggestion] was,"
one member recalled, "but it was mentioned at meetings, and everyone
laughed, but they were more than a little serious."[11]

For Little Rock's activist women, none of this was new; for decades southern women had learned to cajole, dissemble, and playact to get what they
wanted. Men expected it and felt good with themselves when they conceded
to the artifice, even if both sides knew that the display was a charade. Southern society moved along and survived on such fantasies, which covered unpleasant realities and ordered social relations. Each segment of southern
society learned that certain behaviors permitted certain, if restricted, free-

doms, and even rewards, and that the consequences for deviance were deep and lasting.

Sure enough, in January 1959, Grainger Williams, head of the Little Rock Chamber of Commerce and husband of a WEC officer, spoke out publicly for the first time against the school closings. When the segregationist school board fired forty-four teachers in May, three husbands of WEC members formed the Committee to Stop This Outrageous Purge (STOP) to recall the offending school board. The vast majority of STOP members had wives in the WEC. Though the men received the publicity, WEC members provided the organization and the clerical work for the group. Little Rock's public high schools reopened in August.

It is tempting to characterize WEC efforts as promoting the obvious; they never denounced segregation or stressed the morality of their fight to reopen the city's schools. But in the context of the time, their work was courageous and the risks were great. The state police investigated the WEC as a "subversive organization" and jotted down the license plate numbers of members, including Irene Samuel's, which the police noted in parentheses belonged to a Jew. The Nuremburg Laws these were not, of course. But the surveillance, the innuendos, and the implied and implemented threats created a fearful atmosphere in Little Rock and elsewhere in the South.[12]

In Montgomery, Alabama, when black and white churchwomen agreed to initiate an interracial prayer group in the mid-1950s, segregationists published the names of white members. The group quickly dissolved. As Virginia Durr recounted, "The women became frightened when their names were publicized. Even their husbands began getting phone calls from people who threatened to stop doing business with them if their wives went to any more integrated meetings." The women suffered public embarrassment, a high penalty in a region where public behavior reflected status and breeding. A few husbands took out ads in the newspaper disassociating themselves from their wives. As Durr recalled, "One man disassociated himself from his aunt, another disassociated himself from his daughter. They were scared of the repercussions on their business."[13]

Religion played an important role in the women's reform efforts, as it had historically. Methodist and Jewish women in particular dominated the WEC. For the former, the WEC was merely a continuation of the reform tradition dating back to the late nineteenth century; for the latter, traditional liberalism and the sense of minority status propelled their membership. By contrast, many Baptist churches adopted an openly hostile stance toward school integration in Little Rock. Twenty-four Baptist ministers called a Friday-night prayer vigil at the height of the crisis to pray for racial separation.[14]

Adolphine Terry carried with her a good sense of history and what that history had done to the South. Male civic leaders warned her that "blood will flow in the streets" if she and her colleagues persisted, and she worried that history seemed to be repeating itself: "I think the South is acting a hundred years late, just as we did in 1860. We just can't see the future."[15]

After Terry took up the cudgels for a new civil war, her example and that of the WEC spread to other cities, such as Atlanta, Mobile, and New Orleans. On the third anniversary of the group's founding, the local newspaper memorialized: "Looking back now, it is still faintly terrifying to speculate on what Little Rock would have done without the first small gathering together of women who were determined that the schools would be saved. . . . To the Ladies, God bless 'em." The WEC dissolved in 1963, a victim of its own success. But as Sara Alderman Murphy, one of the group's leaders, noted in 1995, "When the WEC finally disbanded . . . it did not actually stop. It had empowered women to know that they could have an impact; it gave us the realization that we could change things." Some of the women, including Murphy, joined a national organization, the Panel of American Women, that worked actively for integration in all aspects of life in Little Rock. And in the mid-1960s the women were instrumental in defeating Faubus and installing the moderate Republican Winthrop Rockefeller as governor.[16]

The majority of WEC women came from prosperous backgrounds; Governor Faubus referred to them derisively as the "Cadillac Brigade."[17] Black women who participated in the movement also came from the elite of their race, but a broader cross-section of African American women participated in the civil rights movement. The key role of the black church, the importance of organizing the black community collectively, and the limits of interracial cooperation moved black middle-class women to recruit leaders from a broad spectrum of the black community.

Freedom's Midwives

Rosa Parks was one of many black church- and clubwomen caught up in the postwar efforts to crash the barriers of white supremacy. She grew up in Montgomery, Alabama, and attended all-black Alabama State College. Although she was college-educated, the only job she could secure as a black woman was as a tailor's assistant in a local department store. Frustrated by her menial job and the daily humiliations of a segregated city, she joined the National Association for the Advancement of Colored People (NAACP), where she met the chapter's president, E. D. Nixon, and Virginia Durr. In the summer of 1955, Nixon and Durr arranged a scholarship for Parks to attend the Highlander Folk School in Monteagle, Tennessee.

The Highlander School, run by Miles Horton, a white Tennessean, provided a unique experience in interracial living for southern blacks and whites (in open violation of Tennessee's segregation statutes). The purpose of the encounter was to inspire the "students" to return home and work for improved race relations by attacking segregation. The atmosphere at the school was relaxed and informal, reflecting Horton's personality. When a skeptical reporter asked him how he managed to get blacks and whites to eat together, he replied, "First, the food is prepared. Second, it's put on the table. Third, we ring the bell."[18]

The two-week session at Highlander impressed Parks, allowing her to see the possibilities for interracial living. The barriers separating black and white, she learned, resulted not from basic differences between the races but rather from artificial distinctions promoted by those with a heavy stake in maintaining white supremacy. When Parks returned to the dull humiliation of life in Montgomery, the contrast with her exhilarating experience in Tennessee was marked. She could not resume her tacit acquiescence in segregation.

On December 1, 1955, Rosa Parks boarded the Cleveland Avenue bus bound for the housing project where she lived with her disabled husband. It had been an especially tiring day for Mrs. Parks: the Christmas rush had just begun, and the heavy pressing irons in her small, stifling workroom aggravated her bursitis. She gratefully took her seat on the bus and relaxed. The bus began to fill up, mostly with blacks heading for the housing project. When a few white men boarded the bus, the driver turned around and shouted, "Niggers, move back!" Parks, seated in the first row of blacks, refused to move. The driver stopped the bus and came over to the seamstress: "Y'all make it nice on yourself and let me have those seats." Parks remained in her seat. The driver, following procedure, called the police, who arrested and jailed her.[19]

The incident might have ended there, as it had on the few previous occasions since the end of the war when black women (men dared not attempt it) defied the bus system's humiliating "rolling" segregation rules, which required blacks to give up their seats and move farther back as whites boarded and places in the front of the bus filled up. But this was no random protest by a tired black woman supporting a household on twenty-three dollars a week.

Parks's friends sprung into action, led by Jo Ann Robinson, an English professor at Alabama State College. Robinson, like so many other black middle-class women, had been active in club and church work through the 1940s. In 1949 she formed the Women's Political Council, an organization that promoted voter registration in the city. Over the next five years, the council evolved into the city's most effective and militant black political voice. Robinson and her colleagues succeeded in electing a sympathetic white politician to the city council and secured the appointment of four black officers to the police force—a significant achievement for a Deep South city. But they could not budge the city on the segregated buses.

Jo Ann Robinson understood that Parks's arrest provided the city's black community with an opportunity both to make a statement on bus grievances and demonstrate their political clout. The day after the incident, Robinson fired up her strongest weapon, her mimeograph machine, and ran off forty thousand handbills calling for a boycott of the city's bus lines. Robinson and her NAACP colleagues distributed the notices at church the next day, a Sunday, and the boycott began on Monday.

Although Robinson and the Women's Political Council had initiated the boycott, neither her group nor E. D. Nixon's NAACP chapter could assume long-term responsibility for sustaining the action, arranging alternative transportation, and rallying the black community. Both the council and the NAACP were middle-class organizations with only loose ties to the mass of Montgomery's black population. They relied on the city's black ministers to recruit the shock troops for the boycott. One of them would be the likely choice to lead and maintain the protest. On the day after the boycott began, Robinson turned over the daily management to the Reverend Martin Luther King Jr. The rest, as they say, is history.[20]

Black women would go on to play significant roles in the struggle for voting rights, a passion that evolved from the late-nineteenth- and early-twentieth-century movements for woman's suffrage to the voter registration drives after World War II and organizations such as Jo Ann Robinson's Women's Political Council. South Carolina's Septima Clark, for example, played a prominent role in that state during the early 1960s in promoting black voter registration. A veteran of the Highlander Folk School who led the workshop Rosa Parks attended in 1955, Clark organized the Citizenship Education Program to build the self-confidence, economic independence, and intellectual base of black women. She successfully disguised her program of providing political information to rural blacks by publicly promoting the education workshops as literacy and home economics programs. Together with her cousin Bernice Robinson, Clark's workshops had successful results in areas down the Carolina and Georgia coasts and along the Alabama-Tennessee border. Through these efforts, Clark hoped to convince black women (and their families) to improve themselves and to link that improvement to political action through the ballot.

Clark, applying the politics of indirection perfected by black women for nearly a century, was always careful to connect her revolutionary politics with traditional elements of southern culture. She offered conferences for ministers on "The Bible and the Ballot" to help overcome the traditional conservatism and wariness of rural pastors. Her work, and the work of other black "teachers" trained at Highlander in 1961, resulted in significant gains in voter registration.[21]

Still, Clark sometimes found gaining the respect and cooperation of black male leaders in the movement as trying as pushing against the boundaries of white supremacy. Martin Luther King Jr. graciously agreed to write the preface for Clark's autobiography, *Echo in My Soul* (1962), but his words reflected the southern black male perception of black women more than Clark's courageous civil rights work. He wrote that the book "epitomizes the continuous struggle of the Southern Negro woman to realize her role as a mother while fulfilling her forced position as community teacher, intuitive fighter for human rights and leader of her unlettered and disillusioned people."[22]

The tension between black women, who had become de facto leaders in the black community following disfranchisement, and black men infected the civil rights movement in the 1960s. Few aspects of the freedom struggle indicated the particular southern grounding of black culture more than the gender relationships, especially at a time when much of the local organizing and leadership came from black women, while the major figures of the regional and national organizations were black men.

Ella Baker, a black North Carolina civil rights activist, assumed the position of acting director of the newly formed Southern Christian Leadership Conference (SCLC) in 1957. Her position testified to her long involvement with organizing civil rights–related activities in the South. During the 1930s she braved hostility from both blacks and whites to organize for the NAACP in the South. Her success resulted in her appointment as National Director of the Branches. But SCLC founders made it clear that her position was temporary while they searched for a more "suitable" leader. Especially frustrating to Baker was the attitude of the black Baptist ministers who dominated the group. They held the same traditional views about women as did many of their white evangelical Protestant counterparts. As Baker explained, "I had known . . . that there would never be any role for me in a leadership capacity with the SCLC. Why? First, I'm a woman. Also, I'm not a minister. . . . The combination of the basic attitude of men, and especially ministers, as to what the role of women in their church setups is—that of taking orders, not providing leadership . . . this would never have lent itself to my being a leader in the movement there."[23]

Baker eventually left the SCLC and in 1960 in Raleigh, North Carolina, founded the Student Nonviolent Coordinating Committee (SNCC). The new civil rights organization differed significantly from the design of the SCLC. Baker ensured that the management structure remained nonhierarchical and that leadership was shared by a group, which would be rotated, rather than dictated by one individual. In its operation SNCC sought to build the movement from the grass roots, that is, to nurture local leadership rather than to move into a community and provide outside leadership. The model proved successful in developing local civil rights organizations and provided a foundation for voting-rights projects in the Deep South during the Freedom Summer of 1964.

In fact, as Baker discovered, it was incorrect to assume that communities lacked the leadership or expertise necessary to mount civil rights campaigns and required a national organization to come in and direct projects. Black women throughout the South had been providing that leadership since early in the century.

Foremost among the diamonds in the rough of the rural South was Fannie Lou Hamer, a black sharecropper from the Mississippi Delta, a land so flat the horizon seems limitless and with soils so rich and black people so poor that the region reminds one of the coffee plantations of Brazil. When Fannie Lou Townsend married Perry Hamer in 1944 and moved with him to the Marlow plantation outside Ruleville, Mississippi, the landlord's dog enjoyed his own bathroom with running water, while the black sharecroppers had neither. Fannie Lou suffered two miscarriages, not an uncommon occurrence among hard-working farm laborers, but filled her need to have children by informally adopting two daughters. Like hundreds of other black families in the Delta, the Hamers eked out a subsistence living and played out their days in anonymity, except to themselves and their kin. Until 1961. In that year,

Hamer underwent routine surgery. She later learned that the surgeon had sterilized her. Sterilization was a common procedure performed on rural black women in the South after World War II, a practice not halted until the 1970s.[24]

The operation led Hamer to question the degree of control white men held over not only her work but also her body. In the summer of 1962, when a young SNCC worker arrived in Ruleville to register blacks to vote, Hamer knew she had found a voice and a cause, and she soon learned at what cost. Along with several other sharecroppers, Hamer joined the young man and attempted to register to vote. Rebuffed, she returned home only to be confronted by Mr. Marlow, who ordered her and her family off the place they had lived for eighteen years.

Inspired by her determination, many of Ruleville's blacks rallied to help the Hamers. The town's middle-class blacks feared a white backlash and unsuccessfully counseled African Americans to drop their support and Hamer to desist from any civil rights activity. The reprisals came swiftly as banks called in loans on black businesses, forcing several to close; the town fired the sole black city worker; and the black church lost its tax exemption. Town officials withheld federal surplus food from blacks, their major winter source of sustenance; banks refused to approve loans for blacks; and ruinously high tax bills were sent to black residents. Fannie Lou received a water bill for nine thousand dollars. She lived in a house without running water. Physical terror accompanied the economic retaliation as blacks sustained sporadic gunfire aimed randomly into their homes.

Hamer persisted. She studied the Mississippi state constitution and passed the exam that measured her understanding of the document. Thus cleared to register to vote, Hamer was again turned away, this time for failure to pay her poll tax, which she could not pay unless she was already registered to vote. Undeterred, she pushed on with her voting-rights activities, attending a workshop at the Highlander Folk School. When she returned to Ruleville, the police savagely beat her and threw her into prison, which steeled her all the more. When in February 1964 civil rights supporters in New England shipped food and clothing to Delta sharecroppers, Hamer organized and controlled the distribution of these items. The position gave her a club over local blacks: if you want to eat and keep warm, you must try to register to vote. When Ruleville's white mayor announced on the radio that Hamer would provide free food and clothing for anyone who showed up at her house, hoping to overwhelm her resources and damage her credibility,

Hamer confronted the hundreds who came and organized them into a voting-rights seminar.

During the Freedom Summer of 1964, when SNCC strategists invited northern college students to join them in a voter-registration drive in the Delta—a drive that yielded few registrants but much national publicity, culminating with the murder of three civil rights workers—Hamer dodged shots fired into her house and the firebombing of her church. One positive result from the tragic summer was the formation of the Mississippi Freedom Democratic Party (MFDP), a political organization Hamer founded to challenge the regular all-white state Democratic Party. She stormed the Democratic national convention in Atlantic City that August, demanding that party leaders seat the MFDP instead of the state's all-white delegation. Fearful of any disruption that could mar the nomination and campaign of Lyndon B. Johnson, convention leaders worked out a "compromise" that allowed two members of the MFDP to be seated with the regular delegation. Hamer rejected the offer and left Atlantic City disillusioned but, as usual, undeterred.

The events of subsequent years vindicated Hamer's persistence; President Johnson signed the Voting Rights Act in the following year, and Mississippi's Democratic Party delegation was considerably more representative of the true racial makeup of the state at the 1968 national convention. Hamer pressed on, founding a bank in the Delta to ensure the type of economic blackmail that ruined black businesses could not recur. She also purchased land to begin Freedom Farm, a cooperative where black managers and laborers could share profits. And in 1970 she filed suit against Sunflower County, Senator James Eastland's bailiwick, demanding the desegregation of the county's schools. Only ill health slowed Hamer's efforts. In 1977 she finally succumbed to cancer and diabetes. Carved on her tombstone is a simple but eloquent epitaph for her and the hundreds of poor blacks who emerged from the veil of fear and invisibility to fashion a movement: "I'm sick and tired of being sick and tired."[25] Hamer could accomplish so much precisely because she was a woman, though obviously an extraordinary woman. If she had been a man, she would have been dead long before.

The good works and leadership of black women from the late nineteenth century through the 1960s did not disappear, of course, after 1970. But the Black Power movement, and what activist Parthia Wynn Hall called "the Black macho rhetoric," overtook the careful bridge building of black women and their organizations.[26] The disintegration of the movement coalition and the disconnection of poor African Americans from other segments of the southern black community reflects, in part, the decline of black women in major leadership roles in communities throughout the region. Male political leaders and their clerical allies dominated the setting of African American agendas in increasingly fragmented southern black communities.

During the 1960s one of the struggles within the struggle for racial equality focused on the reassertion of black male leadership in African American community affairs. Since the turn of the twentieth century, disfranchisement and the cultural animus against the participation of black men in public life in the South had impelled black women to assume leadership roles. After 1965, with the franchise restored and with the leadership experiences gained in the civil rights movement, black men moved to the forefront, both within black communities and as spokespersons to the wider world. The victory of the men did not result in the wholesale withdrawal of black women so much as their assumption of lesser roles, and the black South has been the more impoverished for that trend.

The civil rights movement, in proffering a different historical scenario for the South, consequently altered the image and position of women in southern society, a fitting tribute to the thousands of middle-class white and black women who worked separately for decades to expand the sphere of acceptable activity. What the civil rights movement accomplished was to allow southern women to step out from behind the mask, not necessarily to abandon the role of flirtatious butterfly, but to display more openly their intellectual and intuitive talents. The simultaneous rendering of both belle and brain would confuse outsiders and confound southern white men but would be immensely satisfying to the newest women of a new South. Perhaps the feminist movement in the South has not advanced as much as in other parts of the country because southern white women have less need for it; they have practiced the arts of assertion, leadership, and the assumption of significant responsibilities, all the while denying that they were doing anything of the sort. But the toll in "sheltered lives," as Ellen Glasgow put it, has been frightful. And neither the scars nor the reality of subservience is erased today. The pedestal still stands after a fashion.

Take It Like a Man

The role and status of southern women have changed since the 1960s, not enough to eliminate the South's distinctions from the rest of the country, at least statistically, yet enough to begin making some difference. But statistics do not tell the entire story any more than skylines and demographics imply that the South has melted into America at last; it hasn't done anything of the sort.

At the time of the liberation in 1965, and for some years thereafter, gender roles scarcely changed. Although urban populations grew after World War II, ideals of southern womanhood did not. Urbanization might have provided a cover for new behavior such as Peter Taylor described in "The Old Forest," but as one moved up the social ladder, expectations were layered upon expectations until they smothered the spontaneity of young women. Anne Rivers Siddons, in her 1976 novel *Heartbreak Hotel*, a coming-of-age story of a young white woman caught in the growing drama of civil rights in the 1950s and '60s, wrote, "In the cities of the South—in Atlanta and Birmingham and Charlotte and Mobile and Charleston—there were . . . girls planted, tended, and grown like prize roses, to be cut and massed and shown at debutante balls and cotillions in their eighteenth year. Unlike roses, they did not die after the sowing; instead, they moved gently into colleges and universities and Junior League chapters, and were then pressed between the leaves of substantial marriages to be dried and preserved."[27]

Siddons correctly viewed the process as part of a historical trap: "It was a process of rules, subtle, shaded, iron bylaws that were tacitly drafted in burned and torn households sometime during the Reconstruction," rules that produced women "from identical molds."[28] Many of the women who provided leadership outside the mold were widowed, childless, or never married. Released from expectations, they might encounter less disapproval for their actions beyond the usual headshakers, who agreed that married women with children would never behave like that. These were bright women, to be sure, and in an earlier era a university education and an extensive array of volunteer activities would have reflected a fulfilled life, even if those acquired talents never went beyond reaffirming the basic ideals of southern society.

By the mid-1970s, change was underway. Women's protests, sometimes silent, often covert, became more public. Country music was a cultural genre that occasionally taunted the status quo long before the 1970s. But Loretta Lynn's direct rejection of serial pregnancy in "The Pill" (1975) heralded a more assertive tone among female country artists in the 1980s and '90s. Lynn stated of "The Pill" that "the men who run some of the radio stations, they banned the record because they didn't like what I was saying. But the women knew."[29]

Loretta Lynn's songs demanded respect: "Don't Come Home a-Drinkin' (With Lovin' on Your Mind)." And she informed her man that the times indeed had changed. In "We've Come a Long Way Baby," she declared, "Time to change and I'm demanding satisfaction, too." Yet independence inspired loneliness, and in "When the Tingle Becomes a Chill" and "Somebody Somewhere," lost love and vulnerability still come through. Liberation is not yet an unalloyed joy.[30]

Country music star Dolly Parton reported that growing up in the 1950s she admired the pictures of models in newspapers because "they didn't look as if men and boys could just put their hands on them any time they felt like it, and with any degree of roughness they chose. The way they looked, if a man wanted to touch them, he'd better be damned nice to them." Women should not be apologetic when rejecting male attention, Lorrie Morgan asserts in "What Part of No Don't You Understand."[31]

The ideal of the strong silent type was rejected. At the least, there should be equal communication between men and women. Lorrie Morgan's "Five Minutes," gives her man that much time to figure out "what lovin' me's about." So much for "Stand By Your Man." Even more direct was Michelle Wright's "Take It Like a Man" (1993), which equates manhood with being a good friend as well as a good lover; she complains that contemporary men want maids or mothers, not partners, and challenges them to grow up. When Shania Twain's love-me-or-leave style burst upon the country scene in the mid-1990s with "Any Man of Mine" (1996), her songs left no doubt who was boss, and as for those men wrapped up in their trucks or their hair, well, they could get lost.[32]

The Dixie Chicks, the latest country sensation, combine traditional downhome twang and sentiment with a very modern message. Their very name taunts the feminist ideal, as if to announce that categories and identity trips are not in these southern girls' music or personas. Their music weaves back and forth between traditional love ballads and aggressive, even raunchy anthems of feminine independence, as if southern women were quite accustomed to and comfortable with both sides of femininity. Their hit album *Fly* celebrates freedom as well as getting even. "Goodbye Earl," performed with special relish, tells of an abusive spouse meeting his just desserts (literally—when his wife poisons his dinner). "It turned out he was a missing person nobody missed at all."[33]

This has not become a one-sided debate in Nashville, reflecting only the changing perceptions of women and, not incidentally, their growing buying power. Male country vocalists have responded positively to the sensitivity training imposed on them by female artists. John Michael Montgomery's "I Swear" (1994) is a pledge to remain a true partner in all senses of the word; gone is the macho swagger and devil-may-care attitude toward love and women, and the double-standard such an attitude implies.[34]

Garth Brooks, arguably the most popular of all country vocalists at the turn of the twenty-first century, has tackled such women's issues as domestic violence and date rape. Explaining his 1992 song "We Shall Be Free" to a New York *Times* reporter, Brooks fashioned a new definition of family values, new at least from the perspective of the South: "I think the Republicans' big problem is that they believe family values are June and Walt and 2.3 children. To me it means laughing, being able to dream. It means that if a set of parents are black and white, or two people of the same sex, or if one man or one woman acts as the parent, that the children grow up happy and healthy: that's what family values are."[35]

For many southern women, the changes are not necessarily as dramatic as prefigured by country music artists. Many are still searching for their new roles and are enjoying the expedition. Few writers have captured this transitional period better than Kentucky's Bobbie Ann Mason, who often uses the changing landscape of the New South, the fields receding before subdivisions and K-Marts, to depict the restlessness of the new southern woman. In "The Retreat," Georgeann escapes a retreat workshop on Christian marriage to play a video game. When her perplexed husband asks, "What can I do to make you happy?" she replies honestly, "I'll tell you when I get it figured out. . . . Just let me work on it." The changing roles and the changing South create confusion, but for Mason confusion is a necessary prelude to understanding and lasting change.[36]

In "Shiloh" Mason displays such gender confusion in an early scene in which the heroine, Norma Jean Moffit, "is working on her pectorals. She lifts three-pound dumbbells to warm up, she progresses to a twenty-pound barbell." Meanwhile, her husband Leroy shows his needlepoint pillow cover to his mother-in-law. Trying to revive their failing marriage, Leroy and Norma Jean visit the Shiloh battlefield, a scene that ties the transformation of gender back to the Civil War. As the couple sit silently and gaze at the cemetery for the Union dead, Norma Jean turns to Leroy and says, "I want to leave you," thus connecting the Confederate defeat to Leroy's misfortune.[37]

They may not feel "fulfilled" yet, but southern women are charting new territory for their gender. Some may be using the confrontational means expressed in country songs, or the careful, sometimes painful epiphanies played out in stories like Bobbie Ann Mason's, or more traditional methods of masking new ways with old strategies, what novelist Reynolds Price has called "Mack trucks disguised as powder puffs." As writer James Whitehead has noted, southern women are "calling for change: they have heard all the old myth stories, want some new ones, and are willing to go out and make their own."[38]

Gender Agenda

Clearly, there is still much work to do. The Citadel's battle over the admission of women cadets in 1996 epitomized the persistent strength of patriarchy and the consequent hold of traditional southern history on gender relations. Long after the national service academies had allowed women to enter, southern military schools resisted the trend, well into the 1990s. The last civil case was adjudicated in favor of a female cadet as late as October 1999. Few institutions in the South have a more masculine and historic lineage than the military. The heroics of Virginia Military Institute cadets in the Civil War and The Citadel's heritage as the front line of secession and war are reflected in the traditions of the two schools and in the gray-clad and, until recently, all-male cadet corps. The points of chivalry and manners are as much a part of the curriculum as math and science, and perhaps more important, for judgment in the South has always emphasized outward behavior as a measure of intrinsic worth. But the lessons of chivalry were quickly forgotten in the melee that accompanied the gender integration of The Citadel. Verbal protests turned into physical abuse. Victims suffered burns, bruises, torn clothing, and mental harassment. Not the stuff of gentlemanly behavior, but the cadets would have told you that the women asked for it; they had lost their right of protection by stepping off the pedestal and directly into a southern man's world, directly into conflict with southern history.

The Citadel, a fixture in Charleston, South Carolina, the city that gave us the Civil War, spent nearly four years and $10 million fighting the admission of women cadets. The Citadel began its career as a fortress erected in response to an 1822 slave uprising. Having had mixed success in repulsing slaves and, later, Yankees, it seems that the institution turned its attention to holding back teenage girls. It has been a part of the southern creed that men and women occupy distinctive roles. To have women marching alongside men not only represents an affront to this tradition, but also emasculates the men and defeminizes the women; the result would be chaos, confusion, and humiliation, a collapse of gender roles beyond the wildest dreams of a Bobbie Ann Mason character. As The Citadel's president, Lieutenant General Claudius "Bud" Watts, noted just before he retired, "This country needs to . . . protect and understand the inherent difference between the sexes."[39]

The school's solution was to cajole a compliant South Carolina legislature into appropriating millions of dollars to establish an alternative military program for women at Converse College, an all-female private institution in Spartanburg, but a court ruling in 1996 dashed that idea. While Citadel supporters complained that the school "is the only vestige of the old Confederacy we have left," the state-supported institution succumbed to the court's decision and, after four years of women in the corps, the place is still standing. To their credit, even some of the more conservative lawmakers dropped the fight as a loser. To them, not everything about the past is worth saving; perhaps by adding a new chapter, the whole story can change for everyone's benefit. As Verne Smith, a conservative Democratic legislator from Greenville, explained, "You know I love the history of the South and respect the good things about it. But I don't try to explain away the terrible things. And to ostracize some of our people from that school when it's state-supported, I couldn't go along with that."[40]

The Citadel is a metaphor for the embattled southern white male defending his history from outside marauders—blacks, women, national groups, northern attorneys, and Yankee newcomers. The admissions controversy is yet another opportunity to reenact the great Cause, and like that Cause, the outcome is less important than the good fight itself, a chance against steep odds to hold back the tide that would alter history and therefore the privileged place of white men. Cadets adopted the siege mentality articulated by their superiors; resistance became their focus. The fortress became a place where cadets were "more concerned with survival outside class than a good performance in it. . . . Outside, in a new age molding itself to subtle and difficult new realities, knights were no longer recognized."[41]

If traditional perspectives show signs of moving to the margins rather than sticking in the mainstream of southern thought, actions of southern men, especially southern white men, indicate sharply different perspectives from those of women of both races. Most obvious is the gender gap in politics. Though the political gender gap is a nationwide phenomenon, it is most pronounced in the South, with black and white women tending to favor Democratic candidates, especially those who talk about issues such as education, social services, and health care. In 1997, when North Carolina governor Jim Hunt easily won reelection over his Republican opponent, Robin Hayes, a conservative, born-again Christian touting family values (not to be confused with the domestic issues noted above), Hunt took 56 percent of the white female vote but only 43 percent of the white male vote. Hunt's election actually closed the gender gap a bit. Typically, a slight majority of white women favor Democratic candidates in the South, while white men overwhelmingly support Republicans. Rarely will a Democrat achieve more than 40 percent of the white male vote.[42]

Southern women lag behind those elsewhere in holding elective office. As of 1997, six of the ten states with the lowest percentages of women in state legislatures were located in the South; if you include the border states of Oklahoma and West Virginia, that makes eight out of ten. Only Florida is in the top twenty-five of states with women in elective office. Outside the South, 23 percent of state legislators were women in 1995; less than 14 percent of the lawmakers in the South were women that year. In part this reflects the persistence of small town and rural political power in the South. Women fare better in more urbanized states and in cities. More traditional views on race and gender persist in the countryside. But the country is fast disappearing, or at least transforming. There is no guarantee that the suburban South will be kinder to women's political aspirations, but generally, the less isolation and insulation exist, the more open the South has become.[43]

Female officeholders are a relatively recent phenomenon in the South; it has taken this region considerably longer than the rest of the nation to advance the political careers of women, even in cities. Southern states closed a wide gap during and after the 1992 election. As late as the mid-1980s, there were no female mayors in Tennessee, Louisiana, Mississippi, Georgia, South Carolina, or Virginia.[44]

The relative weakness of women's political power and the traditional antipathy to women's suffrage is reflected in the fact that North Carolina waited until 1971 to ratify the Nineteenth Amendment, while Georgia and Mississippi held out into the 1980s. As for the Equal Rights Amendment, only two southern states, Kentucky and Tennessee, voted to ratify. Lawmakers of those two states, feeling themselves isolated rather than ahead of their time, voted to rescind their decisions.[45]

The relative absence of laws protecting women in the South reflects both the contradictions and the bankruptcy of the pedestal concept. As late as the mid-1990s, a majority of southern states did not recognize marital rape as a crime, and of the eight states without laws prohibiting sex discrimination in employment in 1995, all were located in the South.[46] The dearth of female elected officials has had significant policy implications.

The economic gender gap in the South, greater than in other sections of the nation, both complements and reflects policy shortcomings. Despite substantial gains in professional positions, white women continue to find the greatest share of their work in pink-collar employment ghettoes, and that has remained relatively unchanged since the 1970s. In 1994, 41 percent of employed white women in the South worked in pink-collar occupations, primarily clerical and sales positions; in 1975 that figure stood at 43 percent. Black women have fared scarcely better. In 1994, 50.8 percent of black women held jobs in pink-collar, service, and laborer occupations, compared with 51.4 percent in 1975. Only 5.5 percent of the South's black women held sales jobs in 1975; this figure climbed to 12 percent in 1994. Though black and white women have moved, however slowly, into higher positions since the 1970s, the old adage of last hired, first fired continues to hurt women in the southern work force. In 1993 and 1994, women composed 42.4 percent of workers displaced, up from 34.3 percent during the period 1981 to 1982.[47]

These figures indicate that economic advancement for women is moving slowly in the South. It is not as if women are beginning to enter the work force for the first time. Southern women have worked outside the home, particularly in factories, since the late nineteenth century. But their occupational status has not advanced as rapidly as the Sunbelt economy would imply.

Part of the problem lies in persisting images: of the southern belle, of delicate women far above the hurly-burly of politics and business, the better to perform the role of wife and mother. There is no other region of the country, for example, where beauty pageants continue to play such major roles; just look at the winners of Miss America over the past thirty years. It appears that beauty and talent (the traditional female talents of music and dance, especially) are headquartered below the Mason-Dixon Line, where baton twirlers, drum majorettes, and cheerleaders are idolized and imitated. In what other part of the country would a parent (in Texas) plan a murder to get her daughter on the cheerleading squad? And what is the meaning of the tradition of the popular Rose Festival in Tyler, Texas, in which debs "prostrate themselves camel-like, with their foreheads touching the floor, as their first act of official entrance into adulthood"?[48] Some southern women still define themselves by the sorority, country club, and Junior League, though being a southern belle does not preclude harder and more resourceful interiors. Just ask Margaret Mitchell.

The gender war is already another Lost Cause. It will continue to be fought, of course, as the Civil War continues to have resonance for those who continue to seek the South's redemption in that conflict. Some among an older generation of southern women will continue to find comfort in the traditional perspective and in their status on the pedestal. A new generation of southern women has taken on other traditions—the implied power they have always had and the experience with strategies they have always used to survive and stay sane—and they have run with them. They outperform southern men academically; in the year 2000, women composed nearly 60 percent of the incoming students at the University of North Carolina at Chapel Hill, an institution women could not attend for a time and then were discouraged from enrolling in. And they are pushing inexorably into boardrooms, a longer process to be sure but one that is inevitable. The last vestiges of the Civil War and Reconstruction and the historical myths derived from them will not disappear just because a new history emerges as a written narrative; rather, they will eventually fade away by the practice of change, by demonstrating that women (and African Americans) have a share in the region's past and a stake in its future equal to anybody and everybody else's.

White women of the post–Civil War generation longed for the stability and security the war had taken away; they did not chafe at returning to their dependent status. But, at the same time, they had learned the lessons of the war well: that they could not depend on their men unequivocally, that they would have to make their own way, or at least hone the skills to ensure that they and their children would live in a better world. But they could not make the push for independence too obvious; such a move would prove devastating to their defeated men. They resorted to strategies, an often frustrating maze of attempts to make meaningful lives for themselves and their families. In the process, they became stronger, which accounts for the persisting contradictory national view of southern women as less feminist, but more strong-willed, than their counterparts in the rest of the nation. The "steel magnolia" metaphor fits.[49]

Southern women have been working hard for generations, the plantation myth of leisure and luxury aside. They have shouldered the burdens of a poor, rural society and have experienced the uprooting of the shift to towns and factories. They have raised many children. Southern writer Shirley Abbott bridles at the suggestion that southern women are delicate specimens suited more to the parlor than to public work: "My mother and the other women I knew as a child were farm women. . . . They were not innocent or submissive or delicately constituted, not afraid of balky cows or chicken hawks. . . . They could reason with a mule and shoot a gun. But they also knew just how to take hold of a baby and what to say to a weeping two-year-old."[50]

Southern women also have considerable experience in sisterhood; relating to other women was a powerful elixir in a society that expected little and much of them at the same time. Part of the joy of their reform activities derived from working with other women with whom they could share their dreams and despair, for these revelations were taboo in conversations with men, lest they be made to feel inadequate or even betrayed. As Shirley Abbott explained, "Next to motherhood, sisterhood is what [southern women] value most, taking an endless pleasure in the daily, commonplace society of one another that they never experience in male company."[51]

Southern women have been feminists all along; they just have shown it more discreetly. As southern writer Sharon McKern observed, "Southern women see no contradiction in mixing strength with gentleness." The pedestal was a lonely place, but it offered a commanding view, and women used that perspective strategically to advance their interests inside and outside the household. They do not need courses on assertiveness. The white and black women appearing herein are testimony to that and more. The southern woman, McKern declared, "is not unaccustomed to the uses of power and authority; she has only to learn to exercise these openly, and in her own name."[52] Southern women are in the process of taking that last step.

7 Colors

I have seen a land right merry with the sun, where children sing, and rolling hills lie like passioned women wanton with harvest. And there in the King's Highway sat and sits a figure veiled and bowed, by which the traveller's footsteps hasten as they go. On the tainted air broods fear. Three centuries' thought has been the raising and unveiling of that bowed human heart, and now behold a century new for the duty and the deed. The problem of the Twentieth Century is the problem of the color-line.
—W. E. B. Du Bois, *The Souls of Black Folk*

From the time the first African stepped onto the shores of North America, probably early in the sixteenth century with Spanish explorers, the status of blacks posed a dilemma for European transplants. The relationship between black and white (and red during the relatively brief time that Indians composed a sizeable proportion of the southern population) was always a work in progress. Whites clearly viewed blacks as inferior, but then the English perceived the Irish as less than human. Most Africans arrived in North America in chains, a state of being not calculated to elicit feelings of equality on the part of whites. Slavery, in fact, demanded that whites rationalize the holding of human property, a condition that contradicted both the Enlightenment sentiment of the late eighteenth century and the growth of evangelical Protestantism in the early nineteenth century. Slavery also denied the basis of the American nation, that all men are created equal and that government is derived from the consent of the governed.

The rationalization went something like this: slavery is a civilizing force; without slavery Africans would revert to the barbarism from which they came; under slavery, the African received the Christian religion, which saved his soul and ensured his place in heaven; and slavery allowed white southerners to enjoy unprecedented economic and personal freedom. The status of the slave was conveniently and irrevocably linked to the status of the white, and one could not enjoy a superior status in southern society without the subjugation of the other.

The master, though, did not exercise absolute power. Slavery involved some tacit negotiation between master and slave; abject cruelty did not generate a positive work ethic. The most efficient plantations were those that balanced terror with paternalism: use the whip sparingly but strategically, reward bondsmen with time off, permit them to sell homegrown produce at the local market and keep the profits, and bestow gifts at holidays and other special occasions.

The master's ability to sell the slave loomed as the slave's greatest terror. The domestic slave trade broke hearts and families; a slave could expect to be sold at least once during his lifetime. Circumstances such as a sudden economic reverse, the division of an estate among heirs, or migration to another state undermined even the best-intentioned master's resolve never to sunder families. Especially rebellious slaves, runaways, and chronic malingerers could also expect to be sold. The threat of the auction block weighed more heavily on Africans than the threat of the lash.

No anguish was more heartrending than that of a mother whose child was sold away from her. "Oh, my heart was too full!" recalled Charity Bowery on being told that her boy, Richard, was sold. "[My mistress] had sent me away on an errand, because she didn't want to be troubled with our cries. I hadn't any chance to see my poor boy. I shall never see my poor boy. I shall never see him again in this world. My heart felt as if it was under a great load."[1]

At the end of the Civil War, Union soldiers in the occupied South told of roads clogged with former slaves streaming in both directions. Observers initially attributed the migration to a wanderlust born of slavery's confinement; in fact, the travelers were simply looking for their lost families, for children sold away unexpectedly, for fathers, mothers, husbands, and wives taken to the Deep South to work on plantations or in towns and maybe to start new families, or grieve forever for the ones they had left behind.

As heartbreaking as such occurrences were—and they were more common than not—slaves could do little overtly to combat the system. They recognized the futility of open rebellion. A rebellious slave was a slave sold; for those who refused to reform, a more drastic fate awaited. Richard Bowery's master sold him for his defiance; his new owner in Alabama could not break Richard's will either. When his Alabama master threatened to shoot him if he did not consent to being whipped, Richard replied, "Shoot away, I won't come to be flogged." The master shot and killed him.

For the most part, slaves engaged in small rebellions rather than in large-scale uprisings or massive flight; they saw that whites had the guns, and except in a few districts, whites outnumbered blacks. These factors, as well as the absence of large jungle areas (into which South American slaves sometimes fled) and the distance of mountain hideaways to which slaves could escape, discouraged running away. There were other outlets for expressing discontent that were considerably less dangerous than open rebellion or flight. Taking the master's property was common on plantations, and slaves justified the thievery as merely appropriating the food or material possessions that they had worked for. Withholding or reducing the pace of work, feigning illness, and sabotaging the master's property were other means to alert masters that their charges were not content with their lot.

Still, these were minor annoyances to the master in the larger scheme of things. What gave slaves the will to proceed from day to day and year to year were the lives they fashioned in the quarters: away from white surveillance and in the presence of the love of their families. Their adopted religion, Christianity, provided further solace. Blacks maintained a rich oral tradition in which folktales, such as those based on Brer Rabbit, enabled them to mock powerful whites by identifying themselves with apparently defenseless animals who used wit and cunning to outsmart their stronger enemies. But these were strategies of survival, not existence. There was no substitute for freedom, for owning one's life and labor.

A minority of southern whites owned slaves, never more than one out of four white families in the nineteenth century. Yet the slave regime attained the support of the vast majority of whites, slaveholders or no. Why? Regardless of their social or economic status, whites in the Old South shared one characteristic spread equally across their race: they were not black. In a society where slavery was racial, blackness meant servitude; whiteness, independence. Being white automatically conferred superior status. And whites, regardless of station, guarded their independence fiercely; to lose independence was to slip toward slavery. The set of social rules surrounding the concept of "honor" guarded against such loss. Calling a man a liar, for example, attacked not only his integrity (honor was almost always a male concept), but his status as an equal as well. Inferiority was a badge of slavery, and a white man could not be a slave, so the attack had to be avenged.

Many northerners were aghast when South Carolina congressman Preston Brooks bashed Charles Sumner with a cane as the Massachusetts senator sat at his desk in the Capitol in May 1856. But southerners understood and lauded Brooks for avenging Sumner's verbal attack on Brooks's older cousin, Senator Andrew P. Butler. Butler had a speech difficulty that caused him to drool or spit as he talked. Sumner had mocked Butler's impediment, holding him up to ridicule. To Brooks, Sumner's behavior was not only bad manners, it clearly implied his superiority over the South Carolinian. The South showered Brooks with new canes, and the North hurled volumes of epithets at the offended younger cousin.

Slavery reached far beyond the plantation to affect social relations among whites and bind all whites together. Through this bond, the nonslaveholding white gained a stake in slavery; if he became fortunate enough to earn sufficient money, he and his family might someday own a slave or two themselves. Also, without slavery, as slaveholders often pointed out, the average southern white would be a farm laborer, not a farm owner. Slave owners actively engaged their nonslaveholding neighbors in protecting the institution, enlisting them to serve in slave patrols that fanned out into the countryside hunting down runaways or rounding up slaves out illegally after dark. Blacks learned early in their lives that they could trust few whites, and whites learned from early childhood that they were a master race ordained to control and direct blacks.

Not all whites supported slavery and slaveholding. There existed a small and quiet group of southern whites—Quakers, mountain folk, and some wealthy eccentrics—who prayed for slavery's abolition but would rarely dare to divulge their thoughts publicly. In 1857 North Carolinian Hinton Rowan Helper penned a scathing indictment of slavery's negative economic impact on the South, *The Impending Crisis*, noting especially how it hurt average whites. But Helper was more widely read in the North than in his native region.

It is not entirely correct to see the Old South in the stark terms of black and white. There were shades of color reflecting the sometimes intimate relations between the two races. Sex was closely connected with race, and since race relations derived from the master's power and the slave's weakness, sex was often imposed on slave women. Not all sex between masters and slaves was coerced; some genuinely affectionate and loving relationships evolved, but these were exceptions.

Through much of the first half of the nineteenth century, the Old South was a raw frontier society. Parts of the Lower South states of Alabama, Mississippi, and Louisiana did not open to white settlement until after 1830. Slavery established a racial and gender hierarchy that put black and white, and men and women, in their respective places, and supported a system of honor that governed social relationships with an elaborate etiquette that moderated frontier life. The manners and grace visitors encountered in the South before the Civil War were essential to holding society together, and, like slavery, they reflected the racial and gender hierarchies of southern society.[2]

The Civil War ended both slavery and the order derived from that institution. White men spent much of the next century attempting to restore the racial and gender hierarchy that existed in the South before 1861. Whites could not, of course, reenslave blacks, but they could devise new institutions that would limit the freedom of former slaves and ensure white supremacy.

White southerners lost the war, but they rebelled at losing their superiority over blacks. The Reconstruction era boiled down to a battle over who would rule blacks and under what terms, and who would rule the South. White southerners won in both cases, and in the process of "redeeming" the South from Yankee rule and black ruin, they concocted another heroic chapter in the book of the Lost Cause to bequeath to future generations. The chapter, borrowing liberally from the antebellum rationalizations of slavery, read something like this: blacks, unleashed from the restraints of bondage, relapsed into the barbarism of their ancestors. Federal Reconstruction policies abetted this anarchy until white southerners rose up to save themselves and their civilization: the South Redeemed.

Not all southern whites felt this way. Some welcomed the demise of slavery, an institution they blamed for the destructive war, the planters' domination of political and economic life, and the South's economic weakness. They were willing to grant limited equality to the freedmen. But history overwhelmed them.

Fluid Dynamics

The race issue would not rest, however. Violence and appeals to white solidarity caught up the white South in the vicious vortex of racism. Fealty to race became allegiance to God and country, and above all to the memory of those who fought so bravely for the Lost Cause. The South could not change the verdict of history, but its people could alter its meaning. And the Reconstruction that began so auspiciously for southern blacks turned to Redemption for southern whites. The observation of W. E. B. Du Bois on the situation of southern blacks in 1877 is accurate: "The slave went free; stood a brief moment in the sun; then moved back again toward slavery."[3] History, at least the history written and remembered by white southerners, trivialized blacks' aspirations and condemned their efforts. History provided the foundation for white supremacy over the next century, justifying racial segregation, disfranchisement, lynching, and the erosion of economic and civil rights.

History and how it is remembered cannot totally ground the human spirit. No sooner had the victory of Redemption seemed secure than signs appeared that it was not. During the 1870s and 1880s, despite intimidation and mounting restrictions, race relations remained remarkably fluid in the South. To some extent, this reflected the political situation. Though the Democrats redeemed the South by 1876, Republicans and other political factions continued to challenge the dominant party well into the 1890s. Some blacks continued to vote and hold office, and even a few Democrats courted black voters. Segregation notwithstanding, blacks and whites continued to mingle in public places, do business with each other, and maintain cordial relations on occasion. And some blacks prospered.

In North Carolina, for example, black land ownership increased after Reconstruction as African American families accumulated savings earned from the end of the Civil War and used their nest eggs for down payments on land. By the end of the nineteenth century, black landlords were no longer an oddity. In fact, between 1905 and 1915, black-owned farm acreage statewide rose by 26.4 percent, compared with only .2 percent for whites. Despite these gains, impressive for a people only a generation removed from bondage, rural home ownership by blacks continued to lag well behind the figures for whites. Though 26.2 percent of black heads of household on farms owned their own homes in 1890, and 32.1 percent did so by 1910, the corresponding white figure at that latter date was 66.6 percent.[4]

In the cities, where greater economic opportunities beckoned, North Carolina's black population enjoyed more success. There, black home ownership increased from 15.1 percent in 1890 to 25.8 percent in 1910, considerably closer to the white figure of 37.8 percent. Also in cities, though African

Americans would have preferred greater integration into white society, the emergence of Jim Crow in the urban South actually enhanced black capitalism. In North Carolina this was especially so in the rapidly advancing cities of the Piedmont, such as Durham, Raleigh, Winston-Salem, Greensboro, and Charlotte. Blacks even made inroads into businesses once exclusively controlled by whites. In Winston-Salem, for example, all of that city's twenty general-merchandise firms were owned by whites in 1905; by 1915 there were thirty-seven such firms, five of which were owned by black businessmen. Whites ran all six of Greensboro's hotels in 1905; by 1915 the city boasted nine hotels, and blacks owned two. Durham was a hub of black enterprise, housing as it did the most successful black business in the country, the North Carolina Mutual Life Insurance Company, founded in 1899. By 1925 black sociologist E. Franklin Frazier crowned the city the "Capital of the Black Middle Class."[5]

A few black entrepreneurs catered to a white clientele, such as in the traditionally black service of barbering. John Merrick, who would go on to found North Carolina Mutual from the profits of his barber shop, recognized the tightrope that a successful black businessman must walk when operating in a white community: he could never appear to relish success, much less display it, and must always assume an etiquette that played to white preconceptions of deference and humility. When Merrick took out an ad for his shop in 1900, for example, he noted that the shop was sterilized, "Negro and all."[6]

Most black businesses were service-oriented enterprises requiring low capitalization. The failure rate was high, and periodic economic depressions and the lower consumer spending base of their clientele further hampered the health of black-owned businesses. All the more impressive was how many survived, and even prospered.

Progress was apparent among working-class blacks as well. During the 1880s African Americans joined interracial unions and continued their activities in the Republican Party. They engaged in business with whites. In the countryside, blacks and whites hunted and fished together, worked side by side at sawmills, and traded with each other. In the cities, blacks and whites sometimes lived in the same neighborhoods. To be sure, blacks faced discrimination in employment and voting and suffered random retaliation for perceived violations of racial etiquette. But race relations were by no means fixed in the South.

In 1885 T. McCants Stewart, a black newspaperman from New York, traveled to his native South Carolina expecting rough reception once his train passed south of Washington, D.C. To his surprise, the conductor allowed him to remain in his seat while whites sat on baggage or stood. His entry into the dining car caused little notice among whites, some of whom struck up a conversation. Stewart, who admitted he had begun his journey with "a chip on my shoulder . . . dar[ing] any man to knock it off," now observed that "whites of the South are really less afraid to [have] contact with colored people than the whites of the North." Once in Columbia, South Carolina, Stewart reported his ease of movement through the city. "I can ride in first-class cars. . . . I can go into saloons and get refreshments even as in New York. I can stop in and drink a glass of soda and be more politely waited upon than in some parts of New England."[7] Other blacks corroborated Stewart's experiences of the fluidity of race relations in the years after Redemption.

The lack of certainty about race disturbed many whites, however. A new generation of white men, the first post–Civil War generation, came of age in the South during the 1890s. Unlike their fathers and grandfathers, they had not fought heroic battles, made supreme sacrifices, or redeemed a prostrate region from Yankee and black rule. They had learned these stories from childhood, and this received knowledge became indelible memory. They grew up in the shadow of giants—heroes and Redeemers. The results of these great deeds seemed less secure with each passing year: the Democratic Party, the purity of white women, and the submission of the black race all appeared in jeopardy. Bread and land were taking precedence over white solidarity and threatening the Democratic Party. White and black farmers, pressed by debt, railroad monopolies, and lawmakers who refused to hear their cries for help, joined the Populist Party and challenged Democratic candidates. White women, in whose name white men justified some of the violent excesses of the Reconstruction era and whose honor they had defended during the war, seemed less content with submissive roles as they founded organizations, spoke out on a variety of issues, and pushed against the prevailing notions of gender.

The fact that former slaves refused to submit quietly to their inferior status incensed and alarmed whites most of all. Blacks built lives and careers, held property, and maintained a political voice. A new generation of blacks was emerging: the first generation of freedom. The parents of this new generation had won the battle for liberty; now it was their children's turn to secure the benefits freedom promised. As the young black editor of Nashville's *Fisk Herald* proclaimed in 1889, "We are not the Negro from whom the chains of slavery fell a quarter of a century ago. . . . We are now qualified, and being the equal of whites, should be treated as such."⁸ The dreams of the Reconstruction era may have been denied to their parents, but young blacks refused to accept a servile role in southern society without a contest.

Redeemed, Again

Whites responded forcefully to the assertiveness of the new generation of blacks. They pointed to African Americans like Joseph Charles Price, an educator from North Carolina, who admonished colleagues in 1890 in a tone strikingly similar to the rhetoric of young white men of that era: "If we do not possess the manhood and patriotism to stand up in the defense of . . . constitutional rights and protest long, loud and unitedly against their continual infringements, we are unworthy of heritage as American citizens and deserve to have fastened on us the wrongs of which many are disposed to complain." David Schenck, a Greensboro, North Carolina businessman, spoke for many young whites of his generation in 1890 when he noted that "the breach between the races widens as the young free negroes grow up and intrude themselves on white society and nothing prevents the white people of the South from annihilating the negro race but the military power of the United States Government." Schenck did not endorse annihilation, but concluded, "I pity the Negro, but the struggle is for the survival of the fittest race." At a time when Darwinian metaphors were common throughout society, the implication was that blacks would either toe the color line or disappear from the face of the earth, or at least from the South.⁹

When white Democrats took the stump in the 1890s, they proudly recounted the battles of Reconstruction, flaunting terrorism as a badge of honor both to reaffirm their manhood and to warn against those who would break white solidarity. Places such as Hamburg, South Carolina, and Colfax, Louisiana, where white terrorists murdered opponents or overthrew elected governments, joined the sacred company of Gettysburg and Shiloh. South Carolina Democrat Ben Tillman rode to the State House and later to four terms in the U.S. Senate recounting the Redemption and warning of its fragile legacy. He proudly and openly detailed his participation in the violence at Hamburg in Edgefield County in July 1876 to suppress the black and white Republican vote in statewide elections. "The leading white men of Edgefield," Tillman related, had decided "to seize the first opportunity that the Negroes might offer them to provoke a riot and teach the Negroes a lesson" by "having the whites demonstrate their superiority by killing as many of them as was justifiable."[10]

By keeping the memory of Redemption alive, Tillman kept the state of crisis vivid for the white South. In the 1890s, no less than the 1870s, courageous white men would defend southern honor and take charge. Down with "white negroes," as he called his political opponents. He declared in 1892 that he would "willingly lead a mob in lynching a negro who had committed an assault upon a white woman." The black man, he intoned, "must remain subordinate or be exterminated." Lynchings outnumbered legal executions in South Carolina during the 1890s. Tillman craftily drew together white supremacy and patriarchy, promoting himself as the "Champion of White Men's Rule and Woman's Virtue," and anyone who disagreed challenged not only Tillman but the foundations of southern society.[11]

White southerners intended to secure what their fathers and grandfathers had fought to win. Their legacy to future generations of southerners was a series of political, social, and economic statutes that protected and elevated white supremacy from custom to code. Security was the major thrust of their efforts: to make white women secure from black men; to make white men secure from black economic competition; to make the Democratic Party secure from challenges to its political dominance; and to make whites secure in their supremacy over blacks.

Whites had targeted black political power since the day the Civil War ended, initially through violence and intimidation and later more subtly through legislation. In 1877 North Carolina replaced direct election of county officials with appointments by the state legislature. That same year, the state's lawmakers redrew district lines in cities with large black populations, either concentrating all black voters in one district or dispersing those voters throughout the locality. Centralizing electoral procedures, the North Carolina legislature stacked the state board of elections with sympathetic members who appointed local registrars to impede black registration.[12]

Despite these and other obstacles to voting, blacks continued to cast ballots in North Carolina and elsewhere in the South. In North Carolina, black voters and Republicans staged a political comeback in the mid-1890s, fusing with Populists to challenge Democratic supremacy in the state. The success of the Fusionists prompted Democrats to launch a vicious race-baiting campaign accompanied by violence and triggering the Wilmington race riot in 1898, which overthrew the city's legally constituted government. An editorial in the Charlotte *Observer* blared, "The Anglo Saxon Must Rule." Charles

Brantley Aycock, a young railroad lawyer who would become governor in 1900, told Charlotte audiences that he came "to unite the white people against the negroes, an infamous race." And the Charlotte *News* resorted to poetry to get the point across: "Shall low-born scum and quondam slaves / Give laws to those who own the soil? / No! By our grandsire's bloody graves, / No! By our homesteads bought with toil."

As the 1900 election approached, an election that would reframe the state constitution and disfranchise black voters, "phalanxes of red-shirted marchers, representing 'the best men,' " marched for white supremacy through downtown Charlotte. When the results showed a smashing victory for the Democrats, the Charlotte *Observer* crowed that the "bank men, mill men, and the business men in general—the backbone of the property interest in the State—worked from start to finish and furthermore they spent large bits of money in behalf of the cause. Their opinion must be respected."[13]

Through the next century, white leaders would tell outsiders that only they, the "best men," averted a certain race war in the South. Disfranchisement and Jim Crow, they argued, separated the "lower orders" of whites from blacks, thereby ensuring the peace and prosperity of the region. In truth, white leaders often encouraged violence and used race hatred unabashedly to gain and maintain political and economic power.[14]

Democratic leaders enacted a variety of measures to restore or secure their power. Disfranchisement became a key strategy to that end. To get around the Fifteenth Amendment to the Constitution, which guaranteed every U.S. citizen the right to vote, they employed subterfuges rather than outright prohibition. They complicated the registration and voting processes. States established poll taxes requiring citizens to pay to vote, adopted the secret ballot, which confused illiterate blacks accustomed to using ballots whose color designated the party, set literacy and educational qualifications or required prospective registrants to "interpret" a section of the state constitution, and enacted standards few blacks could fulfill, such as limiting registration to those whose grandfathers had voted. Most grandfathers of black men in the 1890s had been slaves and therefore ineligible to vote.

Laws granted registrars wide latitude in interpreting the accuracy of a prospective voter's understanding of the state constitution. When a journalist asked an Alabama lawmaker if Jesus Christ could pass his state's "understanding" test, the legislator replied, "That would depend entirely on which way he was going to vote."[15] Lawmakers sold white masses on franchise restrictions with the understanding that the measures applied only to blacks, and that their removal from the electoral process would eliminate fraud and corruption.

The voting laws in southern states did indeed limit political corruption, but they also limited voting; turnout dropped dramatically. In Mississippi, for example, voter participation in gubernatorial races during the 1880s averaged 51 percent; during the 1890s the figure dropped to 21 percent. The black turnout in Mississippi averaged 39 percent in the 1880s; it plummeted to near zero in the 1890s.[16]

African Americans attacked disfranchisement. When 160 South Carolina delegates gathered to amend the state constitution in 1895, the six blacks among them mounted a passionate defense of their right to vote. Black delegate W. J. Whipper noted the irony of the clamor for white supremacy at a time when whites held almost all the state's elected offices. He also pointed out that when African Americans formed the majority of voters, they voted with restraint and dignity and frequently elected white candidates. Whipper's appeal failed to move white delegates.[17]

Historians and political scientists have presented the one-party South that reigned from the 1890s to the 1950s as the dominance of rural white elites over their more progressive brethren in the cities. It is true that in most southern states these rural elites, often in heavily black counties, held disproportionate power in the state legislature. State leaders often thrilled their rural constituents with blather about city slickers. Georgia governor Eugene Talmadge was fond of inviting his country backers to Atlanta: "Come see me at the mansion. We'll sit on the front porch and piss over the rail on those city bastards." But neither Talmadge nor any other southern political leader translated antiurban rhetoric into a coherent policy directed against cities. For in the cities, as the Wilmington race riot indicated, they found numerous soul mates in their desire to maintain white supremacy and one-party rule.[18]

Cynicism abounded in the southern political system. A weary Pat Harrison, Democratic senator from Mississippi, capable of better things but tied to the idolatry of white supremacy for his political fortune, related to a New York *Times* reporter from Mississippi that he could be a statesman for five years, but during the sixth—an election year—he went back home to "sling the shit."[19]

Race-baiting became the tried-and-true method of maintaining political office, of solidifying, seducing, or silencing any white opposition and, not incidentally, cowing the black population. As one Deep South senator explained in the mid-1950s, "Give me another issue I can run and be sure of winning out in the counties, and I'll drop the nigger question."[20] Political leaders recognized that white supremacy had an inherent psychological rush for poor whites. Whatever their station, they possessed the South's greatest gift: whiteness. Lillian Smith, a Georgia-born writer and activist for racial justice in the 1940s and '50s, summarized the feeling:

> To be "superior" to be the "best people on earth" with the best "system" of making a living, because your sallow skin was white and you were "Anglo-Saxon," made you forget that you were eaten up with malaria and hookworm, made you forget that you lived in a shanty and ate potlikker and corn bread, and worked long hours for nothing. Nobody could take away from you this whiteness that made you and your way of life "superior." They could take your house, your job, your fun; they could steal your wages, keep you from acquiring knowledge; they could tax your vote or cheat you out of it; they could by arousing your anxieties make you important; but they could not strip your white skin off of you. It became the poor white's most precious possession, a charm staving off utter dissolution. And in devious, perverse ways it helped maintain his sanity in an insane world, compensating him—as did his church's promise of heaven—for so many spiritual bruises and material deprivations.[21]

Purveying the message of white supremacy became one of the few forms of entertainment, aside from religious revivals, in rural areas, where the balance of southern political power resided. Folks came to hear and see a good show and eat and drink at the candidate's expense. They did not come for issues; they did not much care whether these leaders improved their condition, because many believed they were doing fine, and if they were not, they would receive rewards in the great by-and-by. The advice that Jack Burden offered to Louisiana's novice gubernatorial candidate, Willie Stark, in Robert Penn Warren's novel *All the King's Men* (1946), was well taken:

> Hell, make 'em cry, or make 'em laugh, make 'em think you're their weak and erring pal, or make 'em think you're God Almighty. Or make 'em mad. Even mad at you. Just stir 'em up, it doesn't matter how or why, and they'll love you and come back for more. Pinch 'em in the soft place. . . . Hell, their wives have lost their teeth and their shape, and likker won't set on their stomachs, and they don't believe in God, so it's up to you to give 'em something to stir 'em up and make 'em feel alive again. Just for half an hour. That's what they come for. Tell 'em anything. But for Sweet Jesus' sake don't try to improve their minds.[22]

Followers of such advice made good stump speakers but lousy leaders. The highly personalized political process, characteristic of a one-party system, produced an array of colorful characters, to be sure: South Carolina's one-eyed senator, "Pitchfork" Ben Tillman; the "Wild Ass of the Ozarks," Arkansas senator Jeff Davis; the Texas gubernatorial duo of "Ma" and "Pa" Ferguson, the former serving in the state house while the latter served in the state penitentiary; Mississippi's James K. Vardaman, the "White Chief" who campaigned in a white linen suit to offset his shoulder-length black hair; his successor in Mississippi, Theodore "the Man" Bilbo, whose plan for black disfranchisement was to "visit" potential black voters on the night before the election; Alabama's "Kissin' Jim" Folsom, who toured the state with his "Strawberry Pickers" band and a big mop and wash bucket, vowing to sweep the "vermints" out of Montgomery; and the irrepressible Long family of Louisiana, with Huey crying "Every Man a King!" and brother Earl escaping in his pajamas from a mental institution in Houston to resume his duties as governor.[23]

The rollicking nature of southern politics, which straddled an uneasy line between good humor and buffoonery, also had a more serious side. When the entertainers took office and their audiences disappeared, they were often unable or unwilling to address the numerous problems confronting their districts or states. As a legacy of Redemption, governors frequently were weaker than their legislatures, and the legislatures consisted of part-time politicians and full-time lobbyists for the banking industry, public utilities, legal profession, insurance companies, soybean growers, tobacco manufacturers, and the like. Given the one-party system and the power of incumbency, there was little incentive for lawmakers to pay attention to individual citizens in distress, many of whom were black and could not vote in any case. As political scientist V.O. Key Jr. summarized the situation: "The cold hard fact is that the South as a whole has developed no system or practice of political organization and leadership adequate to cope with its problems."[24]

White supremacy was an issue that took the South nowhere but its leaders everywhere. Race became such a staple of southern politics that when, in the 1930s, the national Democratic Party initiated overtures to historically Republican blacks, particularly those who had moved north during the Great Migration after 1915, southern political leaders protested vehemently. When South Carolina senator Ellison D. "Cotton Ed" Smith walked into the 1936 national Democratic Party convention and saw a black minister offering the invocation, he exclaimed, "My God, he's black as melted midnight!" When a black congressman mounted the podium some time later, it was too much for Cotton Ed, and he departed for South Carolina.[25]

For some southern Democrats, the changes in their national party in the 1930s evoked remembrances of Reconstruction and the unholy Republican alliance between blacks and émigré whites. As Virginia senator Carter Glass noted in 1938, the South had better "begin thinking whether it will continue to cast its 152 electoral votes according to the memories of the Reconstruction era of 1865 and thereafter, or will have spirit and courage enough to face the new Reconstruction era that northern so-called Democrats are menacing us with." In a portent of the future, a disgruntled southern Democratic leader informed a *Fortune* magazine reporter touring the South in 1943, "If the Republican party would come out on the issue of white supremacy, it would sweep the South." So strong was the attachment to Negro politics that southern political leaders would even abandon the party of Redemption to maintain its political integrity. All of this led V. O. Key Jr. to pen a concise and apt summary of southern politics during the first half of the twentieth century: "In its grand outlines the politics of the South revolves around the position of the Negro."[26]

Along with exiling blacks from southern politics, whites circumscribed their neighbors from most every other notable participation in regional life. Segregation had existed as a more or less informal separation of the races, North and South, since the Civil War. New generations of blacks and whites and the political turmoil of the 1890s prompted a more formal arrangement. The growth of southern cities and the appearance of new technologies such as the electric streetcar and the elevator brought the races into closer physical contact with each other. The expansion of railroad travel in the South had the same effect.

Exile

The railroad was a symbol of modernity and mobility in the New South. Railroads also increased the potential for interracial contact between black men and white women. Blacks' presence in dining cars and in first-class compartments implied for whites an assertion of economic and social equality. Southern blacks, on the other hand, viewed equitable railroad travel as another step toward fuller participation in national life. When state legislatures initiated segregation on railroads, African Americans protested.

In 1890 Homer Plessy, a Louisiana black, refused to leave the first-class car of a railroad traveling through the state. After he was arrested, he filed suit, arguing that his payment of the first-class fare entitled him to sit in the same first-class accommodations as whites. He claimed that under his right of citizenship guaranteed by the Fourteenth Amendment, neither the state of Louisiana nor the railroad could discriminate against him on the basis of color. The Constitution, in effect, was color-blind.

The U.S. Supreme Court ruled on *Plessy v. Ferguson* in 1896. In a seven-to-one decision, the Court held that segregation laws did not violate the Constitution as long as the railroad or the state provided equal accommodations. What constituted "equal" remained unclear. More important, in the Court's view, "legislation is powerless to eradicate racial instincts," meaning that segregation of the races was "natural" and overrode constitutional considerations. Justice John Marshall Harlan, a Kentuckian and former slave owner, was the lone dissenter. "The destinies of the two races . . . are indissolubly linked together," Harlan declared, "and the interests of both require that the common government of all shall not permit the seeds of race hate to be planted under the sanction of law."[27]

Harlan's dissent was prophetic. The decision encouraged states to enact new segregation laws. In practice, separate facilities (if they existed at all) were rarely equal. A sense of futility, time, expense, and physical danger dissuaded blacks from challenging segregation statutes. By 1900 segregation by law extended to public conveyances, theaters, hotels, restaurants, parks, and schools.

Collectively, these statutes became known as Jim Crow Laws. Jim Crow was a stage persona of Thomas Rice, a northern white minstrel-show performer in the 1820s. Rice depicted Crow as an elderly, lame slave whose murdering of the English language and foolish antics were very popular with white audiences. The Crow character proved so successful for Rice that he changed his name to Jim Crow Rice. The association of Jim Crow with racial segregation reflected popular white stereotypes of blacks.

Economic segregation followed social segregation. Black competition for jobs in towns and cities and their success in various crafts and professions motivated whites to isolate African Americans on the job as they had in schools and public accommodations. After the war blacks entered factory work and occasionally joined white workers to organize against management.

The Knights of Labor, an ill-fated conglomeration of workers and managers from a wide range of enterprises (too wide, as it turned out), enjoyed a spurt of growth and popularity during the 1880s after successes in achieving wage and hour concessions from management in several localities. While the

Knights did not necessarily set out to challenge southern racial traditions, they did not entirely succumb to them, either. They hosted an interracial national convention in Richmond in 1886, and the local white press attempted to stir up indignation. A reporter wrote that black men and women mingled freely, that he witnessed "a bright mulatto girl talking and laughing with a white man" as well as a "colored girl and a white man chatting, the man holding or playing with the girl's hand." Governor Fitzhugh Lee attended and spoke at the opening session, sharing the stage with an African American delegate from New York who introduced the governor. Though the press played up Lee's alleged discomfort, apparently the governor had no such feeling.[28]

The press succeeded in generating sufficient outrage, alleging that as a result of the Knights' stance on race, blacks now viewed themselves as "white man's brudders" and consequently engaged in "race mixing" and "social equality" throughout the two-week meeting. White workers weakened under the pressure and resigned from the Knights; the brief moment of interracial unionism perished. Periodically through the next century, blacks and whites would get together in interracial unions in the steel industry, coal mining, and timbering, achieving a few successes but generally failing to sustain a partnership that would have benefited both.[29]

By the 1890s southern whites were replacing African Americans in some of these trades, anyway, and excluding them from new categories of jobs, such as plumbing and electrical work. Trade unions, composed primarily of craftworkers, excluded African Americans. Although blacks secured employment in the steel and tobacco industries, most employers held that blacks were unfit for manufacturing work. Blacks found themselves increasingly in low- or unskilled positions in railroad construction, lumber camps, and agricultural labor. The new generation of blacks in the 1890s experienced a general "deskilling," or loss of skills, compared to their fathers. Lower incomes from unskilled labor in turn reduced opportunities for better housing and education.

Regardless of where blacks turned in the 1890s, another right, another opportunity, disappeared, all under the cloak of law, though even these measures never totally eliminated meaningful relations between white and black southerners. Humanity occasionally won out over historical artifice. Black and white workers' lives intersected at several points, on the street, in bars, and even in neighborhoods. There were also acts of interracial kindness. Though the paternalism of the plantation and its attendant protection dissipated somewhat in the New South, some white men still felt a sense of noblesse oblige, especially if blacks were willing to assume and maintain an appropriately subservient position. Sometimes these protective relationships could be the difference between life and death. During the bloody Atlanta race riot of 1906, several white employers rushed to their businesses to protect their black workers. Though they obviously had an economic stake in their work force, some of their actions evinced great courage. A white stable owner, for example, saved the lives of two black workers by standing down a mob with a shotgun and "great presence of mind."[30]

There were also less-public displays of interracial kindness: the white librarian who discreetly loaned books to black youngsters; the white political leader who vouched for a black man to a banker; the white woman who brought food to a black family with sick children—these simple acts of compassion occurred throughout the South. Call them paternalistic or even self-serving, but they indicated at least a hint of recognition and understanding that there existed a shared humanity, or at least a shared sense of place, between black and white southerners—that all was not lost behind the legislation, the etiquette, and the perspective of history that enforced the humiliation of one race and the separation of both.

The initiative had to come from the white southerner; the black southerner was an enemy in his own land, such a visible reminder of a tragic history that the white South sought to make him invisible. Perhaps with a sense of irony, some blacks drew the connection between themselves and the defeated Confederates. Black leader Walter White felt that growing up in Atlanta at the turn of the twentieth century he "was . . . part of a history which opposed the good, the just, and the enlightened. I was a Persian, falling before the hordes of Alexander . . . a Confederate at Vicksburg. I was defeated, wherever and whenever there was a defeat."[31]

Black southerners experienced a virtual exile in their own land, forced to play a role to assuage the historical consciousness of the dominant race and take cues from that race lest a false step would remind whites of black humanity and, therefore, of the rotting structure of their past. "The Negro," Du Bois wrote, has a "double consciousness, this sense of always looking at one's self through the eyes of others, of measuring one's soul by the tape of a world that looks on in an amused contempt and pity."[32]

Black southerners learned to become multilingual, to speak the language their white neighbors wanted to hear. They developed a sixth sense that was more than merely functional. The status of blacks meant nothing, and in some cases, behavior of well-to-do blacks had to be more circumspect and staged than that of other segments of African American society, for if blacks generally offered daily reminders of a charred history, then successful blacks demonstrated the lie of white supremacy writ bold. So when C. C. Spaulding, head of North Carolina Mutual and one of the wealthiest black citizens in the United States, sat down in the whites-only section of a Raleigh soda fountain to drink a Coke in 1931, his eminence offered no protection, and he received a brutal beating for his audacity. The average southern white rarely made racial distinctions beyond "good niggers" and "bad niggers," with social status and middle-class values as irrelevant as Druid theology in a Baptist Sunday School class. Good blacks were the ones who minded the racial etiquette and remained in their place; bad blacks challenged the racial status quo, appeared to lust after white women, or deigned to demonstrate ambition.[33]

Southern black leader Booker T. Washington got it mostly wrong when at an Atlanta exposition in 1895 he summoned African Americans to acknowledge and submit to segregation and disfranchisement in exchange for white assistance in gaining educational opportunities and securing job training. His educational mission trained blacks for jobs no longer open to them, or for a life in the countryside, where a depressed agricultural economy and growing racial violence offered little prospect for advancement. Most important, success did not lead to acceptance by the white community; to the contrary, it often led to trouble. Yet Washington's program was probably the best of sorry options open to southern blacks at the turn of the twentieth century.

Even if black southerners adhered to the etiquette and remained dutifully subservient, there were no guarantees that they would escape punishment. Brutality came easier if the dominant race dehumanized their victims. It was not only that the etiquette of white supremacy required a caricature instead of a person, but the cartoons of the era emphasized beastlike characteristics in blacks, such as large lips, narrow head, long arms, and stooped shoulders. Blacks were always perceived as impressionable and gullible. The popular literature played the same theme. Thomas Dixon claimed in his national best seller *The Clansman* (1905) that the assertiveness of blacks during Reconstruction did not occur spontaneously from their own design but from deceptive Yankees who taught the black southerner "to stand erect in the presence of his former master and assert his manhood."[34]

The tendency of whites to identify the African American as a type rather than as a person also held consequences with respect to law enforcement. Authorities rarely applied the standard of presumptive innocence to blacks. As an Atlanta police chief noted in 1900, to be "black was to be marked by fifty percent . . . of the guilt to begin with." Admitting that some black citizens were rounded up and falsely accused of a particular crime, he dismissed any notion of concern because "if the suspect was not guilty of a particular crime he was probably guilty of many other crimes for which he had never been . . . properly punished." And, after all, "one black man was as good as another to play the guilty part," and the broader objective of protecting the general welfare justified his arrest and incarceration.[35]

During times of racial tension, the strategic absence of law enforcement weighed as heavily on blacks as its omnipresence. The ad hoc remedy of lynching was sufficiently widespread to indelibly brand itself in the minds of southern blacks. Just as violence sped the end of Reconstruction, so it hastened the erosion of the remaining vestiges of black civil rights. The rise in lynching during the 1890s reflected the reluctance of blacks to submit quietly to the legislative assault on their rights. Some blacks refused to retreat to their place.

In 1892 three prominent black citizens of Memphis, Tom Moss, Calvin McDowell, and William Stewart, opened a grocery on the mostly black south side of Memphis. The People's Grocery prospered. Across the street, a white-owned grocery that had preceded People's in the neighborhood struggled. The competition, and the effrontery it implied, incensed white proprietor W. H. Barrett. He secured an indictment against his competitors for maintaining a public nuisance. Black community leaders met at the grocery to devise a response. A few at the meeting suggested physical retaliation against Barrett. Learning of the threat, the white grocer notified the police and boasted to the gathering at the People's Grocery that whites would destroy their store. Nine plainclothes sheriff's deputies, all white, approached the store to arrest those who had threatened Barrett. The occupants, unaware of the deputies' identities and fearing an assault, launched a fusillade of shots, wounding three officers. When the deputies identified themselves, thirty blacks surrendered, including Moss, McDowell, and Stewart, and the officers imprisoned them. Four days later, sheriff's deputies removed the three owners from the jail, took them to a deserted area, and shot them dead.[36]

During 1892, 235 racial lynchings (extralegal executions of blacks by whites) occurred in the South. Throughout the decade, whites lynched an average of 150 southern blacks per year. Between 1882 and 1903 whites lynched nearly 2,000 blacks. The men at the People's Grocery had violated two important rules of racial etiquette: they had prospered and they had challenged white authority. The white murderers came from working-class backgrounds and, unable to make a living on their farms, had recently moved to Memphis. This profile fit most lynchers: working-class whites with rural roots struggling in the depressed economy of the 1890s and enraged by the fluidity of urban race relations.[37]

White leaders condoned the orgy of violence through their silence or qualified disapproval. It seemed a cheap price to pay for white solidarity. In 1893 Atlanta's Methodist bishop, Atticus G. Haygood, objected to the torture some whites inflicted on their victims but added, "Unless assaults by Negroes on white women and little girls come to an end, there will most probably be still further displays of vengeance that will shock the world."[38] Yet the men of the People's Grocery had committed no sex crime, and of all the lynchings in the South in the thirty years after 1890, only a quarter had some attributable sexual connection. Sexual "crimes" included remarks, glances, or gestures blacks allegedly made to white women. Lynchers did not carry out their grisly crimes to end a rape epidemic. They killed to keep black men in their place and to restore their own sense of manhood and honor.

Ida B. Wells owned a black newspaper in Memphis and used her columns to publicize the People's Grocery lynchings. The great casualty of the lynchings, she noted, was her faith that education, wealth, and good morals guaranteed blacks the equality and justice they had long sought. The reverse was true. The more blacks succeeded, the greater their threat to whites. She investigated other lynchings and exposed the lie that black rape of white women caused and justified such violence. Suggesting that the attraction of some white women to black men accounted for part of the perceived interracial sexual epidemic, Wells enraged some white Memphians, who destroyed her press and office. Wells fled to Chicago, where she continued to work for racial justice.

The problem was that blacks persevered, and some even thrived. This rankled most of all. Black writer Charles Chesnutt, assessing the bloody race riot in Wilmington in 1898, wrote, "It was a veritable bed of Procrustes, this standard which the whites had set for the negroes. Those who grew above it must have their heads cut off . . . must be forced back to the level assigned to their race."[39]

Historians have noted how after the Civil War segregation represented an improvement over exclusion.[40] In truth, segregation was another form of exclusion—exclusion from a decent education, from public parks, from restaurants, from some theaters and from sections within other theaters, and from the clubs and churches that guided community life throughout the South. As with other elements of racial etiquette, segregation was never rigid and uniform. It was an evolving institution, an accompaniment of modernization that followed the urban and economic development of the region. Regardless of its variations, however, segregation emphasized the inferiority of black southerners.

The words "white" and "colored" now defined African American life in the South, words denoting not only separation but inferiority. The expenditure of funds and the effort to maintain this form of racial charade taxed a poor region. Separate water fountains, rest rooms, entrances, seating, eating facilities, schools, and even days to shop were among the more visible manifestations of segregation. In a southern town before World War II, it was easy to tell where the black neighborhood began and white district ended: the pavement ran out, housing codes went unenforced and dwellings looked more like out-of-place sharecropper shacks than urban residences, city services were sporadic if they existed at all, schools were ramshackle affairs stocked with third-generation hand-me-downs, and hospitals and parks were rare. Many of these districts occupied the lowest-lying areas of the city, where whites would not build; streets often flooded in rain storms. In Memphis, for example, blacks lived in neighborhoods with names such as "Slippery Log Bottoms," "Queen Bee Bottoms," and "Shinertown," indicating their disadvantaged topographical position.[41]

Behind the doors marked "white" and "colored" lay two different worlds, two different qualities of life, and two different opportunities for success. The landscape and etiquette of race spelled inferiority and humiliation on a daily basis. As black writer John Williams remarked, "Nothing is quite as humiliating, so murderously angering, as to know that because you are black you may have to walk a half mile further than whites just to urinate; that because you are black you have to receive your food through a window in the back of a restaurant or sit in a garbage-littered yard to eat."[42]

Reading, Writing, and Race

In the Orwellian world that emerged in the twentieth-century South, the perverse fantasy of white superiority and black inferiority spawned other absurdities. It was an interesting (and unique to the South) feature of southern Progressivism that the most vocal proponents of disfranchisement often wrapped themselves in the reformer's cloak, touting such measures as efficient government, urban beautification, and public-school reform. The last-named crusade was especially noteworthy in the South after 1900, as expenditures for public education soared. Charles Brantley Aycock, North Carolina's "education governor" and a staunch proponent of white supremacy, was among the region's leaders in urging lawmakers to fund education generously. And the South did so, outstripping the percentage increase in northern education expenditures between 1900 and 1930.[43]

Such growth masked a chilling reality: black youngsters fell further behind as black-white differentials in funding seriously hampered African American education. From 1900 onward, black and white school enrollment diverged considerably. In 1900 only 36 percent of black children in the South attended school, and 86 percent of those pupils attended school for less than six months a year. One reason for the poor attendance was the necessity and availability of employment for black children; in 1900, 49.3 percent of boys and 30.6 percent of girls between the ages of ten and fifteen were gainfully employed. A second reason for poor school attendance among black children was that they had fewer schools to attend. Even most cities in the South lacked high schools for blacks into the 1930s; as late as 1920, 95 percent of the South's black children did not attend high school. For elementary schools, only the intervention of northern-based foundations and the hard work and penny pinching of black families contributed significantly to school construction between 1910 and the 1930s. It was not until 1935 that a sufficient number of elementary schools existed in the South to accommodate a majority of the region's black children.[44]

The school construction program did not alleviate the burden of double taxation in the black community. Black taxpayers paid considerably more in taxes than they received in school funds; at the same time they donated money for the construction of black schools. The situation improved somewhat in the 1920s, as white leaders feared that abysmal educational opportunities for blacks, especially in the rural South, would result in labor lost either to southern cities or to the North. As one educator in East Feliciana Parish, Louisiana, noted in 1926, "The parish must provide better schools and longer terms or the exodus of Negroes will continue, perhaps at an increasing rate." The educator's concern did not result in significant improvements. He also noted another economic motive: the relatively high black population in the parish brought in an extra $20,000 in school funding from the state. Although the formula for funding was based on the total number of school-age children of both races, most of the money was expended on white children.[45]

That black education expenditures dropped drastically relative to expenditures for whites after 1900 reflected also the loss of black political power. Black leaders had long assumed a connection between economic well-being and access to the political process. Looking back on four decades of black political involvement and economic progress in 1906, the editor of the *Quarterly Review* of the A.M.E. Zion Church concluded, "All we have and are, came through politics, and it is too late in the day to try to curry favor with somebody by declaring the opposite of a recognized truth." Without decent public education, economic independence was much less likely.[46]

White leaders were not only stingy, they were following the strategy of white supremacy to maintain a dependent work force. In 1890, prior to disfranchisement, expenditures per white pupil exceeded expenditures per black by twofold in Louisiana; in 1910, whites received five and a half times more per pupil than did blacks. Ratios in Alabama were 1.01 to 1 in 1890 and 3.75 to 1 in 1910. Blacks attended school longer than whites in Louisiana in 1890, but in 1910 whites attended school twice as long as blacks during the academic year. In Alabama, the same pattern prevailed, with black children attending school several more days than whites in 1890, but whites reversed the trend, attending one and a third times longer than blacks in 1910.[47]

By the 1930s the disparities had become entrenched in these states. A survey of the 1933–34 school year in Alabama, Louisiana, and Texas revealed that the financial shortcomings and relative disparities in facilities had resulted in 40 percent of eligible white children attending classes compared to 10 percent of eligible black children in Alabama; a 57 percent to 14 percent disparity in Louisiana; and a 59 percent to 35 percent difference in Texas. Only Texas exceeded the southern average differential.[48]

A vicious cycle emerged: a struggling educational system, rife with racial and class distinctions, supported a struggling economy that did not require high educational attainment, which, in turn, justified maintaining rudimentary support for schools. The predominantly rural character of the South until after World War II contributed to the problem. Urban school systems fared better, reflecting the diversity of the economies that supported them. The relatively strong showing of the Texas educational system related to the state's position as the South's most urbanized state from the 1920s onward. Into the 1940s, the one-room school was still the landmark of the rural South, and taxation for the support of rural schools produced considerably lower revenues than amounts available in cities. In 1940 the South spent $26.63 per pupil in rural school districts compared to $46.51 for children in metropolitan counties.[49]

Despite the improvement of school expenditures and school systems, especially in the urban South during the first half of the twentieth century, the region's schools lagged far behind those in the rest of the nation. The ambivalence of white southern leaders toward formal education reflected contentious issues of race, class, and work, and demonstrated another area where the rendering of Civil War and Reconstruction history in the South burdened present and future generations of citizens. White supremacy came with significant costs, and not just for black southerners. The North's educational system supported a diverse economy. In the North education was a necessity; in the South some still considered it an unnecessary luxury. In the 1940s Georgia's governor, Eugene Talmadge, trivialized public education because "it ain't never taught a man to plant cotton." A study conducted during the early 1950s discovered that of every one hundred children entering the first grade in the South, little more than ten graduated from high school.[50]

These figures present an aggregate picture of southern education and its role in perpetuating a dependent economy, the out-migration of the South's best and brightest people, and racial and class disparities. Teacher training was nonexistent outside the cities. So-called eighth-grade scholars often taught rural black pupils, as few blacks advanced beyond that grade. And if they did, they immediately roused the suspicions of local whites: "Why you sending them any farther in school? They can be working here on the farm or they can help Miss So-and-So clean up the house." As black writer Anthony Walton concluded, "You realized that they didn't intend for you to do anything in life."[51]

Black schoolteachers, dealing with as many as two hundred pupils at a time, developed a militarylike rotation, mixing play, instruction, and book work. They used older pupils to help the younger ones. The building they taught in often doubled as a school while its main function, usually as a church, provided the furniture and sustenance for the educational mission. This was so especially in rural areas. Black writer Ernest J. Gaines described a classroom that hosted six grades in his Louisiana parish and was actually a one-room church. The church collection table served as the teacher's desk, and students sat on their knees and used the benches as desks to write upon. Though state law mandated a six-month school year, teachers in Louisiana's rural parishes rarely kept pupils beyond five months, from late October to mid-April, after which time they were needed in the fields.[52]

Even in cities, scholastic arrangements for blacks were likely to be ad hoc and inadequate. Black activist Angela Davis recalled that her elementary school in Birmingham, Alabama, during the late 1940s was actually a cluster of dilapidated wooden frame houses spread over a three-block area. Her history text, a castoff from white schools, referred to the Civil War as the "War for Southern Independence." Other nuggets of knowledge included the "fact" that blacks preferred slavery to freedom; evidence offered included the singing and dancing of slaves in the quarters on Saturday evening.

Davis was grateful for her teachers who taught her about Frederick Douglass, Sojourner Truth, and Harriet Tubman. A Negro History Week was established in her school, though the white school board made certain that the exploits of rebels Nat Turner and Denmark Vesey went unreported. Davis noted the unreality of black education; her teachers consistently preached the value of a strong work ethic and how education would "provide us with the skills and knowledge to lift ourselves singly and separately out of the muck and slime of poverty by our own bootstraps," how this child would become an engineer, that child an accountant, another child a lawyer, and so on. But the reality in Alabama, and in the whole South of that era, was that hard work only begat more hard work; if perseverance paid off, it was more than likely to be resented by the white community. The children could see that reality, and they could see the subservience of their teachers and administrators every time a prominent white person visited the school. "I could not understand," Davis relates, "why we had to behave better for them than we behaved for ourselves, unless we really did think they were superior." White supremacy had a knack for transforming innocuous behavior into mutual reinforcement of its principles.[53]

Yet black southerners made do; one of the remarkable aspects of "separate and unequal" through the first half of the twentieth century was how resourceful black southerners could be when confronting the realities of white supremacy, especially with respect to education. There were special teachers who refused to allow the prevailing wisdom and history of the region to defeat them or their children. Black journalist Carl T. Rowan recalled his high-school history teacher in Tennessee during the early 1940s, Miss Bessie. He balked at her efforts to have him speak correct English, fearful that the boys on the football team, which he desperately wanted to join, would make fun of him and question his manhood. She replied, "Do you know what *really* takes guts? Refusing to lower your standards to those of the dumb crowd. It takes guts to say to yourself that you've got to live and be somebody fifty years after these football games are over." Rowan relented and learned that he did not lose the respect of his buddies, and he graduated as the class valedictorian to boot.[54]

Miss Bessie performed other services for her students besides teaching them history and life lessons. Rowan noted that the town's only public library refused admittance to blacks. Miss Bessie, though, developed a tacit understanding with the white librarian, who smuggled books to her, which she shared with her class.[55] But whites limited the autonomy of Miss Bessie and all other black teachers and administrators. Living in a society that viewed education with ambivalence, and that identified open inquiry with the intrusion of alien and perhaps sacrilegious ideas, whites kept close surveillance on the business of black education. African American novelist Richard Wright recalled his surprise when, after preparing his valedictory address, his high-school principal provided a canned speech that the administrator had written. Wright went on to deliver his own speech but forever forfeited a place in the black leadership in his home town of Jackson, Mississippi, not to mention earning the hostility of local whites.[56]

Black southerners did not merely leave public education to their own initiatives and imaginations. As taxpayers, they pressed local authorities to improve black education even though as disfranchised citizens they could bring relatively little political pressure to bear on elected officials. In 1934, for example, black residents of Lynchburg protested the poor conditions at all-black Dunbar High School. Virginia was ahead of most southern states in providing high schools for blacks during the 1920s and 1930s, but Dunbar was one of only two black high schools in the state without a black principal. The school's white principal worked part time at Dunbar, as she held an assistant principalship at a nearby white elementary school. Dunbar, unlike the white schools, lacked a cafeteria, and its textbooks, according to the petitioners, included the "usual claptrap about shiftless Negroes" and statements about "Nordic supremacy." After four years of quiet but intense protest, Dunbar finally hired its first black principal, Clarence Seay, who would hold the post for the next thirty years. In 1940 the city council approved the construction of a new black elementary school and funded an expansion of Dunbar to relieve overcrowding. The council also voted to reduce the pay gap between black and white teachers.[57]

By the 1940s some white officials recognized the importance of at least a modicum of education for their black citizens as the New Deal and federal expenditures during World War II created a range of employment opportunities and expanded local economies. The NAACP had begun a legal campaign to ensure that if the South insisted on separate facilities for blacks, those facilities must be equal in quality to those of whites. Eventually this campaign would culminate in the *Brown v. Board of Education of Topeka, Kansas* (1954) ruling, which struck down segregated education altogether.

Alabaster Cities

Desegregation, however, lay in the unforeseeable future. In the meantime, blacks endured not only the inequalities and humiliation of a skewed public education system but shortcomings in other public services as well, even in the larger cities such as Atlanta. In 1920, when Atlanta extended sewer and water lines and constructed a broad boulevard to accommodate newly developed white areas of the city, black districts still lacked city water, and 5,000 black children could not attend public school because there was no room. At the end of World War II, only 25 black physicians served Atlanta's 100,000 black citizens; doctors and patients planned hospital stays (if planning was practicable) well in advance because only 50 hospital beds were reserved for blacks. In the place soon to be promoted as "the city too busy to hate," the 1946 capital budget for new school construction showed a 17 to 1 ratio in favor of whites, despite the dilapidated condition of many black schools.[58]

Civic leaders and white residents reinforced patterns of residential segregation, sometimes restricting black citizens within certain neighborhoods and confining them to a particular corridor. Atlanta remains today divided into a white north side and black south side, with Ponce de Leon Avenue as the boundary. In the early twentieth century, white residents north of that divide changed the names of the major streets in their sector so as not to have the same street name as black residents living south of Ponce de Leon. The city enforced the residential patterns, working with developers to ensure racial homogeneity. Of the twenty-eight subdivisions that appeared north of downtown between 1900 and 1936, twenty-six were reserved for whites only. In 1920 black entrepreneur Heman Perry purchased three hundred acres for development on the west side, expanding the already existing southern neighborhoods for blacks. Black and white neighborhoods had racial boundaries designated with "b" and "w" on planning maps. During the late 1940s, when the black west side appeared poised to spill over into a white area, the city refused to allow black developers to build closer than one hundred yards to the dividing line. Officials enforced the decision by warning developers that the city would leave streets unpaved in subdivisions that crossed this line. In the 1950s Atlanta planners dead-ended several arterial roads to restrict the black population, eventually resorting to a barricade across Peyton Road to preserve a white neighborhood. In 1960 the city planned interstate highway routes explicitly to divide black and white neighborhoods, creating an impenetrable barrier to mutual access.[59] Residential segregation existed in northern cities as well. The urban South, though, not only sought legal instruments to ensure separation, but also planned urban services, road extensions, and schools accordingly.

As with the inadequate school system, southern blacks made the best of a bad situation with respect to the skewed geography of segregation. Black neighborhoods housed the major institutions of the black community, including churches and schools. Benefiting from a "protected market," black merchants developed business districts that served a black clientele. These areas boasted shops, hotels, and professional offices, districts such as Sweet Auburn in Atlanta and East Hargett in Raleigh. Blacks took immense pride in building these neighborhoods, physical proof of their success against great odds. As one black Atlantan recalled Sweet Auburn during the 1920s, "You could get anything you wanted on Auburn Avenue, and we owned it."[60] The more-successful black entrepreneurs—morticians, hotel and restaurant operators, realtors, and publishers—benefited financially from the segregated society, and the white community supported the system through bank loans, supplies, and advertising. In a perverse way that typified white supremacy, black enterprise reinforced black subservience.

The separate geography, like the segregated education and work force, also reinforced the invisibility of blacks to whites, and vice versa. Richard Nixon, attending law school at Duke University in Durham, North Carolina, during the late 1940s, recalled, "We had virtually no contact whatever with Negroes. . . . The only time I really saw them was when we would go downtown in Durham on occasion late in the day. The tobacco factories would be having a change of shift. Pouring out of the factories like black smoke from a furnace came the thousands of Negroes who worked there. They walked down one side of the street and we were on the other. . . . No one really seemed to think of them as individuals. They were just a mass of people living their life as a race completely apart from the rest of us."[61]

Invisibility proved convenient when community histories or pageants un-
folded or when monuments were erected and flags unfurled. In the 1920s the
Atlanta Chamber of Commerce published *Atlanta From the Ashes*, touting the
city's virtues. Apparently, no blacks existed or had contributed to the growth
of Atlanta since the Civil War, because they do not appear anywhere in the
book's pages. Perhaps worse than total neglect were the versions of the past
that emphasized the humanity of whites and the inhumanity of blacks, like
the Works Progress Administration guide *Atlanta: Capital of the Modern South*
(1942), which included a segment on the bloody 1906 race riot, "justifiable,"
in the author's view, given the "boldness and insolence of the lower Negro
element."[62]

Mirror Images

When blacks and whites came in contact, the etiquette of race demanded
roles rather than reality, further distancing each from the other. Blacks became a collection of stereotypical characteristics designed by whites' rendering of southern history and confirmed by public behavior, rather than flesh-
and-blood human beings. As Quentin Compson, William Faulkner's tragic
young protagonist in *The Sound and the Fury* (1929), put it nonchalantly, "A
nigger is not a person so much as a form of behavior; a sort of obverse reflection of the white people he lives among." Ralph Ellison's prize-winning 1947
novel, *Invisible Man*, offered the black perspective. He wrote, "I am invisible,
simply because people refuse to see me. . . . When they approach me they
only see my surroundings, themselves, or figments of their imagination—
indeed, everything and anything except me."[63]

Yet white southerners constantly proclaimed their consummate knowledge
of blacks, particularly to outsiders who questioned regional racial patterns.
But a few whites, even those who supported the system wholeheartedly, saw
through the claim. Will Percy, scion of a prominent Mississippi Delta planter
family, wrote in his poignant autobiography, *Lanterns on the Levee*, "It is true
in the South that whites and blacks live side by side, exchange affection liberally, and believe they have an innate and miraculous understanding of one
another. But the sober fact is we understand one another not at all."[64]

The racial etiquette of white supremacy that rendered blacks invisible and
whites unknowing exacted a heavy toll on both races and on the South. In a
region where informal contact was a way of business and of life, where con-

versation and sociability softened the intruding edges of competition and anonymity, blacks and whites were cut adrift from each other's fellowship, and
they and the South were the poorer for it. As Du Bois articulated it in 1903,
"In a world where it means so much to take a man by the hand and sit beside
him, to look frankly into his eyes and feel his heart beating with red blood;
in a world where a social cigar or a cup of tea together means more than
legislative halls and magazine articles and speeches,—one can imagine the
consequences of the almost utter absence of such social amenities between
estranged races."[65]

The white man lost the black man as a resource. Blacks had worked whites'
land for three centuries and had developed an intimate knowledge of its idio-
syncrasies and of the technologies best suited to cultivate it. Whites consulted
them occasionally but most often did not, and blacks rarely volunteered advice. Wisdom and knowledge were the province of one race, so ignorance
covered both and the South.

The consequences fell harshest on southern blacks. Etiquette required
them to live and act down to white expectations. Richard Wright recalled the
time when he was a boy that he confided to a white woman his ambition to
be a writer. The woman replied angrily, "You'll never be a writer. . . . Who
on earth put such ideas into your nigger head?" Somewhat later, Wright
nearly received a severe beating when, working at an optical company, he
asked one of the white employees to show him the trade. Racial etiquette in
the South turned the American Dream on its head; it devalued education and
ambition and rewarded its opposite. When blacks fulfilled these low expectations, they merely reinforced white perceptions. Etiquette trapped blacks in
a role that robbed them of the opportunity to attain an identity, an intellectual and social potential, and the dignity that comes with a sense of self-
worth. As Wright summarized his experience, "Not only had the southern
whites not known me, but more important still . . . I had not had the chance
to learn who I was. The pressure of southern living kept me from being the
kind of person that I might have been. I had been what my surroundings had
demanded."[66]

The racial etiquette and the white supremacy that drove it was, in the end,
an unnatural pattern of human relations. Segregation not only impressed inferiority on blacks but also required whites to uphold illogical principles that
children would have intuitively discarded. Blacks could purchase toothpaste
in the local drugstore, but not a hamburger. Black maids and cooks came into
intimate contact with white children, prepared food, and laundered clothing

and linens, yet whites barred blacks from public swimming pools and dining rooms and prohibited them from trying on clothing in stores, as if such casual contact would contaminate whites. Black women developed genuine bonds with the children they cared for, yet the parents rarely inquired about the families these women left in order to tend to whites, nurse them to health, and teach them right from wrong. These aspects of segregation were not only humiliating; they were plain stupid. And when African Americans finally exposed the stupidity, segregation crumbled; whites confronted by such illogic could no longer sustain the fiction that segregation was the most logical method for ordering the relations of blacks and whites in the South.

The etiquette was corrupting in part because it denied feelings of love and intimacy. White children often developed close relationships with blacks in their earliest years, but these relationships could never be fulfilled as white children internalized the etiquette of race relations. As Virginia Durr recalled of her Alabama childhood, "[I was] taught little by little that it was a relationship [I] couldn't have. I was just as intimate with Sarah and Nursie and the tall yellow man as if they were members of my family. Yet I literally never knew their names."[67]

White supremacy was ordained by a historical consciousness at once incomplete and inaccurate, and as both races played out their roles, the play itself reinforced the beliefs of the dominant race. These roles, unnatural as they were, had to be learned, and whites who thought about it, and almost every black, could recall the day or event when the realization came that race mattered in their small universe, and that white mattered most of all. For whites, it was the realization and then the internalization that they had power; for blacks, that they had none.

White children learned these lessons early. Former president Jimmy Carter recalled the day he discovered the finality of white supremacy. Though he attended the segregated white high school in Plains, Georgia, his best friends remained two black boys, A. D. and Edmund, on a neighboring farm. "One day, A. D., Edmund and I approached the gate leading from our barn to the pasture. To my surprise, they opened it and stepped back to let me go through first. I was immediately suspicious that they were playing some trick on me, but I passed through without stumbling over a tripwire or having them slam the gate in my face. It was a small act, but a deeply symbolic one. After that, they often treated me with some deference. I guess that their parents had done or said something that caused this change in my black friends' attitude. The constant struggle for leadership among our small group was resolved, but a precious sense of equality had gone out of our personal relationship, and things were never again the same between them and me."[68]

By the time whites attained adulthood, most were inured to the injustice. They came to accept the inferior, demeaning status of blacks as a natural element of the southern landscape, and they looked through or past or not at all at the contradictions of the system. The maintenance of white supremacy dominated southern institutions and thought, and whites tried to eradicate blacks completely from public discourse and life. Blacks were ignored in school texts, the press shunned them (but not their criminal behavior), and discussions of public issues treated blacks as nonpersons. Except as occasional caricatures, blacks were absent from public displays of history in monuments, memorials, and museums. Even whites who wondered about the discrepancies between reality and history feared speaking out. Eugene Gant, the protagonist in Thomas Wolfe's 1929 novel, *Look Homeward, Angel*, delighted in debunking southern myths from his voluntary exile in New York, but he acknowledged the irresistibility of historical traditions and the danger of opposing them at home. Rationally, he could call the South a "barren spiritual wilderness." Yet "so great was his fear of the legend, his fear of their antagonism, that he still pretended the most fanatic devotion to them."[69]

Southern whites were basically decent people; that is important to say, because the inherent evil of white supremacy derives not from whites' hostile intentions but from their reading of their own past, a reading considered so accurate, so obvious, so sacred that most scarcely questioned the result. Mississippi writer Elizabeth Spencer recalled growing up on a plantation during the 1930s and the ease and grace of life, of gauzy days and firefly nights, a peace built to some extent on the backs of the black people who worked her family's land. "It was an ugly system, of course. . . . But in that childhood time of enchantment and love, it never seemed to me anything but part of the eternal. Might as well question why the live oaks were there, or the flowers in Aunt Esther's garden, or the stars in the sky."[70]

The "better" white families taught their children never to say "nigger" and to treat blacks with respect, albeit within the boundaries of prevailing racial etiquette. But as adolescents, whites earned the respect of their peers by assuming the racial customs of the time. As another Mississippi writer, Melany Neilson, noted of her teenage years, "Every time we spoke the word 'nigger,' each time with a little more in condescension, we began to feel some power in the word itself." She confessed to achieving "some kind of dim satisfaction" in using the word.[71]

Eventually, conscious became unconscious, and like Elizabeth Spencer, southern whites merely went about their business assuming that what prevailed in race relations was the natural order of things. Lillian Smith asked in the late 1940s, "What white Southerner of my generation ever stops to think consciously where to go or asks himself if it is right for him to go there! His muscles know where he can go and take him to the front of the streetcar, to the front of the bus, to the big school, to the hospital, to the library, to the hotel and restaurant and picture show, into the best that his town has to offer its citizens. These ceremonials in honor of white supremacy, performed from babyhood, slip from the conscious mind down deep into muscles and glands and become difficult to tear out."[72]

For blacks, however, the sudden first knowledge of separation and difference was often accompanied by terror or deep sadness, or a combination of the two. On the surface, an incident could be innocuous, but in the context of white supremacy it assumed especially hurtful connotations. Mary Mebane remembers from her Durham childhood in the early 1940s her brother's playing with a fancy cup, far more stylish than anything the Mebanes owned. A white woman had offered a drink and told him to keep the cup. Mary understood that this act of kindness was mixed with the practical knowledge that the neighbor no longer wanted the cup after a black person drank from it.[73]

Daisy Bates, the architect of the desegregation of Little Rock's Central High School in 1957, grew up in the small Arkansas town of Huttig in the 1920s. She told of a time she went down to the market to buy a pound of center-cut pork chops. Not understanding why the clerk first waited on a white girl who came into the store after her, Daisy complained. The butcher replied angrily, "Niggers have to wait 'til I wait on the white people. Now take your meat and get of here!" But the butcher gave her fatty chops, and when she returned home, Daisy asked her parents to take them back. She recalled that her father dropped to his knees in front of her, placed his hand on her shoulders, and began shaking her and shouting, "Can't you understand what I've been saying? There's nothing I can do! If I went down to the market I would only cause trouble for my family." Daisy's father had tears in his eyes. She asked, "Daddy, are you afraid?" He jumped to his feet and displayed "an anger I had never seen before. 'Hell no! I'm not afraid for myself. I'm not afraid to die. I could go down to that market and tear him limb from limb with my bare hands, but I'm afraid for you and your mother.' "[74]

Black parents sought to shield their children as much and as long as possible from the soul-drenching effects of white supremacy. Sometimes parents made light of incidents or turned them into positives, such as the practice of going to the back door of a restaurant to receive food interpreted as special treatment and an opportunity for extra helpings, rather than acknowledged as the discriminatory practice it was. Most often, black parents sought to limit their children's contacts with white adults as much as possible. In cities this proved easier, with separate neighborhoods, schools, and churches, but even in rural areas older blacks employed devices of avoidance for their young-sters. The Reverend Ralph David Abernathy, who would go on to head the Southern Christian Leadership Conference (SCLC), one of the major civil rights organizations of the 1950s and '60s, noted the difficulties of negotiat-ing the racial minefields of Alabama's black belt, where he grew up in the 1930s. His father simply instructed young Ralph never to talk to a white man. As Abernathy explained, "white men would ask me something and I'd just shake my head, so I got the reputation of being dumb. That was my father's way of protecting me. . . . I would sit in the wagon and hold the reins, but if a white man said anything to me, I'd just be dumb. So I never had any contact with white people at all. I went to a black school. I went to a black church. I was surrounded by black people."[75]

Perhaps the greatest gift black parents could impart to their children was a sense of self-worth, the very attribute white supremacy sought to destroy. As Anthony Walton's mother related, "Even in Mississippi I was never raised to think I was second class, even when I was walking behind the white folks' bus. They used to ride past us every morning while we walked, but it didn't occur to us that we weren't as good as those kids riding. It was just a myth of white folks. They were mean and they wouldn't let us ride, but we were taught we were as good as them."[76]

Other black parents would pursue a more tragic, if perhaps more realistic, path and discourage their children from attainment, from dreaming about something better. They would squelch ambitions of college, professional ca-reers, and status, and they would instead promote the importance of recti-tude, mechanical skills, and domestic chores. Writers Richard Wright and Mary Mebane both had parents and relatives deride their literary aspirations. Mebane remembered her mother scolding her: "You somewhere with your head in a book and you let my okra burn." As Mebane interpreted the event: "For unspoken was the knowledge that . . . black girls were really being trained to work as domestics."[77]

Like southern women, southern blacks had limited options within the roles society assigned to them. Ralph Ellison described three ways black youngsters could handle the revelation of their inferior position in the society of white supremacy: "They could accept the role created for them by the whites and perpetually resolve the conflicts through the hope and catharsis of Negro religion; they could repress their dislike of Jim Crow social relations while striving for a middle way of respectability, becoming—consciously or unconsciously—the accomplices of whites in oppressing their brothers; or they could reject the situation, adopt a criminal attitude, and carry on an unceasing psychological scrimmage with the whites that often flared forth into physical violence." These options account in part for the preeminence of the black church as both refuge and release in the black community, as well as the level of violence directed less at the whites—that, after all, was a dangerous strategy—than at their fellow blacks. Angela Davis described "the inner-directed violence which was so much a part of our school lives . . . to the point where it verged on fratricide. Hardly a day would pass without a fight—in class or outside." These actions merely confirmed whites in the belief of black inferiority, lawlessness, and the need for retributive justice. The system perpetuated stereotypes and continually confirmed them.[78]

The shame of it, for Mississippi writer David Cohn, was that "members of two races lived out their lives on parallel lines, to meet but in infinity, each with a wound in his heart and a torment in his mind. . . . Living, their ways were separate. Dying, they became a common but not commingled dust."[79] History as it was lived in the South created both a barrier to racial reconciliation and a daily reminder of racial distinctions. The poem "The Tall Men," by Donald Davidson, testifies to this tangible impediment: "There is a wall between us, anciently erected. / Once it might have been crossed, men say. / But now I cannot / Forget that I was master, and you can hardly / Forget that you were a slave."[80]

In a society predicated on separating them, both blacks and whites were trapped together in the same fantasy of history. The Lost Cause had elevated the fight for independence and the preservation of slavery to a holy endeavor, enshrining the Old South as a halcyon era of grace, order, and righteousness. Reconstruction threatened to disgrace, discredit, and disrupt this vision. Redemption offered the hope of setting things right again, of putting Yankees and blacks in their proper places: in the North and under the whites, respectively. Southerners of both races stumbled through the twentieth century compelled to play out a historical fantasy that knew no end or alteration. When Swedish economist Gunnar Myrdal toured the South during the late 1930s gathering material for his epic volume on race relations, *An American*

Dilemma (1944), he was astonished to find how deeply white supremacy was embedded in the historical consciousness of southerners and contended that as long as the perception of history went unchanged, race relations would remain the same as well. As Myrdal noted, "History [in the South] is not used, as in the North, to show how society is continuously changing, but rather on the contrary, to justify the status quo and to emphasize society's inertia."[81] These historical myths not only inhibited change but denied that there was anything that required change.

To depict the period from the 1890s to the 1950s as a racial dark age in the South is to neglect the persistent protest that arose from the black community. Despite personal peril and the likelihood of failure, some blacks refused to acquiesce to white supremacy and the historical consciousness from which it derived. To do otherwise would confirm white prejudices and expectations of their black neighbors; to suffer silently meant to assume a role someone else had imposed.

African Americans initiated more than a dozen streetcar boycotts in the urban South between 1896 and 1908, although segregated public transportation held fast. Black leaders throughout the country formed the Afro-American Council in 1890 to protest the deteriorating conditions of black life, but the council accomplished little and disbanded in 1908. W. E. B. Du Bois organized an annual Conference on Negro Problems at Atlanta University beginning in 1896, but participants presented research, not plans of action.

World War I spurred black southerners to more-direct action; black families had sent their young men to make the world safe for democracy, and they demanded the same at home. At a postwar rally in an A.M.E. Church in Kildare, Texas, the speaker urged fellow blacks not to "close ranks" with whites but to demand their rights, even if it meant opening "another war for Democracy, right here at home." He warned that black veterans were returning experienced "in killing white men." The fledgling NAACP welcomed thousands of new members in the region during the year after the war ended and filed suits against egregious cases of racial discrimination, which they occasionally won. When a clerk in a San Antonio shoe store struck a black woman with a shoe, an NAACP attorney succeeded in getting the clerk arrested, fined, and fired. But by 1920 state and local officials, as well as violent reprisals, had closed down a majority of the NAACP branches in the South.[82]

Still, the NAACP persisted. During the 1930s its lawyers began to chip away at *Plessy v. Ferguson*'s "separate but equal" dictum. Although the U.S. Supreme Court did not overturn that ruling until the *Brown* decision of 1954,

NAACP litigation had so narrowed *Plessy* by the early 1950s that its downfall became inevitable.

More numerous than the organized challenges to white supremacy were the ad hoc instances of defiance. Individuals who refused to sit in the back of the bus or in Jim Crow waiting rooms provided lonely witness to the fact that, surface appearances to the contrary, blacks opposed the indignity of segregation. In 1932 a group of black ministers in Raleigh, North Carolina, boycotted the dedication of a war memorial after officials ordered them to sit in the back of the auditorium. A few years later, black students in Greensboro, North Carolina, boycotted movie theaters when owners issued a statement condemning "the appearance of colored people in scenes with whites on an equal basis."[83]

But the average southern white male was not a gradualist, not a believer that eventually black southerners would attain the proper accoutrements of civilization to take their place alongside the region's whites. White supremacy was a heady tonic; it gave whites, no matter how poor or despised, an automatic superiority. Whatever misfortune occurred, the white southerner would never be a nigger. And since "nigger" implied a certain behavior and status, any movement from that expectation threatened the racial hierarchy and white civilization itself. When white southerners advanced the notion in the 1950s that the goal of integrationists was interracial sex, most Americans scoffed at that conclusion. Yet the progression was perfectly logical; move one inch from the rules of segregation, and the barriers, all the barriers, between the races come tumbling down, and with them, the South.

The Citadel cadets celebrate the resignation of female cadet Shannon Fulkner, 1996, but their cause was lost as the state military school was ultimately forced to admit female students. *Courtesy Mic Smith*/The Post and Courier

Many whites believed that former slaves were incapable of assuming the responsibilities of freedom. The belief became part of the standard historical perspective of Reconstruction and was expressed as early as 1862 in this illustration from *Harper's Weekly*.

Advertisement for Luzianne coffee, Gastonia (N.C.) *Gazette*, 1918. The faithful servant is but one of several caricatures whites made of southern blacks by the early 1900s. The construction implied both good race relations and the clear superiority of whites while also evoking nostalgia for the Old South. *Courtesy Gastonia* Gazette

Ben Tillman regaling South Carolina voters, ca. 1900. Few southern politicians approached the skill of South Carolina's "Pitchfork" Ben Tillman in weaving together the themes of pure white womanhood and white supremacy. The appeal resonated not only with rural whites but also with an urban middle-class constituency, as this photograph indicates. *Courtesy Special Collections, Clemson University Libraries, Clemson, South Carolina*

Educating the South, 1925. These advertisements for southern literature and history for use primarily in the South's public schools reinforced prevailing historical perspectives for both white and black students. *Courtesy Atlanta History Center*

Photo montage from a Richmond promotional brochure, 1932. The images and texts of materials advertising southern cities scarcely acknowledged the presence of blacks in their midst. *Courtesy Virginia Historical Society*

Segregation on public transit, Birmingham, Alabama, 1933. Before the 1950s, the words "white" and "colored" governed the daily lives of all southerners. *Courtesy Birmingham Public Library (#30.47)*

Blues passed down from generation to generation, Eatonville, Florida, 1935. Many of its practitioners were self-taught or learned from a relative. The blues influenced jazz, country music, and rock 'n' roll. *Courtesy Library of Congress*

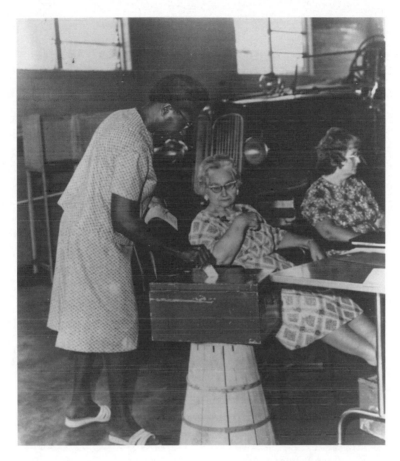

Voting, Jackson, Mississippi, 1966. The 1965 Voting Rights Act changed the South's political landscape. Since prevailing historical perspectives reflect prevailing political power, black ballots also brought contesting views of the past into the public arena. *Courtesy AP/Wide World Photos*

Up from invisibility. Telling African American history in the South across the urban landscape is one strategy to resurrect the buried history of the region's African American population. A new monument on the grounds of the South Carolina state capitol in Columbia, dedicated in March 2001, depicts black history in the South and in South Carolina in particular. This representation joins a half-dozen Confederate monuments nearby. *Photo by Melinda H. Desmarais*

How far have we come? Waving the Confederate battle flag at Woodlawn High School in Birmingham, 1963, in a rally to keep that school racially pure. Woodlawn today is an over-whelmingly African American high school. *Courtesy Birmingham Library (#1076.1.59). Copyright, photo by the Birmingham* News, *2001. All rights reserved. Reprinted with permission.*

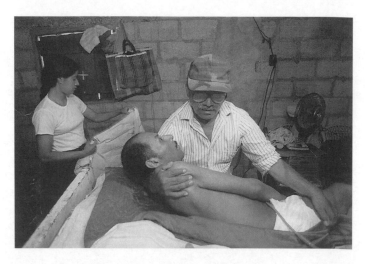

Porfirio Fuentes cradles his son, Carmelo, who suffered heat stroke picking tomatoes in eastern North Carolina, 1998. The old black/white divisions in southern society will change in the coming decades with the increased presence of Latinos. But will the South overcome its tradition of worker exploitation and weak government regulation? *Photo by Gayle Shomer; Courtesy Charlotte* Observer

Casual interracial contact in Birmingham's Linn Park, 2001, reflects positive changes in the city's race relations since the 1960s. But the contact rarely extends beyond the end of the workday. A United Daughters of the Confederacy Civil War monument stands in the background. *Photo by Melinda H. Desmarais*

Gone With the Wind became an international sensation after it opened in Atlanta in 1939 at this glitzy premiere. To this day, many white southerners still adhere to the film's depiction of race relations, the Civil War, and Reconstruction. *Courtesy Atlanta History Center*

The grief is real after all these years. The reinterment of Confederate sailors from the submarine, CSS *Hunley*, Charleston, South Carolina, 2000. *Photo by Diedra Laird; Courtesy Charlotte Observer*

The "compromise" over removing the Confederate battle flag from atop the capitol dome in Columbia, South Carolina, was hardly that, as this 2000 Kevin Siers cartoon illustrates. *Courtesy Kevin Siers and the Charlotte* Observer

Still fighting the Civil War. The Confederate battle flag flies alongside the Confederate monument on the capitol grounds in Columbia, South Carolina. The soldier gazes across at a bank building, 2001. *Photo by Melinda H. Desmarais*

8 Sharings

We knew that probably the most powerful and potent weapon that people have literally no defense for is love, kindness.
> —Franklin McCain, "The South's First Sit-in," February 1, 1960

By God, maybe the South will save us all. Maybe the South contains the real American future.
> —Peter Schrag, "A Hesitant New South: Fragile Promise
> on the Last Frontier"

The great tragedy was that southern blacks and whites had touched each other in so many ways over the centuries, but the artifice of history obscured the common bond of place, blood, and culture. Deeper than the casual contacts of workers, and more lasting than the occasional, yet genuine, kindnesses that occurred between black and white, the very essence of southern culture knew no racial boundaries. The amalgam produced a unique Afro-European culture in the South before the Civil War, and the strictures of racial segregation did little to reverse the connections. Thus the great tragedy produced a great irony: two peoples, forced to live separate lives, joined in countless ways to produce one culture. The human spirit triumphs over its folly.

Few aspects of southern culture demonstrate this black-white amalgam better than southern music; the whole repertoire of it, from blues to rock 'n' roll, reflects the numerous crossings between the two communities. The blues emerged from the Deep South at about the same time that states hardened the color line, though the music probably evolved much earlier. Charles Peabody, a Harvard archaeologist, wrote about the strange music he heard in Mississippi during an excavation of Indian mounds in the late nineteenth century. Unaccompanied and improvisational singing coupled with melody lines borrowed from white ballads characterized this new music. Instruments, especially the guitar, livened the tunes, and soon blacks throughout the South used the wail of the blues to express their feelings, tell a story, or just have fun. W. C. Handy introduced the blues to white audiences in Memphis, and it became immensely popular in the Beale Street bars and honky tonks before it spread to the North along with southern black migration during World War I.

Jazz, kin to blues but different in its rhythms and complexity, had an even more diverse southern lineage. According to historian John Boles, jazz emerged as "a creative blending of African, Caribbean, and European; religious music, secular music; minstrelsy, ragtime, blues, and brass marching bands." The blues came out of the cotton fields; jazz flourished in the cities of the Deep South in the 1890s, and in New Orleans most of all, where blacks put European instruments through syncopated paces, none better than trumpeter Charles "Buddy" Bolden. Within a generation, George Gershwin had adapted the rhythms of jazz for "serious" music, with his "Rhapsody in Blue" in 1924.[1]

White adaptations of black music were common, just as blacks borrowed from white culture, playing European instruments and using extant sacred and secular music to construct blues and jazz. Country-music star Hank Williams borrowed blues rhythms and movements that scandalized the country establishment but delighted a new generation of fans. Rock 'n' roll demonstrated the most obvious cross-fertilization between black and white southern music.

Sam Phillips owned a small recording studio in Memphis in the early 1950s. Although Phillips was white, he believed that so-called race music, rhythm and blues numbers recorded by black musicians, could find a white audience. In March 1951 he recorded Jackie Brenston and his Delta Cats singing "Rocket 88," perhaps the first rock 'n' roll record ever made. Not too far away, in Tupelo, Mississippi, a young Elvis Presley listened to "race music" on his radio. When he moved to Memphis, Presley persuaded Phillips to record him. His first single, "That's All Right Mama," combined the styles of black blues (the song was originally recorded by black blues artist Arthur "Big Boy" Crudup) and white country music, a mixture that would stamp rock 'n' roll as a new and vital musical form.[2]

Just as the air waves carried "race music" into white homes, it also wafted the Grand Ole Opry and country music into countless black homes in the South, influencing such young blues artists as Ray Charles Robinson (Ray Charles) and Richard Penniman ("Little Richard"). Presley's success opened the mass market for black blues performers such as Chuck Berry and Fats Domino, in addition to Charles and Penniman. When Presley performed gyrations he had witnessed at a black Pentecostal church, the musical miscegenation was complete, shocking many Americans, particularly southern whites.

Rock 'n' roll emerged just at the beginning of the civil rights movement, and perhaps the juncture was more than coincidence. White segregationists understood that young people of both races were promiscuously crossing an aural color line. Segregationists cited the NAACP "as the evil force behind rock 'n' roll." The Alabama White Citizens' Councils, groups of middle-class white men who militantly upheld segregation, went so far as to set up a committee "to do away with this vulgar, animalistic, nigger rock & roll bop." Council members condemned the new music as a plot to "mongrelize America," claiming its subliminal messages and beat produced "animalism and vulgarity" in listeners. They induced disc jockeys to stop playing Jerry Lee Lewis's "Whole Lotta Shakin' Goin' On" because radio stations "didn't play songs by niggers," a mistaken reference to the singer's race.[3] Needless to say, the councils received little cooperation from the state's white teenagers. It was impossible to segregate the air waves.

Nor was it possible to segregate food. Africans taught white southerners about rice, new uses for corn, and together blacks and whites devised new ways to eat and serve pig flesh—especially barbecue. As Raleigh journalist Jonathan Daniels noted in the 1940s, "Barbecue is the dish which binds together the taste of both the people of the big house and the poorest occupants of the back end of the broken-down barn."[4]

To both black and white southerners, eating was not merely about consuming a meal; it was a ritual of fellowship. Breaking bread is the lubricant to conversation, a substitute for words understood in the offering of sustenance. The Reverend Will Campbell remarked about the tradition among both races of showering bereaved families with casseroles: "It means, 'I love you. And I am sorry for what you are going through, and I will share as much of your burden as I can.' And maybe potato salad is a better way of saying it." Cooking in the South, a region of small towns and rural neighborhoods, where kitchen technology came last and late, was often burdensome. As novelist Kaye Gibbons stated in *A Cure for Dreams*, "Pies and cakes take a great deal of trouble and historically have never been viewed as something merely to eat."[5]

Whether it is the New Year's Day ritual of hoppin' john, the casserole parade of mourning, dinner on the church grounds, or the covered-dish bonanza of family and neighborhood gatherings, food is the symbol of community, of shared joys and sorrows, and of mutual commitment. Fannie Flagg's *Fried Green Tomatoes at the Whistle Stop Café* (1987) and Anne Tyler's *Dinner at the Homesick Restaurant* (1982) both depict the transcendent nature of southern cooking and eating. As one reviewer noted, "Cooking is not simply a task or a chore; it is a mission that fulfills a sense of belonging as one earns a reputation for being at least a caretaker for her family, and at best, a very good cook. It is also a ministry that nurtured people's emotional and spiritual needs as much as their physical ones." Despite the fast-food invasion, southerners still take great pride in the slow track: the slow fire in the barbecue pit, the slow baking of pies and cakes, and the slow simmering of collards. As black barbecue maven Sy Erskine explained, "Southerners have been known to be slow traditionally in doing certain things. It transfers right on to the cooking of the food. . . . It is a tradition strictly of the South."[6] Distinctive cuisine for a distinctive people, black and white.

Because the meaning of food transcended eating and reflected the shared culture of black and white southerners, few aspects of the convoluted customs and laws of segregation drew more attention than how and where people consumed food and drink. Most restaurants barred blacks outright. Breaking bread in the same building held implications that overcame any segregated seating arrangements. Some eateries offered take-out service for blacks through a side or back window. Department stores and drugstores forbade blacks to sit at lunch counters. Black maids, cooks, and other servants took their meals in the kitchen, never in the dining room where white folks ate.

For a white to sit down and share a meal with a black person, no matter how close and friendly the relationship, resulted in social death and perhaps worse. Southern whites never forgave Teddy Roosevelt for the seemingly innocent gesture of inviting black leader Booker T. Washington to the White House for tea. Most white southerners could distinctly remember the first time they sat down to eat with a black person; that was how memorable and traumatic the experience could be. When Katharine Du Pre Lumpkin left her native South Carolina to enroll in Columbia University in 1915, she attended a tea at which black women were present—and not as servers. "When it was over," she recalled, "I found the heavens had not fallen, nor the earth parted asunder to swallow us up in this unheard of transgression." But few white southerners dared avail themselves of either the opportunity or the circumstance. Cultural taboos and the consequences that followed their violation proved too powerful to take the chance, if the thought should ever enter the white mind.[7]

These cultural commonalities notwithstanding, from the vantage point of the early 1940s, white supremacy seemed a permanent condition in the South. Yet, since the barriers went up in earnest in the 1890s, there had never been regional unanimity on the subject. Some southerners, white and black, male and female, had resisted, or at least had implicitly challenged the status quo, through their churches, through tentative connections between black and white organizations, through common workplace experiences, and, increasingly, through the courts. The spirit of inquiry, never a hardy plant in the South, showed signs of life at a few institutions of higher education, particularly the University of North Carolina at Chapel Hill, where a group of social scientists in the 1930s set about to study the South's problems, a remarkable achievement for a region that proclaimed itself the best place on earth. But the Regionalists, as the Chapel Hill social scientists were called, generally avoided linking the South's deep economic and political shortcomings to race; at most, they expressed regret about how the dual system of education drained resources from an already poor region.

This is not to say that some white southerners did not connect race with the South's troubled economy. In 1938 a North Carolina senator attributed the region's chronically poor economy to the presence of "two and a half millions of negro workers, many of whom are not disposed to work constantly, very few of whom are disposed to try to accumulate." Thus, African Americans, not the system of white supremacy, were to blame for the South's plight. W. E. B. Du Bois mocked these explanations and stated the obvious, that "the South cannot go about its business without first looking into the race angle. It is so busy keeping the Negro down that it has let everything else go to wreck and ruin, asking only that the Negro be kept *under* the ruin."[8]

Academics did not challenge the sacrosanct color line, but they at least exposed readers to the fact that serious problems existed in a region whose experiences, especially economic, diverged so greatly from the course of the nation. Perhaps their readers, or at least a few of them, would draw the conclusion that white supremacy accounted in no small part for this discrepancy. But the weight of history bore heavily on the South, and whatever great change could occur in race relations had to offer up an alternative vision, or at least the promise of such.

An incident at Chapel Hill in 1938 highlighted the difficulty of effecting such an alternative historical perspective. Pauli Murray, a native North Carolinian who would become one of the more prominent black writers in the postwar era, applied for admission to the all-white state university. Predictably, the university denied her entrance. In supporting the decision, the student newspaper, an enlightened organ that had promoted the progressive research agenda of the school's social scientists, remarked, "North Carolina, with its history colored by the story of a defeated Southern Confederacy and a long association with Negroes and their habits, 'does not believe,' in the words of Governor [Clyde] Hoey, 'in social equality between the races.' "9 The matter seemed so obvious.

So who would or could effect a change? The federal government or Yankee reformers were unlikely candidates, however sympathetic they may have been, for in the 1930s a sympathy (of a sort) for racial equality emerged in Washington. That was also the decade of the great film triumph of *Gone With the Wind*, which displayed the southern historical perspective for an entire nation uninterested in or unaware of contending views. White southerners would have been surprised to learn that a racial problem existed. They may have read the works of the Chapel Hill crowd, but they figured the remedy for the struggling agricultural sector, the weak industrial economy, and the public-health and public-educational problems lay in a bit more imagination, a great deal more education, and leaders who could and would address these issues. Race scarcely entered the picture, and when it did, most would agree with the *Daily Tar Heel*'s assessment of race relations: White supremacy was a given, and you don't mess with the natural order of things; nor do you defy the precedent of history and defile your ancestors, and God in the bargain.

Revelation

It would fall to blacks to redeem the South, to demonstrate how southern history could bind as much as it broke apart and distracted blacks from whites. South Carolina writer James McBride Dabbs projected this scenario:

"A despised minority, excluded from the common life returns at last more in love than in hatred to reveal . . . not only that possibility of community that has always haunted the mind of the South, but also . . . a vision of the universal meaning of failure and defeat."[10]

Even the most enlightened southerners agreed that a solution to racial problems, assuming such problems existed, must come from within; yet when they said that they assumed that progressive whites, the same group that had initiated interracial dialogues beginning in the early 1900s, would lead the way. They could not conceive of blacks effecting even modest reforms, both because of the limitations Jim Crow had placed on their educational and political skills and because of the sharp reaction likely to occur in the white community, which would destroy any attempt at change. But building on the fight against fascism during World War II, southern blacks sprung to the initiative, startling (and troubling) some of their white colleagues.

Carl Rowan expressed the more assertive attitude that the war inspired among black southerners: "It has been said—correctly—that war is hell. This war turned out to be the great liberator, for it gave me a national mission of honor that would open up new horizons of opportunity and potential achievement."[11] Southern black leaders sought to hasten that liberation by pressing for frequent and meaningful interracial dialogues and a public condemnation of white supremacy from prominent figures of both races. Returning black servicemen would demand nothing less, and already signs were appearing—violence, recriminations in the press, and warnings from political leaders—that blacks' expectations from the war, derived from both their personal experiences and the general aims of the country in the war, heightened racial tensions significantly.

Not surprisingly, a white woman provided the bridge to effect both objectives. Jessie Daniel Ames invited black and white leaders to a series of conferences in Durham, Atlanta, and Richmond between 1942 and 1944. At Durham, the conferees issued a bold statement calling for a "New Charter of Race Relations in the South," one that was "fundamentally opposed to the principle and practice of compulsory segregation in our American society." Since the days of the Southern Sociological Congress and the Commission on Interracial Cooperation, members strove to make separate as equal as possible; now, for the first time, they attacked the root of the problem. In 1944 they formed a new, more-activist interracial body, the Southern Regional Council, with Chapel Hill Regionalist Howard W. Odum as president. The council would not formally renounce segregation until 1951. The difficulty of reaching an interracial consensus identifying segregation as a fundamental obstacle to black advance and regional development led a group of black conferees, chaired by Howard University professor Rayford Logan, to publish a book, *What the Negro Wants* (1944), which attacked segregation and called for racial equality across the board. The hesitancy of white friends to embrace the new, forthright stand of their black brethren portended the difficulties blacks would encounter over the next two decades in waging a battle for racial equality in a region where whites had a great stake in retaining sharp racial distinctions.[12]

Events outside the South boosted southern blacks' resolve. In 1944 the U.S. Supreme Court in *Smith v. Allwright* struck down the "white primary" in the South. The decision energized blacks in the same manner that emancipation spurred freedmen after 1865 to form Union Leagues and register to vote. Often initiated by black women who built on their organizational experiences and contacts, Negro Voters Leagues sprung up across the South, especially in cities.

The promise of political power had instant results in the urban South. In Atlanta Mayor William B. Hartsfield acknowledged the growing power of the Negro Voters League there and helped to establish an interracial political coalition in 1949 that lasted for twenty years. When the League demanded that the city hire black police officers, Hartsfield replied that he would do so once the League registered ten thousand black voters; when it had done so, the mayor carried out his part of the bargain.[13]

President Truman submitted a civil rights package to Congress in 1948. His efforts went nowhere, but for the first time since Reconstruction, a president specifically targeted blacks for ameliorative legislation. In the meantime, the NAACP stepped up its assault on the fiction of separate but equal, until, in 1954, the Supreme Court struck down the *Plessy* precedent in *Brown v. Board of Education of Topeka, Kansas*.

The events of the civil rights movement seemed to flow like strong rivers into a mighty ocean of justice following the *Brown* decision. The Montgomery bus boycott in 1955 thrust Martin Luther King Jr. into the national spotlight. In 1960 four black college students from Greensboro, North Carolina, sat in at a Woolworth's lunch counter and launched a regionwide movement that drew in a new generation of blacks: less afraid, more idealistic (as young people are wont to be), and impatient to wait for their ideals to become reality. The bloody Freedom Rides of 1961, which limped across the Deep South, laying bare the violence that had been there all along but had remained hidden from the glare of national publicity, ended segregated inter-state travel and raised the awareness of people across the country that segregation was not merely a racial accommodation but a brutal system of denial and oppression. In Birmingham in 1963 school children placed their bodies in the line of high-pressure fire hoses and police dogs to demand the simple right to eat in downtown restaurants, try on clothing in department stores, and sit wherever they wanted to in movie theaters. A few months later, four young girls were brutally ambushed in a black church preparing for Sunday morning services. The fall of Birmingham spelled the death knell of segregation; a year later, President Lyndon B. Johnson, moving the federal government behind the protestors more vigorously than had his predecessor, signed the Civil Rights Act of 1964, officially outlawing segregation in public accommodations. Within a year the last formal bastion of white supremacy fell with the passage of the 1965 Voting Rights Act.

Looking back at this moral crusade—for that is what it was—it all seems so inevitable, a tide of events washing over the ramparts of white supremacy. But to participants who endured the daily struggle, the periodic despair, and the numerous failures, the outcome seemed far from certain. The president's signature translated a dream into a law. White supremacy may have been an unnatural, illogical system based on a skewed reading of the past, but it had created a master race and a political system to support it, and neither would relinquish their prerogatives easily. The white South drew within itself, launched vigorous censorship campaigns on campuses, in the press, on the job; a few Deep South states funded state-supported secret service apparatuses, such as the Sovereignty Commission in Mississippi, that gathered mostly useless information but that further undermined democratic institutions and civil liberties in the South. Mississippi writer Elizabeth Spencer recalled the state's collective mentality in 1955 just as the movement began: "Mississippi was pulling inward, the wagons were making a tight little circle, the feather had showed up behind the rock, every night sound was a threat. The closed society was bolting and barring every door and chinking every window." The irony was that the threat did not come from outside the South; the federal government—the Congress, the President, and the judiciary—moved ponderously, indecisively, and sometimes not at all. The galling aspect of it all was that the revolution, when it reared, came from within, and from the least likely source: the region's black population.[14]

The extreme conservative segregationists are not noteworthy, for they have always and ever challenged difference. Rather, it is the resistance, or silence, of the "good" white people that stands out—the ministers who clammed up, the civic leaders who moved only when profits were threatened, and the politicians and law-enforcement officials who worked more to foment strife than to stifle it. We can understand the silence even as we question it: the historical record provided vivid proof of the dangers of stepping forward and onto the platform of racial justice. But those who fired black employees, who condemned violence while publicly threatening it if blacks persisted in their protests, who railed from the soap box or the floor of Congress in the rhetoric of states' rights, or who invoked the name of God to justify racial separation and sanctify a historical vision with little substance—their blind eyes to the justice of the cause is less understandable. Had the system so corrupted them that they saw it as not only natural, but right? Or, minor, private misgivings aside, was it a matter of civic virtue, of duty, of religious faith to maintain the status quo?

The resistance unwittingly revealed the rotted philosophical underpinnings of white supremacy, as when lawmakers hurriedly implemented outlandish electoral laws, suddenly wiping registration lists clean, requiring impossible literacy tests, and moving or closing polling places arbitrarily. As one Georgia sheriff announced in 1962 after he broke up a peaceful voting-rights meeting, "We want our colored people to go on living like they have for years." Both the proprietary nature of race relations and the caricature that black southerners had become are clear-cut in his statement.[15]

Standing in the South in 1965 was akin to standing in Germany in 1945. The collapse of the Third Reich had not magically rid the country of Nazis. But it did provide a hope to start anew, ever mindful of the horrible past and ever hopeful for a better future. White supremacy was not the Holocaust, and southern whites were not Nazis—not even close. But the civil rights movement provided a golden opportunity for the region to place the past in perspective and derive a new meaning from it, to shape a future in which both races could participate. The manner in which blacks conducted the movement—as a moral, religious crusade rather than as a war of retribution and vindication—offered the promise of reconciliation. Blacks were the new Redeemers, more legitimate than the white supremacists who had claimed that title. But would that Redemption hold? Would it spread? Was the salvation merely cosmetic and superficial? Would it hold beyond the immediate euphoria of a fight well fought, or would it turn into a new struggle?

The Offering

It is a testament to the genius of the black-led movement that in the process of destroying the visible structures of white supremacy, an occurrence that just a few years earlier had seemed impossible, blacks did not destroy any hope of a lasting reconciliation with southern whites. Martin Luther King Jr., who perhaps more than anyone else epitomized the movement, always stressed the importance of distinguishing the sin from the sinner. He studiously avoided portraying the issue as a black-white struggle. As he explained during the Montgomery bus boycott, "This is not a war between the white and the Negro but a conflict between justice and injustice."[16] That position not only elevated the struggle to a higher plane but left open the opportunity for a reconciliation once the battle was won. In addition, it framed black hopes in terms that whites understood as southerners, even if they found it difficult to hear. King's message not only fell within the evangelical tradition but spoke to the shared history of southerners—a people who had experienced injustice, second-class citizenship, and numerous indignities inflicted by a powerful oppressor. His gospel was directed not at divesting the white southerner of his religion and history, but rather at fostering a closer, more inclusive connection with that culture.

In other words, King and the hundreds of black leaders and followers in the towns and cities of the South engaged whites directly. The success of the movement depended both on federal intervention and the campaign of moral persuasion waged by blacks on behalf of whites and the South in general. The process did not work only one way, of course. Black southerners derived significant benefits from the movement apart from the obvious important gains. They achieved a sense of community as they overcame class, color, and geographic distinctions. They also attained a sense of self-worth, which the system of white supremacy had constantly denied. As Franklin McCain recalled his feelings after the initial sit-in in Greensboro in 1960, "I probably felt better that day than I've ever felt in my life. I felt as though I had gained my manhood, so to speak, and not only gained it, but had developed quite a lot of respect for it." Discussing the impact of the sit-ins and the demonstrations that followed, *Ebony* magazine summarized the transformation of southern blacks: "The Negro has lost some of his former virtues and a good many illusions. Gone is his celebrated patience, his childlike obedience, and his colossal fear. He has waited ninety-eight years. . . . The day he stopped being a good old Negro was the day he became a man." The emasculating nature of white supremacy suddenly appeared less threatening. Even if many whites regarded black men with greater hostility now, a big step forward had been taken in transforming all blacks from caricatures into people. As Leslie Dunbar of the Southern Regional Council observed in 1961, "At least Negroes are not regarded as instruments and tools, but as antagonists. That, in itself, is a higher status."[17]

Southerners attach a considerable weight to public behavior as a reflection of breeding and status. The calm, nonviolent, prayerful, typically well-dressed black protestors represented a sharp contrast to their often scruffy, thuggish white antagonists. The protestors' methods gave some whites pause, and their direct and simple demands generated a public reassessment of segregation. Black southerners had surprised their white neighbors by revealing blacks' antipathy toward segregation and the hypocrisy and contradictions of the system. As the Greensboro *Daily News* editorialized directly after the sit-ins there, "There are many white people in the South who recognize the injustice of the lunch counter system. It is based on circumstances which may have made sense 100 years ago; today it has a touch of medievalism. It smacks of Indian 'untouchables' or Hitlerian Germany's Master Race Theories."[18]

The laying bare of "injustice," as the newspaper called segregation, implied that a moral issue was at stake. White southerners, once they recognized it as such, must either reconcile their deep religious faith to a new social order or live with and explain away the increasingly uncomfortable contradiction between faith and reality. As theologian James Sellers noted in 1961, the sit-in demonstrations provided a swift "updating into reality" for many white southerners. When Fisk University student and Nashville sit-in leader Diane Nash confronted Mayor Ben West with the question, "Do you feel it's wrong to discriminate against a person solely on the basis of race or color?" the moral absurdity of the proposition forced West from behind the barrier of tradition: "I couldn't agree it was morally right to sell them merchandise and refuse them service. . . . It was a moral question."[19]

The civil rights movement also divested the white southerner from other misconceptions: the notion of what blacks ought to look and behave like and the idea that blacks were content with the system of segregation. James A. Rogers, editor of the Florence (South Carolina) *Morning News*, considered himself a moderate, even a liberal on racial issues, in the late 1950s and early '60s. He supported segregation, he explained, not "because I was against the black, but because I was for him. . . . not because I wished to keep him in his place, but because I wished for him to have every opportunity that I had to make a place for himself." That place was behind the color line, where, Rogers believed, there existed "no social tension" that would retard blacks' development. The movement taught Rogers otherwise: that segregation generated considerable tension by perpetuating a permanent second-class citizenship.[20]

It is true that such awareness and repentance may not have been general among white southerners, but numbers were not that important at the time. What was important, especially for the continuation of racial reconciliation, was that at least a few whites attained enlightenment. Referring to God's pledge in Genesis not to destroy Sodom if only ten righteous people could be found there, German theologian Dietrich Bonhoeffer observed that God "is able to see the whole people in a few, just as he saw and reconciled in One the whole of humanity."[21]

By moderating the public obsession with race that dominated political campaigns, social relations, and patterns of work, residence, and education, blacks enabled whites to achieve a truer sense of past and place. As James Sellers noted, that obsession had diverted southerners from the enjoyment and learning derived from their land and history. The "domain of superior status" was a great temptation to the white southerner, but now he had the opportunity, courtesy of his black neighbors, to pursue his true destiny. The South could leaven "the nation with its sense of the land, personal relations, [and] the past."[22] The movement had taught that white supremacy was not synonymous with southern history; in fact, it was inhibiting a more accurate perspective on that past. Perhaps now the South could give up fighting the Civil War and discover its truer meaning within the context of a biracial society.

The belief in the inferiority of blacks was at the center of the southern historical perspective, but the events of the 1960s demonstrated, as James McBride Dabbs argued, that blacks and whites had been "fused by the fires of history."[23] They had shared the same land, defeat, poverty, ignorance, and exploitation. And now blacks offered the lessons of that past to whites in order to remove the burdens of history from both races. With blacks as partners instead of objects, whites could allow their historical perspective to gain a maturity and an understanding that would liberate the future. The movement, by debunking one important myth of that perspective—black inferiority—called into question the meaning of other historical myths, such as those of the nature and role of black and white women, the Old South, and the Civil War and Reconstruction. The movement provided an alternative interpretation. It was no coincidence, for example, that white academic southern historians launched major revisions on these themes in the 1950s and '60s.[24]

Whether or not southern whites would assume a new perspective on the past was a problematic question. Southern blacks had altered regional race relations less through moral suasion and the promise of redemption—though they were important factors—than through the compulsion of federal law. Civic leaders who quickly endorsed desegregation and called for peace did so more in the name of profits than prophecy, which is not to deny genuine feelings of remorse. Also, instead of interpreting events of the 1960s as liberating, whites could very well perceive a massive defeat. The surrender a century earlier led to a society that was not so much closed as truncated, locked in an orthodoxy that restricted everyone and everything to varying degrees. Perhaps, as historian Joel Williamson noted, "The Southern white psyche in 1965 had reached a new low." The reason for this depression, Williamson maintained, was that "the Southern psyche was long driven to seek respect from the North and love from the Negro. Southerners might survive a lack of respect from the North, but they could not survive continuing manifestations of hate from black people."[25] In short, the victory could produce a backlash.

Signs

In the immediate aftermath of the legislative victories, such a scenario seemed unlikely. The South appeared as one euphoric entity, basking in its newfound racial accommodation and enjoying unprecedented prosperity, which many observers linked to civil rights legislation. Southern pundits, mostly white, predicted an extraordinary era of moral, economic, and political leadership in the South. These boosters, not unlike the economic propagandists that elevated a few textile mills into a great industrial revolution nearly a century earlier, ran happily through the southern press and numerous national publications proclaiming the dawn of a new era. National audiences believed these regional theorists all the more as northern cities, and the blacks within them, came down upon each other.

Indeed the South, like Ebenezer Scrooge rediscovering the meaning of Christmas after being scared nearly to death, bounded about in giddy fashion in the decade after 1965. It was, as writer Walker Percy termed it in 1966, "an almost invincible happiness." Southern politicians and journalists not only waxed ecstatic at the South's liberation but offered the region as a national model. A rejuvenated New South Creed emerged, touting the former Confederacy as both an economic miracle *and* a paragon of racial peace and harmony. Anniston, Alabama, journalist H. Brandt Ayers proclaimed a "postracial South" in 1971. Former North Carolina governor Terry Sanford, referring to improved race relations in 1970, declared that "now is the time, and the South can lead the way. . . . The South's time has come after a century of being the whipping boy and the backward child." Writer and publisher Willie Morris promised that the South could offer "more than a few crucial lessons to other Americans."[26]

The national press picked up the refrain, eager to pursue a new angle, especially one laden with irony, and the South, if nothing else, was and is ironic. The South was "in." Its music, folklore, literature, and political leaders attained national exposure and admiration. The Sunbelt had replaced the Old South in national imagery. A series of complimentary articles in the New York *Times* in 1976 and the presidential candidacy of former Georgia governor Jimmy Carter that same year sealed the region's image as a national poster child for what was right in an America just emerging from a disastrous war and an equally debilitating scandal in the White House. Never mind that scholars pounced on the concept of the Sunbelt and riddled it with holes, exposing persistent poverty, racism, voting-rights abuses, and religion run amuck; the very disdain of academics merely served to elevate the South even further in national estimation. It was *Gone With the Wind* all over again, only this time it wasn't a movie, it was the real thing. If, as the saying goes, Americans vote with their feet, then the South was turning up a big victor. In the 1970s, for the first time since the Civil War, the South ceased being a net exporter of its people. No longer did northerners check their accents, ethnic customs, or beliefs at the border and hope to plunge into anonymity. Everyone seemed welcome in the South, black and white, native and nonnative.

Of course, contrary evidence could be found if only one looked. The white supremacists had not suddenly disappeared, and black southerners did not automatically join the southern mainstream fully prepared to enter into partnerships with their white neighbors. Nor did it appear likely that, given decades of scrupulous cultivation of historical, religious, and political orthodoxy, that the South would now become a bastion of freethinking, honest debate, and democracy.

The most obvious and immediate change occurred in the dismantling of the signs that divided the South for nearly a century. Blacks no longer walked through their towns and cities perpetually reminded that the terms "white" and "colored" defined their lives for the worse. Though the signs came down, changed practice sometimes came later. Blacks kept their sixth sense of how much to push the new legislation and how much to hold back and go about their business as before. Many factories and businesses in the South continued to maintain separate facilities, though management no longer formally designated them as such. Blacks also knew which bars, restaurants, and hotels they could enter safely. Yet outward compliance with the public-accommodations features of the 1964 Civil Rights Act was widespread, and open defiance was minimal.

White businessmen seemed weary of defending an indefensible system, especially one that unsettled the local economy. Andrew Young, a 1960s civil rights activist and former U.S. congressman and mayor of Atlanta, recalled returning to a St. Augustine, Florida, motel five days after the act's passage. Just the previous week, a waitress had poured hot coffee over Young and his group, who were seeking service in the motel restaurant, and the manager had laced the swimming pool with hydrochloric acid just as Young prepared to wade in. "We went back to that same restaurant," Young related, "and those people were just wonderful. They were apologetic. They said, 'We were just afraid of losing our business. We didn't want to be the only ones to be integrated. But if everybody's got to do it, we've been ready for it a long time. We're so glad the president signed this law and now we can be through these troubles.'"[27] It is not clear whether such attitudes reflected a genuine embrace of integration or a great relief that the demonstrations had ended and the South could go about its business without the distractions of racial strife. In the short run, it did not much matter, because doors closed for decades suddenly opened for blacks, especially middle-class blacks, and there was hope that other segments of black society would follow.

Equally impressive was the death knell to the one-party South, a moribund system by 1965 anyway, one whose usefulness had clearly passed its time. Two major shifts occurred, both replete with ironies. First, southern blacks, protected by the 1965 Voting Rights Act, registered in droves and overwhelmingly supported the Democratic Party, which led the fight for racial equality in the Congress and at the White House but historically had been the political engine of white supremacy. Second, southern whites began to desert the party of Redemption for their historic enemies, the Republicans.

In economic terms, benefits began to accrue to blacks with sufficient education and background to take advantage of the affirmative-action provisions of the 1964 Civil Rights Act and the establishment of the Equal Employment Opportunity Commission (EEOC). For the first time, black workers moved into factory floor positions in the textile industry. As federal and local governments expanded and black political power advanced, public-sector hiring of blacks rose as well. The old black middle class of teachers and preachers now expanded to include government workers and an array of white-collar positions in the growing cities of the South as the region's economy mirrored the national trends toward service employment. The formal denouement of school segregation and the opening up of top-flight state institutions to all qualified citizens boosted job prospects as well. It was typical for black high-school students to head up north after graduation to seek education or employment opportunities; more began to stay in the South, and by the 1970s more came back, or moved to the region for the first time. Given these serial blows to white supremacy, the euphoric rhetoric is hardly surprising. These were not pie-in-the-sky speculations; these were real and dramatic examples of what, just a short decade earlier, would have been unthinkable.

The historic lesson of the first Reconstruction, however, was that it was possible to overcome harsh legislation and political and social upheaval. Though the type of vigilante violence that undid the first Reconstruction would not be possible in the age of television, mass journalism, and a national economy, there were strategies whites could implement that would stay, moderate, or even reverse the intent of the civil rights legislation and of the movement in general.

Black southerners had offered up an alternative historical vision. The next three decades demonstrated that its acceptance throughout the region varied and that the traditional perspective on the past showed remarkable vitality. The mentality that forged white supremacy and one-party rule, that condemned dissent and promoted orthodoxy, is more widespread than the glass and steel towers of the sparkling and sprawling cities would lead us to believe. The region's promoters in the 1970s heralded the onset of the Southern Century; the nation as a whole may be less thankful for that prospect once it recognizes that although the civil rights movement ended in 1965, the struggle for the regional soul and control of its past has continued.

9 New Battlegrounds, Old Strategies

> In the South, we are two cultures, one black and the other white, and yet we
> are one culture. That is the essence of our southern lives, a tension-laden
> contradiction, an apparent impossibility which is the root of our being.
> —Joel Williamson, "The Oneness of Southern Life"

Reminiscent of the hopeful freedmen who lined up by the registration desks in the tumultuous days following the Confederacy's surrender, African Americans after the Voting Rights Act passed stood in registration lines, carefully filling out forms with whatever writing implements they had at hand. One hundred years had passed, and nothing, it seemed, had happened. But 1965 was not 1865; there would be no hooded hooligans roaming the night, no extralegal legislatures sealing off blacks from the ballot box, and no creative accounting of votes or voters. Maybe.

The immediate results of the 1965 Voting Rights Act sufficed to stifle thoughts that the second Reconstruction would unfold as the first—an initial ray of hope followed by darkness and despair. Changes were especially notable in the Deep South, where the most egregious restrictions on the voting rights of black citizens existed. By 1967 black registration had jumped from 19 percent to 52 percent in Alabama and from 7 to 60 percent in Mississippi.[1] By the mid-1970s African Americans accounted for one-fifth to one-fourth of the electorate in the Deep South, and politicians responded accordingly. The open race-baiting of the one-party era subsided. Andrew Young spoke about the new political arithmetic in 1976: "It used to be Southern politics was just 'nigger' politics—a question of which candidate could 'outnigger' the other. Then you registered 10% to 15% in the community, and folks would start saying 'Nigra.' Later you got 35% to 40% registered, and it was amazing how quick they learned how to say 'Nee-grow.' And now that we've got 50%, 60%, 70% of the black votes registered in the South, everybody's proud to be associated with their black brothers and sisters."[2]

Election results reflected the new political era as Dale Bumpers, touting a race-neutral populism, became governor of Arkansas in 1970, handily defeating Orval Faubus. The following year, William Waller won election as governor of Mississippi on a platform of racial moderation. In Georgia, Jimmy Carter replaced rabid segregationist Lester Maddox in the State House. As Carter's successor in Georgia, George Busbee noted in an appropriate metaphor: "The politics of race has gone with the wind."[3]

Voting Rights and Wrongs

If the history that prevails reflects the power that is wielded, then black southerners have become important players in shaping the South's new historical context. The congressional roll call on the voting-rights extension in 1975 revealed the impact of black enfranchisement on southern congressmen. In the House, the 1974 class of southern Democrats voted twelve to one in favor of extension; the 1972 group supported the measure by a ten-to-two margin. In the Senate, southern Democrats voted for the extension nine to six. Those Democratic senators elected after 1966 supported the bill by a vote of eight to one; those elected prior to 1966 opposed the extension by a margin of five to one.[4]

By 1995 African Americans held 16 percent of all seats in southern state legislators while constituting 16 percent of the total population. In the thirty years since the passage of the Voting Rights Act, black representation in southern state legislatures increased more than sixteenfold, surpassing the rate of increase in the North (35 percent), where only 4.7 percent of the legislators are black, compared with a black population proportion of 9 percent.[5]

There is also evidence that the extreme racial polarization in southern voting is moderating somewhat. In the 1998 congressional elections, after court reversals reduced black congressman Mel Watt's thin black majority to a decided minority of 34 percent, he won reelection with 56 percent of the vote over a white Republican opponent. Similar results occurred in redrawn congressional districts in Georgia, where black representatives Cynthia McKinney and Sanford Bishop easily won reelection in 1998. The black electorate in their districts accounted for roughly one-third of the eligible voters. All three incumbents achieved relatively easy victories in the 2000 elections as well. Some attribute these striking victories to the power of incumbency and its benefits, including fund-raising and exposure, or to the fact that Republican opponents have not been strong or have run weak campaigns. Regardless, the fact is that black candidates are winning in majority-white districts.[6]

These gains have not occurred without a fight, and the battle is ongoing. From the outset of the Voting Rights Act's implementation, states and localities have attempted to dilute the black vote. Until the 1970s and early 1980s, when the federal courts struck down at-large voting in certain jurisdictions, lawmakers abolished districts and wards in order to spread the black vote throughout one large district. In 1966 the Mississippi state legislature, for example, resurrected the post-Reconstruction era strategies of "cracking, stacking, and packing." Lawmakers drew some districts to split heavy black concentrations (cracking); in others they concentrated large numbers of blacks with even larger numbers of whites (stacking); and they prepared a few totally black districts (packing) where it was impossible to leaven black voters with whites due to a high concentration of blacks. These packed districts ensured that adjacent areas would remain in white control. Also in 1966—and the timing is not fortuitous—a special legislative session in North Carolina authorized forty-nine boards of county commissioners to switch from district to at-large electoral systems. The state also required at-large elections for all school boards.[7]

Runoff primaries proved another popular technique to limit black electoral success. Lawmakers mandated a majority vote in order for a candidate to win a primary. In multicandidate fields, this proved well nigh impossible. Blacks who survived the first primary, even if they had finished first but with under 50 percent of the vote, typically failed to win the runoff primary, especially in at-large districts or statewide elections. (Most of these majority runoff statutes remain on the books in the South.) When redistricting time came around, as required after every decennial census, through the 1980s lawmakers protected racial, partisan, and incumbent interests. It would not be until well into the 1980s that most at-large systems were abolished, either through settlement or adjudication.[8]

Annexations also proved a popular mechanism to dilute the growing number of black votes in cities. Even before the Voting Rights Act, white leaders understood the political value of incorporating white suburban areas. When Atlanta mayor William B. Hartsfield annexed Buckhead in 1952, he added 100,000 whites to the city's population.[9]

Baton Rouge, Louisiana, pursued an active annexation policy during the 1960s and 1970s. The city annexed twenty-seven areas during the 1960s and forty-three in the 1970s. Through the middle of the 1970s, whites composed more than 80 percent of the population annexed into the city since 1947. During this nearly thirty-year period, sixty-one subdivisions and areas were annexed into the city; only six possessed black populations of over 4 percent of the total. Without the annexations, the city of Baton Rouge would have been nearly half black by 1980; the black population instead stood at slightly over one-third at that date. But the city suddenly turned cautious when confronted with an annexation request from black residents of an unincorporated area in the mid-1970s. That area came into the city in three separate annexations over the course of five years, as white local officials called for a reassessment of annexation policy, expressing concern about the financial implications of adding new territory to the city.[10]

When these mechanisms no longer worked because of demographic changes, lawmakers adopted more-drastic measures. In 1980 white civic leaders in Baton Rouge revived a plan to abolish the city council and expand the parish (county) council to take jurisdiction over the city. Though promoted as an efficiency move, in fact no major services were consolidated. The African American population of the city had grown from 28 percent in 1970 to 37 percent in 1980, and that growth would be reflected in the composition of the city council, where at least three out of seven, and perhaps four out of seven, seats could be occupied by blacks. The scenario had significant implications for the disbursement of urban services and patronage. Under the new parish council, blacks controlled four out of twelve seats, a decided minority compared with the balance of power they might have held on the city council.[11]

The 2000 presidential election in Florida cast light on the dark shadows of electoral politics in a southern state: ballots arrived late at Bethune-Cookman College, a predominantly black institution in Daytona Beach; there was sudden police presence in Tampa's black neighborhoods on election day; laptop computers were provided to Cuban American (mostly Republican) precincts in Miami-Dade County to facilitate communication with the central voter registry to resolve questions and disputes expeditiously, but to only one black precinct; computers for the same purpose were sent to selected precincts in Tampa, but not one black precinct received the machines; and there were widespread reports of police roadblocks and sweeps for no apparent reason on election day. Doubtless part of the difficulty resulted from the unprecedented black turnout, but questions of intent surface when such patterns are so widespread.[12]

The continuing conflict over black voting rights reflects the resurgence of the Republican party in the South since the 1960s. While pundits praised the race-sanitized campaigns of the 1970s, a new, more subtle language was emerging that employed code words, such as "forced busing," "law and order," and "job quotas." Each phrase assumed a corresponding image in white minds. When Republican candidates talked about the need for teacher testing and accountability in education, the image was of an incompetent black teacher dismissed; when candidates mentioned welfare reform, the white voter imagined the black welfare queen dethroned; and toughness on crime conjured up images of black criminals behind bars.

The revitalized Republican Party in the South has been the primary beneficiary and instigator of the camouflaged racial rhetoric. Southern Republican leaders before the 1960s presented themselves legitimately as moderate alternatives to most white Democrats, especially for urban voters more interested in economic opportunity than racial politics. Their traditional political base in the mountain regions of the South also typically eschewed racial issues for the simple reason that very few African Americans resided in those districts. But the transformation of southern politics precipitated by the Democratic-sponsored civil rights legislation of the mid-1960s drew conservative white Democrats into the Republican Party.

Actually, the desertion of white southern Democrats began long before the 1965 Voting Rights Act. In 1948, when President Truman presented a civil rights package to Congress, a number of southern Democrats bolted and formed the Dixiecrat Party, which captured the electoral votes of several Deep South states but did not derail Truman's reelection. In 1952 and 1956, reflecting the growing urbanization in the region, more southerners left the party to vote for the Republican presidential candidate Dwight D. Eisenhower. At the local and statewide level, however, the South remained solidly Democratic.

The civil rights movement changed all that. As early as 1962, several Republican gubernatorial candidates ran unsuccessful race-based campaigns but demonstrated sufficient strength on which to build should whites become

more disaffected with the national Democratic Party. Some previews of future Republican campaigns occurred in South Carolina in 1962. In that year
William D. Workman Jr., a journalist, ran for the U.S. Senate against Democratic incumbent Olin D. Johnston, a segregationist. Yet Workman managed
to stake out a position to Johnston's right in the campaign. He complained
that blacks who were offended by the term "nigger" were "too sensitive." As
for the Civil War, that conflict demonstrated "who was stronger, not necessarily who was right." Workman also managed to throw in some praise for
the Reconstruction-era Ku Klux Klan, though he admitted the most recent
iteration of the group was "unpleasant." Though he lost, he managed to receive 44 percent of the vote.[13]

In 1964, when the Republicans nominated as their presidential candidate
Arizona senator Barry Goldwater, a conservative who had voted against the
Civil Rights Act, the "great white switch" was underway in earnest. When
Congress passed the 1964 Civil Rights Act, President Johnson remarked to a
confidante, "I think we just delivered the South to the Republican Party for
some time to come." Subsequent events proved the accuracy of Johnson's
prediction. In 1984 political scientist Earl Black spoke to a group of Republicans in South Carolina on the nature and prospects of the party in the South.
After his talk, a few businessmen came up to say that they had enjoyed the
presentation though they felt that he had overstated the party's racial appeal.
They suggested that race was, at best, a minor factor in the party's southern
success and that economic reasons were paramount. Before Black could reply,
another businessman approached the group and interjected, "Enjoyed the
talk. Why don't you leave the niggers behind and come and join us?"[14]

Though Republican leaders would repudiate the latter sentiment, race and
economics not only became central to party strategy in the South but merged
to some degree. A lifelong Democratic voter from Mississippi explained his
shift to the Republican camp: "It's all this 'gimme' business. . . . What we
need now is for the black race to pull themselves up by their own bootstraps."
This comment could be neatly cataloged as a reaffirmation of the Republican
Party's free-enterprise philosophy; Democratic Party leaders, however, read
other meanings into this and similar statements. As former Democratic Mississippi congressman Wayne Dowdy observed, "Republicans in Mississippi
are . . . [in the GOP] because they like what they think the Republican Party
now stands for in a racial sense. And that's a strong part of the Republican
Party in Mississippi. In my district, a lot of the people who are in the Republican Party are racists."[15]

Some credit should also go to Democrat George Wallace as an architect of the modern Republican Party in the South. By the late 1960s the Alabama governor had moderated his raw, racist appeals, though race still played a crucial role in his statewide and national campaigns. Much as white southerners claimed that states' rights drove the Confederate cause during the Civil War, Wallace framed his racial rhetoric as an issue of state sovereignty. The rough translation was that states knew best how to order their own race relations, and those who heard Wallace's message grasped the subtext clearly. He employed states' rights, crime, and welfare as surrogate issues for race. He understood the alienation of the white working class and tapped into their fears and frustrations. The Republicans would do the same.[16]

Louisiana's David Duke embodied the logical conclusion of Republican politics and rhetoric in the South. This is not to say that Duke's Nazi and Klan past and his career of purveying racist and anti-Semitic literature reflected anything typical about southern Republicans. Duke carefully kept some of these biographical details hidden or explained them away as youthful indiscretions. But his message of white victimization—especially as related to affirmative action, the importance of getting tough on crime and welfare fraud, and the promotion of low taxes and family values that stress heterosexual relationships and two-parent households—differed little from standard Republican campaign fare. Duke appealed not only to blue-collar whites but also to middle-class suburban homeowners fearful of slipping back or behind and resentful of what they viewed as unfair government intervention on behalf of African Americans.

The message, coupled with an economic downturn in Louisiana's critical petroleum industry, catapulted Duke in 1989 to a narrow and surprising victory in a race for a seat in the Louisiana House of Representatives. Duke's past became an asset. As a Duke supporter explained, "We need him now. We have to send a message to the blacks." While national Republicans denounced and distanced themselves from Duke, their party colleagues in Louisiana did not. The Reverend Billy McCormack of the state's Christian Coalition, responding to charges that Duke's message contradicted the Gospel, declared that Duke represented less of a threat to Christianity than the Jewish lawyers of the American Civil Liberties Union.

The following year, Duke took on incumbent U.S. Senator J. Bennett Johnston in the open primary (Republicans and Democrats run in the same primary in Louisiana) for Johnston's U.S. Senate seat. Though Johnston won easily, Duke polled nearly 60 percent of the state's white vote. Of Louisiana's

140-member Republican central committee, only two individuals spoke out against Duke's candidacy, and one, Beth Rickey, was nearly expelled from the group. In 1991 Duke surprised political experts by finishing second in the gubernatorial primary, outpolling incumbent governor Buddy Roemer. In the runoff against Democrat Edwin Edwards, the moral and economic consequences of Duke's candidacy mobilized a broad coalition of business and political leaders, particularly after details emerged indicating that Duke's "youthful indiscretions" with Nazism persisted well into the 1980s.[17]

David Duke continued to roil the waters of Louisiana politics. Though he also continued to lose, his performance consistently exceeded the predictions of polls and pundits. In May 1999 he fell just short of qualifying for a runoff for the U.S. Congress, finishing a close third in a race where all five candidates held conservative Republican credentials. Unlike in his previous campaigns, Duke made little attempt to hide his Aryan-supremacy views from the public, having recently published a book calling for an Aryan resurgence and the establishment of voluntary homelands for minorities. During the campaign he denounced Kwanzaa celebrations and Malcolm X postage stamps. In the nation's second-poorest state, the only southern state where more people moved out than migrated in during the 1990s, these issues hardly seem compelling. But the white-supremacy campaigns of the first half of the twentieth century also bore little relation to the problems of white constituents. In his postelection "victory" speech, Duke declared, "This has got to say something very powerful about the issues I represent. These people did not go into this unaware." Only one of his opponents denounced him, and he finished dead last. Governor Mike Foster, a Republican, said nothing; in fact, he purchased Duke's mailing list for his first gubernatorial campaign.[18] The point is not that southern Republicans are edging toward Aryan-supremacist views but that the rhetoric of their campaigns and some of their political bedfellows create an atmosphere that implicitly condones more-extreme representations of their message.

Trent Lott did not bring the burden of a David Duke–type résumé to his position as U.S. Senate Majority Leader. Lott is a southern Republican who epitomizes the rise of the party in the region, as well as the rise of the South within the national party and the nation. Yet his fellow travelers in Mississippi include a group, the Council of Conservative Citizens, whose members descend directly from the White Citizens' Council, the regionwide organization that served as the coordinating force for massive resistance to desegregation during the 1950s and 1960s. The refurbished council includes five thousand members statewide, including nearly three dozen members of the state legislature. Confederate battle flags festoon its meetings, and members stand for "Dixie" and sit for "My Country, 'Tis of Thee." The council supports "Southern cultural issues" as well as restrictions on immigration and an end to busing to achieve school desegregation, issues within the Republican mainstream. Council newsletters feature regular columns by the venerable founder of the White Citizens' Council, Robert Patterson, who writes, "Western civilization, with all its might and glory, would never have achieved its greatness without the directing hand of God and the creative genius of the white race. Any effort to destroy the race by a mixture of black blood is an effort to destroy western civilization itself." The council's fund-raiser is a required stop on the campaign tour for the state's Republican politicians.[19]

Much as the South became the bellwether of the national Democratic Party after 1900, the region is now the dominant partner in the Republican coalition. And as Democrats in other parts of the country sustained the racial status quo in deference to their southern colleagues, the racial and religious conservatism of southern Republicans has a controlling influence on the national party. For all the talk about the South as the nation's race leader, the growth and strength of the Republican Party indicates a different track, one that maintains the South's divergence from the rest of the country.

At the same time, the political landscape of the South is changing. There are simply fewer good ole boys and good ole girls than in the 1970s; not that they have disappeared, but they have been joined by millions of migrants from the North who bring with them not so much different historical perspectives as no perspective at all. From these newcomers is most often heard the plaint that "*they* are still fighting the Civil War." The refrain is uttered more in exasperation and a dash of incomprehension than in outright hostility. The migrants are much less susceptible to appeals, subtle or otherwise, of the white-supremacist and biblical roots of that history, though they may be Republicans. They are also generally more aggressive in spending tax money, and they are prominent among the reasons why the South today is dotted with so many Democratic "education governors."

A measure of the growing political power of migrants was the defection in 2000 of Republican Randy J. Sauder of Cobb County, Georgia, to the Democratic Party. Though hardly presaging another "great white switch," the move is indicative of changes in southern demography. Sauder serves in the Georgia House of Representatives and promoted conservative causes so faithfully that, in his first term beginning in 1994, a national Republican organization voted him the top freshman state legislator in the nation. Cobb County, the former stronghold of Newt Gingrich, hardly seems like a Democrat-friendly venue. But Cobb County is part of the vast Atlanta metropolitan area, which, in turn, is the epicenter of a southeastern migration stream that brought 2.5 million Americans to the region during the 1990s. Though most of these new residents are white and typically Republican, they do not share the religious and historical perspectives of longtime residents. They are much less interested in the coded issues of lower taxes, welfare reform, and crime than they are in managed growth and education, issues that tend to favor southern Democrats more than southern Republicans. Sauder explained, "My district has changed so dramatically since I was first elected. The people moving in want to see action on issues like education and sprawl, and it's the Democrats that have grabbed those themes and delivered." Also, these once solidly Republican suburban metropolitan districts are now experiencing black in-migration for the first time. By the year 2000, 12 percent of Cobb County's population was African American, compared to just 4 percent in 1980.

Sauder's conversion may not signal the beginning of a Democratic tide so much as the moderating of the southern Republican Party. If so, that would remove a considerable obstacle to the redefinition of the southern past. As John N. Davis, executive director of a nonprofit research group in North Carolina, noted, "These [newcomers] are pro-government Republicans, who want the best soccer fields, schools and police departments that government money can buy. And suddenly you see formerly conservative candidates for office pushing education and environment programs that they would have tried to cut ten years ago." During the last three years, residents in nineteen of the twenty counties in metropolitan Atlanta have voted to raise sales taxes to pay for schools and other projects.[20]

Equally indicative of the changing political landscape was the Florida campaign conducted by 2000 Democratic presidential candidate Al Gore. By traditional political analysis, Florida should have gone easily for Governor George W. Bush. It is a prosperous Sunbelt state with huge populations of affluent suburban whites, many from the North and typically Republican, coupled with more traditional conservative elements in north Florida and the Panhandle, as well as the Cuban American community in Miami. Successful Democrats running for statewide office in Florida (or in any other southern state) usually cobble together a coalition of African Americans and enough suburban and blue-collar whites to secure victory. Florida Democrats such as

Reubin Askew, Lawton Chiles, and Bob Graham achieved statewide victories by picking off enough good ole boys and girls to go along with the traditionally Democratic black and Jewish vote. But, as political analyst Jonathan Cohn noted, Gore's Florida campaign wrote off the "southerner vote" and pieced together a coalition of everyone else, including Jewish voters, non-Cuban Hispanics, African Americans, and young suburban independents, all groups whose numbers are growing rather than receding in Florida and elsewhere in the South. After peaking at 43 percent in 1996, Republican registration has declined in the state. Although the southern establishment still runs the state, their time in power may be limited.[21]

The South's changing demography may help African American residents to lift the burdens of history, which their political participation has lightened but not banished. The key political issues that could effect this political transformation include education and the environment foremost. In both cases, the historical burdens have fallen most heavily on black southerners, and if racial politics can recede in importance, they would be the greater beneficiaries of new policies in these areas.

Schools: Burdens of Race and History

Few public institutions in the urban South have reflected racial policy divisions more in the years after 1965 than the public-school system. By the 1980s most white civic leaders in the urban South had already abandoned the public schools. What began with such high hopes in the aftermath of the *Brown* decision ended in a resegregation of the school system.

The historical context is important in considering the fate of public education in the South and its relationship to race. The white construction of southern history suggested not only that African Americans lacked the intellectual capacity for learning, but that attempts to educate that population were both futile and dangerous. Too much education for too many of either race could challenge prevailing historical and racial dogmas, as well as the leaders who profited from maintaining these regional orthodoxies. As W. J. Cash wrote in 1929, "A thinker in the South is regarded quite logically as an enemy of the people." Religious attitudes reinforced secular suspicion of formal education. The received truths of history blended with the divinely inspired truths of biblical text to abjure doubt, inquiry, and ambiguity. These attitudes extended to the use of textbooks, the hiring of teachers, and the extent to which local educators permitted outside influences to enter the class-room, a process that continues to the present. In the late 1980s, for example, the Bay County, Florida, school board banned sixty-four books, including works by Shakespeare and Sophocles, that they deemed to contain obsceni-ties. The superintendent said that he "hopes to restore Christian values" to the school system.[22]

School expenditures, especially low teacher salaries, and a greater neglect for elementary education has reflected such attitudes. As one Louisiana edu-cator commented in the 1970s, elementary schools in that state have histori-cally been accorded "the short end of the stick as to building facilities, qualifications, pay, and workload of the teachers." Significant change would not occur any time soon: "It would be pleasant to record the fact that enlight-ened change has brought an end to such practices [but] such desirable evi-dence of progress is less than complete." The school population became whiter and wealthier as it moved up to secondary education, which received greater resources.[23]

Since World War II, educators throughout the South have understood that a good public school system requires an open mind and supportive atti-tudes. A Florida educator wrote in 1945 that "the chief problem to be solved [with respect to public education] . . . is the problem of improving the under-standing and changing the attitude of the people" toward formal education. In 1974 a Louisiana educator noted that "basic to establishing, maintaining, and improving a system of education is favorable public sentiment. . . . Its development has not come easily." A special task force on southern education advised in 1991, "We must increase the public's commitment to education." Finally, a 1996 report placed the issue in historical context, concluding, "The South's further advancement will depend on its shedding vestiges of old atti-tudes and mind-sets that have stereotyped blacks, women, and rural residents and channeled them into lower-skill, lower-pay jobs."[24]

A key factor in changing these attitudes is local leaders' perception of eco-nomic development, in much the same way as improved economic prospects softened segregationist sentiment among the South's urban business leaders during the 1960s. Historically, selling the South did not require an elaborate or refined educational system. In fact, too much education could lead to worker agitation or out-migration. The South found its wealth in things: oil, gas, cotton, and tobacco. Education was a cost. But times have changed, and now things are less important. As a 1996 report on economic conditions in the South put it, "What people know builds economies and individual wealth these days, not what they can coax from the earth. Education is a necessary investment in the well-being of individuals, the wealth of a community and the future of the South's economy. How that investment is made—how priorities are drawn and ordered—is the most important decision the region will make."[25]

Good education has become good business. The general value of a liberal education to a society is scarcely considered, any more than the moral dimension of the civil rights movement received priority among whites who wished to accommodate change without extending themselves too much. But for some localities, it is too late for that decision. Hostile racial attitudes combined with historic ambivalence over public education has already seriously compromised many urban school systems in the South.

The U.S. Supreme Court's decision in *Swann v. Charlotte-Mecklenburg Board of Education* (1971) required southern school districts to initiate desegregation immediately (typically accomplished through busing). The ruling had a significant impact. Relatively few black pupils attended majority-white schools as late as a decade after the *Brown* decision. By 1972, though, 36 percent of the region's blacks attended majority-white schools, reaching a high of 44 percent in 1983. But after that date, the South reversed itself, proving that revolutions can indeed go backwards; the figure declined to 39.2 percent in 1991, to 36.6 percent by 1994.[26]

There are numerous reasons for the decline. The increasing black population in central cities such as Atlanta and Birmingham renders integration with whites more difficult, especially since courts have not required black city and white suburban schools to merge for the purpose of achieving racial integration. In a few cases, black leaders have not pursued the option to voluntarily initiate cross-suburban busing. In the late 1960s, in what became known as the "Second Atlanta Compromise," the city's black leaders agreed not to press for suburban busing in return for greater control of the city's school system. Blacks certainly control Atlanta's schools today, but they are presiding over a troubled enterprise that has lost all possibility for integrated education. It is difficult to desegregate when more than 90 percent of the school population consists of black children.[27] Some cities, such as Little Rock, Arkansas, and Norfolk, Virginia, have ended or modified busing (with the blessings of federal courts), relying on magnet schools, voluntary assignments, and the pairing of districts to achieve modest desegregation. A primary objective in many urban school systems is to prevent the erosion of the white middle-class population, an essential component for quality education, not only because of the children's educational background but also because of parental involvement. Many whites still equate black schools with inferiority and hesitate to send their children to school with too many black youngsters. They favor integration, but not too much of it.

Statistical profiles indicate that southern schools are more integrated than schools elsewhere in the country. Much of the integration occurs, ironically, in the rural South, where there is often only one school for all to attend. Historically, there may have been one black and one white school. When forced to desegregate, rural school districts typically closed black schools and merged the black student body into the white school. The advantage of the larger consolidated school for high-school sports, especially for football, has kept white attendance fairly stable in rural areas.[28]

As the South becomes more urbanized, the outlook for integrated education is bleak. Some blacks and whites question the educational value of desegregated schools. Significant educational disparities continue to separate black and white students. In 1996, for example, the Charlotte-Mecklenburg school system reported that 39 percent of black third graders read at or above grade level, compared to 76 percent of whites. There is a direct correlation in Charlotte-Mecklenburg between the percentage of black enrollment at a particular school and the performance of its students on standardized tests. But integrated schools may not boost black test scores anyway; there is evidence that cultural and environmental factors are more important in determining black academic achievement than the racial composition of a particular school. There is no easy answer, either to the continued struggles of public education in the South generally or to the increase in segregated schools. Historical legacies, both of attitudes toward education and of racial perceptions, are difficult to overcome.[29]

Natural and Unnatural

If southern history is a tar baby that the present generation of southerners finds difficult to grasp or release, the metaphor is more than figurative. The legacy of racially skewed public policy is especially evident in recent years with respect to the natural environment. Historically, southerners, especially southern leaders, have rarely placed concerns about the natural environment as a high priority. The region was too poor, it seemed, to afford the luxury of conservation. Clear-cutting of forests, gouging mines out of mountains and streams, belching pollutants into the air and water, and cluttering pristine beaches and waterfronts with visual eyesores and dangerous chemicals proved tolerable as long as jobs and economic development accompanied the effluvia of modernization. Selling the South has involved auctioning not only its labor but the land and resources as well. The folks who have taken advantage of state and local generosity have generally not been good custodians of their properties and surroundings. When the resource or the business played out, when better opportunities opened elsewhere, they were gone. "Captains of Second Class Industry and First Class Extortion," Robert Penn Warren called them, but, in truth, there was often little persuasion required. The South opened its arms willingly to those who sought to despoil it.[30]

The eagerness with which governments solicited exploitive activities reflects more than the poverty of the region. It belies a defensiveness that somehow the South was not part of the American industrial enterprise but instead an inferior colony that would never be quite good enough to join the great march of progress. So, as the weaker sibling, the South tried that much harder to seek approval and inclusion. The smokestack did not represent a trade-off; it represented progress and participation. The South did not invent wide-eyed boosterism, but it took the genre to a new level of excess, throwing in subsidies, land write-offs, and outright gifts that caused even a few courted executives to blush. The booster-driven economy proved not only compatible with white versions of southern history but essential to its fulfillment.

Poor, rural counties continue to sell their health for dollars in a devil's choice between poverty and temporary solvency. Of the nation's 179 toxic waste dumps, 108 of them are located in the South. The region continues to lead the nation in industrial emissions of toxic chemicals.[31] Louisiana has been especially assiduous in courting polluting industries as it has transformed itself from a poor agricultural state to a poor industrial state. "Cancer alley," a corridor stretching along the Mississippi River from Alsen in suburban Baton Rouge down past New Orleans, has become a notorious metaphor for unchecked corporate pollution. Louisiana has consistently scored at the bottom of the *Green Index*, an annual standard of environmental health in the South published by the Durham-based Institute for Southern Studies in their magazine, *Southern Exposure*. The state also ranks at or near the bottom in basic lifestyle indicators such as infant mortality, households without plumbing, and the number of workers in high-risk jobs. The state has been historically generous to the petrochemical firms. During the 1980s, for example, the thirty largest corporations in the state, many of them petrochemical operations, received $2.5 billion in Louisiana property-tax exemptions. These exemptions did not necessarily result in more work for the state's labor force; relatively few new permanent positions were created by the windfall.[32]

The vast majority of residents living near the petrochemical plants along "cancer alley" are black, a population historically restricted in both political and economic arenas in Louisiana. Concerns about "ecoracism" emerged from both the civil rights movement of the 1960s and '70s and the environmental movement of the 1970s and '80s. Louisiana has become a battleground against such exploitation. Along cancer alley, hazardous waste facilities are often located adjacent to black communities like Alsen. During the mid-1980s local residents successfully organized, with the help of the Sierra Club and Greenpeace, to block the incineration of polychlorinated biphenyls (PCBs) in their neighborhood. A report issued by the Environmental Protection Agency in 1993 confirmed residents' suspicions of a strong correlation between the location of polluting plants and waste facilities and black districts. Several international conglomerates, such as Georgia Gulf, Dow Chemical, and Placid Refining Company, have dealt with the problem by purchasing entire black districts near the facilities. Similar organized activities of poor black and Hispanic residents occurred in Brownsville, Texas, in 1983, to protest the burning of carcinogenic wastes near their coastline in the Gulf of Mexico. In June 1997 the Louisiana NAACP organized a demonstration for ecojustice in Baton Rouge that drew ten thousand participants.[33]

In 1998 black Louisiana residents waged battle against a Japanese firm called Shintech. The company hoped to build the nation's largest polyvinyl chloride (PVC) production plant. PVC is used in a wide range of products, including pipes, wire coating, credit cards, and packaging materials. Black citizens in Convent, Louisiana, in St. James Parish, where the proposed plant would be built, organized the St. James Citizens for Jobs and the Environment to oppose plant construction. They were up against formidable odds. Nearly half of the parish population lacked a high-school education, and many were reluctant to step forward for fear of losing or being denied a job. Shintech launched an extensive advertising campaign in the local newspaper to discourage potential protesters. The parish president anonymously sent out four hundred letters urging recipients to lobby the state's Department of Economic Development to support Shintech. The people who received the letters were those on a job waiting list. A Baton Rouge public relations firm distributed a study conducted by Louisiana State University researchers on the Shintech payroll demonstrating that the high incidence of cancer among employees resulted from smoking and poor diets, not from industrial pollutants. Several independent researchers challenged both their methodology and findings.

Jobs generated the enthusiasm for Shintech among parish and state leaders, specifically 165 for local residents and millions of dollars in revenue for the local economy. But Shintech would receive more than it gave. The state donated a ten-year property-tax exemption, amounting to a savings for the company of $94.5 million. The state also declared the site of Shintech's proposed facility an enterprise zone, entitling the company to a rebate of $35 million, plus a corporate income-tax credit of $2,500 for each new job created, or a total of $412,500. Altogether, the incentives amounted to a savings of $129.9 million for Shintech, while the parish received $18 million. The black neighborhoods near the plant would gain pollution and few, if any, jobs, as most of the residents lacked a high-school diploma. Shintech ultimately pulled out of the site, not wanting to offer itself as the nation's first test case on environmental racism.[34]

Majority-black counties in the South lead the nation in hazardous-waste sites. It is not that the soil or the strategic location qualifies these districts for such placements; it is the fact they are mostly poor and mostly black and hence historically mostly powerless to object, especially when jobs and tax dollars are at stake. In the early 1990s, Mississippi state officials selected majority-black and poor Noxubee County (the county's name in Choctaw means, fittingly, "stinking creek") as the site of a hazardous-waste facility. The poor black residents opposed the facility, but their opposition probably would have produced few results if a white woman from a prominent family had not joined their cause and, with some other affluent whites, formed "Protect the Environment of Noxubee" (PEON). The local NAACP had initially endorsed the project, as it promised new job opportunities for poor blacks in the area.[35] The battle against environmental racism in most instances is no longer a conflict of poor, powerless African Americans against a white-supremacist power structure. Black political power, a greater inclination of whites to cross the color line to support black neighbors, and a general increase in environmental awareness have combined to generate interracial cooperation.

In the South, exploitation of land and labor have proved mutually reinforcing, and not just for black southerners. In recent years, the booster economy has struck especially hard at immigrant labor. The cucumber fields of North Carolina are filled with Latino workers on early spring mornings, more than ten thousand of them. The workers typically live in small, cinder-block cabins furnished with four or five beds each. A wash basin stands outside the cabins serving as the laundry and cleaning facility for the men inside. In the hot fields, quotas are weighed against water breaks, and slackers are let go; at a wage rate of seven times what a worker can make in Mexico, there are many willing to take the place of a discharged field hand. But some employers use creative accounting methods, as did one crew leader of Hispanic workers in southwest Florida convicted of violating the Thirteenth Amendment to the Constitution—the one outlawing slavery.[36] Recent investigations have uncovered fraudulent mine-safety testing in Kentucky, where miners continue to succumb to black lung. As one former inspector noted in 1999, "The health of the men never entered into it."[37] The South is still fighting the Civil War, still killing its people.

The environmental battles reflect the fact that in the South at the beginning of the twenty-first century, poverty as much as race is the debilitating feature of the economic and social landscape. Yet race, and the historical baggage accompanying it, compounds the problem. Some parts of the South are still awaiting the economic liberation prefigured by the civil rights victories of the mid-1960s.

Work: Ebb and Flow

It is true, though, that the rising tide of the Sunbelt economy has lifted numerous urban blacks into the middle class. The black middle class in North Carolina, for example, grew from 21 percent of the black population in 1969 to 44 percent in 1989; in South Carolina, it increased from 17 percent to 38 percent. Though these figures lag behind the white middle-class percentage, which is closer to 60 percent in North Carolina and about 50 percent in South Carolina, the advances are impressive. These figures are reflected regionwide in the fact that the black population is the fastest suburbanizing group in the South, and that movement into private-sector management positions is beginning to grow alongside the relatively high visibility of African Americans in local, state, and federal positions.[38]

Significant economic gaps still exist between black and white southerners reflecting a historical heritage of inadequate education, discrimination, and low expectations. Black advances have not come without white resistance. Black entrance into the textile industry, for example, saw a pattern of evasion, obstruction, and eventual reluctant acceptance of minority workers. Historically, blacks worked in the textile mills only in the most menial positions and away from the shop floor. The textile industry employed large numbers of white women and children, and mixing blacks with this work force would have been impossible given the prevailing racial views during the first half of the twentieth century. Also, the belief was widespread among mill owners and other white leaders that blacks did not possess either the dexterity or the skill to operate machinery. When black southerners attempted to enter the mill work force after the passage of the 1964 Civil Rights Act, these excuses emerged again as justification for barring blacks from textiles. Even when federal authorities invoked the new civil rights statutes, bosses used various means to limit black employment and reduce the attraction of mill work for African Americans.[39]

During the late 1960s and 1970s, African American workers entered the textile industry in appreciable numbers for the first time. Textiles offered better wages, job security, benefits, and working conditions than most unskilled African Americans could secure through other employment. In the small southern Piedmont towns and villages where many textile enterprises were located, job alternatives were scarce and textiles offered the best opportunity for achieving modest economic independence. But when few mill owners voluntarily complied with the provisions of the 1964 Civil Rights Act, prospective black workers filed suit, a sometimes dangerous process in small communities. The suits revealed a systematic pattern of discrimination against black workers into the early 1980s.

After 1964 companies removed "white" and "colored" signs from the plant. But owners often retained the separate facilities, and black workers used them "out of custom and fear." White workers refused to train blacks for higher-paying positions. Managers rarely promoted black workers, and when they did, they typically selected the most "cooperative" laborer. Personnel officers usually hired blacks at the lowest entry levels, regardless of skills. They justified such practices by claiming it minimized opposition from whites, which would harm productivity.[40]

The formal complaints against textile companies did not diminish over time; the level remained fairly constant until the 1980s. "Very significant" pay disparities between blacks and whites doing similar work persisted, according to government records. Sometimes, companies such as Cannon Mills in Kannapolis, North Carolina, simply refused to implement consent decrees (formal settlements between the federal government and an offending corporation that set specific remedies to redress violations). In the mid-1970s Cannon maintained ninety-four all-white job classifications, and thirty departments were closed to black employment. The federal government concluded that Cannon had made "next to no progress" in opening up white-collar jobs to blacks.[41]

Some employers made the best of what they considered a bad situation and used black employment to spur greater productivity among whites. In 1969 a "confidential strategy paper" prepared by the South Carolina State Committee for Technical Education endorsed integration as a means of inspiring both black and white workers: "One does not want to be outdone by the other, for the Negro wants to prove himself and the white does not want to be outperformed." Also, since black employees tended to be more sympathetic to unionization, managers could play the race card against the union, charging that unionization would threaten white jobs. The tactic persists. Union organizer Bruce Raynor noted in 1995 that "to this day [in] every campaign we run the company makes race an issue, every single one. The company will tell the whites, 'The union's going to force us to give the good jobs to blacks.' . . . It's still a big weapon against us."[42]

Still, textile employment generated some positive gains, both in blacks' economic situation and in race relations generally. In 1964 less than 5 percent of South Carolina's mill work force was black; by 1976 that figure had risen to above 30 percent. Throughout the South by the end of the 1970s, blacks held one-quarter of all textile jobs. Textile work had a profound impact on black communities in terms of education, stability, and economic independence. As one black textile worker in Rock Hill, South Carolina, noted, "Once the '60s came along the high school people, they stayed here. They became a more stable part of the community, they had better employment, they could encourage their children to go on to school, and they could pay for their education. And, you know, it improved things, it uplifted the whole community. . . . In this area textiles led the way."[43]

Black employment occasionally generated closer bonds between black and white textile workers, especially women. As their well-to-do counterparts discovered earlier in the century, black and white working-class women found a common cause in the textile mills. Ora Lee Smith, a white textile worker from Tarboro, North Carolina, explained that the hiring of black women "changed the attitudes of the whites a whole lot, because I mean at one time I guess everybody felt like we were supposed to have the better jobs, but if a person's capable of doing a job, let them have it, whoever. That's the way I feel about it now; maybe I didn't years ago." Louise Peddaway, a black Tarboro employee, recalled that "the people there really cared. They acted like they really wanted me to learn." Ollie Seals, a black worker at a Columbus, Georgia, textile plant, also remembered her initiation fondly: "At the time I was real young . . . and most of the white people looked at me as being their baby. . . . White women took care of me. They looked out and made sure that none of the other people mistreated me." Despite the hard work, the bonding with white women at some of the plants enabled black women workers to post the best attendance and retention rates of any group of workers in the textile industry. The recollections of black women stand in stark contrast to the experiences of black men with respect to their fellow white employees. Perhaps the white women saw an ally in the common fight against a male-dominated managerial staff.[44]

Some of the most effective collaborations between black and white women occurred with respect to job actions and union organizing. Women composed more than 85 percent of the work force at Oneita Knitting Mills in Andrews, South Carolina. In 1973 black and white women struck the plant, successfully underscoring the positive impact of black hiring on unionization as well as the power of interracial cooperation. The strike was a good learning experience in race relations generally. As white striker Mary Cox related, "One thing that I thoroughly enjoyed when I was out, I didn't know a lot of the women, especially the colored women, and I learned to know them, and I learned to like a lot of them that I really didn't think I could like. But I found out that they're colored people and that doesn't matter at all, they're just like we are."[45]

The increase in union activity in the textile industry after 1970 confirmed the worst fears of managers: that black workers were more amenable to both unionization and job actions. Fresh from the civil rights movement, accustomed to networking and organizing against powerful forces, African Americans approached unionization as a natural extension of their struggle for social and economic justice. Eventually, white workers who believed in the benefits of unionization but who were concerned about jobs, family, and community reaction, appreciated black workers' willingness to organize collectively. A new era of interracial unionization began to take shape.

The cruel irony of textiles, as well as of steel, in the South, is that just as blacks gained a foothold and began to achieve comparable jobs and wages, the industry faltered from an assault of overseas competition and technological change. The machine has had a serious impact on the black economy since

World War II generally, beginning in agriculture. In 1940 one-quarter of Mississippi's black population farmed; by 1990 that figure had declined to less than 1 percent. Yet many blacks (in South Carolina's case, 50 percent) continue to live in rural areas. Without farm work, and dependent on foot-loose industries, black unemployment in the rural South is high. By 1967 only 5 percent of the cotton in Mississippi was picked by hand; also by that year, the black sharecropper had just about disappeared. As late as 1959, more than seventeen thousand blacks sharecropped in the state. While there was little to recommend sharecropping as an economic activity for southern blacks, the absence of work in the rural South has resulted in chronic poverty, high illiteracy, and high infant mortality. As the industrial economy has weakened and new jobs require at least some education, rural blacks are even less suited for employment now than they were a generation ago.[46]

It is easy to pick on Mississippi, where welfare checks are the main economic activity in some predominantly black Delta counties. North Carolina is a progressive southern state with the high-tech-friendly Research Triangle Park, several top-notch public and private universities, and a reputation for moderate race relations. Eastern North Carolina, a part of the state that made national headlines in 1999 as a sodden victim of Hurricane Floyd, struggled long before the storm. A combination of mechanization in agriculture and industry, as well as the departure or closure of several manufacturing firms, cut short the revival in black employment that occurred in the decade after 1965. By 1980 Halifax County had the highest poverty rate in the state, with Duplin County close behind. The chicken-processing plants and the electrical-appliance and furniture factories have neither absorbed the surplus rural labor force nor boosted consumer income sufficiently to generate other enterprises. In November 1982, when Perdue Farms advertised for 200 workers for its new chicken-processing plant in rural Martin County, 1,400 residents applied, mostly blacks.[47]

The economic problems of blacks in eastern North Carolina reflect and reinforce significant racial disparities. Statewide, 17.8 percent of the black population and 11.3 percent of whites possess an eighth-grade education or less; in Halifax County those figures are 31.2 percent and 13.1 percent, respectively. Black per capita income was 54.9 percent that of whites in North Carolina in 1990, 42.2 percent in Halifax County. The figures in some other eastern North Carolina towns were as follows: Kinston, 38.8 percent; Roanoke Rapids, a major textile center, 39.8 percent; Scotland Neck, 33.3 percent; and Warsaw, 23.6 percent. Throughout the state, 40.9 percent of black children lived below the poverty line. In Roanoke Rapids that figure climbed to 68.2 percent, and in Warsaw to 87.4 percent. In Kinston 53 percent of black children fell under the poverty line, compared to 6.1 percent of white children. Infant mortality, taken as a ratio of infant deaths per one thousand births, also reflected the historical legacy of racial disparities: in Roanoke Rapids the figure was 42.1 for blacks, 0 for whites; in Kinston, 69.8 for blacks, 5 for whites. The Sunbelt economy has not, for the most part, brightened rural South, especially the black rural South.[48]

While textiles remain North Carolina's largest industrial employer, it is a ng industry in terms of jobs. What historian Robert J. Norrell has out the steel industry in Birmingham applies to the textile business Carolina: "Most of the jobs to which they [black workers] had just g. s now disappeared." And although black textile employment may ha appreciable positive impact on racial attitudes and perceptions amc nd white women, and even among some men, this has not sprea der community, as blacks and whites continue to live separate lives i -town South. One black worker described Stanley, North Carolin n where "the black people stay to themselves and white people stay to themselves." Truly interracial work forces in the mills are becoming less common. Some predict that within a decade or so most of the mills in the South may have all-black work forces in production jobs; some already do. As one white worker explained, "I think overall the black and white people are working more together now than we did back then, but also I would have to say that most of the white people are getting out of the mills. They're going on to easier jobs like the banks . . . and I feel before the end of time that the mills are going to be all predominantly black except for white supervisors, I think that's the way we're heading now."[49]

With blacks employed in shrinking industries and unemployable in growth occupations, they are increasingly pushed to the margins of the Sunbelt economy. The plight is especially noticeable in rural areas, where traditions inveighing against black employment are most entrenched. In the 1960s, the first decade of the South's economic boom, white workers gained 287,000 jobs in Deep South nonmetropolitan areas, while blacks lost 97,000 jobs. Even in new activities, such as catfish farming in Mississippi, blacks dominate in the toughest and most menial jobs. As Anthony Walton described a fish factory, "The . . . women stand ankle deep in water all day and are surrounded by fish guts and scales as they cut and gut and slice. Workers complain of carpal tunnel syndrome and are allowed only two bathroom breaks per eight-to-ten-hour shift. The fish factories look like nothing more than a new kind of plantation." In 1967 Senator Robert F. Kennedy toured the Mississippi Delta, where the living conditions of blacks shocked him: "My God, I did not know this kind of thing existed. How can a country like this allow it?" Anthony Walton toured the same area more than twenty-five years later and wrote, "The same statement could be made today." As Martin Luther King Jr. wrote in 1967, "With the Voting Rights Act one phase of development in the civil rights revolution came to an end. A new phase opened. . . . White America was ready to demand that the Negro should be spared the lash of brutality and coarse degradation, but it had never been truly committed to helping him out of poverty. . . . Jobs are harder and costlier to create than voting rolls." But the problem in the South today is less about creating jobs that blacks can fill as it is about better preparing blacks to fill the jobs that already exist.[50]

Though African American economic problems are greatest in rural areas, they are not confined there. A 1994 report revealed that Atlanta, arguably the southern showcase for black enterprise, ranked only ninth nationally in levels of black entrepreneurship, behind such cities as Columbus, Ohio, and Sacramento, California. Most of the city's black-owned firms are heavily dependent on public-sector contracts. Disparities in southern cities between black and white participation in the highest-paid category of white-collar occupations—managers and professionals—are greater than elsewhere. Nearly 30 percent of white males worked in such positions, compared to 8 percent of blacks in 1994. By contrast, more than 40 percent of black males toiled in laborer or service positions, compared to 13 percent of white men. And because blacks have come lately to the general job market in the South, they face more than whites the prospect of layoffs and dismissals in these days of corporate mergers and overseas flight. During the 1980s black men were about 20 percent more likely to lose their jobs for these reasons than were white men.[51]

In the bubbling economy of the urban South, the cost of housing has risen beyond the means of many black families, including the working poor; minimum wages remained fairly stagnant during the 1990s. Poor families, even when they find shelter, are typically on the move again after a short time. It is possible in prosperous Charlotte, North Carolina, for example, to find children who have attended six elementary schools in a single year.[52]

Black economic status in the South since 1965 has been so variable that it is difficult to conclude a discussion of it with a general statement. Statistical measures point in two directions. Without the landmark legislation of the mid-1960s, many positive economic gains, such as the growth of the black middle class and the opening of more diverse job opportunities for black men and women workers, would have taken longer, if they would have occurred at all. The erosion of black industrial employment; the persistent poverty of the rural South with the accompanying educational, health, environmental, and occupational shortcomings; and the racial gap with respect to types of work reflect both a changing international economy and the burdens of southern history. It is one thing to have new laws, and even new attitudes; it is another to escape the bonds of the past. That is not done so readily.

10   *Measures*

I know you are asking today, "How long will it take?" I come to say to you
this afternoon however difficult the moment, however frustrating the hour,
it will not be long, because truth pressed to earth will rise again.
　　　—Martin Luther King Jr., "Our God is Marching On!"

Measuring racial progress in the South since 1965 is a tricky business; there are abundant examples to satisfy both the optimists and the pessi-
mists. How the races perceive each other today reflects to a great extent how
each race perceives southern history, how the Civil War and Reconstruction
have burrowed into the consciousness of black and white, and how they re
main two distinctive events for each. Not that black and white southerners
go around musing about those events as they would ruminate about the stock
market or last night's basketball game. But the Civil War and Reconstruction
persist and permeate nonetheless in the legacy they have left for both the
South and southerners. The old white version lingers, a more hearty perennial than most think, while the new version exposed by blacks in the civil
rights movement, and written into textbooks and professional historical
works, struggles for acceptance and public visibility.

The record of race relations in the South more than a generation after the
civil rights movement ended is mixed, but disturbing trends indicate both the
pull of the past and the uncertainty of the future. In 1997 the Charlotte *Observer* conducted a poll of blacks and whites in Mecklenburg County and

compared it with a similar poll conducted in 1987. Charlotte, one of the country's most prosperous cities during the 1990s, with its history of relatively benign race relations, albeit within the framework of prevailing southern traditions, could be expected to deliver a generally positive view of racial issues. The poll results, however, revealed wide racial disparities on most issues and perceptions. The one area of general agreement was in response to the question as to whether race relations in the county had improved, remained the same, or had gotten worse since 1987: 36 percent of black respondents and 35 percent of whites agreed that race relations had improved in the county in the previous decade, while 27 percent and 29 percent, respectively, held the opposite view.

In response to the statement "Most people regard blacks as inferior to whites," only 6 percent of whites strongly agreed, compared to 32 percent of blacks. Ninety percent of black respondents declared that the issue of racial discrimination was "very important" to them, compared to 47 percent of white respondents. Not surprisingly, 84 percent of blacks indicated some or considerable interest in becoming involved in efforts to improve race relations, compared to 62 percent of white respondents. These figures do not necessarily reveal lingering racial prejudices among whites as much as they reflect the historical trend of whites' not perceiving race as a major issue. For example, 24 percent of white respondents claimed they were discriminated against in the previous year because of their race, compared to 55 percent of black respondents. At the same time, 29 percent of whites reported that they knew a black person who was discriminated against, compared to 67 percent of black respondents who knew of such an individual. While an equally high percentage of blacks and whites stated they would welcome a member of the opposite race in their neighborhood, 52 percent of whites would oppose interracial dating in their families compared to only 19 percent of blacks. These positions mark some progress since the 1987 poll for whites, but blacks felt more discriminated against in 1997 than in 1987. On the whole, most responses differed little from the earlier poll.

Polling data on race, however, is slippery. Pollsters understand that respondents want to give the "right" answers and look good or be helpful to the pollsters (the latter a particularly southern phenomenon), so the numbers might be inflated toward the positive. Generally, the polls indicate that race relations have improved slightly in some areas, regressed in others, but overall still reveal a gap in perception. If whites do not perceive a problem, or at least a significant one, then there is no need to propose or implement remedies, and those who clamor for change and action are consequently perceived as whiners or ingrates.[1]

Over the long haul, though, a discernible change has occurred in attitudes, at least as measured in the polls. In 1966 pollster Louis Harris found that 39 percent of white southerners agreed with the *Brown* decision; nearly thirty years later, this figure had increased to 87 percent. But by the time of the latter poll, the *Brown* decision had become largely irrelevant, as many children in the South's urban public school systems attended mostly segregated schools. This circumstance was reflected in a 1994 University of North Carolina poll in which a majority of blacks agreed that desegregated schools were required to achieve equal opportunity for all races and two-thirds of the white respondents disagreed. In the abstract, whites are committed to desegregation; in actual implementation, there is considerably more wariness. It may be comforting to know that the "right" or the "acceptable" answer today is no longer what was right and acceptable a generation or more ago, but the translation from polls to reality is more difficult.[2]

Polls may be inconclusive, inaccurate, or an ideal representation of what the reality ought to be, but the key to understanding race relations in the South at the beginning of the twenty-first century remains understanding the extent to which nineteenth-century historical perceptions remain in place. The alternative history offered by the civil rights movement has produced significant changes in regional historical consciousness, but mostly among black southerners. The descendants of slaves could now claim the South as their own. Before 1960, "South," and particularly "southerner," had distinctly white connotations. As invisibles, written out of the region's history and banished from consciousness except as performers in a historical drama directed by whites, southern blacks lived as strangers in their homeland. But the civil rights movement and its results have helped blacks come home again, some literally, to the region of their ancestors. As southern black writer Alice Walker noted in her memorial to Martin Luther King Jr., the fallen civil rights leader battled against those who sought "to disinherit" her. "He gave us back our heritage. . . . He gave us continuity of place. He gave us home."[3]

Southerners

Television journalist Charlayne Hunter-Gault returned to the University of Georgia, the scene of her turbulent arrival in January 1961 when she and

Hamilton Holmes broke the color barrier at the school, to address the graduating class of 1988, relating that it was "good to be back home again in a place that I have always thought of as 'our place.' " To make no mistake as to whom she included in "our place," Hunter-Gault explained that since her graduation, "through the events of our toil and our tumultuous history," southerners have become "a definable people."[4]

Many blacks, in fact, identify themselves as southerners, a designation most of those would not have offered forty years ago. In a 1992 Atlanta *Constitution* poll of those born in the South, 78 percent of whites and 76 percent of blacks considered themselves southern. A 1993 University of Virginia survey found that black southerners were even more likely than white southerners to take pride in their southern background. None of this is surprising; blacks have inhabited the region for generations, longer than most whites, and their ancestors remain in the soil of the South. Migration elsewhere did not dim their love for the region, even as southern whites did their best to make it otherwise. In the late 1980s pioneer black historian John Hope Franklin moved from Chicago to Durham, North Carolina, a migration hardly conceivable a few decades earlier. As he explained in 1995, the move was natural to him as a native of the region: "The South, as a place, is as attractive to blacks as it is to whites. Blacks, even when they left the South, didn't stop having affection for it. They just couldn't make it there. Then they found the North had its problems too, so you look for a place of real ease and contentment where you could live as a civilized human being. That's the South. It's more congenial; the pace is better; the races get along better. It's a sense of place. It's home."[5]

Part of the black embrace of the South results from the civil rights movement's exposure of the fact that black and white heritage in the region is closely intertwined, through blood and history, fulfilling James McBride Dabbs's prophecy "that Southern history was God's way of leading two originally opposed people into a richer life than either could have found alone." Perceptive whites understood the interconnectedness of blacks and whites in the South and the tragedy of their separation. W. J. Cash wrote, "In this society in which . . . nearly the whole body of whites, young and old, had constantly before their eyes the example, had constantly in their ears the accent, of the Negro, the relationship between the two groups was, by the second generation at least, nothing less than organic. Negro entered into white man as profoundly as white men entered into Negro—subtly influencing every gesture, every word, every emotion and idea, every attitude."[6]

The civil rights movement possessed this distinctive proselytizing element, not surprising in an ostensibly religion-led and religion-inspired affair that preached this common heritage to both blacks and whites; to blacks so they would not turn away and cast down their birthright in cynicism or flight, and to whites so that they could see white supremacy as a false mirror of what and who they really were. This sentiment among blacks did not, of course, originate with the civil rights movement. They had sought, through example and what modest protests they could generate, to enlighten their white neighbors since the end of the Civil War. Black writer Ernest J. Gaines recalled an exchange between himself and his creative-writing professor, Wallace Stegner, at Stanford in the late 1950s:

> Stegner asked: "Ernie, who do you write for? Who do you want to read your books?"
> "I don't write for any particular group, Mr. Stegner. I just try to write well and hope that somebody will buy it."
> "Suppose someone held a gun to your head and asked you again: Who do you write for?"
> "Well, I probably would say I write for the black youth in the South. I hope that in my writing I can help them find themselves."
> "Suppose the gun were still there, and he asked you who else you wish to reach."
> "In that case, I would have to say I wrote also for the white youth of the South. To help them see that unless they know their neighbors of three hundred years, they know only half of their own history."[7]

The acknowledgment of "southerness" among blacks is also due to the very real changes in the South since 1965. One who watches a child grow up daily misses the subtle changes in his development; so is progress best measured by those not closest to the situation. There is the temptation to use yesterday as the yardstick, when months or even years would do much better. Historian Vernon Burton left the town of Ninety Six, South Carolina, in 1965 to attend college. When he left, the public schools were totally segregated and whites held all the seats on the at-large-elected city council. Thirty years later, Burton found the schools fully integrated, and blacks, who composed 20 percent of the town's population, had elected one of their own, Charles Harts, to the city council, which voters now chose from districts rather than from at-large constituencies. In 1995 Harts, who returned south after spending his adult life in Buffalo, New York, prevailed in a three-man race for mayor, winning a majority of all votes cast. Explaining his victory, Harts stated, "I felt I could relate to them by being a country boy who grew up in a poor, struggling family."[8]

Visitors to southern cities today will note and often remark on the casual interracialism of social scenes, at coffee breaks, in luncheon places, and in general life around town. It seems natural enough yet a world away from the strictly segregated South of just a generation before. Matthew Cooper, a New Jersey native, covered the 1996 Summer Olympic Games for *The New Republic* and was struck by "Atlanta's common black-white Southern culture. At cafeteria-style restaurants . . . there's a comfortable mixing found less often in the North. Over heaping plates of fried chicken and greens, you'd see black cops and white businessmen happily digging in."[9]

Nor is this simply an Atlanta phenomenon. Walter Edgar, director of the Institute of Southern Studies at the University of South Carolina and a keen observer of southern life and culture, reeled off several incidents that occurred in the Columbia, South Carolina, area in 1997: an interracial Cub Scout day camp in Orangeburg is led by a black female director with a white female assistant; a party for a state army reserve unit in Darlington featured an interracial line dance led by the white mayor of the city and a black woman; and the son of a prominent Low Country family and member of the Kappa Alpha Order, a fraternity whose rituals evoke the Old South, married a black woman at Bethel A.M.E. Church in Columbia, with every event a biracial affair and the entire wedding written up with a two-column photograph in the Calhoun County *Times*.[10]

In the same area of South Carolina, at the same time, other incidents also occurred that indicated more than the mere lingering of a racist hangover. A restaurant in Aiken County refused to serve black patrons; a swimming pool operated by the Saluda County jaycees turned away an interracial youth group; in Orangeburg County, a charity softball tournament rejected an integrated team; and thrown into the mix were several church burnings tied to the Ku Klux Klan between 1991 and 1996. What is particularly noteworthy about these incidents, though, is not that they contradict or cancel out the positive racial examples, but the swiftness with which community institutions and individuals came together to denounce the actions. The state attorney general revoked the restaurant's license, the governor of the state invited the youth group over for a pool party, and the mayor of the Orangeburg County town issued a public apology.[11]

One of the more gruesome racial crimes in the twentieth century occurred in June 1998 in Jasper, Texas, as three young white men beat James Byrd, a black man, tied him to the back of a pickup truck, and dragged him for two miles, severing one of his arms and his head. Byrd had not been suspected of any crime—except that of being black. Jasper, a town thirty miles west of Louisiana, had a history of white vigilantism and was a center for lynch-law justice earlier in the century. But the town, black and white, immediately rallied around the Byrd family and each other. A white pharmacist noted, "This is not Jasper. This is a bunch of idiots. . . . Everybody here's just upset." The town, 45 percent black and 55 percent white, where blacks hold elective office and several executive positions in private, white-owned businesses, had enjoyed relatively placid race relations in recent years. Sheriff Billy Rowles noted that "the white community is just as appalled about this as the black community." In less than a year, Jasper juries convicted all three white men of capital murder, sentencing two of them to death. Both black and white residents of Jasper talked about "reconciliation" and rededication to tolerance and brotherhood.[12]

The brutal lynching in Texas demonstrated the revulsion of both black and white citizens to extreme racism. But the act itself, and the ties of the convicted men to white-supremacist groups, revealed another uncomfortable fact: the increasing tolerance and openness in the 1990s of antiblack rhetoric. This is not to say that such sentiments appeared suddenly in the 1990s, but public opinion had kept them suppressed—for the most part.

The trend to espouse racist attitudes publicly in the 1990s is reminiscent of the 1890s. There is the same connection to a white history that rephrases but does not reinterpret the Civil War and Reconstruction, especially in smaller communities, an unwillingness to accept the results of new historical visions and realities that have emerged in the South since 1965. In 1995 two whites burned the Reverend Terrance Mackey's church to the ground in the South Carolina Low Country town of Greeleyville. By a tradition extending back to the Jim Crow era, black people would shop in the lone grocery store in the morning, and whites purchased their groceries in the evening. Mackey decided to shop in the evening. On one occasion he overheard a white man mutter to his friend, "That's the nigger preacher causing the trouble." As of 2000, "little has changed" in Greeleyville, Mackey noted. "Blacks outnumber whites, but the few whites with wealth control the county."[13]

These are not rare and random occurrences reflecting a small blind spot in the South's new vision of itself. Beneath the occasional overt act of hate lies a deeper and broader wellspring of traditional white perspectives that percolate to the surface more often in hostile rhetoric. In October 1997 the Charlotte *Observer* inadvertently revealed the persistence of the traditional historical view and the willingness to express it. Charlotte is a hotbed of stock car racing, and NASCAR events attract a broad cross-section of (mostly white) southerners. Though NASCAR is a national organization and holds events all over the country (and occasionally abroad), the South remains its heartland. In an article on the sport, the *Observer* noted that relatively few blacks are involved in NASCAR, whether as drivers, members of pit crews, garage employees, or team owners, and wondered if the association should actively recruit black drivers. Most of the callers and writers, many of whom identified themselves by name, were white men, and the depth of their reaction reflected the same state of siege that some white evangelical Protestants demonstrate and that many working-class whites feel in the South. For despite Republican overtures, most GOP leaders care little about this group in terms of protecting their financial, educational, and occupational interests. Working-class whites have seen southern blacks advance to positions of leadership in southern political and economic life while they have experienced the disappearance of blue-collar work, the decline of public education, and a service economy that has not kept pace with wage levels in white-collar occupations. They perceive such programs as affirmative action and set-asides as additional advantages to a group that is already advantaged by government support and the backing of major political and economic institutions. They have also seen women advance, enjoy better economic opportunities, and become increasingly unimpressed with the macho image of the southern male. They hear that attitude in the new country songs and they see it where they work. The *Observer*'s simple and seemingly innocuous proposal unleashed a torrent of frustration that continues to seethe, below and sometimes above the surface of the Sunbelt South.

Here are some of the responses: "NO! We don't need blacks in race cars. They have every other sport. Let the white people have at least one sport." A Charlotte resident stated, "Sure, go ahead and recruit black drivers, and while you're at it, be sure to set up a black drivers' association. And maybe we could set aside five out of the first ten starting positions for black folks. I mean, we do it for everything else." Another Charlotte man chastised the paper along the same lines: "I think you people don't understand that the age of political correctness is past us. If black race car drivers want to succeed, let them do it on their own. Maybe you think we should establish quotas and goals for blacks in NASCAR like we have everything else in this country." A

Lancaster, South Carolina, reader complained, "We already give blacks everything they want. . . . I just don't think we should have black people in racing. If you bump 'em on the track they're gonna holler racist. If they don't win a race they're gonna holler racist. If NASCAR does something—new rules—they'll be hollering racist. The blacks as you call them (I call 'em n———) are gonna be hollering racist about everything." One reader tied the race and gender issues together neatly: "For the *Observer* to even ask the question is absurd. It's just another example of a bunch of bull dykes, women, feminized politically correct men trying to go out and seek more welfare for black folks." All of these respondents signed their names. Interestingly, the newspaper never intimated any quota or affirmative action program; the editors merely suggested a recruitment effort.[14]

The openness of these declarations is as disturbing as the content. Yet observers who have traveled through the South in recent years have reported similar incidents of whites who are no longer guarded in expressing racist views. One journalist visiting Greenwood, Mississippi, in 1998 reported that "whites in Greenwood are much more likely today than they were ten years ago to openly admit that they send their children to Pillow Academy not because it is a better school but because of its racial composition."[15] Perhaps this is a good sign, a step toward greater candor in race relations. But it is also indicative of greater public acceptance, at least in the white community, of racist rhetoric.

Silences

There are, then, sufficient examples to support both cases: that race relations in the South are steadily improving, or that the advances of the 1960s are slowly eroding under political and economic pressures. But the prevailing race relations in the South today are actually none at all. The instances of interracial contact that we see all around us, in restaurants, businesses, and schools, are for the most part superficial. There is no denying that some interracial friendships have blossomed and that interracial marriages have increased, where neither would have been thinkable a generation before. But the races generally pass each other with almost the same character of invisibility that existed in the formal era of white supremacy. Atlanta, often held up as a model of race relations in this newest South, is a place where blacks and whites still live on different sides of town, and though they may work with each other, genuine interracial friendships are rare. "Race relations?" asked a prominent white Atlanta liberal. "We don't have race relations in Atlanta anymore." As one journalist put it, what prevails in Atlanta is not "racial harmony" but "peaceful coexistence—a wary truce between two groups who believe they are fundamentally different and will always live separately."[16] Part of this reflects the national balkanization that has occurred in recent decades; we talk about "communities" instead of one community, and with each community comes a particular culture that must be advanced, defended, and protected. In the South, such separatism is especially dangerous because of the region's distinctive history: not only is separate never equal, but it reifies racial stereotypes that in turn enforce separateness and inequality.

The separateness is apparent not only in the large cities but also in the smaller towns of the South. "The peace in Greenwood is . . . thoroughly separate," a journalist observed. When Anthony Walton visited Mississippi in the early 1990s, he saw scenes that scarcely would have been possible a few decades earlier: "I saw blacks and whites sharing public space peacefully, moving among and around each other easily, without friction." Yet he also noted that they did not talk to each other "except in superficial transactions. . . . So if there was no apparent rancor, still this affability didn't extend far beyond the surface." At the high school in Yazoo City, students elect black and white favorites for each class, and black and white homecoming queens, a practice that is not unique to Mississippi. Perhaps in terms of the broad perspective of where Mississippi *was*, this is progress, imperfect as it is. But it is also avoidance, a tacit agreement to go separate ways, not to know each other or care much about it. It discards the very core of the historical lesson imparted by the civil rights movement, that of a shared past that could only attain fruition if both races joined in the present to understand their mutual history.[17]

The geography of contemporary metropolitan areas in the South helps the avoidance strategy. These sprawling metropolises are in reality collections of enclaves, some nominally integrated but most not, tied together by ribbons of highways. We live our lives in sealed environments, offices, cars, and climate-controlled homes. When we come together in malls, there is only the most casual interaction; in churches, another community gathering spot, we are as separate racially as we have ever been. This reflects a national pattern and not an exclusive indictment of southern living. But, as writer Benjamin Schwarz has noted, "This new, informal segregation, regrettable everywhere, is especially tragic in the South, since by giving up their close coexistence, white and black southerners will inevitably lose a vital part of what makes them who they are."[18] Ironically, the older generation of black and white southerners, particularly those who lived in small towns or rural areas, had more contact with each other than many black and white city dwellers experience today.

Much of this separateness is by mutual consent and is indicative of the broader problem: our inability to understand each other's history, find common ground, and respect our differences. That attitude is perhaps not surprising on the part of southern whites, but blacks as well increasingly prefer to keep to themselves, to avoid "white folks overload," as some put it. A black woman in Greenwood, Mississippi, sent her son to a mostly white school across the Yazoo River, but she now sends him to a neighborhood school that is 98 percent black. "I would rather send my son to Davis, because he is happier with his own kind. I think the whites feel the same way. I sent my son to Bankston because he's not going to be able to go through life without dealing with white people. I pulled him out because he's had enough togetherness."[19]

In fact, the burden of integration had fallen mostly on blacks. When the white Y and hospitals became integrated, the corresponding black institutions typically closed. In smaller communities, school desegregation invariably resulted in the abandonment of black public schools. More often than not, black children experienced the burdens of busing. One former student of all-black Williston High School in Wilmington, North Carolina, recalled: "We were in a cocoon bathed in a warm fluid where we were expected to excel . . . and then something called desegregation punctured it. We went from our own land to being tourists in someone else's. It never did come together, and I think it's on the verge of falling apart altogether now."[20]

When downtown businesses, theaters, restaurants, and hotels opened their doors to blacks, the black business communities that had survived urban renewal withered away, wiping out the black entrepreneurial class in the process. Black money that had remained in the community is now scattered about. The economy generated by these businesses paled, of course, in comparison to that of the white business sector, but the enterprises afforded a modest element of independence for both consumer and owner alike. As an elderly black Jacksonville resident recalled of that city's once-thriving black business district, "We didn't have to ask the white man for nothin'. Nothin'!" The Afro-American Life Insurance Company, an enterprise that owed its success to the refusal of the major white-owned life insurance companies to cover blacks, formed the centerpiece of that district. In 1987 the company declared bankruptcy. The cityscape along Ashley Street, the main thoroughfare of Jacksonville's black business district, disappeared. "The urban boulevard, once flourishing," a reporter observed, "is along most of its length a ragged pasture of uncut grass."[21]

The fond remembrance of black Jacksonville reflects a growing nostalgia among southern blacks for the segregation era and derives in part from a need to possess a valid cultural heritage, the physical remnants of which have disappeared as a result of neglect, urban renewal, highway construction, and integration. Part of that cultural heritage is also found in the sense of community and self-help that characterized the separate neighborhoods of the past and now have regrettably followed the national trends of crime, drugs, and dispersal. Black educator Johnnetta Cole recalls in her 1993 memoir, *Conversations*, "Prior to integration, self-help was a way of life. During times of more overt and more brutal oppression than we now experience, we possessed a reservoir of values, that enabled us to survive and in many instances thrive."[22]

In recent years, several black memoirists have manifested a warm remembrance of growing up in the days of Jim Crow amid the paraphernalia, physical and mental, of white supremacy. Writer and academic Henry Louis Gates's *Colored People: A Memoir* (1994) depicts his childhood village in West Virginia as a self-enclosed community where children grew up surrounded by supportive family, teachers, preachers, and friends. Gates's town is like the womb the Williston High School student described: secure, warm, and comforting. A similar text of memory is Raymond Andrews's *The Last Radio Baby* (1990), about growing up "colored" in Georgia in the 1930s and '40s. He nostalgically evokes the respect for elders and kin, the cotton-picking contests, songfests, and the excitement of weekly trips to town. These memoirs stress the togetherness, community, mutual respect, and, above all, the safety of blackness that enveloped such enclaves.[23]

These memoirs are more reflective of the present than they are of the reality of the past; in their own way, they are as insidious as the white remembrances of the Civil War and Reconstruction, selective memories that exalt a certain era and a particular people to the misunderstanding of both. They miss the sharp divisions that existed in black communities, the distinctions of class and color. Such memories also work as barriers to inhibit confronting some of the unpleasant realities of the present. They relieve thinking and working; they are comforting when things aren't going well enough. But they are wrong. The filter of memory forgets that these districts were not self-contained enclaves secreted away from the white South. As black writer Gerald Early commented, "In such a reading of American social history, black communities before 1954 were, segregation notwithstanding, or perhaps owing to segregation, the American equivalent of an Edenic Africa before the coming of the white man. . . . If the black world before integration was so attractive, why was there a civil rights movement?"[24]

Historian Saul Friedländer's 1997 book, *Nazi Germany and the Jews: The Years of Persecution, 1933–1939*, about the fate of the Jews in Nazi Germany before the Second World War and before the implementation of the Final Solution, contains a pertinent lesson for segregation nostalgiasts. Jewish culture flourished under the Nazis, Friedländer noted, as the authorities drove them out of theaters, orchestras, and schools, and off editorial boards. "German Jews educated and entertained each other, producing fine works of art, drama, fiction and scholarship." But Friedländer recounts these "golden" years more with a sense of tragic irony than with fond nostalgia. We know, of course, what awaited these Jews, and we also know their resourcefulness occurred out of necessity, out of their powerless and submissive relationship to Aryan Germany. The full life they had led before 1933 may have lacked the brilliant luster of the cultural outpouring that occurred after 1933, but it was a life lived whole with little compromise and participation in the larger German society on their own terms. After 1933 the Jews became increasingly invisible to the average German, increasingly confined to their own neighborhoods and institutions. Out of sight, they drifted out of mind. What the years before the Holocaust underscored was not the virulent hatred and anti-Semitism of average Germans but their profound indifference once German Jews disappeared from participation in the broader society.[25]

The growing sequestration of southern blacks gives southern whites one less issue to contend with, and they do not really mind. Most whites would say race relations are fine, but they made the same declarations during the Jim Crow era. The polls show a strong majority of whites in favor of integration, but don't expect them to do much about it. And blacks, in any case, are sending out increasingly mixed messages about whether or not they care, whether or not the struggle to achieve a biracial society is worth it.

Black leaders promote group ideology, group entitlements, and group identity. To be sure, the movement that destroyed segregation by law focused on the civil rights of a group, but King and his colleagues always emphasized that the movement was about the dignity of individuals as much as the uplift of any group. As black sociologist Shelby Steele has noted, "being 'black' in no way spared the necessity of being myself." More to the point, Frederick Douglass lectured that "the only excuse for pride in individuals . . . is in the fact of their own achievements. If the sun has created curled hair and tanned skin, let the sun be proud of its achievement." The focus on group exclusivity and uniqueness hampers integration efforts if difference becomes the sole definition of identity.[26]

The withdrawal of blacks and whites from each other occurs at an inopportune time for black southerners. The South is becoming a multiethnic environment, and not only in south Florida and Texas. The evidence of substantial immigration from Latin America and Southeast Asia is apparent on supermarket shelves, in restaurants, school curricula, social services, and public programs and festivals in every major southern city today. These newcomers, while they are not interested in divesting themselves of their native cultures, are very much striving to join the American mainstream as quickly as possible. It is not an either-or proposition; one does not need to bargain away cultural identity to attain full partnership in American society. Southern blacks should understand that embracing cultural identity to the exclusion of integration results in an incomplete and stunted identity. It also undermines the historical lessons of the civil rights movement.

Black isolation has political and economic consequences as southern urban populations become more diverse ethnically. The Hispanic surge in jobs and in politics has hurt both the economic and political power of blacks in Miami. Black-Hispanic tensions exist in cities such as Atlanta and Charlotte over jobs and cultural misperceptions. In politics, Houston offers a portent of future alignments in other southern cities. During the 1980s there were indications that blacks and Latinos might take on a common political cause, but that appears no longer to be the case. As one analyst explained, "Blacks and Latinos [in Houston] don't live the same sort of lives." In terms of employment, family structure, crime, and attitudes toward the police, a vast gulf exists between blacks and Latinos in Houston.[27]

These patterns reflect national phenomena: the disintegration of black communities, the coalescing of immigrant economic and political power, and the indifference of whites. But southerners above all Americans know the costs of separation. During the heady years following the mid-1960s, southerners of both races approached racial reconciliation with a sense of mission; they touted their region as a national trendsetter in putting things right, in acting as a beacon to an America beset with burning cities and broken lives.

It is rare to find such pronouncements, such bravado, today. We are finding out that we are no better than anyone else.

We can renew the South's commitment to an integrated society dreamed of in 1865, promised in 1965, yet still elusive today. The leadership will not come from government, as both political parties have a vested interest in separatism; leadership probably will not emerge from established institutions, black or white, both of which have stakes in maintaining the separate identities of the southern population, however well-meaning their outlook. For all the publicity of Martin Luther King Jr. and national civil rights organizations, the movement was, in its essence, a grass-roots affair. One of the great accomplishments of the civil rights movement was to organize local black communities, generate a sense of empowerment, and secure some real gains, whether it was the first sidewalk or the last place on the ballot.[28] Perhaps the South's religious institutions can play a role—that is, those that are focused on improving society rather than on changing government policy. People will say that the greatest shortcoming in the black community in the South and elsewhere is economic, but until a more integrated and interrelated society emerges, those problems will persist.

A considerable part of the problem is that it is difficult for blacks and whites to talk about themselves, especially their pasts. Teachers find it awkward to deal with slavery; topics related to the Civil War and Reconstruction that reflect poorly on one race or the other are glossed over or skipped; segregation is often dealt with in the abstract or with an example that points up the absurd (like separate water fountains), but without a context, so it seems like another century and another planet instead of right here a generation ago; and students learn the civil rights movement as an event of great men and great legislation. We don't want to offend anyone, so we educate no one. It is possible, even probable, to find black and white students totally ignorant of the civil rights movement and what it stood for, what the stakes were, what preceded it, and how as southerners we are better off for it. The reporter who visited Greenwood, Mississippi, in 1998 found that "younger blacks . . . don't know much about the civil rights movement, and often don't seem to care." As for slavery, the Civil War, and Reconstruction, candid classroom discussions are increasingly rare. High schools in Alabama, Texas, and several other southern states avoid those "divisive" topics by beginning American history in 1877. It is not likely that southerners, black *or* white, will learn more than received myths about the Civil War and Reconstruction. We are still fighting the Civil War because we have not yet learned that it is OK to stop.[29]

The current state (or nonstate) of race relations in the South does not present an insurmountable problem. Conventional wisdom fifty years ago was that segregation would last a long time. In our own lifetimes we have seen the Berlin Wall go up and then come down, the Soviet Empire collapse, men walk on the moon, and blacks have lunch at Ollie's Barbecue in Birmingham. The seemingly impossible can become the probable very quickly and unexpectedly. It does not take a large army to effect such "miracles," just the good will of some dedicated men and women of both races who can put aside the posturing, the suspicions, and take up again the program of recovery and reconciliation begun a generation ago. Fashioning a new historical consciousness in the South is difficult; the old one proved especially comforting and right to whites, just as it proved despicable to blacks. The wounds of that perspective have not yet healed and, in fact, are opened at frequent intervals. What is needed is not so much a merger of Robert E. Lee and Martin Luther King Jr. as a better understanding of both, an appreciation that one can accept the past without distorting it or denigrating others. By knowing each other's past, black and white southerners will have a better appreciation by which to share their common elements without forsaking the special and particular meanings of each. Cherished southern values such as family, place, community, and religion have a special resonance for both blacks and whites in the South; they are not race-specific but the indigenous characteristics of all southerners.

Georgia congressman John Lewis, who still bears the scars of his civil rights crusading, may be, as historian Sean Wilentz asserts, "The Last Integrationist." If that is the case, then it is a sad commentary on our progress since 1965 in refashioning southern history and southern society in a broader, more inclusive image. Lewis argues, "You can have an integrated society without losing diversity. But you can also have a society that transcends race, where you can lay down the burden of race—I'm talking about just *lay it down*—and treat people as human beings, regardless of the color of their skin." Lewis knows well the horror of segregation as the handmaiden of white supremacy, the teacher of inferiority, the enforcer of humiliation, the siren of a false sense of security, and the killer of dreams. Yet Lewis admits that his vision is "old-fashioned," that "it's out of date—that for a black person, it's Tommin', it's weak, it's passive. It is a radical idea. It's revolutionary to talk about the creation of a beloved community, the creation of a truly interracial democracy, a truly integrated society."[30]

Revolutions have occurred in our lifetime, in the South and elsewhere. We can and must speak with the confidence and commitment of Frederick Douglass when he posed the question in June 1863: "Can the white and colored people of this country be blended into a common nationality, and enjoy together . . . under the same flag, the inestimable blessing of life, liberty, and the pursuit of happiness, as neighborly citizens of a common country?" Douglass answered his own question unequivocally: "I believe they can."[31]

11   Histories

Who controls the past controls the future; who controls the present controls the past.
>   —George Orwell, *Nineteen Eighty-Four*

Is there nothing about the South that is immune from the disintegrating effect of nationalism and the pressure for conformity? . . . There is only one thing that I can think of, and that is its history. . . . I mean . . . the collective experience of the Southern people. It is in just this respect that the South remains the most distinctive region of the country.
>   —C. Vann Woodward, *The Burden of Southern History*

So what is left? A region that is still burying its Civil War dead. Since the 1920s, southern writers, William Faulkner in particular, have demonstrated that the creation of a new perspective would be difficult. The old view was corrupt and corrupted; the new version of modern America lacked spiritual and social conscience. Like Will Barrett in Walker Percy's *The Last Gentleman* (1966), the southerner is either fixated upon the past and therefore immobilized by it, or is a total amnesiac and therefore destructive. As Percy asked in another novel, *Lancelot* (1977), "What is worse, to die with Stonewall Jackson at Chancellorsville or to live with Johnny Carson in Burbank?"[1]

For some, and their numbers are not as small as one would think, the old myths are still operative. When outsiders note that southerners are still fighting the Civil War, they are not just referring to the small but vocal coterie who gather like relics of ancient clans at Sons of Confederate Veterans conclaves, battle reenactments, or meetings of the United Daughters of the Confederacy, not so much to learn history as to repeat it. These and more private memorialists scarcely view their commemorations and remembrances as historical artifacts. The war and its legacies are living witness to their lives and those of their ancestors, real or imagined. It is all around them, living and breathing. Southern writer Rick Bass explained how the war imprints itself on the contemporary Mississippi landscape: "I don't care if it was a hundred and twenty years ago, these things still last and that is really no time at all, not for a real war like that one, with screaming and pain. The trees absorb the echoes of the screams and cries and humiliations. Their bark is only an inch thick between then and now: the distance between your thumb and forefinger. The sun beating down on us now saw the flames and troops' campfires then, and in fact the warmth from those flames is still not entirely through traveling to the sun. The fear of the women: you can still feel it, in places where it was strong."[2]

It is not difficult during an average week to pick up a southern newspaper and see history's battles unfold. Mostly they are fought in the letters to the editor. The correspondence mixes combativeness, defensiveness, self-righteousness, and direct or indirect references to the Civil War—all familiar characteristics of a traditional South neither gone nor forgotten, but waning nonetheless. A Charlotte native opined that "many Northerners are now experiencing a resolve by Southerners to no longer back down from their repeated attacks on our way of life. The battle lines being drawn here have nothing to do with the War Between the States, but rather with a determination to maintain our cultural identity." Another Charlotte resident adopted the same tone, complaining that northerners "seem far too willing to remind me who won the Civil War. The War for Southern Independence has long since been over—and we're painfully aware of its outcome!" But it isn't over, and he, for one, is still fighting.[3]

Northerners, especially transplants, find such declarations a tad ridiculous, which stirs the vitriol of southerners even more. Responses display an exasperation that such an ancient conflict continues to preoccupy southerners, and, besides, they ought to be thankful for the migration of northerners, as it has contributed significantly to southern prosperity and intellectual advancement. Neither of these suggestions is calculated to make a positive imprint on the mind of the southerner. "I've had it," wrote one exasperated transplant from the West Coast to Charlotte. "Why is it so hard for the people around here to get on with life? Every time I read the paper I'm left with a horrible taste of hatred, whether it be the 'North-South' thing or the 'black-white' thing or the 'you're-not-from-here' thing. The history around is interesting and abundant. But why must I watch the worst parts of it being recreated daily? Didn't we learn?" Another northerner living in Statesville, North Carolina, offered this advice to his neighbors: "I believe it is time to stop fighting the ci. . . , oops, the 'War of Northern Aggression,' and join the rest of the nation. The South which was an inbred society forty years ago when I first moved here, owes a lot of its success to the diversification it has experienced since then." And, finally, a Pittsburgh transplant of Polish extraction extols the American "melting pot" to his neighbors, explaining that it "enriches our lives with tradition and food, and the diversity expands our minds and increases our ability to accept others as they are. . . . I have been in North Carolina for eight years, and not once have I heard a Southerner speak of his or her heritage or ancestors in any way other than in reference to the Civil War (by the way, it's over!)."[4]

Few things will raise contemporary white ire in the South more than northerners' assertions that they are the prime architects of the current Sunbelt prosperity, which lifted the region from its chronic poverty and ignorance. Rodney J. Woods of Charlotte, a northern transplant, suggested as much in a letter to the Charlotte *Observer*. Here are some responses: "A typical Yankee of Mr. Woods' outlook is best described by his reference that Charlotte citizens are just too dumb and backwards to get along without him and his likes. He also wonders what would happen if all Northern industries and businesses were not here. . . . If [his] company does not appreciate cheap labor and citizens who still believe in the old-fashioned work ethic, then perhaps the company and Mr. Woods should pack up and return to the land of ice, snow, air pollution, crime and everything else that they came down here to get out of." For good measure, the writer added, "And don't call the war between the states the Civil War. It was a war between two nations. . . . If you want to live here, at least learn the language."

Another respondent took exception to Mr. Woods's comparison between New York City and Charlotte, a comparison that Woods thought was complimentary to both. Not so, charged a Hickory, North Carolina, resident who wrote that Woods exhibited "prejudice" in his comparison by stating that "he loves both Charlotte and New York but in different ways: Charlotte for its open spaces, relaxed pace and moderate climate; New York, for its variety and culture. The underlying bias is obvious. New York may not have open spaces, but Charlotte certainly has both variety and a rich culture."

Ultimately, Mr. Woods's comments reflected his unfamiliarity with southern history, or at least the folkloric version articulated by some white southerners. Jim Price of Huntersville, North Carolina, set him straight: "Had Mr. Woods studied his history . . . he'd know that after the war, carpetbaggers came South to rape and plunder our people, land and culture."[5]

The sharp exchanges are not limited to the newspapers; they occur at parties, at work, at school, often cloaked in good-natured jibes but always with a sense of difference and a hint of superiority on both sides. This is not surprising. Southerners shaped their historical identity in part based on their opposition to the Yankee. The North was always a key reference point, albeit in a negative sense. When northerners began to arrive in significant numbers, the reference point moved much closer. On the one hand, it sharpened southern identity for many, but on the other, it became increasingly clear that aside from food and accents, it was not certain what that identity meant. Northerners had a clue, and most of the readings were unflattering: that southerners were always fighting the Civil War; that ethnic and religious diversity were unwelcome; that southern charm and hospitality were false veneers under which lurked hostility and bigotry. Southerners, for their part, tended to view these migrants as pushy intruders, arrogant, and just plain different, which was the most threatening characteristic of all. The great migration from the North tended less to vitiate southern distinctiveness than to bring into bolder relief.

Not Forgotten

Some southerners will take it very personally; it is not only their history but themselves under attack, for how can you separate one from the other? They will rail against the new history and the new society forming around it, and will rail ever more fiercely because they know it is well past two in the afternoon on that hot July day that swung the balance of history against them for all time. Some will let go; no longer blind, they will see that there is life after loss, that they are still southerners by the grace of God, not by dint of a past not whole. That is a hope, not a promise.

Some will not let go, the southern patriot groups forming in the 1990s like phalanxes of a ghost army exactly one hundred years after a new generation of southern whites saved the Redemption for history and memory. Their re-appearance reflects the state of crisis. But this time, they cannot drown the new history nor sequester women and deprive blacks of their past. It is too late for that, but too early to surrender.

The League of the South, formed in 1994 as "an activist organization of unreconstructed Southerners pursuing cultural, social, economic and politi-cal independence for Dixie," and composed primarily of academics and ama-teur historians, publishes books such as *The South Was Right!* explaining that "the War of Northern Aggression was not fought to preserve any union of historic creation, formation, and understanding, but to achieve a new union by conquest and plunder." As for the abolitionists, they were a collection of socialists, atheists, and "reprehensible agitators."[6] League members promise to "teach the truth about Confederate history." And what is that? "We envi-sion a free and prosperous Southern republic. . . . A bold, self-confident civili-zation based on its cultural and ethnic European roots." And of the millions of Africans who gave their culture, bodies, and lives to the South and to white southerners, there is no accounting.[7]

These views perpetuate the fantasies of the redeemers and their heirs. The diaries and papers left behind by Union fighting men rarely reveal a thirst for booty. Rather, they fought for the ideals their leaders had articulated—the Union and, later, freedom. And the abolitionists, though insufferable, self-righteous prigs in some cases, were far from godless men; they were deeply religious evangelical Protestants who viewed slavery as a sin against God.

Like their predecessors, these groups merge history and faith, the one jus-tifying, requiring, the other. League member Charles Davidson, an Alabama state senator carrying on the tradition of his ancestors, pointed out that since slavery is in the Bible, it is wrong to "call something evil that God obviously allows." He continued, "To say that slaves were mistreated in the Old South is to say that the most Christian group of people in the entire world, the Bible Belt, mistreated their servants and violated the commandments of Jesus their Lord. Anyone who says this is an accuser of the Brethren of Christ. Not a very good position to take." Make no mistake: these are not the much-maligned "redneck" elements; these are southern leaders proving that the shelf-life of southern history extends considerably beyond its expiration date. As Alabama writer Diane Roberts noted, "The stuff . . . isn't biodegradable. It's right under the floorboards, *down there*; you don't even have to dig to find it."[8]

The recent emergence of journals such as the *Southern Partisan*, which stresses "the centrality of the Confederacy to the Southern identity," and other "historical" publications such as *Southern Heritage, Confederate Underground, The Journal of Confederate History, The Confederate Sentry,* and *Counterattack,* reflect the tenacity of traditional perspectives on the Civil War and Reconstruction, as well as the racial and gender implications derived from those views. These are not white supremacy publications, but they portray the Confederacy and Reconstruction in ways that gloss over the realities of slavery, romanticize the Old South, and distort the record of Reconstruction. The journals exhibit a strong-willed intention to "set the record straight," to counter histories that have infiltrated textbooks, museums, and other public venues and materials.[9]

Then there are the Confederate reenactors, those in it for the military and historical aspects and those in it to promote the Lost Cause and who call themselves "freedom fighters." These folks are literally still fighting the Civil War, though less its outcome than its history. Artifacts sold at reenactment events include an image of Abraham Lincoln with a red bullet hole in the middle of his forehead over which is emblazoned the slogan "Sic Semper Tyrannis," the "Death to Tyrants" oath delivered by John Wilkes Booth after he assassinated the president at Ford's Theater in April 1865. Some reenactors have held memorial services for the likes of Henry Wirz, the notorious commander of Andersonville Prison whom federal authorities executed as a war criminal. The hope of memorialists is to have the government exonerate Wirz. When that day arrives, they noted with perhaps intended irony, "We can hold hands and sing, 'Free at Last! Free at Last!' "[10]

These are not large groups, and their publications do not have massive circulations, but there is a broader white support in the South, within the Republican Party and among some evangelical Protestants, for example. These are not fringe people. The groups publicly disavow white supremacy, yet the history they resurrect and purvey reinstalls the white South as the arbiter of regional society and relegates blacks to a subsidiary role, if any at all.

As these views indicate, it is a mistake to assume that education and the rewriting of texts will change historical views, for to change history one must contemplate changing one's self. Today most southern students first encounter detailed information on Reconstruction in high school, if they encounter it at all. Most districts use current historiography to demonstrate that the prevailing myth of the era as an oppressive time for the South and for southern whites in particular is just not so. However, these interpretations have often proved impervious to the prevailing folklore. As one student explained to a faculty member at a southern university, "You'll never believe all the stuff I learned in high school about Reconstruction—like it wasn't so bad, it set up school systems. Then I saw *Gone With the Wind* and learned the truth about Reconstruction." As Robert Coles recently lamented, "One can only wonder how it has been possible for so many extraordinarily eloquent and powerful books, all so carefully written and meticulously documented, to avail so little."[11]

It is easy to dismiss these folks as nostalgia-laden boobs at best, racists and sexists at worst, but it is also a distortion. Remembering may have virtues, even if what is remembered is skewed or just plain wrong. It may be easier to alter interpretations than to imbue a society with the importance of the past to begin with. Remembering is the only redoubt against those who would erase the past altogether.

There is a touching innocence in the belief that it is possible to recapture the past and everything good with it. The same search for simplicity that moved the Confederate soldier to embrace the Old South and create the Lost Cause and the Redemption motivates white southerners still clinging to the traditions of their ancestors. Those literally still fighting the Civil War, the reenactors, described in Tony Horwitz's *Confederates in the Attic* (1998), claim they are after innocence, not blood. A woman cooking before the reenactment of the Battle of the Wilderness laments, "We lost the art of conversation, of just being neighbors. . . . You climb back in your car and head back home, and the twentieth century starts flooding in again. It's depressing." Another woman agrees: "It's an era lost that we're trying to capture. Men were men and women were women. It was less complicated." "I think," a male reenactor concluded, "there's a lot of people like me who want to get back to a simpler time. Sandlot baseball, cowboys and Indians, the Civil War." Underlying these sentiments are the significant changes that have occurred in southern society over the past thirty years: things happening too quickly; a society that always changed, to be sure, but at its own pace with many of the familiar guideposts still intact. Now the direction is unclear, and fighting the war is one of the few activities where absolutes still prevail.[12]

In August 1996 about two dozen Sons of Confederate Veterans gathered in Spotsylvania Courthouse, Virginia, to bury a soldier killed in a fierce battle that occurred there in May 1864. They laid to rest the last remains of a Confederate known only as "Rebel Butler." Rebel Butler's skull had been on display at a museum in New Castle, Indiana. A member of the burial party defensively assured a reporter, "This has nothing whatsoever to do with slavery. This is a burial for a soldier who gave the full measure for his cause." We have not come to the point where giving a soldier an honorable burial is seen solely as a gesture of doing what is right rather than indicative of baser motives.[13]

Inclusion

To reach this point, we need to display, acknowledge, and debate southern history in all its variations, as painful as that might be. In this way we engage each other, reach a fuller understanding of ourselves, and hopefully learn to live, if not appreciate, our differences as well as commonalities. Some well-intentioned southern civic leaders have attempted to jump-start the process by layering black history on the white history that already exists throughout the South. The organizers of the 1996 Summer Olympic Games in Atlanta, for example, presented a laser-light show on Stone Mountain that concluded with the image of Martin Luther King Jr. superimposed on the starkly incomplete sculpted likenesses of Robert E. Lee, Jefferson Davis, and Stonewall Jackson. As one observer wrote, "On one hand the juxtaposition was disturbing: the Civil War and civil rights had been rendered morally equivalent. But it was also a wonderful bit of myth-making, too. The city has superimposed King over the soldiers of the Confederacy, allowing both parts of the past to form the myth of a tolerant, biracial metropolis."[14]

Some (predominantly whites) have called for an even greater merger of historic symbols. They advocate joint celebrations of King's and Lee's birthdays, which fall near each other. Arkansas journalist Paul Greenberg contends that the South will never attain peace with its past until "southerners, black and white, accept the same symbols." Instead of tearing down the Confederate battle flag, Greenberg advocates keeping the flag flying and erecting a statue of Martin Luther King Jr. on the same site. "The South will rise again," he wrote in 1988, "when it rises as one—when we rise together, not against each other. The South will be one when a march celebrating King's birthday is led by some brave and discerning soul carrying the Confederate battle flag."[15]

I would not hold my breath waiting for that parade. The danger is that both visions will reside, as do the races, in parallel universes, with parallel misunderstandings, separate but equal and never coming together. There is no need for either race to relinquish sacred symbols, merely the need to understand them and each other better. Better history, rather than better symbols, is what we need. Such an education may not result in a merger but a new common vision that dismisses the ancient myths in favor of a new, as-yet unconceptualized historical consensus.

Such layering of histories, commendable though the intent may be, do not close the wide gap in black and white perspectives on southern history. They also assume that any black history will do as long as it relates to Dr. King, ignoring a rich yet mostly buried past of black life in the South. Consider the common exercise in many southern communities of renaming a street for Martin Luther King Jr. More than one hundred southern cities have done so. But the streets so named offer witness less of racial reconciliation than of indifference. Most of these avenues run through dilapidated black neighborhoods, where few, if any, whites ever travel. One observer designated the King thoroughfares as "Boulevards of Broken Dreams." Also, renaming assumes that the previous street name had little resonance for residents; it denies or dismisses another history. In 1992, when Athens, Georgia, leaders proposed to change the name of Reese Street in a black neighborhood to King Street, homeowners in the area protested. As one wrote, "I respect what Dr. King stood for . . . but I think it is an injustice to his name to want to name any street at random after him and feel something has been accomplished. . . . The residents feel some sense of loyalty to their present [street] names because of their long existence and family heritage."[16]

At least the good intentions behind these shotgun marriages of black and white southern history have the virtue of bringing black southern history to a broader public. The southern landscape for generations reminded citizens of the grace of the Old South, the honor of the Lost Cause, and the glory of the Redemption. Absent is not only the black perspective on these events and eras but a more honest portrayal of white southern history. Errors, omissions, and outright lies abound in the public display of the white southern past. And in being wrong, this public history is hurtful; it perpetuates a historical perspective that all the history texts and learned lectures cannot erase. It is in these public venues that the Old South, the Civil War, and Reconstruction achieve the exaggeration and mythologizing that, rather than honoring those who fought and died with courage, cheapens and trivializes their sacrifice.

The sum message of public markers to various Civil War battles in the South is that the Confederacy chalked up huge victories but somehow lost the war. The markers suspend not only time but belief as well. At Appomattox the United Daughters of the Confederacy erected a marker that claims, "Here on Sunday April 9, 1865 after four years of heroic struggle in defense of principles believed fundamental to the existence of our government Lee surrendered 9,000 men, the remnant of an army still unconquered in spirit, to 118,000 men under Grant." The editorial aside, the figures are wildly inaccurate. Documents, including the parole slips that Grant handed to departing Confederate soldiers, indicate that Grant had 63,000 troops at Appomattox and Lee commanded about 30,000 soldiers. Instead of a 13 to 1 advantage, the Union possessed little more than a 2 to 1 superiority. The larger number certifies the heroism against unsurmountable odds that became a major feature of Lost Cause history. But the accurate number would not diminish either General Lee or the Confederacy. It would say that Lee, outnumbered but yet unvanquished, recognized the futility of carrying on the struggle and generating more carnage for a cause already lost.

Worse is the history that never gets told. Kentucky remained tenuously in the Union during the Civil War; the state sent 90,000 of its sons to fight for the Union, and 35,000 men from Kentucky joined the Confederate cause. Yet throughout Kentucky today, seventy-two Confederate monuments stand, while there are but two Union markers. What difference does that make? Todd County, Kentucky, citizens supported the Union. But on Jefferson Davis's birthday, the county still crowns a "Miss Confederacy," judged worthy of that honor by her "poise, hair, hooped skirt, and answers to questions such as, 'What will you do while holding the title to promote and defend Southern heritage?'" The school sports teams are known as the Rebels. In 1995 four black youths shot into a white-driven pickup truck flying a large Confederate battle flag. One of the white youths allegedly shouted "nigger" at the black youngsters. The shots killed Michael Westerman, a white teenager, and the truck's owner.[17]

Twenty years ago the average plantation tour in the South placed slaves, or "servants," as they were called, squarely in the background. Loyal, hardworking, and trustworthy, they were shadow figures. Even when their humble dwellings survived on the grounds, tourists rarely visited them or found anyone to interpret them and the people who lived there. This is changing, especially at popular sites such as Williamsburg and Thomas Jefferson's Monticello. It is not a comfortable change, either for descendants of the slaves or those of their masters.

Betty Hertzog owns a plantation, evocatively called "Magnolia," in Natchitoches, Louisiana, a town with an equal number of black and white residents. Ask most citizens about race relations, and they would call them "good." There are few surface tensions but instead a gentleman's agreement to avoid the subject of race. We must be pleasant. Civic leaders, promoting what is popularly called "heritage tourism," convinced Hertzog to turn over some of her land to the National Park Service to create the Cane River Creole National Historical Park. The plan would preserve the plantation that Hertzog, a descendant of the original antebellum owners, found difficult and expensive to manage, and it would generate tourist revenue for the town. The Park Service placed ranger Carla Cowles, a black woman, at the site to interpret the plantation. As she noted simply, "I'm here to tell the whole story." But from Betty Hertzog's perspective, the whole story was no longer necessary, if it ever was. "A lot of people around here have put slavery behind them," she explained. "It is a part of the history here, and no one wants to ignore it. But I don't want to talk about slavery and get stuck on that."[18]

Cowles, using the acting technique she had learned at Williamsburg, portrayed the life of slaves on Magnolia plantation in a rich tapestry of storytelling, religion, and family life. The harsher aspects of the system—work, punishment, and the sale and sundering of families—emerge only indirectly. The idea is to show the slave as a person and to introduce whites, who compose the vast majority of visitors, to a history they did not know, or worse, thought they knew. As Cowles put it, "We can't heal old wounds until we look at the way life was and all its problems."[19]

In the meantime, Betty Hertzog shows the plantation house and leaves the discussion of slavery to Cowles in the slave cabins. Separate pasts, a buried history, is exposed. Hertzog is considering turning over the house to Mary Catalo, a relative. Catalo, a realtor in New Orleans, is from a younger generation of southern whites who grew up in the post–Jim Crow era, after 1965. She is uneasy about the history of the plantation and the role of her family on it, but she is determined to live with whatever the land divulges. "It is not a comfortable thing for me to come out and say that my relatives owned slaves, but it is important that we all openly acknowledge where we came from so we can start to work through the problems that were created in the past. Racism is a difficult thing to deal with because it runs so deep. To me this park offers a chance to at least help start a dialogue that doesn't exist right now." Out of conflict, a history more whole will emerge. The result may be a reconciliation of a people with their history and with each other.[20]

As part of this process, cities across the South are memorializing the civil rights movement as part of broader heritage-tourism campaigns. Civil rights venues are becoming the urban version of the Civil War battlefield—not as heavily visited but just as firmly placed in the landscape and consciousness of a place and a people. Birmingham offers visitors tours of the Sixteenth Street Baptist Church, the site of the brutal September 1963 bombing that claimed the lives of four young black girls; the civil rights museum and research center across the street; and Kelly-Ingram Park, where Bull Connor trained his fire hoses and police dogs on peaceful demonstrators. The Edmund Pettus Bridge in Selma, scene of the bloody voting-rights confrontation in March 1965, has become an official stop on that city's historic tour. In 1984 the city donated five thousand dollars toward the restoration of Brown's Chapel, the spiritual headquarters of the voting-rights movement in Alabama.[21] And in the Shrine of the Confederacy, its most holy corridor, Monument Avenue, there now stands, not far from the famous equestrian statue of Robert E. Lee, a statue of Arthur Ashe, though the black tennis star and community leader deserved a better sculptor.

Encouraging is the fact that some southern towns off the beaten track, away from the spotlight of the civil rights movement and the tourist dollars to sustain a symbol or a monument, are nonetheless awakening to their own biracial heritage. Over the past decade, more than one hundred markers and monuments to black history have appeared throughout the state of Tennessee, where statues and memorials dedicated to Confederate general and Ku Klux Klan founder Nathan Bedford Forrest still outnumber those of Andrew Jackson. Inclusion may not necessarily mean a new historical perspective, but it is an important step in that direction.

Settling old historical accounts is the corollary to inclusion. Bringing closure to the open wounds of history is part of the healing process. Byron De La Beckwith, a white middle-class Mississippian, a Sunday school teacher, escaped two hung juries for the 1963 slaying of Mississippi civil rights leader Medgar Evers after two white policemen provided him with an alibi. But in 1994, with testimony from a witness to whom Beckwith had bragged about the murder, he was finally convicted and imprisoned for life. Four years later, also in Mississippi, former Imperial Wizard of the White Knights of the Ku Klux Klan Sam Bowers was finally convicted, after four unsuccessful tries, of the firebomb murder of voting-rights advocate Vernon Dahmer Sr. in 1966. The jury, unlike previous panels, consisted of six blacks, five whites, and one Asian American. Bowers had already served six years for his part in the slaying of three civil rights workers near Philadelphia, Mississippi, during Freedom Summer of 1964. But that was a federal conviction. Bowers often boasted that no Mississippi jury would ever convict a white man of killing a black man in that state. He is currently serving a life sentence for Dahmer's murder.[22]

By the year 2000 southern states had reopened seven long-dormant cases from the civil rights era, including the most notorious: the bombing of the Sixteenth Street Baptist Church in Birmingham. The outcome of these cases will test not only the will of the South to fashion a new history but also its ability to confront the old past squarely and honestly. Bob Helfrich, the assistant district attorney who prosecuted Sam Bowers, admitted that some of his white friends have chided him, "Haven't we spent enough money on this?" And some blacks have wondered whether it might not be a better idea to just let things lie. Helfrich responded, "You can't put a price on justice." Or on history.[23]

Sometimes it is not possible to tie up history's loose ends so neatly or deal with the wrongs so directly. But allowing forgetfulness to bury the past is worse. What past gets remembered and memorialized reflects those who control the present; what is forgotten reflects power also. Better late than not at all. In January 1923 a mob of whites descended on the black section of Rosewood, Florida, laying siege to the neighborhood for two days in response to rumors that a black man had attacked a white woman. The mob destroyed every home in the black community and killed at least six black men. Not until 1994, after a four-year pro bono investigation undertaken by one of the state's leading law firms, did Florida acknowledge the tragedy of Rosewood and offer $1.2 million and a formal apology to the three hundred direct descendants of the Rosewood community.

In 1921 Tulsa, Oklahoma's, black business district promoted itself as the "Negro Wall Street of America," a prosperous thirty-five-block area that reflected the savings and hard work of the city's black population. But, as in Rosewood, a rumor alleging an assault by a black man on a white woman precipitated a white rampage led by the Ku Klux Klan that burned the district to the ground and murdered 250 black residents. Unlike in Rosewood, white civic leaders in Tulsa and in the state of Oklahoma made little effort to hide the incident, or at least their interpretation of it. Instead, they promoted an official version contending that the city's African American population had instigated the conflagration. To seal this version, articles about the riot were cut from the newspapers archived in the city library. Not until 1996, when an interracial committee held commemorative services and prepared a memorial for the site, did a different perspective on the incident achieve a wide circulation.

Perhaps the most dramatic reconciliation and remembrance event occurred in Wilmington, North Carolina, a century after a devastating race riot terrorized the city's black community. As in Tulsa, an interracial committee, including a noted southern historian, University of North Carolina, Wilmington, professor Melton McLaurin, cleared the public historical record of rumor and replaced it with fact. The 1898 Centennial Foundation sponsored a play on the riot at Thalian Hall, where angry whites gathered a century earlier to adopt a "White Man's Declaration of Independence," calling for the subjugation of the black population. After the performance, the audience signed "The People's Declaration of Racial Interdependence," summoning the community to work for racial equality and economic justice. The foundation continues to sponsor interracial programs and encourage community organizations to exchange visits and memberships, and promotes linkages between Wilmington's black heritage and the city's tourist industry.[24]

The commemoration of these events brought together black and white southerners in love, mutual respect, and reconciliation. The conflict over the Confederate battle flag has generated few, if any, of these attributes. But it is a necessary first step in bringing the unpleasant aspects of southern history to the surface. Once exposed to the light, the healing process can begin, and it has begun.

For most people outside the South, the passions evoked by a flag from a long-ago war to which only a minority of southerners can claim any ancestral connection is nothing short of bizarre. Except, of course, the war isn't long ago. The battle flag's defenders claim that it represents heritage, not hate—that it was not so much the emblem of the Confederacy as it was the standard of the soldier who fought heroically for a lost cause. And although it is unfortunate that extremists have waved the flag to promote bigotry, such defilement should not detract from its historic meaning to a people and a region. The flag's modern-day significance, its supporters claim, is as a symbol of freedom against oppression and for individual rights and self-determination. As an Atlanta factory worker stated, the battle flag "ain't got nothing to do with hating black people or any of that KKK stuff. All they mean to me is 'get the hell off my back and leave me the hell alone.' " Which may be why, if you travel in Europe, especially eastern Europe, you will occasionally see the emblem on cars or in taverns and on clothing as an expression of defiance against authority.[25]

Opponents say that's precisely the point. It *is* a flag of defiance, a treasonous standard that bears the indelible taint of slavery; it is a standard for human bondage, and it has remained a banner of white supremacy since the first deep blue St. Andrews cross on a red field appeared in battle. Despite disclaimers, it is a symbol of hate, they argue, not heritage, and they point to statements such as one made by a flag waver in Forsyth County, Georgia, in 1987: "It stands for the rights of white people. Call it a symbol of white supremacy if you like. It's a carryover from the Civil War."[26]

For nearly eighty years after the war, the battle flag appeared primarily at Confederate memorial events. But even during this benign era in the emblem's career, its supporters associated the flag with white supremacy. During the 1890s, when states all across the South passed restrictive racial legislation, Mississippi and Alabama redesigned their state flags to more closely resemble the battle flag. The Alabama state flag is the same as the battle flag except in color: it has a red cross on a white field, a scheme consciously employed to evoke white supremacy. As a historian of the Alabama flag wrote, its purpose was "reminding white people of their common nationhood and common ethnicity," a purpose "*identical* with the writing of segregation into statute books." For black Alabamians watching their civil rights evaporate, the connection was unmistakable. The flag confirmed the legislature's message that the state's black population was invisible and of no account.[27]

The genuine article remained mothballed, except for special occasions, until the 1940s, when it made a dramatic resurgence just as President Harry Truman prepared the first civil rights legislative package since the Reconstruction era. It became the unofficial symbol of the "Dixiecrat Party," the breakaway faction of southern Democrats during the 1948 presidential campaign. That same year, the rebel flag waved as the official symbol of the University of Mississippi. The battle flag emerged as a standard accessory to the segregationist rallies of the 1950s, especially after the 1954 U.S. Supreme Court decision in *Brown v. Board of Education of Topeka, Kansas* toppled segregation in public education and, by implication, threatened it everywhere else. In an official act of defiance, the Georgia legislature incorporated the emblem into its state flag in 1956.[28] When South Carolina raised the battle flag over its State House in Columbia in 1962, the purported excuse was to celebrate the Civil War centennial. Yet, the flag persisted on its lofty perch long after the commemoration of the hundredth anniversary of the war's putative end in 1865.

In the fall of 1996, South Carolina's Republican governor David Beasley, who had entered office two years earlier as a flag-supporting southern patriot, decided that the time had come to lower the banner. Whatever his motives—to broaden his political base, to mollify anxious business leaders, or as a stroke of conscience—the decision provoked a controversy. The firestorm of protest from many of the governor's white constituents caused him to reverse his position, a move that fanned rather than quelled the flames of the debate. The reversal came too late, though, to save his 1998 reelection bid; many voters no longer trusted him on the issue. His opponent, Democrat Jim Hodges, preferred a compromise on the flag issue.[29]

In July 1999 the NAACP announced a national boycott of South Carolina beginning in January 2000. Facing the loss of convention revenues, business groups across the state pleaded with lawmakers to lower the flag. Forty-eight of the sixty-five surviving members of the 1962 legislature signed a petition saying they never intended for the flag to fly beyond the end of the centennial.

In late 1999 flag proponents launched a counterattack with a series of television commercials designed to rebut both the historical and economic arguments posed against the flag. One ad noted that the state had prospered during the three decades the flag had flown above the Capitol, and that "the Confederate flag is not about race. It represents a state with a tradition of independence, an entrepreneurial spirit that believes economic rewards will follow hard work." The battle flag meets the New South, and both prosper. That is an interesting reading of South Carolina history since the 1960s but consistent with earlier readings of southern history. The ad is instructive, though, in underscoring how a particular rendering of the Civil War and Reconstruction can influence one's perspective on more-recent history. Seeing history through the lens of myth distorts the viewer's perception of everything else.[30]

Flag supporters believed that the assault on the banner atop the State House represented part of a concerted campaign to banish the symbols and historical treasures of white southern history from sight and, therefore, render both the artifacts and white southerners invisible. Another commercial asks, "Will the Civil War monuments at the State House and across South Carolina be next for attack? Will we be forced to change the names of our roads and schools? Make no mistake about it, the extremists who are viscerally attacking the Confederate flag will not be happy until all records and remembrances of those days are obliterated." Though hyperbolic, the ad accurately reflected the trend in some communities to rename schools and public buildings and replace or modify monuments. Perhaps each generation should be allowed to exalt its own heroes. But we would lose more than conti-nuity with our past if such a pattern developed. At times the rhetoric of well-intentioned black organizations implies an exclusion of Confederate history that is just as discriminatory as the manner in which black southerners have been written out of southern history for the past century. Burying or running away from history is as bad as reifying it. For if you deny it, you will not deal with it, and if you do not deal with it, history will continue to wound society.

Governor Beasley's original suggestion to lower the flag and place it over a Civil War museum on the Capitol grounds seemed about right. It places history where it ought to be—in the past—and it allows South Carolina to move and look forward, where it ought to move and look, without denigrat-ing a part of its heritage. General Robert E. Lee's advice, after all, as he left the battlefield for the last time was "Furl the flag, boys."

The compromise the legislature worked out and implemented in July 2000 lowered the flag from the dome and placed it instead by a Confederate monu-ment on the Capitol grounds, plainly visible to anyone walking or driving down Main Street. As Republican state senator Glenn McConnell, a flag sup-porter, intoned, "If there's one thing we learned at Gettysburg, it's occupy the high ground and don't leave it."[31] To the NAACP, the battle flag's new, more public, if less exalted, position, hardly represented a compromise, and they maintained their call for a boycott.

Still, the debate resulted in some rethinking, even soul searching, on both sides of the issue, a process ultimately more important than the battle flag itself. Ron Neal, a native of Spartanburg, South Carolina, who traveled to Columbia to watch the lowering of the battle flag from the State House dome in July 2000, struggled to find a way out, to keep his heritage without dese-crating his neighbor: "There are decent people on both sides. To me, that flag represents the blood of my ancestors. But I can understand how some people feel different. What would be great is if they could agree on a flag, and we could put both of them up on the dome." Bert Davis, a black truck driver from Columbia also attending the flag ceremony, had no problem with fellow South Carolinians expressing pride in ancestors who fought for south-ern independence: "I know that's the war those [white] people fought for. . . . I don't mind them honoring their people, but they worry about their ances-tors, and don't think about what they did to *our* ancestors." Reconciliation, historian James C. Cobb noted, depends "less on their [blacks' and whites'] ability to agree than on their willingness to tolerate disagreement about an identity that, to preserve, they must first learn to share."[32]

More encouraging was Georgia's handling of their persistent battle-flag controversy in 2001. Working away from the glare of publicity that produced posturing on both sides of the issue in South Carolina, a small interracial group of Georgia legislators designed a new flag for the state. Threats of an economic boycott, subtle pressure from popular Governor Roy E. Barnes, and a growing understanding on both sides of the historical validity of diverse historical perspectives pushed the small group to a compromise. The new Georgia banner does include the Confederate battle flag, but as part of an array of flags that have flown over the state in its history. The flags are displayed over a narrow ribbon at the bottom of the new design. The legislators sought not to eliminate the flag that is still important to many Georgians but rather to place that history in its appropriate historical context.

During the negotiating process, it became clear that once-bitter opponents had undergone an epiphany of sorts, brought together by a divisive symbol and frank discussion that opened minds and even hearts to other histories in this formerly exclusive historical province. Larry Walker, a white legislator from Perry County, in central Georgia, entered the negotiations as a strong battle-flag advocate, admitting that, had he been a lawmaker in 1956, he would readily have voted with the majority to replace the old Georgia flag with the new standard that included the battle flag. "Even now," he confessed, "I still have deep feelings for my Southern heritage and for the Confederacy, which for a lot of us was the defining moment of the South. But now I think it is time we started to move away from that moment." When a white southerner stops fighting the Civil War, the conflict's personal meaning does not necessarily come to an end as well.

Tyrone Brooks, a black state representative from Atlanta who has fought to excise what he called the "Georgia Swastika" from the state standard for more than two decades, also rejected compromise at first. But as each side probed personal emotions and learned about differing historical perspectives, Brooks's viewpoint changed. "What I finally had to acknowledge was that Confederate history is a part of our history. We cannot erase it, and it needs to be preserved for history's sake." Advocating the compromise on the House floor, Walker agreed, declaring that it was time to consider "the Georgians who were forced here, and who are just now beginning to share in the wonderful bounty of this country; Georgians who at least until recently have received little respect and much ridicule and deriding." This is coming to terms with the past, not erasing, whitewashing, or ignoring it. And coming to terms does not mean embracing; simply acknowledging and understanding the past will suffice.[33]

Why now? Why reopen painful criminal investigations, redesign or redeploy state banners that proudly proclaimed a particular historical perspective, commemorate embarrassing civil disorders, and provide public funds for racial outrages committed years and decades ago? To some extent it reflects the same generational phenomenon that has propelled the resurgence of Confederate heritage groups. These contestants over the past are responding as much to each other as to the histories they champion. Much like the first post–Civil War generation of black and white southerners in the 1890s fought the battle of freedom versus exclusion, the first post–civil rights generation of black and whites has arrived to fight a similar conflict. The generation that led or resisted the civil rights movement is passing on. The great black leaders of the movement, such as Martin Luther King Jr., Ralph David Abernathy, and Hosea Williams, have died; as have white allies, such as Judges Frank M. Johnson and Terry Sanford; and white adversaries, such as George Wallace. A new generation of blacks and whites leads a new South, unencumbered by Jim Crow yet still groping for answers to the region's persistent historical dilemmas. History is both the problem and the answer. There is a strong desire to get it right, to sweep away the cobwebs, drown the lies, uncover the truth, and bury the ghosts. And move on. This is a prosperous region, perhaps too fixated on grabbing the next economic bonanza but also coming to realize the value of education, investment in human capital, and the dignity of the individual—all individuals, due in no small part to the increase in black political and economic power since the mid-1960s. Southern blacks are now in a position to influence state legislatures, city commissions, and, therefore, history itself.

In Bobbie Ann Mason's "Shiloh," there at the battlefield—where the horrors of war were brought home to Union and Confederate soldiers, many for the first time in 1862, a place where more than 3,500 young men gave their lives—a southern family plans a picnic. The party, consisting of a matriarch, her daughter, and her daughter's husband, interpret the battle through the prism of their own lives, diminishing the significance of that history in the process. As Mason writes of Mabel's thoughts, "General Grant, drunk and furious, shoved the Southerners back to Corinth where Mabel and Jet Beasley were married years later, when Mabel was still thin and goodlooking." Her son-in-law is startled by the size of the battlefield: "Shiloh is an immense place, and Leroy cannot see it as a battleground. It is not what he had expected. He thought it would be like a golf course." Mason's explanation underscores the feelings of many white southerners, caught as they are in this era of historical uncertainties in their region: "I don't think the people I write about are obsessed with the past. I don't think they know anything about the Civil War, and I don't think they care. . . . But I think they reflect that tension that's in the culture between hanging onto the past and racing toward the future."[34]

The historical reassessment, which also is inextricably connected to the identity of black and white southerners, will be difficult. As long as history envelopes the South and southerners, there will be myriad issues and questions to resolve. At what point, for example, does one's history become another's pain? Is preserving and showing off the gracious antebellum mansions of Natchez a tacit approbation of the slave labor that accounted for such wealth and finery? Or is it an example, like the Roman Forum or the doors of Dublin, of a bygone culture that speaks to us of beauty, form, and function but that is devoid of deeper meaning? Is memorializing the Confederate war dead an act of racism, or is it homage to brave young men who fought for a flawed cause but nevertheless fought bravely and honorably? Should a Works Progress Administration mural in a Gastonia, North Carolina, post office be removed because, in this cotton textile town, the painting depicts black people picking cotton, a scene accurate historically and necessary to the production of textiles, but a scene, as one black resident anguished, "that . . . cries slavery forever"?[35]

As southern urban school systems become increasingly black, how appropriate is it to change the names of these schools from those of white southerners to black southerners, as much to honor deserving but heretofore invisible African Americans as to wipe out the historical connection to segregation and slavery? In 1997 the Orleans Parish School Board voted unanimously to change the name of George Washington Elementary to Dr. Charles Richard Drew Elementary. There is no mistaking Drew's credentials; he is widely credited for developing methods to preserve blood plasma. But Washington was our first president and the leader of the American Revolution. Yet, as one black leader in New Orleans explained, "Why should African Americans want their kids to pay respect or pay homage to someone who enslaved their ancestors?"[36] Is it appropriate to apply the litmus test of the late twentieth century to a long-dead patriot who was troubled enough by the institution to emancipate his slaves after his death? Do we trash or ignore the white history of the South as we did black southern history? Or is there a common ground we can stand on and simply call it "southern history," encompassing blacks and whites, together and separate?

In the meantime, southerners continue to fight the Civil War. Even for those not actively engaged in the struggle, the war may still tug at their hearts; it is embedded in their blood, and rationality has little to do with it. Hodding Carter III, whom no one would mistake for an unreconstructed southerner, acknowledges that opponents of the rebel flag are right but confesses, "It still grabs me. . . . Right or wrong, our ancestors fought, suffered, retreated, died, and were overcome while sustained by those same symbols."[37]

It is this experience with defeat and the building of an elaborate rationale for that defeat and its aftermath that sets the South apart from the rest of the American nation. White southerners lived in mytholand in order to survive the harsh postwar environment, an environment of poverty and struggle that did not really cease to exist as the norm until well into the twentieth century. As W. J. Cash wrote, "The peculiar history of the South has so greatly modified it from the general American norm that, when viewed as a whole, it decisively justifies the notion that the country is—not quite a nation, but the next thing to it."[38]

If history has defined the South, it has also trapped white southerners into sometimes defending the indefensible, holding onto views generally discredited in the rest of the civilized world and holding on the fiercer because of that. The extreme sensitivity of some southerners toward criticism of their past (or present) reflects not only their deep attachment to their perception of history but also their misgivings, a feeling that maybe they've fouled up somewhere and maybe the critics have something. Southerners may be loyal to their past, but they are not stupid. When the weight of reality presses in on the myth too heavily, southerners may abandon the myth and acknowledge, if not embrace, the reality. The civil rights movement is testimony to this trait. As we try to understand the South today, almost every aspect of its being relates to the region's peculiar history or, more properly, to what white southerners made of that history, the history of the Civil War and Reconstruction.

It is not yet clear what, if anything, will replace the Lost Cause as the operating historical myth of the South, or even if the Lost Cause is finally lost rather than merely refurbished. What southern society will become in this new century, especially given the growing economic and political importance of the region, and what America will become as well, will depend largely on how southerners reconstruct their past. Will that reconstruction be inspired *by* the changes that have occurred since 1965 or *in spite of* them? Now, amid sharpening discourses over heritage and hate, the growing separateness of black and white, it is yet possible to absorb George Santayana's truism that "loyalty to our ancestors does not include loyalty to their mistakes." Then we can declare an end to the Civil War; then how we made peace will become the definitive tradition of southern history; and then the historic burdens on southerners, black and white, male and female, and on the land, will be lighter. History will still matter, because that is the South's immutable distinction, but it will matter differently.

Notes

Introduction

1. Phyllis Trible, "God's Ghostwriters," *New York Times Book Review*, February 4, 2001; see also Israel Finkelstein and Neil Asher Silberman, *The Bible Unearthed: Archaeology's New Vision of Ancient Israel and the Origin of Its Sacred Texts* (New York: The Free Press, 2001).

2. Trible, "God's Ghostwriters."

3. Leon Wieseltier, "Sorry," *The New Republic* 222, March 27, 2000, p. 6.

4. George B. Tindall, *The Ethnic Southerners* (Baton Rouge: Louisiana State University Press, 1976), 21.

5. Michael O'Brien, "On Observing the Quicksand," *American Historical Review* 104 (October 1999): 1203.

6. Pamela L. Moore, "Banking in a Backwater?" Charlotte *Observer*, April 19, 1998.

7. *Ibid.*

8. Kim McLarin, "Feeling at Home South of the Mason-Dixon," New York *Times*, December 13, 1998.

9. Larry J. Griffin, "Southern Distinctiveness, Yet Again, or Why America Still Needs the South," *Southern Cultures* 6 (Fall 2000): 57.

10. Flannery O'Connor, "Some Aspects of the Grotesque in Southern Fiction," in *Flannery O'Connor: Mystery and Manners*, ed. Sally and Robert Fitzgerald (New York: Farrar, Straus & Giroux, 1979), 40; see also Albert Mobilio, "Biloxi Bound," *New York Times Book Review*, April 9, 2000, p. 18, Larry Brown, *Fay* (Chapel Hill: Algonquin Books of Chapel Hill, 2000).

11. John Shelton Reed, "Where is the South?" *Southern Cultures* 5 (Summer 1999): 117.

12. O'Brien, "On Observing the Quicksand," 1202; the quiz can be accessed at http://www.ibiblio.org/uncpress/quiz/.

13. Fox Butterfield, "The Curse of the South," Charlotte *Observer*, August 2, 1998; see also, Bertram Wyatt-Brown, *Southern Honor: Ethics and Behavior in the Old South* (New York: Oxford University Press, 1982).

14. John Shelton Reed, "The Central Theme," *Southern Cultures* 5 (Winter 1999): 96–8; Ed Williams, "The Bible Belt on the Cusp of the Millennium," Charlotte *Observer*, May 16, 1999.

15. Yoder quoted in James C. Cobb, *Redefining Southern Culture: Mind and Identity in the Modern South* (Athens: University of Georgia Press, 1999), 142; C. Vann Woodward, *Thinking Back: The Perils of Writing History* (Baton Rouge: Louisiana State University Press, 1986), 108.

16. Cobb, *Redefining Southern Culture*, 142.

17. U.S. National Emergency Council, *Report on Economic Conditions of the South* (Washington, D.C.: Government Printing Office, 1938), 1.

18. One of the best-argued recent works of this genre is Peter Applebome's *Dixie Rising: How the South is Shaping American Values, Politics, and Culture* (New York: Times Books, 1996). Historian Michael O'Brien has offered a telling critique of the view that southern culture and politicians are taking over America. O'Brien asserts that "southern ideological exports tends to have their labels removed. Southern religion becomes in California a blow-dried evangelicalism, the neo-Confederate becomes in Arizona genetically conservative, the Arkansas governor becomes a president of multicultural vagueness, the old blunt talk about 'slew-footed Senegambians' . . . becomes the oblique codes of the Willie Horton advertisement. . . . If the South were to show up on the doorstep of American culture and openly say, I'm here, move over, imitate me, southerners know that doors would slam in their faces." O'Brien, "The Apprehension of the South in Modern Culture," *Southern Cultures* 4 (Winter 1998): 11.

19. Warner quoted in Paul M. Gaston, *The New South Creed: A Study in Southern Mythmaking* (New York: Knopf, 1970), 334; George B. Tindall, "Beyond the Mainstream: The Ethnic Southerners," *Journal of Southern History* 40 (February 1974): 1.

Chapter 1: The Past Is

1. Barry Hannah, *Ray* (New York: Knopf, 1980), 41.

2. William Faulkner, quoted in Lewis P. Simpson, "William Faulkner and Yoknapatawpha," in *The American South: Portrait of a Culture*, ed. Louis D. Rubin (Baton Rouge: Louisiana State University Press, 1980), 243.

3. Ben Robertson, *Red Hills and Cotton: An Upcountry Memory* (1942; rev. ed., Columbia: University of South Carolina Press, 1960), 245.

4. Edward L. Ayers, Patricia Nelson Limerick, Stephen Nissenbaum, and Peter S. Onuf, *All Over the Map: Rethinking American Regions* (Baltimore: Johns Hopkins University Press, 1996), 12.

5. On this point, see Michael O'Brien, "On Observing the Quicksand," *American Historical Review* 104 (October 1999): 1204.

6. Frank W. Owsley, quoted in Charles F. Roland, *An American Iliad: The Story of the Civil War* (New York: McGraw-Hill, 1991), 113.

7. Warren, quoted in Grace Elizabeth Hale, "We've Got to Get Out of This Place: Tony Horwitz Tours the Civil War South," *Southern Cultures* 5 (Spring 1999): 58.

8. Quoted in David Goldfield et al., *The American Journey: A History of the United States*, 2d ed. (Upper Saddle River, N.J.: Prentice Hall, 2001), 509.

9. Ibid., 515.

10. Two excellent works that offer detailed analyses of how white southerners spun defeat

into a golden memory are Gaines M. Foster, *Ghosts of the Confederacy: Defeat, the Lost Cause, and the Emergence of the New South* (New York: Oxford University Press, 1987); and Charles Reagan Wilson, *Baptized in Blood: The Religion of the Lost Cause, 1865–1920* (Athens: University of Georgia Press, 1980).

11. On the stabilizing properties of tradition, see Eric Hobsbawm, "Introduction: Inventing Traditions," in *The Invention of Tradition*, ed. Hobsbawm and Terence Ranger (Cambridge: Cambridge University Press, 1983), 1–2.

12. On the disconnection between war and peace in the South, see Howard Bahr, *The Year of Jubilo: A Novel of the Civil War* (New York: Henry Holt, 2000).

13. George W. Bagby, quoted in Leo Glazer and Susan Key, "Carry Me Back: Nostalgia for the Old South in Nineteenth-Century Popular Culture," *Journal of American Studies* 30 (April 1996): 1.

14. David S. Cecelski, "Oldest Living Confederate Chaplain Tells All?—Or, James B. Avirett and the Rise and Fall of the Rich Lands," *Southern Cultures* 3 (Winter 1997): 5–24.

15. Henry Grady, quoted in Charles Reagan Wilson, "The Myth of the Biracial South," in *The Southern State of Mind*, ed. Jan Nordby Gretlund (Columbia: University of South Carolina Press, 1999), 5–6; see also Paul M. Gaston, *The New South Creed: A Study in Southern Mythmaking* (New York: Knopf, 1970).

16. Philip Alexander Bruce, quoted in James C. Cobb, *Redefining Southern Culture: Mind and Identity in the Modern South* (Athens: University of Georgia Press, 1999): 169.

17. See Robert F. Durden, "Electrifying the Piedmont Carolinas: The Beginning of the Duke Power Company, 1904–1925, Part 1," *North Carolina Historical Review* 76 (October 1999): 410–40; "Electrifying the Piedmont Carolinas: The Beginning of the Duke Power Company, 1904–1925, Part 2," *North Carolina Historical Review* 77 (January 2000): 54–89.

18. W. J. Cash, *The Mind of the South* (New York: Knopf, 1941), 65–6.

19. William Faulkner, *Absalom, Absalom!* (New York: Random House, 1936).

20. Margaret Mitchell, *Gone With the Wind* (New York: Macmillan, 1936), 608.

21. James McBride Dabbs, *Who Speaks for the South?* (New York: Funk & Wagnalls, 1964), 111; William Alexander Percy, *Lanterns on the Levee: Recollections of a Planter's Son* (New York: Knopf, 1941), 286.

22. Jefferson Davis, quoted in Richard D. Starnes, "Forever Faithful: The Southern Historical Society and Confederate Historical Memory," 2 (Winter 1996): 188.

23. Mary Johnston, quoted in Sarah E. Gardner, "Every Man Has Got the Right to Get Killed? The Civil War Narratives of Mary Johnston and Caroline Gordon," *Southern Cultures* 5 (Winter 1999): 17.

24. Caroline Gordon, quoted in ibid., 27.

25. Willie Morris, *North Toward Home* (Boston: Houghton Mifflin, 1967), 63.

26. James Eleazar, quoted in Edward L. Ayers, *The Promise of the New South: Life After Reconstruction* (New York: Oxford University Press, 1992): 27.

27. Shirley Abbott, *Womenfolks: Growing Up Down South* (New Haven: Ticknor & Fields, 1983), 14.

28. Howell Raines, "George Wallace, Segregation Symbol, Dies at 79," New York *Times*, September 15, 1998.

29. Kevin Thornton, "The Confederate Flag and the Meaning of Southern History," *Southern Cultures* 2 (Winter 1996): 233.

30. Jacquelyn Dowd Hall, " 'You Must Remember This': Autobiography as Social Critique," *Journal of American History* 85 (September 1998): 448.

31. See Daniel W. Stowell, *Rebuilding Zion: The Religious Reconstruction of the South, 1863–1877* (New York: Oxford University Press, 1998).

32. Wilson, *Baptized in Blood*, 59.

33. James Branch Cabell, *Let Me Lie* (New York: Farrar, Straus and Co., 1947), 74.

34. C. Vann Woodward, *Thinking Back: The Perils of Writing History* (Baton Rouge: Louisiana State University Press, 1986): 15, 27; see also Bruce Clayton, *W. J. Cash: A Life* (Baton Rouge: Louisiana State University Press, 1991).

35. Ellen Glasgow, *The Sheltered Life* (1932; reprint, Charlottesville: University Press of Virginia, 1994), x, 120.

36. Florence King, *Southern Ladies and Gentlemen* (New York: Bantam, 1976), 27.

37. Abbott, *Womenfolks*, 3; Percy, *Lanterns*, 345.

38. "Eudora Welty," in *Growing Up in the South: An Anthology of Modern Southern Literature*, ed. Suzanne W. Jones (New York: Penguin, 1991), 71.

39. Wilma Dykeman and James Stokely, *Neither Black Nor White* (New York: Rinehart, 1957), 16.

40. John R. Gillis, "Heritage and History: Twins Separated at Birth," *Reviews in American History* 25 (September 1997): 377.

41. Ibid., 376; John Stuart Mill, quoted in Glenn C. Loury, "Exclusionary Rule," *The New Republic*, November 24, 1997, p. 13.

42. Ralph Waldo Emerson, quoted in William H. Nicholls, *Southern Tradition and Regional Progress* (Chapel Hill: University of North Carolina Press, 1960), 131.

43. Cash, *Mind of the South*, 429, 66.

44. Hannah Arendt, quoted in Jean Bethke Elshtain, "Authority Figures," *The New Republic*, December 22, 1997, p. 12.

45. Cash, *Mind of the South*, 429.

46. John Gunther, *Inside U.S.A.* (New York: Harper and Brothers, 1947), 657–8.

47. Stark Young, "Not in Memoriam, but in Defense," in Twelve Southerners, ed., *I'll Take My Stand* (1930; reprint, New York: Harper, 1962), 355. Young and eleven colleagues comprised a group called the Agrarians. They were among the few white Southerners of the era to offer a different perspective on southern history on which to build contemporary society. They discarded the moonlight and magnolias history of the Old South and elevated the yeoman farmer and his simple virtues, which stood as ramparts against "our urbanized, anti-provincial, progressive, and mobile American life." But this new version of the Old South did not so much change history as shuffle the characters. It was incomplete and omitted the millions of people—slaves—who had made the Old South a viable enterprise.

48. George Orwell, quoted in Benjamin Schwarz, "The Idea of the South," *Atlantic Monthly*, December 1997, p. 118; Mark Twain, quoted in Lee Glazer and Susan Key, "Carry Me Back: Nostalgia for the Old South in Nineteenth-Century Popular Culture," *Journal of American Studies* 30 (April 1996): 23.

49. Katharine Du Pre Lumpkin, *The Making of a Southerner* (1946; reprint, Athens: University of Georgia Press, 1991), 206; Louis D. Rubin Jr., *The Faraway Country: Writers of the Modern South* (Seattle: University of Washington Press, 1963), 14.

50. Ellen Glasgow, quoted in Carol S. Manning, "Afterward," in Ellen Glasgow, *Sheltered Life*, 300.

51. R. W. Hayes and Helen Dortch Longstreet, quoted in John Egerton, "Days of Hope and Horror: Atlanta after World War II," *Georgia Historical Quarterly* 78 (Summer 1994): 305.

Chapter 2: God-Haunted

1. See Cynthia Lynn Lyerly, *Methodism and the Southern Mind, 1770–1810* (New York: Oxford University Press, 1998).

2. Rhys Isaac, *The Transformation of Virginia, 1740–1790* (Chapel Hill: University of North Carolina Press, 1982), 175.

3. R. Drew Smith, "Slavery, Secession, and Southern Protestant Shifts on the Authority of the State," *Journal of Church and State* 36 (Spring 1994): 265, 267. On the distinctions between antebellum northern and southern evangelicals, and on the conversion of slaves to Christianity, see John B. Boles, ed., *Masters and Slaves in the House of the Lord: Race and Religion in the American South, 1740–1870* (Lexington: University Press of Kentucky, 1988); Christine Leigh Heyrman, *Southern Cross: The Beginnings of the Bible Belt* (New York: Knopf, 1997); Frederick A. Bode, "The Formation of Evangelical Communities in Middle Georgia: Twiggs County, 1820–1861," *Journal of Southern History*, 60 (November 1994): 711–48; William W. Freehling, "James Henley Thronwell's Mysterious Antislavery Moment," *Journal of Southern History* 57 (August 1991): 383–406; Eugene D. Genovese, "Black Plantation Preachers in the Slave South," *Southern Studies* 2 (Fall/Winter 1991): 203–9; Barry Hankins, "Southern Baptists and Northern Evangelicals: Cultural Factors and the Nature of Religious Alliances," *Religion and American Culture* 7 (Summer 1997): 271–98; Daniel Walker Howe, "The Evangelical Movement and Political Culture in the North during the Second Party System," *Journal of American History* 77 (March 1991): 1216–39; Bill Leonard, "Southern Baptists and Southern Culture," *American Baptist Quarterly* 4 (June 1985): 200–12. For an excellent overview of differences between southern and northern religion from the colonial era to the present, see John B. Boles, "The Southern Way of Religion," *Virginia Quarterly Review* 75 (Spring 1999): 226–47.

4. Paul Goodman, "Moral Purpose and Republican Politics in Antebellum America, 1830–1860," *Maryland Historian* 20 (Fall/Winter 1989): 6.

5. Drew Gilpin Faust, "Christian Soldiers: The Meaning of Revivalism in the Confederate Army," *Journal of Southern History* 53 (February 1987): 65, 84.

6. David Goldfield et al., *The American Journey: A History of the United States* (Upper Saddle River, N.J.: Prentice Hall, 1998), 531.

7. Charles Reagan Wilson, *Baptized in Blood: The Religion of the Lost Cause, 1865–1920* (Athens: University of Georgia Press, 1980), 61, 60, 71.

8. Ibid., 73.

9. Ibid., 98.

10. Thomas Nelson Page, quoted in Lewis P. Simpson, "The Southern Republic of Letters and *I'll Take My Stand*," in *A Band of Prophets: The Vanderbilt Agrarians after Fifty Years*, ed. William C. Havard and Walter Sullivan (Baton Rouge: Louisiana State University Press, 1982), 82.

11. Wilson, *Baptized in Blood*, 23.

12. Ibid., 25, 26, 27.

13. Ibid., 32, 33.

14. Ibid., 25.

15. Howard W. Odum, *The Way of the South: Toward the Regional Balance of America* (New York: Macmillan, 1947), 151.

16. An exhibit of these chilling photographs went on display in New York and toured nationally during the year 2000. See Roberta Smith, "An Ugly Legacy Lives On, Its Glare Unsoftened by Age," New York *Times*, January 13, 2000.

17. Mark Twain, quoted in Joel Williamson, "Wounds, Not Scars: Lynching, the National Conscience, and the American Historian," *Journal of American History* 83 (March 1997): 1221.

18. Thomas Landess, "A Note on the Origin of Southern Ways," in Fifteen Southerners, *Why the South Will Survive* (Athens: University of Georgia Press, 1981), 162.

19. Willie Morris, *North Toward Home* (Boston: Houghton Mifflin, 1967), 54, 55.

20. Kathleen Minnix, "The Atlanta Revivals of Sam Jones: Evangelist of the New South," *Atlanta History* 33 (Spring 1989): 8.

21. Ibid., 21.

22. Ibid., 22.

23. "Dr. Dixon Claims Evolution Started in Unscientific Age," Raleigh *News & Observer*, December 31, 1922.

24. See Willard B. Gatewood Jr., *Preachers, Pedagogues and Politicians: The Evolution Controversy in North Carolina, 1920–1927* (Chapel Hill: University of North Carolina Press, 1966).

25. See Edward L. Ayers, *The Promise of the New South: Life After Reconstruction* (New York: Oxford University Press, 1992), 399–408.

26. *Discipline of the Pentecostal Holiness Church* (Franklin Springs, Ga., 1937): 11–4, 41–3.

27. See T. Harry Williams, "Trends in Southern Politics," in Frank E. Vandiver, ed., *The Idea of the South: Pursuit of a Central Theme* (Chicago: University of Chicago Press, 1964), 61.

28. Frank W. Barnett, quoted in Wallace M. Alston, Jr., and Wayne Flynt, "Religion in the Land of Cotton," in *You Can't Eat Magnolias*, ed. H. Brandt Ayers and Thomas H. Naylor (New York: McGraw-Hill, 1972), 115–16.

29. Ibid.

30. The social program of the congress, as outlined in its 1914 proceedings, can be found in James E. McCulloch, ed., *Battling for Social Betterment: Southern Sociological Congress, Memphis, Tennessee*, May 6–10, 1914 (Nashville: Southern Sociological Congress, 1914), 9.

31. Nancy Keever Andersen, "Cooperation for Social Betterment: The Intellectual and Theological Rationale of Southern Methodists Associated with the Southern Sociological Congress, 1912–1914," *Methodist History* 34 (October 1995): 37.

32. See Elizabeth Anne Payne, "The Lady Was a Sharecropper: Myrtle Lawrence and the Southern Tenant Farmers' Union," *Southern Cultures* 4 (Summer 1998): 5–27.

33. Andersen, "Cooperation for Social Betterment," 32.

34. Katharine Du Pre Lumpkin, *The Making of a Southerner* (1946; reprint, Athens: University of Georgia Press, 1991), 238.

35. Mark Newman, "The Mississippi Baptist Convention and Desegregation, 1945–1980," *Journal of Mississippi History* 59 (Spring 1997): 2.

36. Ibid., 1–32.

37. Gunnar Myrdal, *An American Dilemma: The Negro Problem and Modern Democracy* (New York: Harper & Row, 1944), 873n.

38. Ibid., 876.

39. Ralph McGill, quoted in Marshall Frady, "God and Man in the South," *Atlantic Monthly*, January 1967, 38.

40. Ralph McGill, "The Agony of the Southern Minister," New York *Times*, September 27, 1959.

41. See Will D. Campbell, *The Stem of Jesse: The Costs of Community at a 1960s Southern School* (Macon, Ga.: Mercer University Press, 1995).

42. Pat Watters, *The South and the Nation* (New York: Pantheon, 1969), 10.

43. Billy Graham, quoted in Frady, "God and Man in the South," 40.

44. Martin Luther King Jr., "Letter from Birmingham City Jail" (1963), in *A Testament of Hope: The Essential Writings of Martin Luther King, Jr.*, ed. James Melvin Washington (New York: Harper & Row, 1986), 289–302.

45. Carlyle Marney, quoted in David Goldfield, *Black, White, and Southern: Race Relations and Southern Culture, 1940 to the present* (Baton Rouge: Louisiana State University Press, 1990), 137; Walker Percy, "Mississippi: The Fallen Paradise," *Harper's*, April 1965, p. 171.

46. King, "Letter from Birmingham," in *A Testament of Hope*, ed. Washington, 289–302.

47. Ibid.

48. "U.S. Pauses to Honor King, His Legacy," Charlotte *Observer*, January 21, 1986.

49. Dietrich Bonhoeffer, quoted in James Sellers, *The South and Christian Ethics* (New York: Association Press, 1962), 38–9.

Chapter 3: Culture Protestants

1. Samuel S. Hill Jr., "The South's Culture-Protestantism," *Christian Century* 79 (September 12, 1962): 1094–6.

2. Daniel L. Turner, *Standing Without Apology: The History of Bob Jones University* (Greenville, S.C.: Bob Jones University Press, 1997), 32.

3. Ben Robertson, *Red Hills and Cotton: An Upcountry Memory* (1942; reprint, Columbia: University of South Carolina Press, 1960), 129–30.

4. Myra Macpherson, "The Many Voices of Jerry Falwell," Charlotte *Observer*, October 7, 1984; John B. Judis, "Crosses to Bear," *The New Republic*, September 12, 1994, 21–5.

5. Judis, "Crosses to Bear," 23.

6. Leighton Ford, "Merry Who-mas?" Charlotte *Observer*, December 25, 1999.

7. See Michael Novak, "It's Not All Relative," New York *Times*, October 16, 1998.

8. James C. Cobb, ed., *The Mississippi Delta and the World: The Memoirs of David L. Cohn* (Baton Rouge: Louisiana State University Press, 1995), 139; see also Wilmer C. Fields, "On Jordan's Stormy Banks: Religion in a Changing South," in John B. Boles, ed., *Dixie Dateline: A Journalistic Portrait of the Contemporary South* (Houston: Rice University Press, 1983), 65–79.

9. W. J. Cash, *The Mind of the South* (New York: Knopf, 1941), 90.

10. "Homosexual Lifestyle Exacts High Toll," letter to editor, Charlotte *Observer*, February 26, 1995; "God Will Destroy Sinful Nation," letter to editor, ibid.

11. Ken Garfield, "Baptists Stir Debate in Bid to Convert Jews," Charlotte *Observer*, June 15, 1996; Garfield, "Religion a Daily Reality of Life in the Bible Belt," ibid., December 20, 1982.

12. Jay Reeves, "Suit Alleges Religious Harassment," Charlotte *Observer*, August 26, 1997.

13. For a discussion of the *Santa Fe* case, as well as the transcript of Justice John Paul Stevens's majority opinion, see Linda Greenhouse, "Student Prayers Must be Private, Court Reaf-

firms," New York *Times*, June 20, 2000. On the harassment of the Jewish student, see the column by Rowland Nethaway, senior editor of the Waco (Texas) *Tribune-Herald*, "Taking Sides Can Promote Intolerance," Charlotte *Observer*, June 26, 2000.

14. Jon Christensen, "Teachers Fight for Darwin's Place in U.S. Classrooms," New York *Times*, November 24, 1998.

15. Tom Ehrich, "Deeds of Love, Not Political Platforms Identify Christians," Charlotte *Observer*, July 29, 1996.

16. "Readers Debate Conversion of Jews," Charlotte *Observer*, July 29, 1996.

17. "Crevices," *The New Republic*, July 24, 2000, p. 9.

18. "Baptists in Texas Reject a Call for Wives to 'Submit' to Husbands," New York *Times*, November 10, 1999; "Southern Baptists Pass Resolution Opposing Women as Pastors," ibid., June 15, 2000; Gustav Niebuhr, "With Texas Group's Proposal, Struggle Among Baptists Enters a New Phase," ibid., October 28, 2000.

19. Kathleen Curry, "No Job Lined Up—Just a Hope and a Prayer," Charlotte *Observer*, September 21, 1997.

20. "Crevices," 9.

21. Bill Moyers, "America Searches for a New Vision," speech delivered at Wake Forest University, November 19, 1997, excerpted in the Charlotte *Observer*, December 8, 1997.

22. David Mathews, "Coming to Terms with Another New South," in *The Rising South: Changes and Issues*, ed. Donald R. Noble and Joab L. Thomas (University: University of Alabama Press, 1976), 101.

Chapter 4: Pretty Women

1. C. Vann Woodward and Elisabeth Muhlenfeld, eds., *The Private Mary Chesnut: The Unpublished Civil War Diaries* (New York: Oxford University Press, 1984), 21.

2. George Fitzhugh, quoted in Stephanie McCurry, "The Two Faces of Republicanism: Gender and Proslavery Politics in Antebellum South Carolina," *Journal of American History* 78 (March 1992): 1249, 1254; see also McCurry, *Masters of Small Worlds: Yeoman Households, Gender Relations, and the Political Culture of the Antebellum South Carolina Low Country* (New York: Oxford University Press, 1995).

3. John B. Boles, *The South Through Time: A History of an American Region* (Englewood Cliffs, N.J.: Prentice Hall, 1995), 222.

4. David Goldfield et al., *The American Journey: A History of the United States* (Upper Saddle River, N.J., 1998), 543.

5. Joan E. Cashin, *A Family Venture: Men and Women on the Southern Frontier* (New York: Oxford University Press, 1991), 57, 65.

6. Jerrold Hirsch, "Grassroots Environmental History: The Southern Federal Writers' Project Life Histories as a Source," *Southern Cultures* 2 (Fall 1995): 132.

7. Suzanne Lebsock, *The Free Women of Petersburg: Status and Culture in a Southern Town, 1784–1860* (New York: Norton, 1984), 215.

8. Harriet A. Jacobs, *Incidents in the Life of a Slave Girl*, ed. Jean Fagan Yellin (Cambridge, Mass.: Harvard University Press, 1987), 12.

9. Ibid., 27.

10. Drew Gilpin Faust, "Altars of Sacrifice: Confederate Women and the Narratives of War," *Journal of American History* 76 (March 1990): 1204, 1207.

11. Goldfield et al., *The American Journey*, 512.

12. Faust, "Altars of Sacrifice," 1210.

13. Marlene Hunt Rikard and Elizabeth Crabtree Wells, " 'From It Begins a New Era': Women and the Civil War," *Baptist History and Heritage* 32 (July/October 1997): 63.

14. Ibid., 66.

15. Ella Lonn, *Desertion during the Civil War* (New York: Century, 1928), 12.

16. Faust, "Altars of Sacrifice," 1224.

17. Ibid., 1224. Some of the excellent works on the role of southern women during the Civil War that have informed this section of the chapter include Catherine Clinton, *Tara Revisited: Women, War, and the Plantation Legend* (New York: Abbeville Press, 1995); Drew Gilpin Faust, *Mothers of Invention: Women of the Slaveholding South in the American Civil War* (Chapel Hill: University of North Carolina Press, 1996); George C. Rable, *Civil Wars: Women and the Crisis of Southern Nationalism* (Urbana: University of Illinois Press, 1989); LeeAnn Whites, *The Civil War as a Crisis in Gender: Augusta, Georgia, 1860–1890* (Athens: University of Georgia Press, 1995); Edward D. C. Campbell Jr. and Kym S. Rice, eds., *A Woman's War: Southern Women, Civil War, and the Confederate Legacy* (Charlottesville: University Press of Virginia, 1996).

18. Faust, *Mothers of Invention*, 231, 137, 134.

19. Alice Fahs, "The Feminized Civil War: Gender, Northern Popular Literature, and the Memory of the War, 1861–1900," *Journal of American History* 85 (March 1999): 1492.

20. See Faust, *Mothers of Invention*, 247.

21. For a full discussion of these and other post–Civil War novels by southern women writers, see Jane Turner Censer, "Reimagining the North-South Reunion: Southern Women Novelists and the Intersectional Romance, 1876–1900," *Southern Cultures* 5 (Summer 1999): 64–91.

22. Bobbie Ann Mason, *Clear Springs: A Memoir* (New York: Random House, 1999), 148–9.

23. Virginia I. Burr, "A Woman Made to Suffer and Be Strong: Ella Gertrude Clanton Thomas, 1834–1907," in *In Joy and Sorrow: Women, Family, and Marriage in the Victorian South, 1830–1900*, ed. Carol K. Bleser (New York: Oxford University Press, 1991), 222, 224.

24. Ibid., 227.

25. Ibid., 231.

26. Alan Grubb, "House and Home in the Victorian South: The Cookbook as Guide," in *In Joy and Sorrow*, ed. Bleser, 166, 174.

27. For a discussion of some of these issues, see Martha Hodes, "The Sexualization of Reconstruction Politics: White Women and Black Men in the South after the Civil War," *Journal of the History of Sexuality*, no. 3 (1993): 59–74; see also Laura F. Edwards, *Gendered Strife and Confusion: The Political Culture of Reconstruction* (Urbana: University of Illinois Press, 1997).

28. Karin L. Zipf, " 'The WHITES shall rule the land or die': Gender, Race, and Class in North Carolina Reconstruction Politics," *Journal of Southern History* 65 (August 1999): 499.

29. See Diane Miller Sommerville, "The Rape Myth in the Old South Reconsidered," *Journal of Southern History* 61 (August 1995): 481–518.

30. Winfred B. Moore Jr. et al., eds., *Developing Dixie: Modernization in a Traditional Society* (Westport, Conn.: Greenwood Press, 1988), 215; on the connection between gender and the maintenance of the antebellum power structure, see Laura F. Edwards, *Gendered Strife & Confusion: The Political Culture of Reconstruction* (Urbana: University of Illinois Press, 1997).

31. Jacquelyn Dowd Hall, " 'You Must Remember This': Autobiography as a Social Critique," *Journal of American History* 85 (September 1998): 448.

32. Ellen Glasgow, quoted in Carol S. Manning's "Afterward," in Ellen Glasgow, *The Sheltered Life* (1932; reprint, Charlottesville: University Press of Virginia, 1994), 308. See also Howard N. Rabinowitz, *The First New South, 1865–1920* (Arlington Heights, Ill.: Harlan Davidson, 1992), 177; Cheryl Thurber, "The Development of the Mammy Image and Mythology," in *Southern Women: Histories and Identities*, ed. Virginia Bernhard et al. (Columbia: University of Missouri Press, 1992), 97.

33. Florence King, quoted in Drew Gilpin Faust, "Gender and the Lingering Burden of Southern History," in *The Future of the South* (Research Triangle Park, N.C.: National Humanities Center, 1995), 23; Shirley Abbott, *Womenfolks: Growing Up Down South* (New Haven, Ticknor & Fields, 1983): 84; Anne Goodwyn Jones, *Tomorrow is Another Day: The Woman Writer in the South, 1859–1936* (Baton Rouge: Louisiana State University Press, 1981), 4.

34. Margaret Mitchell, *Gone With the Wind* (New York: Macmillan, 1936), 616.

35. Elizabeth Robeson, "The Ambiguity of Julia Peterkin," *Journal of Southern History* 61 (November 1995): 767, 769.

36. Darden Asbury Pyron, "Nell Battle Lewis (1893–1956) and 'The New Southern Woman,' " in *Perspectives on the American South*, ed. James C. Cobb and Charles R. Wilson (New York: Gordon and Breach, 1985), 63–85.

37. Hollinger F. Bernard, ed., *Outside the Magic Circle: The Autobiography of Virginia Foster Durr* (University: University of Alabama Press, 1985), xi.

38. Glasgow, *The Sheltered Life*, x; Elizabeth Spencer, quoted in Polly Paddock Gossett, "Recalling a Home Place That Is No More," Charlotte *Observer*, January 25, 1998.

39. Lorraine Gates, "Power from the Pedestal: The Women's Emergency Committee and the Little Rock School Crisis," *Arkansas Historical Quarterly* 55 (Spring 1996): 35.

40. Florence King, *Southern Ladies and Gentlemen* (New York: Stein & Day, 1975), 33.

41. Stephen Vincent Benét, *John Brown's Body* (1927; reprint, New York: Holt, Rinehart, and Winston, 1968), 159–60.

42. Robeson, "The Ambiguity of Julia Peterkin," 767; Anne Firor Scott, "Women, Religion, and Social Change in the South, 1830–1930," in *Religion and the Solid South*, ed. Samuel S. Hill Jr. (Nashville: Abingdon Press, 1972), 94.

43. Connie L. Lester, " 'Let Us Be Up and Doing': Women in the Tennessee Movements for Agrarian Reform, 1870–1892," *Tennessee Historical Quarterly* 54 (Summer 1995): 90.

44. See Maurice M. Manring, "Aunt Jemima Explained: The Old South, the Absent Mistress, and the Slave in a Box," *Southern Cultures* 2 (Fall 1995): 19–44.

45. Zora Neale Hurston, *Their Eyes Were Watching God* (1937; reprint, New York: Negro Universities Press, 1969), 69, 74.

46. Ibid., 85.

47. Mary Mebane, "Mary," in *Growing Up in the South: An Anthology of Modern Southern Literature*, ed. Suzanne W. Jones (New York: Penguin, 1991), 452.

48. Mary Mebane, *Mary, Wayfarer: An Autobiography* (New York: Viking, 1983), 16, 17.

49. Hall, " 'You Must Remember This,' " 450; see also the UDC Web site: http://www.hqudc.org

50. Hall, " 'You Must Remember This,' " 451.

51. Ibid., 458.

52. Joan Marie Johnson, " 'Drill into us . . . the Rebel tradition': The Contest over Southern Identity in Black and White Women's Clubs, South Carolina, 1898–1930," *Journal of Southern History* 66 (August 2000): 534, 543.

53. Ibid., 545.

54. On the development of a woman's political culture during this era, see Judith N. McArthur, *Creating the New Woman: The Rise of Southern Women's Progressive Culture in Texas, 1893–1918* (Urbana: University of Illinois Press, 1998).

55. The Wilmington race riot is also an interesting example of how history is recorded for posterity. The revolutionary aspect of the violence in Wilmington received little coverage in the state's press, which focused on the actions of black newspaper editor Alexander Manly. The Raleigh *News & Observer*, on November 11, 1898, led with the headline, "Negroes Precipitate Conflict by Firing on the Whites—Manly, the Defamer of White Womanhood Escapes." On the same day, the New York *Herald* carried the story under the following lead: "By Revolutionary Methods White Citizens of North Carolina Overturn Existing City Government and at Once Establish Their Own."

56. Andrea Meryl Kirshenbaum, "The Vampire That Hovers over North Carolina: Gender, White Supremacy, and the Wilmington Race Riot of 1898," *Southern Cultures* 4, no. 3 (1998): 23, 22.

57. Ibid., 23. Apparently, Rebecca's entreaties took. Waddell became the mayor of Wilmington's revolutionary government.

58. Ibid., 25.

59. Dewey W. Grantham, *The South in Modern America: A Region at Odds* (New York: HarperCollins, 1994), 71.

60. Elizabeth Hayes Turner, " 'White-Gloved Ladies' and 'New Women' in the Texas Woman Suffrage Movement," in *Southern Women*, ed. Virginia Bernhard et al., 144.

61. Catherine Clinton, "Bloody Terrain: Freedwomen, Sexuality and Violence during Reconstruction," *Georgia Historical Quarterly* 76 (Summer 1992): 330.

62. Elna C. Green, "From Antisuffragism to Anti-Communism: The Conservative Career of Ida M. Darden," *Journal of Southern History* 65 (May 1999): 294.

63. Ibid., 302, 314.

64. Mary Martha Thomas, "The Ideology of the Alabama Woman Suffrage Movement, 1890–1920," in *Southern Women*, ed. Bernhard et al., 121.

65. Turner, " 'White-Gloved Ladies' and 'New Women,' " in ibid., 135.

66. Ibid.

67. Edward L. Ayers, *The Promise of the New South: Life after Reconstruction* (New York: Oxford University Press, 1992), 319.

68. Ibid., 233.

Chapter 5: Lady Insurrectionists

1. Nanci Kincaid, *Crossing Blood* (New York: Putnam, 1992), 164.

2. Edward L. Ayers, *The Promise of the New South: Life after Reconstruction* (New York: Oxford University Press, 1992), 170.

3. Anne Firor Scott, "How Women Have Changed Georgia—and Themselves," *Atlanta History* (Summer 1990): 8.

4. Ibid., 9.

5. Ayers, *Promise of the New South*, 181.

6. Ibid., 321.

7. Scott, "How Women Have Changed Georgia," 10; Frances Mitchell Ross, "The New Woman as Club Woman and Social Activist in Turn-of-the-Century Arkansas," *Arkansas Historical Quarterly* 50 (Winter 1991): 324; Ayers, *Promise of the New South*, 78–9.

8. Ross, "The New Woman as Club Woman," 317–51.

9. Elizabeth Hayes Turner, " 'White-Gloved Ladies' and 'New Women' in the Texas Woman Suffrage Movement," in *Southern Women: Histories and Identities*, ed. Virginia Bernhard et al. (Columbia: University of Missouri Press, 1992), 134.

10. Mary Martha Thomas, "The Ideology of the Alabama Woman Suffrage Movement, 1890–1920," in ibid., 116.

11. Josephine Henry, "The New Woman of the New South," *Arena* 11 (1894–95): 334.

12. Amy Thompson McCandless, "Progressivism and the Higher Education of Southern Women," *North Carolina Historical Review* 70 (July 1993): 302–25.

13. James L. Leloudis, *Schooling the New South: Pedagogy, Self, and Society in North Carolina, 1880–1920* (Chapel Hill: University of North Carolina Press, 1996).

14. Nancy Keever Andersen, "Cooperation for Social Betterment: The Intellectual and Theological Rationale of Southern Methodists Associated with the Southern Sociological Congress, 1912–1914," *Methodist History* 34 (October 1995): 29–41.

15. O. Latham Hatcher, *Rural Girls in the City for Work* (1930; reprint, New York: Garland, 1986), 68–9.

16. Peter Taylor, "The Old Forest," in *Growing Up in the South: An Anthology of Modern Southern Literature*, ed. Suzanne W. Jones (New York: Penguin, 1991), 318–19.

17. Richard Love, "The Cigarette Capital of the World: Labor, Race, and Tobacco in Richmond, Virginia, 1880–1980," unpublished Ph.D. dissertation, University of Virginia, 1998, p. 120; see also Lucy Randolph Mason, *To Win These Rights: A Personal Story of the CIO in the South* (Westport, Conn.: Greenwood Press, 1970).

18. See Jacquelyn Dowd Hall et al., *Like a Family: The Making of a Southern Cotton Mill World* (Chapel Hill: University of North Carolina Press, 1987).

19. See Jacquelyn Dowd Hall, "Private Eyes, Public Women: Images of Class and Sex in the Urban South, Atlanta, Georgia, 1913–1915," *Atlanta History* 36 (Winter 1993): 24–39; Gretchen E. Maclachlan, "Atlanta's Industrial Women, 1879–1920," *Atlanta History* 36 (Winter 1993): 16–23.

20. See Hall, "Private Eyes, Public Women."

21. Nancy MacLean, "The Leo Frank Case Reconsidered: Gender and Sexual Politics in the Making of Reactionary Populism," *Journal of American History* 78 (December 1991): 917–48.

22. Love, "The Cigarette Capital of the World," 112.

23. Patrick Huber, "Battle Songs of the Southern Class Struggle: Songs of the Gastonia Textile Strike of 1929," *Southern Cultures* 4 (Summer 1998): 109–22.

24. See Jacquelyn Dowd Hall, *Revolt Against Chivalry: Jessie Daniel Ames and the Women's Campaign Against Lynching* (New York: Columbia University Press, 1979); Hall, "Women and Lynching," *Southern Exposure* 21 (Spring/Summer 1993): 46–7.

25. Lillian Smith, *Killers of the Dream* (1949; reprint, New York: W. W. Norton & Company, 1978), 145.

26. Kathleen Atkinson Miller, "The Ladies and the Lynchers: A Look at the Association of Southern Women for the Prevention of Lynching," *Southern Studies* 2 (Fall/Winter 1991): 266.

27. Jacquelyn Dowd Hall, "Partial Truths: Writing Southern Women's History," in *Southern Women*, ed. Bernhard et al., 25.

28. See Stewart E. Tolnay and E. M. Beck, *A Festival of Violence: An Analysis of Southern Lynchings, 1882–1930* (Urbana: University of Illinois Press, 1995).

29. Dorothy Sterling, "To Build a Free Society: Nineteenth-Century Black Women," *Southern Exposure*, 12 (March/April 1984): 5.

30. Catherine Clinton, "Bloody Terrain: Freedwomen, Sexuality and Violence during Reconstruction," *Georgia Historical Quarterly* 76 (Summer 1992): 318.

31. Sterling, "To Build a Free Society," 6.

32. See Glenda Elizabeth Gilmore, *Gender and Jim Crow: Women and the Politics of White Supremacy in North Carolina, 1896–1920* (Chapel Hill: University of North Carolina Press, 1997); Anastatia Sims, *The Power of Femininity in the New South: Women's Organizations and Politics in North Carolina* (Columbia: University of South Carolina Press, 1997).

33. See Scott, "How Women Have Changed Georgia," 8.

34. Beverly Washington Jones, *Quest for Equality: The Life and Writings of Mary Eliza Church Terrell, 1863–1954* (Brooklyn: Carlson Publishers, 1990), 26.

35. Ardie Myers, review of Lillian Serece Williams and Randolph Boehm, eds., *National Association of Colored Women's Clubs, 1895–1992* (Bethesda, Md.: University Publications of America, 1994. Part 1: *Minutes of the National Conventions, Publications, and President's Office Correspondence*), *Journal of American History* 84 (June 1997): 260.

36. Joan Marie Johnson, " 'Drill into us . . . the Rebel tradition': The Contest over Southern Identity in Black and White Women's Clubs, South Carolina, 1898–1930," *Journal of Southern History* 66 (August 2000): 551.

37. Tera W. Hunter, *To 'Joy My Freedom: Southern Black Women's Lives and Labors after the Civil War* (Cambridge: Harvard University Press, 1997), 178–9.

38. Linda Gordon, "Black and White Visions of Welfare: Women's Welfare Activism, 1890–1945," *Journal of American History* 78 (September 1991): 561.

39. Johnson, " 'Drill into us . . . the Rebel Tradition,' " 555.

40. Charlotte Hawkins Brown, "Clippings," Charlotte Hawkins Brown Papers, Reel 2, Schlesinger Library, Radcliffe College, Cambridge, Mass; see also Constance Hill Mareena, *Lengthening Shadow of a Woman: A Biography of Charlotte Hawkins Brown* (Hicksville, N.Y.: Exposition Press, 1977).

41. Daniel Levine, "A Single Standard of Civilization: Black Private Social Welfare Institutions in the South, 1880s–1920s," *Georgia Historical Quarterly* 81 (Spring 1997): 71.

42. Scott, "How Women Have Changed Georgia," 11.

43. Darlene Clark Hine, "Race and the Inner Lives of Southern Black Women: Thoughts on the Culture of Dissemblance," in *Southern Women*, ed. Bernhard et al., 187.

44. Mary Church Terrell, "The Duty of the National Association of Colored Women to the Race," in *Mary Church Terrell: Selected Essays* (Brooklyn: Carlson Publishers, 1990), 148.

45. Mary Church Terrell, "First Presidential Address to the NACW," in ibid., 134.

46. Sterling, "Nineteenth-Century Black Women," 12.

Chapter 6: A Woman's Movement

1. Arnold Shankman, "Dorothy Tilly and the Fellowship of the Concerned," in *From the Old South to the New: Essays on the Transitional South*, ed. Walter J. Fraser Jr. and Winfred B. Moore Jr. (Westport, Conn.: Greenwood Press, 1981), 247.

2. Hollinger F. Bernard, ed., *Outside the Magic Circle: The Autobiography of Virginia Foster Durr* (University: University of Alabama Press, 1985), 171–2.

3. Sara Alderman Murphy, *Breaking the Silence: Little Rock's Women's Emergency Committee to Open Our Schools, 1958–1963* (Fayetteville: University of Arkansas Press, 1997), 7.

4. Ibid., 11.

5. Ibid., 21.

6. Ibid., 67.

7. Lorraine Gates, "Power from the Pedestal: The Women's Emergency Committee and the Little Rock School Crisis," *Arkansas Historical Quarterly* 55 (Spring 1996): 35.

8. Ibid., 37, 39.

9. Ibid., 45.

10. Murphy, *Breaking the Silence*, 118.

11. Gates, "Power from the Pedestal," 45.

12. Murphy, *Breaking the Silence*, 218.

13. Bernard, ed., *Outside the Magic Circle*, 244–5.

14. Murphy, *Breaking the Silence*, 148.

15. Ibid., 217.

16. Ibid., 221, 232.

17. Ibid., 139.

18. David Goldfield, *Black, White, and Southern: Race Relations and Southern Culture, 1940 to the Present* (Baton Rouge: Louisiana State University Press, 1990), 96; see also Darlene Clark Hine, "Lifting the Veil, Shattering the Silence: Black Women's History in Slavery and Freedom," *The State of Afro-American History: Past, Present, and Future*, ed. Hine (Baton Rouge: Louisiana State University Press, 1986), 245–6.

19. Goldfield, *Black, White, and Southern*, 95.

20. See J. Mills Thornton III, "Challenge and Response in the Montgomery Bus Boycott of 1955–1956," *Alabama Review* 33 (1980): 163–235; Martin Luther King Jr., *Stride Toward Freedom: The Montgomery Story* (New York: Harper, 1958); "Montgomery Bus Boycott," *Southern Exposure* 9 (Spring 1981): 13–21.

21. Belinda Robnett, "African-American Women in the Civil Rights Movement, 1954–1965: Gender, Leadership, and Micromobilization," *American Journal of Sociology* 101 (May 1996): 1681–2.

22. Ibid.

23. Quoted in ibid., 1671.

24. See Anthony Walton, *Mississippi: An American Journey* (New York: Vintage, 1996), 140–6.

25. Ibid., 146.

26. Belinda Robnett, *How Long? How Long? African-American Women in the Struggle for Civil Rights* (New York: Oxford University Press, 1997), 180.

27. Anne Rivers Siddons, *Heartbreak Hotel* (New York: Simon & Schuster, 1976), 4.

28. Ibid., 5.

29. Pamela Fox, "Recycled 'Trash': Gender and Authenticity in Country Music Autobiography," *American Quarterly* 50 (June 1998): 252.

30. See Jon Pareles, "When Country Sang to Just Plain Folks," New York *Times*, May 15, 1999.

31. Fox, "Recycled 'Trash,' " 258.

32. Curtis W. Ellison, "Keeping Faith: Evangelical Performance in Country Music," *South Atlantic Quarterly* 94 (Winter 1995): 151; Bruce Feiler, "Gone Country," *The New Republic*, February 5, 1996, pp. 19–20, 22–4.

33. See Jon Pareles, "If Your Man Treats You Bad, It's Great to Break Loose but Even Better to Get Even," New York *Times*, July 24, 2000.

34. Ellison, "Keeping Faith," 152.

35. Ibid., 160.

36. Harriet Pollack, "From *Shiloh* to *In Country* to *Feather Crowns*: Bobbie Ann Mason, Women's History, and Southern Fiction," *Southern Literary Journal* 28 (Spring 1996): 98.

37. Bobbie Ann Mason, "Shiloh," in *Shiloh and Other Stories* (New York: Harper and Row, 1982), 14.

38. Reynolds Price, quoted in Sharon McKern, *Redneck Mothers, Good Ol' Girls and Other Southern Belles: A Celebration of the Women of Dixie* (New York: Viking, 1979), 3; James Whitehead, quoted in Stephen A. Smith, *Myth, Media, and the Southern Mind* (Fayetteville: University of Arkansas Press, 1985), 112.

39. Henry Eichel, "Another Southern Lost Cause," Charlotte *Observer*, September 1, 1996.

40. Ibid.

41. Nathaniel Tripp, "Men Behaving Badly," review of Catherine S. Manegold's *In Glory's Shadow: Shannon Faulkner, The Citadel and a Changing America* (New York: Knopf, 1999), *New York Times Book Review*, January 23, 2000.

42. Ferrel Guillory, "A Political Paradox: North Carolina's Twenty-Five Years Under Jim Hunt and Jesse Helms," *Southern Cultures* 4 (Spring 1998): 52–61; see also Paul Luebke, *Tar Heel Politics 2000* (Chapel Hill: University of North Carolina Press, 1998), especially chapter 10.

43. Sue Tolleson-Rinehart, "Can the Flower of Southern Womanhood Bloom in the Garden of Southern Politics?" *Southern Cultures* 4 (Spring 1998): 78–87; Gerald Ingalls et al., "Fifty Years of Political Change in the South: Electing African Americans and Women to Public Office," *Southeastern Geographer* 37 (November 1997): 140–61.

44. Ingalls et al., "Fifty Years of Political Change," 148; Drew Gilpin Faust, "Gender and the Lingering Burden of Southern History," in *The Future of the South* (Research Triangle Park, N.C.: National Humanities Center, 1995), 23.

45. Maxine P. Atkinson and Jacqueline Boles, "The Shaky Pedestal: Southern Ladies Yesterday and Today," *Southern Studies* 24 (Winter 1985): 405; Tolleson-Rinehart, "Flower of Southern Womanhood," 84.

46. Faust, "Gender and the Lingering Burden," 23.

47. Anne Eckman and Jordan Green, "Job Equity in the Downsized South: A Special Report on Work in the 1990s," *Southern Exposure* 25 (Fall/Winter 1997): 9, 11.

48. Vernon Chadwick, "Twirling Fire: Can Southern Beauty Survive as a Radical Political Value?" *Southern Reader* 1 (Summer 1992): 1, 5.

49. See Faust, "Gender and the Lingering Burden," 23.

50. Shirley Abbott, *Womenfolks: Growing Up Down South* (New Haven, Conn.: Ticknor & Fields, 1983), 6.

51. Ibid., 167.

52. McKern, *Redneck Mothers*, 253.

Chapter 7: Colors

1. David Goldfield et al., *The American Journey: A History of the United States* (Upper Saddle River, N.J.: Prentice Hall, 1998), 390–1.

2. The literature on slavery is voluminous. The preceding paragraphs reflect recent scholarship, especially Ira Berlin, *Many Thousands Gone: The First Two Centuries of Slavery in North America* (Cambridge: Belknap Press of Harvard University Press, 1998); John B. Boles, *Black Southerners, 1619–1869* (Lexington: University Press of Kentucky, 1983); Edward D. C. Campbell Jr. and Kym S. Rice, eds., *Before Freedom Came: African-American Life in the Antebellum South* (Charlottesville: University Press of Virginia, 1991); Peter Kolchin, *American Slavery, 1619–1877* (New York: Hill and Wang, 1993); Albert J. Raboteau, *Slave Religion: The "Invisible Institution" in the Antebellum South* (New York: Oxford University Press, 1978).

3. W. E. B. Du Bois, *Black Reconstruction in America* (New York: Harcourt, Brace, 1935), 30.

4. Robert C. Kenzer, *Enterprising Southerners: Black Economic Success in North Carolina, 1865–1915* (Charlottesville: University Press of Virginia, 1997), 27.

5. Ibid.; E. Franklin Frazier, "Durham: Capital of the Black Middle Class," in *The New Negro*, ed. Alain LeRoy Locke (New York: A. & C. Boni, 1925), 339.

6. Jean B. Anderson, *Durham County* (Durham: Duke University Press, 1990), 222; see also Walter B. Weare, *Black Business in the New South: A Social History of the North Carolina Mutual Life Insurance Company* (Urbana: University of Illinois Press, 1973).

7. C. Vann Woodward, *The Strange Career of Jim Crow* (New York: Oxford University Press, 1974), 82.

8. Howard N. Rabinowitz, *The First New South, 1865–1920* (Arlington Heights, Ill.: Harlan Davidson), 145.

9. Joseph Charles Price and David Schenck, quoted in Edward L. Ayers, *The Promise of the New South: Life After Reconstruction* (New York: Oxford University Press, 1992), 428.

10. Stephen Kantrowitz, *Ben Tillman and the Reconstruction of White Supremacy* (Chapel Hill: University of North Carolina Press, 2000), 261.

11. Ibid., 169.

12. See William R. Keech and Michael P. Sistrom, "North Carolina," in *Quiet Revolution in the South: The Impact of the Voting Rights Act, 1965–1990*, ed. Chandler Davidson and Bernard Grofman (Princeton: Princeton University Press, 1994), 155–90.

13. Thomas W. Hanchett, *Sorting Out the New South City: Race, Class, and Urban Development in Charlotte, 1875–1975* (Chapel Hill: University of North Carolina Press, 1998), 86–7.

14. Joel Williamson distinguishes between "Conservative" and "Radical" southern white mentalities with respect to race, with the former exhibiting a more civil, moderate tone and stance, while the latter is synonymous with rabid racism. While the distinctions are helpful in

sorting out white attitudes toward race, I would argue that the differences are more of style than of substance. And, in some respects, the "Conservative" outlook was more nefarious, in that it was often cynical and corrosive. See Joel Williamson, *The Crucible of Race: Black-White Relations in the American South since Emancipation* (New York: Oxford University Press, 1984).

15. Goldfield et al., *The American Journey* , 582.

16. Rabinowitz, *First New South*, 114–5.

17. Columbia *State*, October 27, 1895.

18. William Anderson, *The Wild Man from Sugar Creek: The Political Career of Eugene Talmadge* (Baton Rouge: Louisiana State University Press, 1978), 209.

19. Earl Black and Merle Black, *Politics and Society in the South* (Cambridge: Harvard University Press, 1987), 7.

20. David Goldfield, *Black, White, and Southern: Race Relations and Southern Culture, 1940 to the Present* (Baton Rouge: Louisiana State University Press, 1990), 83.

21. Lillian Smith, *Killers of the Dream* (New York: Norton, 1961), 164–5.

22. Robert Penn Warren, *All the King's Men* (New York: Harcourt, Brace & World, 1946), 77.

23. See, for example, Raymond Arsenault, *Wild Ass of the Ozarks: Jeff Davis and the Social Bases of Southern Politics* (Philadelphia: Temple University Press, 1984); Carl Grafton and Anne Permaloff, *Big Mules and Branchheads: James E. Folsom and Political Power in Alabama* (Athens: University of Georgia Press, 1985); William F. Holmes, *The White Chief: James Kimble Vardaman* (Baton Rouge: Louisiana State University Press, 1970); T. Harry Williams, *Huey Long* (New York: Knopf, 1969).

24. V. O. Key Jr., *Southern Politics in State and Nation* (New York: Knopf, 1949), 4.

25. George B. Tindall, *The Disruption of the Solid South* (New York: Norton, 1972), 31–2.

26. Carter Glass, quoted in Dewey W. Grantham, *The South in Modern America: A Region at Odds* (New York: HarperCollins, 1994), 131; "The Deep South Looks Up," *Fortune*, July 1943, 220; Key, *Southern Politics*, 5.

27. *Plessy v. Ferguson* (163 U.S. 537), in *Cases Argued and Decided in the Supreme Court of the United States* (Rochester, N.Y.: The Lawyers Cooperative Publishing Company, 1920), 264–5.

28. Richmond *Dispatch*, October 5, 1886.

29. Richmond *Whig*, October 7, 1886; see also Daniel Letwin, *The Challenge of Interracial Unionism: Alabama Coal Miners, 1878–1921* (Chapel Hill: University of North Carolina Press, 1998).

30. Charles Crowe, "Racial Massacre in Atlanta, September 22, 1906," *Journal of Negro History* 54 (April 1969): 162.

31. "Walter White," in *Growing Up Black*, ed. Jay David (New York: Avon, 1992), 9.

32. W. E. B. Du Bois, *The Souls of Black Folk* (1903; reprint, Millwood, N.Y.: Kraus-Thomson, 1973), 180.

33. Osha Gray Davidson, *The Best of Enemies: Race and Redemption in the New South* (New York: Scribner, 1996), 42.

34. "The Clansman," Atlanta *Journal*, June 10, 1905.

35. Gregory L. Mixon, " 'A Memorandum to Armageddon': Violence, Race, and Class in a New South City," manuscript in author's possession, 1998, chapter 7, p. 42.

36. Mildred I. Thompson, *Ida B. Wells-Barnett: An Exploratory Study of an American Black Woman, 1893–1930* (Brooklyn: Carlson Publishing, 1990), 27–8; Kenneth W. Goings and Gerald L. Smith, " 'Unhidden' Transcripts: Memphis and African American Agency, 1862–1920," *Journal of Urban History* 21 (March 1995): 372–94; see also W. Fitzhugh Brundage, ed., *Under Sentence of Death: Lynching in the South* (Chapel Hill: University of North Carolina Press, 1997).

37. See Grace Elizabeth Hale, *Making Whiteness: The Culture of Segregation in the South, 1890–1940* (New York: Pantheon Books, 1998).

38. Thompson, *Ida B. Wells-Barnett*, 39–40.

39. Andrea Meryl Kirshenbaum, " 'The Vampire That Hovers Over North Carolina': Gender, White Supremacy, and the Wilmington Race Riot of 1898," *Southern Cultures* 4 (Fall 1998): 11.

40. The best statement of this perspective is found in Howard N. Rabinowitz, *Race Relations in the Urban South, 1865–1890* (New York: Oxford University Press, 1978).

41. Goldfield, *Black, White, and Southern*, 27.

42. Ibid., 11–2; see also Bertram W. Doyle, *The Etiquette of Race Relations in the South: A Study in Social Control* (Chicago: University of Chicago Press, 1937).

43. See Dewey W. Grantham, *Southern Progressivism: The Reconciliation of Progress and Tradition* (Knoxville: University of Tennessee Press, 1983); Jack Temple Kirby, *Darkness at the Dawning: Race and Reform in the Progressive South* (Philadelphia: Lippincott, 1972); James L. Leloudis, *Schooling the New South* (Chapel Hill: University of North Carolina Press, 1996); William A. Link, *A Hard Country and a Lonely Place: Schooling, Society, and Reform in Rural Virginia*, 1870–1920 (Chapel Hill: University of North Carolina Press, 1986); Link, *The Paradox of Southern Progressivism, 1880–1930* (Chapel Hill: University of North Carolina Press,1993); J. Morgan Kousser, "Progressivism—For Middle-Class Whites Only: North Carolina Education, 1880–1910," *Journal of Southern History* 46 (May 1980): 169–94.

44. James D. Anderson, *The Education of Blacks in the South, 1860–1935* (Chapel Hill: University of North Carolina Press), 149, 150, 152, 181.

45. J. M. Foote and M. Robertson, *The Public Schools of East Feliciana Parish* (Baton Rouge: State Department of Education, 1926), 20–1.

46. Kenzer, *Enterprising Southerners*, 87.

47. Robert A. Margo, *Disfranchisement, School Finance, and the Economics of the Segregated Schools in the United States South, 1890–1910* (New York: Garland, 1985), 8–9.

48. Anderson, *Education of Blacks*, 236–7; see also Charles C. Bolton, "Mississippi's School Equalization Program, 1945–1954: 'A Last Gasp to Try to Maintain a Segregated Educational System,' " *Journal of Southern History* 46 (November 2000), 793.

49. Truman M. Pierce, *White and Negro Schools in the South: An Analysis of Biracial Education* (Englewood Cliffs, N.J.: Prentice Hall, 1955), 119, 161.

50. Numan V. Bartley, *The New South: 1945–1980* (Baton Rouge: Louisiana State University Press, 1995), 148–52.

51. Anthony Walton, *Mississippi: An American Journey* (New York: Vintage, 1996), 62.

52. Ernest J. Gaines, *A Lesson Before Dying* (New York: Vintage, 1994), 34.

53. "Angela Davis," in *Growing Up Black*, ed. David, 210, 211, 213, 214.

54. "Carl T. Rowan," in ibid., 124.

55. Ibid., 126.

56. Richard Wright, *Black Boy* (1945; reprint, New York: Harper, 1993), 206–11.

57. Charles Scott Wright, "Creating a New Deal: The Importance of Black Self-Help Organizations in Lynchburg, Virginia, 1930–1940," M.A. thesis, University of North Carolina at Charlotte, 1998, p. 87.

58. John Egerton, "Days of Hope and Horror: Atlanta after World War II," *Georgia Historical Quarterly* 78 (Summer 1994): 290, 291.

59. Ronald H. Bayor, *Race & the Shaping of Twentieth-Century Atlanta* (Chapel Hill: University of North Carolina Press, 1996). Other southern cities devised equally elaborate schemes for maintaining segregated residential areas. See, for example, the Richmond *Times-Dispatch*, April 29, 1911; Christopher Silver, *Twentieth-Century Richmond: Planning, Politics, and Race* (Knoxville: University of Tennessee Press, 1984).

60. Harvey K. Newman, "Southern Hospitality: A History of the Growth of Atlanta and its Hospitality Business," manuscript in author's possession, 93.

61. Davidson, *Best of Enemies*, 31.

62. Works Progress Administration, *Atlanta: Capital of the Modern South* (Washington, D.C.: WPA, 1942), 31.

63. William Faulkner, *The Sound and the Fury* (New York: Random House, 1929), 106; Ralph Ellison, *Invisible Man* (1947; reprint, New York: Vintage, 1972), 3.

64. William Alexander Percy, *Lanterns on the Levee: Recollections of a Planter's Son* (1941; reprint, Baton Rouge: Louisiana State University Press, 1991), 299.

65. Du Bois, *Souls of Black Folk*, 185.

66. Wright, *Black Boy*, 162–3; 284.

67. Hollinger F. Bernard, ed., *Outside the Magic Circle: The Autobiography of Virginia Foster Durr* (University: University of Alabama Press, 1985), 18–19.

68. Jimmy Carter, *An Hour Before Daylight: Memories of a Rural Boyhood* (New York: Simon & Schuster, 2001), 229–30.

69. Thomas Wolfe, *Look Homeward, Angel: A Story of the Buried Life* (New York: Scribners, 1929), 155.

70. "Recalling a Home Place That Is No More," Charlotte *Observer*, January 25, 1998.

71. Melany Neilson, *Even in Mississippi* (University: University of Alabama Press, 1989), 38–9.

72. Smith, *Killers of the Dream*, 96.

73. Mary Mebane, *Mary* (New York: Viking Press, 1981), 51–2.

74. "Daisy Bates," in *Growing Up Black*, ed. David, 172.

75. Goldfield, *Black, White, and Southern*, 10.

76. Walton, *Mississippi*, 58.

77. Mary Mebane, *Mary, Wayfarer* (New York: Viking, 1983), 103–4.

78. Walton, *Mississippi*, 31; "Angela Davis," in *Growing Up Black*, ed. David, 220.

79. James C. Cobb, ed., *Cosmopolitan Provincial: The Delta and World According to David L. Cohn* (Baton Rouge: Louisiana State University Press, 1996), 6–7.

80. Donald Davidson, "The Tall Men," in *Poems, 1922–1961* (Minneapolis: University of Minnesota Press, 1966), 140.

81. Gunnar Myrdal, *An American Dilemma: The Negro Problem and Modern Democracy* (1944; reprint, New York: Harper & Row, 1962), 441.

82. Steven A. Reich, "Soldiers of Democracy: Black Texans and the Fight for Citizenship, 1917–1921," *Journal of American History* 82 (March 1996): 1479, 1494, 1500.

83. Davidson, *Best of Enemies*, 77.

Chapter 8: Sharings

1. John B. Boles, *The South Through Time: A History of an American Region* (Englewood Cliffs, N.J.: Prentice Hall, 1995), 437–48; see also Edward L. Ayers, *The Promise of the New South: Life after Reconstruction* (New York: Oxford University Press, 1992): 380–92; William Ferris, *Blues from the Delta* (New York: Anchor Books, 1979).

2. Shane Maddock, " 'Whole Lotta Shakin' Goin' On': Racism and Early Opposition to Rock Music," *Mid-America* 78 (Summer 1996): 186; see also James C. Cobb, *Redefining Southern Culture: Mind and Identity in the Modern South* (Athens: University of Georgia Press, 1999): 36, 118–9; Brian Ward, *Just My Soul Responding: Rhythm and Blues, Black Consciousness, and Race Relations* (Berkeley: University of California Press, 1998); Courtney Haden, "Dixie Rock: The Fusion's Still Burning," *Southern Exposure* 5 (Summer/Fall 1977): 37–43.

3. Maddock, " 'Whole Lotta Shakin' Goin' On,' " 78.

4. S. Jonathan Bass, " 'How 'bout a Hand for the Hog': The Enduring Nature of the Swine as a Cultural Symbol in the South," *Southern Cultures* 1 (Spring 1995): 314.

5. Will Campbell, quoted in James C. Cobb, "Community and Identity: Redefining Southern Culture," *The Georgia Review* 50 (Spring 1996): 15; Kaye Gibbons, *A Cure for Dreams* (New York: Vintage, 1991), 44.

6. Angeline Godwin Dvorak, "Cooking as Mission and Ministry in Southern Culture: The Nurturers of Clyde Edgerton's *Walking Across Egypt*, Fannie Flagg's *Fried Green Tomatoes at the Whistle Stop Café* and Anne Tyler's *Dinner at the Homesick Restaurant*," *Southern Quarterly* 30 (Winter/Spring 1992): 90; Bass, " 'How 'bout a Hand for the Hog,' " 314.

7. Katharine Du Pre Lumpkin, *The Making of a Southerner* (1946; reprint, Athens: University of Georgia Press, 1991), 193.

8. David L. Carlton and Peter A. Coclanis, "Another 'Great Migration': From Region to Race in Southern Liberalism," *Southern Cultures* 3 (Winter 1997): 46, 51.

9. "Mills of the Gods," *Daily Tar Heel*, January 6, 1939.

10. James McBride Dabbs, *Who Speaks for the South?* (New York: Funk & Wagnalls Co., 1964), 381.

11. "Carl Rowan," in *Growing Up Black*, ed. Jay David (New York: Avon, 1992), 134.

12. Carlton and Coclanis, "Another 'Great Migration,' " 51–4.

13. Ronald H. Bayor, *Race & The Shaping of Twentieth-Century Atlanta* (Chapel Hill: University of North Carolina Press, 1996), 21–9.

14. Bill Minor, "Grand Opening: The Mississippi Sovereignty Commission," *Southern Changes* 20 (Summer 1998): 20–2; "Recalling a Home Place That Is No More," Charlotte *Observer*, January 25, 1998.

15. J. Morgan Kousser, *Colorblind Injustice: Minority Voting Rights and the Undoing of the Second Reconstruction* (Chapel Hill: University of North Carolina Press, 1999), 202.

16. David Goldfield, *Black, White, and Southern: Race Relations and Southern Culture, 1940 to the Present* (Baton Rouge: Louisiana State University Press, 1990), 103.

17. Franklin McCain, quoted in "I'm Gonna Sit at the Welcome Table One of These Days," *Southern Exposure* 9 (Spring 1981): 22; "The Image Makers," *Ebony*, April 1961, p. 88; Leslie Dunbar, "The Annealing of the South," *Virginia Quarterly Review* 37 (Autumn 1961): 499.

18. Goldfield, *Black, White, and Southern*, 121.

19. James Sellers, *The South and Christian Ethics* (New York: Association Press, 1962), 119.

20. James A. Rogers, "Striking the Balance in the Sixties," *Furman Magazine* 22 (Spring 1985): 3, 6.

21. Sellers, *The South and Christian Ethics*, 138–9; see also Fred Hobson, *But Now I See: The White Southern Racial Conversion Narrative* (Baton Rouge: Louisiana State University Press, 1999).

22. Sellers, *The South and Christian Ethics*, 65.

23. Goldfield, *Black, White, and Southern*, 170.

24. Although historian C. Vann Woodward began writing a new perspective on southern history during the 1930s, he published two influential works in the 1950s that reoriented professional historical interpretations on events during and after Reconstruction, *Origins of the New South, 1877–1913* (Baton Rouge: Louisiana State University Press, 1951) and *The Strange Career of Jim Crow* (New York: Oxford University Press, 1957). The institution of slavery also came under thorough reinspection in the 1950s. See especially Stanley M. Elkins, *Slavery: A Problem in American Institutional and Intellectual Life* (Chicago: University of Chicago Press, 1959) and Kenneth M. Stampp, *The Peculiar Institution: Slavery in the Antebellum South* (New York: Random House, 1956).

25. Goldfield, *Black, White, and Southern*, 172.

26. Walker Percy, *The Last Gentleman* (New York: Signet, 1968), 150; H. Brandt Ayers, "You Can't Eat Magnolias," in *You Can't Eat Magnolias*, ed. Ayers and Thomas H. Naylor (New York: McGraw-Hill, 1972), 24; Terry Sanford, "The End of the Myths: The South Can Lead the Nation," in ibid., 329; Willie Morris, introduction, to ibid., ix.

27. Goldfield, *Black, White, and Southern*, 145; see also David R. Colburn, "The Saint Augustine Business Community," in Elizabeth Jacoway and Colburn, eds., *Southern Businessmen and Desegregation* (Baton Rouge: Louisiana State University Press, 1982), 211–35.

Chapter 9: New Battlegrounds, Old Strategies

1. J. Morgan Kousser, *Colorblind Injustice: Minority Voting Rights and the Undoing of the Second Reconstruction* (Chapel Hill: University of North Carolina Press, 1999), 55.

2. Charles Reagan Wilson, "The Myth of the Biracial South," in *The Southern State of Mind*, ed. Jan Nordby Gretlund (Columbia: University of South Carolina Press, 1999), 9.

3. David Goldfield, *Black, White, and Southern: Race Relations and Southern Culture, 1940 to the Present* (Baton Rouge: Louisiana State University Press, 1990), 179.

4. Steven F. Lawson, *In Pursuit of Power: Southern Blacks & Electoral Politics, 1965–1982* (New York: Columbia University Press, 1985), 252.

5. Gerald L. Ingalls et al., "Fifty Years of Political Change in the South: Electing African Americans and Women to Public Office," *Southeastern Geographer* 37 (November 1997): 146.

6. "Election Notebook," *The New Republic*, November 23, 1998, 8, 10.

7. William R. Keech and Michael P. Sistrom, "North Carolina," in *Quiet Revolution in the South: The Impact of the Voting Rights Act, 1965–1990*, ed. Chandler Davidson and Bernard Grofman (Princeton: Princeton University Press, 1994), 162.

8. Ibid., 167, 188–9.

9. Christopher Silver and John V. Moeser, *The Separate City: Black Communities in the Urban South, 1940–1968* (Lexington: University Press of Kentucky, 1995), 112–3.

10. Data provided by Charles M. Tolbert, Ph.D., Senior Research Scientist, Louisiana Population Data Center, Louisiana State University. The series of events related to the annexation may be followed in the press: "Scotlandville Residents Ask Annexation," Baton Rouge *State-Times*, August 6, 1978; "C-P Committee Recommends Suspension of Annexation," ibid., September 7, 1978; "Annexation Talk Provokes 'Words,' " ibid., October 19, 1978; "Scotlandville Annexation Voted," ibid., October 26, 1978.

11. "U.S. OK's Councils Redistrict," Baton Rouge *State-Times*, June 22, 1982; "Councils Set Election on Merger," Baton Rouge *Morning Advocate*, June 24, 1982.

12. Mireya Navarro and Somini Sengupta, "Arriving at Florida Voting Places, Some Blacks Found Frustration," New York *Times*, November 30, 2000.

13. Russell Merritt, "The Senatorial Election of 1962 and the Rise of Two-Party Politics in South Carolina," *South Carolina Historical Magazine* 98 (July 1997): 285; see also Earl Black and Merle Black, *Politics and Society in the South* (Cambridge: Harvard University Press, 1987); Dan T. Carter, *From George Wallace to Newt Gingrich: Race in the Conservative Counterrevolution, 1963–1994* (Baton Rouge: Louisiana State University Press, 1996); Alexander Lamis, *The Two-Party South* (New York: Oxford University Press, 1984).

14. Lyndon B. Johnson, quoted in John B. Boles, *The South Through Time: A History of an American Region* (Englewood Cliffs, N.J.: Prentice Hall, 1995), 499; Haynes Johnson, "The South's Racial Climate Turns Ugly and Raw," Charlotte *Observer*, October 7, 1984.

15. Lamis, *Two-Party South*, 256n.

16. Dan T. Carter, *The Politics of Rage: George Wallace, the Origins of the New Conservatism, and Transformation of American Politics* (New York: Simon & Schuster, 1995).

17. For an excellent discussion of the Duke phenomenon, see Lawrence N. Powell, *Troubled Memory: Anne Levy, the Holocaust, and David Duke's Louisiana* (Chapel Hill: University of North Carolina Press, 2000), 436–99.

18. Kevin Sack, "David Duke Misses Louisiana Runoff but Has Strong Showing," New York *Times*, May 3, 1999.

19. John Kifner, "Lott, and Shadow of a Pro-White Group," New York *Times*, January 14, 1999.

20. David Firestone, "Population Shifts in the Southeast Realign Politics in the Suburbs," New York *Times*, June 3, 2000.

21. Jonathan Cohn, "Dixieland," *The New Republic*, December 25, 2000, p. 42.

22. W. J. Cash, "The Mind of the South," *American Mercury* 17 (October 1929): 191; "The Censorship Monopoly," *Southern Exposure* 16 (Fall 1988): 15.

23. Rodney Kline, *Education in Louisiana—History and Development* (Baton Rouge: Claitor's Publishing Division, 1974), 66–7.

24. Edgar L. Porphet, ed., *Building a Better Southern Region Through Education: A Study in State and Regional Cooperation* (Tallahassee, Fla.: Southern States Work-Conference on School Administrative Problems, 1945), 2; Kline, *Education in Louisiana*, 171; MDC, Inc., *The State of the South* (Chapel Hill: MDC, Inc., 1996), 77.

25. MDC, Inc., *State of the South*, 53.

26. Gary Orfield et al., "Deepening Segregation in American Public Schools," *Southern Changes* 19 (Summer 1997): 14.

27. Charles Rutheiser, *Imagineering Atlanta: The Politics of Place in the City of Dreams* (London: Verso, 1996), 61.

28. See David S. Cecelski, *Along Freedom Road: Hyde County, North Carolina, and the Fate of Black Schools in the South* (Chapel Hill: University of North Carolina Press, 1994).

29. Tom Bradbury, "Revolutionary Hopes: Goals for Schools Imply Drastic Improvements," Charlotte *Observer*, November 9, 1996.

30. Robert Penn Warren, *Flood* (London: Collins, 1964), 29; see also James C. Cobb, *The Selling of the South: The Southern Crusade for Industrial Development, 1936–1980* (Baton Rouge: Louisiana State University Press, 1982).

31. Otis L. Graham, "Again the Backward Region? Environmental History in and of the American South," *Southern Cultures* 6 (Summer 2000): 50–72.

32. Robert D. Bullard, *Dumping in Dixie: Race, Class, and Environmental Quality* (Boulder: Westview Press, 1994), 55–8; "Toxic Struggles," *Southern Exposure* 21 (Winter 1993): 21–2; "Gold and Green," ibid., 22 (Fall 1994): 49.

33. Robert Lee Maril, *Cannibals and Condos: Texans and Texas along the Gulf Coast* (College Station: Texas A&M University Press, 1986); William R. Freudenburg and Robert Gramling, "Socioenvironmental Factors and Development Policy: Understanding Opposition and Support for Offshore Oil," *Sociological Forum*, no. 3 (1993): 341–64; see also Eileen Maura McGurty, "From NIMBY to Civil Rights: The Origins of the Environmental Justice Movement," *Environmental History* 2 (July 1997): 301–23.

34. The Shintech story is told in Ron Nixon, "Toxic Gumbo," *Southern Exposure* 26 (Summer/Fall 1998): 11–5; "Company Evades 'Environmental Racism' Test," New York *Times*, September 20, 1998.

35. Colin Crawford, *Uproar at Dancing Rabbit Creek: Battling over Race, Class, and the Environment* (Reading, Mass.: Addison-Wesley Publishing Co., 1996).

36. "Florida Farmworkers Bust Modern-Day Slaveholders," *Southern Exposure* 27 (Summer 1999): 10.

37. Gardiner Harris, "Dust, Deception and Death," *Southern Exposure* 27 (Fall 1999): 34–9.

38. Jeff Diamant, "Middle Class, and Neighbors," Charlotte *Observer*, September 14, 1997.

39. This discussion on the integration of southern textile mills relies on Timothy J. Minchin, *Hiring the Black Worker: The Racial Integration of the Southern Textile Industry, 1960–1980* (Chapel Hill: University of North Carolina Press, 1999).

40. Minchin, *Hiring the Black Worker*, 102.

41. Ibid., 159.

42. Ibid., 257.

43. Ibid., 33.

44. Ibid., 181.

45. Ibid., 202.

46. Orville Vernon Burton, "Race Relations in the Rural South Since World War II," manuscript in author's possession, 9–11.

47. Linda Flowers, *Throwed Away: Failures of Progress in Eastern North Carolina* (Knoxville: University of Tennessee Press, 1990), 4, 168, 182.

48. All data, except infant mortality rates, were taken from the 1990 U.S. Census for North Carolina [*http://venus.census.gov/cdrom/lookup*]. Infant mortality data were taken from the North Carolina Department of Human Resources, *North Carolina Vital Statistics*, Vol. 1 (Raleigh: Department of Human Resources. 1997).

49. Minchin, *Hiring the Black Worker*, 271.

50. Robert Kennedy, quoted in Anthony Walton, *Mississippi: An American Journey* (New York: Vintage, 1996), 254; Martin Luther King Jr., *Where Do We Go From Here: Chaos or Community?* (New York: Bantam Books, 1967), 4, 6.

51. Anne Eckman et al., "Job Equity in the Downsized South: A Special Report on Work in the 1990s," *Southern Exposure* 25 (Fall/Winter 1997): 9–11.

52. Jason De Parle, "Workers Seek Help in Charlotte," Charlotte *Observer*, October 25, 1996.

Chapter 10: Measures

1. Bob Meadows, "Race Divide Still Evident in our Lives," Charlotte *Observer*, September 14, 1997; Foon Rhee, "Race Relations Strained," Charlotte *Observer*, December 30, 1993.

2. "South Adjusts Its Attitude," Charlotte *Observer*, May 15, 1994; "The State of Race Relations," ibid., September 14, 1997; "What Southerners Think About the South," Atlanta *Journal and Constitution*, February 16, 1992.

3. James C. Cobb, "Community and Identity: Redefining Southern Culture," *Georgia Review* 50 (Spring 1996): 12.

4. Ibid., 10.

5. "What Southerners Think," Atlanta *Journal and Constitution*; Benjamin Schwartz, "The Idea of the South," *The Atlantic Monthly*, December 1997, p. 122; Peter Applebome, "Keeping Tabs on Jim Crow: John Hope Franklin," *The New York Times Magazine*, April 23, 1995, p. 38.

6. James McBride Dabbs, *Who Speaks for the South?* (New York: Funk & Wagnalls Co., 1964), 381; W. J. Cash, *The Mind of the South* (New York: Knopf, 1941), 13.

7. Ernest J. Gaines, "Bloodline in Ink," *Georgia Review* 50 (Fall 1996): 532.

8. Orville Vernon Burton, "Race Relations in the Rural South since World War II," manuscript in author's possession, 33.

9. Matthew Cooper, "Welcome to the Olympic Village," *The New Republic*, July 15 & 22, 1996, p. 16.

10. Walter Edgar, "Beyond the Tumult and the Shouting: Black and White in South Carolina in the 1990s," in *The Southern State of Mind*, ed. Jan Nordby Gretlund (Columbia: University of South Carolina Press, 1999), 95–106.

11. Ibid., 96–7.

12. Michael Graczyk, "East Texas Town Says Race Problems Were in the Past," *Associated Press*, June 1998 [http://www.reporternews.com/texas/dd-race0611.html].

13. Peter St. Onge, "Beyond the Flag," Charlotte *Observer*, February 6, 2000.

14. Fannie Flono, "Race and NASCAR: Gentlemen, Start Your Dialogue," Charlotte *Observer*, October 12, 1997.

15. Richard Rubin, "Should the Mississippi Files Have Been Reopened?" *The New York Times Magazine*, August 30, 1998, p. 36.

16. Tamar Jacoby, "The Next Reconstruction," *The New Republic*, June 22, 1998, p. 20.

17. Rubin, "Mississippi Files," 36; Anthony Walton, *Mississippi: An American Journey* (New York: Vintage, 1996), 21.

18. Schwarz, "The Idea of the South," 125; on this point of mutual estrangement, see Charles M. Payne, *I've Got the Light of Freedom: The Organizing Tradition and the Mississippi Freedom Struggle* (Berkeley: University of California Press, 1995).

19. Sam Fulwood, "Up Against a Wall," Charlotte *Observer*, February 23, 1992; Rubin, "Mississippi Files," 36.

20. Cobb, "Community and Identity," 13.

21. Russ Rymer, "Integration's Casualties," *The New York Times Magazine*, November 1, 1998, p. 50.

22. Ibid.; see also Onita Estes-Hicks, "The Way We Were: Precious Memories of the Black Segregated South," *African American Review* 27 (Spring 1993): 9–18.

23. Henry Louis Gates, *Colored People: A Memoir* (New York: Knopf, 1994); Raymond Andrews, *The Last Radio Baby* (Atlanta, Ga.: Peachtree Publishers, 1990).

24. David Goldfield, "Segregation and Racism: Taking Up the Dream Again," in *Understanding the Little Rock Crisis: An Exercise in Remembrance and Reconciliation*, ed. Elizabeth Jacoway and C. Fred Williams (Fayetteville: University of Arkansas Press, 1999), 39.

25. Saul Friedländer, *Nazi Germany and the Jews: The Years of Persecution, 1933–1939* (New York: HarperCollins, 1997), 6.

26. Shelby Steele, quoted in Marvin Caplan, *Farther Along* (Baton Rouge: Louisiana State University Press, 1999), 320; Frederick Douglass, quoted in Randall Kennedy, "My Race Problem—and Ours," *The Atlantic Monthly*, May 1997, p. 56.

27. Mireya Navarro, "Black-Hispanic Rift in Miami," Charlotte *Observer*, February 18, 1997; Phuong Ly, "Life in City's Global Village," Charlotte *Observer*, September 14, 1997; Peter Beinart, "New Bedfellows," *The New Republic*, August 1 & 18, 1997, p. 24.

28. See, for example, John Dittmer, *Local People: The Struggle for Civil Rights in Mississippi* (Urbana: University of Illinois Press, 1994); Robert J. Norrell, *The Civil Rights Movement in Tuskegee* (New York: Random House, 1985).

29. Rubin, "Mississippi Files," 31; Robert E. Bonner, "Rebels With Causes, Now and Then," *Reviews in American History* 27 (June 1999): 236.

30. Sean Wilentz, "The Last Integrationist," *The New Republic*, July 1, 1996, p. 22.

31. Kennedy, "My Race Problem—and Ours," 66.

Chapter 11: Histories

1. Walker Percy, *The Last Gentleman* (New York: Farrar, Straus Giroux, 1966); Walker Percy, *Lancelot* (New York: Farrar, Straus Giroux, 1977), 158.

2. Rick Bass, *The Watch* (New York: Norton, 1989), 172–3.

3. Letters to the editor, Charlotte *Observer*, November 19, 1996.

4. Letters to the editor, Charlotte *Observer*, November 29, 1996; February 7, 1998.

5. "A Few Thoughts on Carpetbaggers," Charlotte *Observer*, March 12, 1985.

6. Diane Roberts, "A League of Their Own," *Southern Exposure* 25 (Spring/Summer 1997): 18–23.

7. Barbara Thiede, "Southern 'Heritage' Groups Distort History for Political Ends," Charlotte *Observer*, October 23, 1998.

8. Charles Davidson, quoted in Jessica Saunders, "Old South Slavery Defender Drops his Bid for Congress," Charlotte *Observer*, May 12, 1996; Diane Roberts, "A League of Their Own," 23.

9. Charles Reagan Wilson, "The Myth of the Biracial South," in *The Southern State of Mind*, ed. Jan Nordby Gretlund (Columbia: University of South Carolina Press, 1999), 17–8.

10. Michael O'Brien, "On Observing the Quicksand," *American Historical Review* 104 (October 1999): 1206; Tony Horwitz, *Confederates in the Attic: Dispatches from the Unfinished Civil War* (New York: Pantheon, 1998), 331.

11. Paul M. Gaston, "After Jim Crow: Civil Rights as Civil Wrongs," in *Southern State of Mind*, ed. Gretlund, 45.

12. Horwitz, *Confederates in the Attic*, 134, 139. For two perceptive commentaries on Horwitz's book, see W. Fitzhugh Brundage, "Commemoration and Conflict: Forgetting and Remembering the Civil War," *Georgia Historical Quarterly* 82 (Fall 1998): 559–74; Grace Elizabeth Hale, "We've Got to Get Out of This Place: Tony Horwitz Tours the Civil War South," *Southern Cultures* 5 (Spring 1999): 54–66.

13. Anne Gearan, "Soldier's Remains Buried, 132 Years After Battle," Charlotte *Observer*, August 25, 1996.

14. Matthew Cooper, "Welcome to the Olympic Village," *The New Republic*, July 15 & 22, 1996, p. 20.

15. Wilson, "Myth of the Biracial South," 16.

16. Derek H. Alderman, "Creating a New Geography of Memory in the South: (Re)naming of Streets in Honor of Martin Luther King, Jr.," *Southeastern Geographer* 36 (May 1996): 61.

17. I am indebted to James W. Loewen for these examples of misused southern history; see "Lies Across the South," *Southern Exposure* 28 (Spring/Summer 2000): 33–48.

18. Ginger Thompson, "Reaping What Was Sown on the Old Plantation," New York *Times*, June 22, 2000.

19. Ibid.

20. Ibid.

21. David Goldfield, *Black, White, and Southern: Race Relations and Southern Culture, 1940 to the Present* (Baton Rouge: Louisiana State University Press, 1990), 272.

22. Doris Betts, "Killers Real and Imagined," *Southern Cultures* 5 (Winter 1999): 5–13; Rick Bragg, "32-year Wait for Justice is Over," Charlotte *Observer*, August 22, 1998.

23. Emily Yellin, "A Changing South Revisits Its Unsolved Racial Killings," New York *Times*, November 8, 1999.

24. Melton A. McLaurin, "Commemorating Wilmington's Racial Violence of 1898: From Individual to Collective Memory," *Southern Cultures* 6 (Winter 2000): 35–57; see also H. Leon

Prather, *We Have Taken a City: Wilmington's Racial Massacre and Coup of 1898* (Teaneck, N.J.: Fairleigh Dickinson University Press, 1984).

25. John M. Coski, "The Confederate Battle Flag in American History and Culture," *Southern Cultures* 2 (Winter 1996): 205.

26. Ibid., 221.

27. Kevin Thornton, "The Confederate Flag and the Meaning of Southern History," *Southern Cultures* 2 (Winter 1996): 239.

28. Ibid., 238.

29. See David Broder, "Stakes Are High in S.C. Flag Fight," Charlotte *Observer*, January 15, 1997; see also Allan Gurganus, "At Last, the South Loses Well," New York *Times*, December 8, 1996.

30. Henry Eichel, "NAACP Calls on Nation to Give S.C. a Wide Berth," Charlotte *Observer*, January 1, 2000.

31. Ibid.

32. Tommy Tomlinson, "They Share More Than They Know," Charlotte *Observer*, July 2, 2000; James C. Cobb, *Redefining Southern Culture: Mind and Identity in the Modern South* (Athens: University of Georgia Press, 1999), 149.

33. David Firestone, "The New South: Old Times There Are Not Forgotten," New York *Times*, January 28, 2001.

34. Bobbie Ann Mason, "Shiloh," *Shiloh and Other Stories* (New York: Harper and Row, 1982), 15–6; 13; Mason, quoted in Wendy Smith, "*Publisher's Weekly* Interview with Bobbie Ann Mason," *Publisher's Weekly*, August 30, 1985, p. 425.

35. Kevin Chappell, "Cotton Mural Spurs Anger," Charlotte *Observer*, July 3, 1994.

36. Kevin Sack, "It's 'Washington' No More," Charlotte *Observer*, November 16, 1997.

37. Hodding Carter III, "Looking Back," *Southern Cultures* 2, no. 3/4 (1996): 286.

38. W. J. Cash, *The Mind of the South* (New York: Knopf, 1941), viii.

Index

African Americans: divergence from white historical perspective, 5–6, 37; aspirations of, 19, 192, 194, 217, 220; white fears of, 19; and evangelical Protestantism, 46–8, 63–4, 69–74, 188; and role of church, 63–4, 170, 222; and impact of World War II, 70; and gender conflicts, 109–10, 153–4, 173–4; middle-class women, 153–61; working-class women, 157, 184; in slavery, 187–91; during Reconstruction, 192; economic status of, 192–3; 202–3, 254–5, 273–80; disfranchisement of, 197–8, 210; segregation of, 201–8; and organized labor, 202–3, 275–6, as white construction, 205–6, 216, 250–1; and police, 205–6; education of, 209–14, 266–9; neighborhoods of, 214–5; and racial etiquette, 216–9; and environmental racism, 272; and textile work, 274–6; rural poverty of, 277–9; identification as southerners, 283–5; migration to South, 284; segregation nostalgia, 291–3; and Hispanics, 294
Alabama: anti-Semitism in, 82; woman's suffrage in, 118; women's clubs in, 142; racial disparities in public education in, 210; and Confederate battle flag, 312; mentioned, 295
Ames, Jessie Daniel: and the ASWPL, 150–2; and work in founding Southern Regional Council, 163, 245

Andrews, Raymond, 292
Arkansas: Civil War in, 17; women's clubs in, 141
Association of Southern Women for the Prevention of Lynching (ASWPL), 88, 150–2, 163, 166
Atlanta: 1996 Summer Olympic Games in, 9, 305; Sam Jones's revivals in, 59–60; and WCTU, 139; women's clubs in, 140–1, 157; and black institutions, 157; civil rights movement in, 170; 1906 riot in, 204; segregation in, 214–5, 216, 289–90; public schools in, 268; black economic status in, 279; race relations in, 286; black-Hispanic relations in, 294; mentioned, 100, 145, 198, 245
Atlanta Neighborhood Union, 159
Aycock, Charles Brantley, 196–7, 209

Baker, Ella, 173–4
Barnett, Frank W., 64–5
Barrett, Jane Porter, 158–9
Baton Rouge, La.: black vote dilution techniques in, 259; environmental pollution in, 270, 271
Benét, Stephen Vincent, 107
Birmingham, Ala.: black education in, 212; civil rights demonstrations in, 247; heritage tourism in, 309; settling historical accounts, 310; mentioned, 145, 278